Herbert Burke

Historical portraits of the Tudor dynasty and the reformation period

Herbert Burke

Historical portraits of the Tudor dynasty and the reformation period

ISBN/EAN: 9783337104436

Printed in Europe, USA, Canada, Australia, Japan

Cover: Foto ©ninafisch / pixelio.de

More available books at **www.hansebooks.com**

HISTORICAL PORTRAITS

OF

THE TUDOR DYNASTY AND THE REFORMATION PERIOD.

BY

S. HUBERT BURKE,

AUTHOR OF THE MEN AND WOMEN OF THE REFORMATION.

"Time unveils all truth."

VOL. III.

JOHN HODGES,
13, SOHO SQUARE, LONDON.

1883.

Dryden Press:
J. DAVY AND SONS, 137, LONG ACRE, LONDON.

INTRODUCTION.

It was originally intended that this work should be brought to a close in three volumes; but such a concourse of characters, and so many important events occurred in England and other countries, during the Tudor dynasty, that it appeared to me impossible to bring the events of many years —or a portion of them—into the space intended for the results of my inquiries. I have been compelled, therefore, to extend the work to four volumes, and even then to use more brevity than the importance of the various incidents might seem to permit.

It has been contended by some Reviewers, that " I have concerned myself too much with the statements of modern writers." But, I beg respectfully to reply, that the great object of my work is to remove the false impressions made upon the English reader by sectarian and party writers, remote and more recent. The second volume of this work has been condemned by some journals, for no other reason than that of placing before the world an honest record of the deeds of the public men of the reigns of Henry VIII., Edward VI., Queen Mary, and Elizabeth. It has been the unhappy feeling of too many English writers to suppose, that to foster sectarian prejudice was the proper mode of writing History—perhaps, because such a course of action was successful in a financial point of view. I have not written for Party, but for Equity, and have eschewed religious controversy as foreign to a work wholly devoted to the elucidation of historical truth.

Amongst the criticisms upon the second volume of this work I have been accused of "having an insuperable objection to calling people by their right names." I select one remarkable case from the list:—"The author calls Lady Jane Grey *Lady Dudley.*" My answer to this "correction" is brief and conclusive. In the indictment for high treason preferred against the lady in question, she is styled *Jane Dudley, the wife of Guildford Dudley.** From the period of her marriage to her execution she was *legally* known as the wife of Guildford Dudley. Here is another proof of her being the wife of Dudley, which I extract from the work criticised by a certain Reviewer. It is taken from a note to the second volume (p. 492) of the "Historical Portraits":—

"There is a beautiful little illuminated Prayer-book in Latin, enclosed in a well-preserved morocco case, in the British Museum, which book Lady Jane Dudley had with her on the scaffold. On

---

* Statute IV., p. 217 ; Journal of Council ; Archæologia, VIII., Vol. V., p. 407.

the fly-leaf is some writing of Lady Dudley's, in a fine bold hand :
—"*Lord, I trust in Thee: let me never be confounded.*" The writing concludes :—"*Yours, as the Lord knoweth.*

"(Signed)   JANE DUDLEY."

In no one action of her political life does she appear on the page of History as *Jane Grey*. Why Jane Dudley has been misrepresented and deprived of her *lawful* title of Dudley, by so many writers, it might *now* be difficult to ascertain. The Reviewer to whom I have just referred ought not, however, to be unacquainted with a fact which so many writers have ignored.

Were the olden custom of dedication now in existence, I would have earnestly sought the honour of dedicating this particular volume of my work to the Most Honourable Henry, Duke of NORFOLK, Earl Marshal of England.

The Duke of NORFOLK'S personal kindness to me can only be forgotten when I cease to live.

The noble House of NORFOLK has, in bygone times, done much to promote the cause of Historical Truth. "Dodd's Ecclesiastical History" would never have been published were it not for the timely aid of Edward, Duke of NORFOLK, who lived in the days of the Penal Laws.*

I cheerfully assign their full share of merit to those who

---

* See Vol. IV., p. 274, of the "Historical Portraits," for the narrative concerning Dodd's History.

have in any way assisted in my labours. To the officials of the Literary department of the British Museum I would be more diffuse in my thanks, as they one and all deserve, did not the experience of nearly two-and-twenty years prove that courtesy, kindly attention, and delicate consideration seem to be such unavoidable attributes to the gentlemen who officiate in that important department of an unrivalled Institution as to render the expression of individual gratitude superfluous.

S. H. BURKE.

London : November 6th, 1882.

CONTENTS OF VOL. III.

		PAGE
Chapter I.	Cardinal Pole's Mission—(Pole's Mission Continued)	1
" II.	Archbishop Cranmer arraigned for Heresy	10
" III.	A Challenge to Dr. Cranmer	17
" IV.	The Archbishop Degraded	24
" V.	The Recantations—the Sequel	28
" VI.	Clerics of the "New Learning"	39
" VII.	Clerical Reformers—Calvin and Servetus	94
" VIII.	Queen Mary's Consort	108
" IX.	The Poet Surrey	122
" X.	England described by Foreign Contemporaries	135
" XI.	Men of the "New and the Old Learning"	143
" XII.	Persecution of Conscience	212
" XIII.	Last Days of Queen Mary	238
" XIV.	Death of Cardinal Pole	257

			PAGE
Chapter	XV.	Accession of Elizabeth	262
„	XVI.	The Marian Bishops	278
„	XVII.	Change of Religion in England	298
„	XVIII.	Elizabeth and her Suitors	316
„	XIX.	The Royal Favourite	325
„	XX.	Diplomatic Revelations	340
„	XXI.	(1561)—The Social and Religious Aspect of England	353
„	XXII.	Queen Elizabeth's Foreign Policy	366
„	XXIII.	The Results of "Royal Progresses"	373
„	XXIV.	The Reformation in Scotland	379
„	XXV.	Mary of Lorraine	390
„	XXVI.	The Families of De Clifford and Holles	408

VOL. III.

CARDINAL POLE'S MISSION.

CHAPTER I.

(POLE'S MISSION *continued*).

CARDINAL POLE was not many weeks in England before he realized the difficulty of his situation, yet he persevered in the labours of his mission. He called upon the bishops and clergy to "go amongst their flocks and speak kindly words to them; reminding the young and the old what a glorious Catholic country England had been in past ages." Pole's "England of the Past" was a faithful copy of the beautiful original. But now everything was changed. The people, however, seemed more inclined to rush into controversy about creeds than to engage in the practice of any religion, Christian or otherwise.

Again, I must remark that the politicians of Edward's reign had brought the country to the verge of ruin. They acted with a hypocrisy that dishonoured the character of public men. But the most noted feature in their conduct was the indifference with which they betrayed and assassinated one another, whilst impiously invoking the blessing of the Almighty upon their actions. With such examples in high places, it was no wonder that the lower classes became violent, debased, and reckless.

The Queen was suffering from a severe heart illness on the day she had appointed to introduce Cardinal Pole to her Parliament, and to explain to them the exact nature of his mission. Her Highness could not go, as usual, to Westminster, and was, therefore, compelled to take the privileges of an invalid; and convene the Lords and Commons in the Presence Chamber of Whitehall Palace. The Queen was carried to the throne in a kind of stupor, attended by a large number of ladies, who, according to the observant George Ferrers, " were a-weeping for their good mistress." At this remarkable assembly King Philip was seated under the same canopy as the Queen, but at her left hand; on her right, a chair of state was placed for Cardinal Pole. When the Lords and Commons were all seated, and " sympathy expressed for the Queen's illness," the Lord High Chancellor of the realm (Gardyner), rose to address the " assembled wisdom " in the following fashion :—

Most grave Lords of the Upper House, and my worthy and honourable maisters of the nether House of Parliament, here all assembled in the name of God Almighty, I now present and introduce to you all, the Lord Cardinal, Reginald Pole, *Legate-a-latere*, from the Apostolic See of Rome, as Ambassador to the King and Queen's Majesties, upon one of the weightiest causes that ever happened in this old realm of ours. It is the pleasure of their Majesties that you listen attentively with your ears to all my Lord Cardinal has to relate for the good of your sowles and bodyes, and the honour of our brave old realm, and the prosperitie of all therein, with God's blessing upon our actions.

Dr. Gardyner's speech was well received; and the Cardinal was much pleased at the penitential appearance of many of those who were the determined enemies of Rome a few months previously. Pole believed that this assembly of hypocrites and knaves was sincere; but Gardyner who looked upon them, as an old politician might, doubted the honesty that caused tears to come upon the cheeks of such men as Lords Winchester and Pembroke, or William Paget, or the grave and astute William Cecil.

The Cardinal addressed the assembled Parliament for two hours. He gave them an interesting account of his "long exile from his beloved country, and the many privations he occasionally underwent." "He always prayed that he might end his days in dear old England." In eloquent language he reviewed the history of Catholicism in England for so many ages; pointed out the services the monastic houses had rendered to the people, both in a religious and social point of view. He also referred to the means resorted to by Crumwell for the destruction of those time-honoured institutions. He uttered terrible words of malediction against Cranmer and all those who had acted with him.*

Looking towards the Queen, Pole spoke with considerable emotion. "For several years" said he, "Her Majesty has been marked out for persecution of the most unmanly and unkind description. Her father was opposed to her; she was not allowed to see her sainted mother. But her worst and most cruel enemies were those in power during her brother's reign. They were the persecutors of liberty of conscience, but the Princess stood by her religion with a

---

*Cranmer was at this time a prisoner in the Tower, forgotten by his former colleagues who were now "joyous at the reconciliation with Rome." Notwithstanding the desertion of his friends, it is certain that Gardyner and Pole did not desire to be the legal instruments for his prosecution. I have already remarked, in the second volume of this work, that Cranmer was three times absent from the Tower on his "word of honour." It is very unlikely that the Governor of the Tower granted this liberty without a special order.

heroic feeling amidst plots and threats against her life. So great was the Queen's attachment to her religion that he felt certain, that if her persecutors sent her to the stake she would have gone thither singing hymns of glory to God for having been given an opportunity to die for His faith. The continued persecutions the Queen experienced at the hands of the Reformers stamped upon her heart the certainty of the Eternal Truth, and holiness of the Church in which she was born, and would, without fail, end her days. Helpless and unarmed, the Queen came forward to seek her lawful inheritance. Her title was denied by a combination of unscrupulous rebels; her honour stigmatized by cowards, and her legitimacy denied by such a being as Thomas Cranmer. The honest hearts of England were not to be controlled by the rebellious leaders of a family conspiracy. The people rushed to the Royal standard, and, in a short time, the whole country acknowledged the royal lady as their lawful Sovereign. The Queen had immense faith in the loyalty and chivalry of Englishmen."

It was no wonder that immense excitement pervaded the assembly when Pole resumed his seat, for his eloquence was of the most impassioned type, and his exquisitely modulated voice and magnificent figure, carried his hearers to a pitch of wild enthusiasm. In the course of his speech the Cardinal intimated that he had power from Pope Julian to absolve the realm without previous restitution of the Church lands, confiscated by Henry VIII. The immediate consequence of this undertaking was, that the Houses of Parliament, by general consent, proposed a petition to the throne, praying for reconciliation with the Court of Rome.

On the following morning the Queen, King Philip, and the Cardinal took their places as on the previous day, when the Lords and Commons were again summoned. Pole's commission from the Pope having been read, the Peers and Commons *fell on their knees,* and the Cardinal pronounced the benediction. The whole assembly accompanied the Queen and Philip to St. Stephen's Chapel, where *Te Deum* was sung, which ended the ceremony.

Subsequent events, however, proved the utter dishonesty and hypocrisy of nine-tenths of the assembled politicians on this occasion. Religion and honour were pledged by perjured lips, for very few amongst them cared for any creed, unless to promote their own personal interests by becoming its advocates for a season; or to resist another religious revolution to be brought about, perhaps, by chosen agencies. Let it be remembered, that nearly all the principal men present were either members of Somerset's Government, or supporters of it.

The fatigue caused by the state ceremonies brought a dangerous illness on the Queen, from which, however, in a few weeks she was restored.

The Christmas holidays were approaching, and the Queen's Treasurer was commanded to make preparations for a series of entertainments. The festivities were on a grand scale, and much excited the austere Puritan censors. One remarkable incident was apparent—namely, that the reconciliation between the Queen and her sister seemed to be complete. Leti states, that Queen Mary, placing a ring of great value upon Elizabeth's finger, impressively said, " Well, sister, whether you have done me wrong, or otherwise, I now *freely forgive you!* "

The great hall of the palace was lighted with one thousand lamps of various colours, artistically disposed. Here the Queen, Philip, the Princess Elizabeth, and a splendid assembly of English, Flemish, and Spanish nobles supped. Elizabeth was likewise present at the grand tourneys that took place five days subsequently.

About the time of these festivities (1554), Courtney, Earl of Devon had been released from Fotheringay Castle, and was introduced at Court with the honours due to his rank. In one of Noailles' despatches to the French Government, he states that Courtney was connected with a conspiracy for the assassination of Lord Arundel and Sir William Paget, but, as usual, one of the conspirators' letters betrayed his companions. At his own desire the Queen allowed him to travel, that he might improve his mind. His timid, shifting, and unpractical character, made him unpopular with the English nobles and knights, for a want of physical courage was deemed by those fearless squires a greater disgrace than all the murders and treasons committed by Courtney's great uncle, King Richard the Third.

When Courtney was discharged from prison he frequented the society of women of bad repute. His conduct became so abominable that the French and Venetian ambassadors admonished him as to the consequences.* But he was reckless as to the value of his honour. He was some thirty years of age at this period. His portrait, by Antonio More, presents the grand outlines of the Plantagenets. The expression of the face is penetrating and majestic; the features high and exquisitely moulded; the forehead lofty and noble, and decorated by a rich *chevelure* of light brown curls. An engraving from this portrait is to be seen in Horace Walpole's Anecdotes of Paintings. Courtney's "last days are shrouded in obscurity." He is supposed to have died in a monas-

---

* "Noailles' Secret Despatches."

tery near Milan. He is said to have been attended during his last illness by Father Vaughan, an English Franciscan.

Amongst the distinguished foreigners who visited the English Court in 1555 were the Prince of Orange, and Count Egmont; there also appeared in all the grace of manly beauty, Alva, who subsequently won in the Low Countries a notoriety which, evil as it was, has been exaggerated, according to the evidence of the recent State Papers. There might, likewise, be seen about this period in Whitehall a youthful gallant named Ruy Gomez, who, in time became a celebrated prime minister of Spain; and, as if to complete the historic group, there arrived soon after Phildibert Emmanuel, Duke of Savoy, the suitor of Elizabeth, and the future conqueror of St. Quintin.

In a few months later, the Queen's health, which had been long sinking, gave way. The Sovereign was merely alive, and her Council began that reign of terror which closed in the darkest gloom—in disgrace and horror to all concerned. Cardinal Pole was likewise in the decline of years, but at best he possessed no political influence in the country, and had no party. He was quite sad over the condition to which religion had become reduced. A combination of circumstances decided that Pole's mission was an utter failure.* To add to his difficulties and misfortunes, there was no friendly understanding between Pole and Paul the Fourth. The Pope's Italian ideas of politics were very unpopular with Englishmen, and had a mischievous effect, as far as the promotion of Catholicity in England was concerned.

---

* State Papers of Mary's reign ; Holingshed's Chronicle ; Tytler's Edward and Mary, vol. 2 ; Archbishops of Canterbury, vol. 8.

Paul the Fourth resolved to involve Pole in the same disgrace with his friend, Cardinal Morone, and to subject the orthodoxy of both to the investigation of such a tribunal as the Inquisition. The Pontiff ordered a letter to be prepared, announcing to Cardinal Pole that his Legatine authority was set aside, and commanding him quickly to return to Rome. Queen Mary and Philip disapproved of the policy pursued by the Pope at this critical moment. Mary and King Philip "protested against it"; the English prelates and nobility complained of the injury which religion would receive from this mode of action. But the Pontiff was unmoved. He immediately transferred to the newly-created Cardinal (Peto), then in his eighty-second year, all the powers which had hitherto been exercised by Cardinal Pole.*

In this emergency, Queen Mary's respect for the Papal authority did not prevent her from having recourse to the precautions which had often been employed by her predecessors. Orders were issued that every messenger from foreign ports should be detained and searched. The bearer of the Papal letters was arrested at Calais; his despatches were privately conveyed to the Queen in Council, and the letters of revocation were destroyed. Thus it happened that Peto never received any *official* notice of his preferment, nor Pole of his recall. Pole, however, ceased to exercise the legatine authority.†

Queen Mary boldly replied to Paul the Fourth that she would not permit Cardinal Pole to leave her realm.‡ To the next Papal message on this subject the Queen became more firm, and gave proof that she had a dash of the Tudor blood in her veins.

---

* Cardinal Pole, Ep. 5, p. 144. † Lingard, vol. 5, p. 517.
‡ Pallavicino, vol. 2, p. 500.

Proceedings were already commenced in Rome against Reginald Pole. The Cardinal, in strong though respectful language, remonstrated and protested against the injustice which was done to his character.* Peto soon after died, and the question remained in suspense, till it was set at rest, in the course of a few months, by the deaths of all the parties concerned.

* Cardinal Pole, vol. 5, p. 31-36.

CHAPTER II.

ARCHBISHOP CRANMER ARRAIGNED FOR HERESY.

IN the first and second volumes of this work I have chronicled a record of the proceedings of Archbishop Cranmer as the clerical and political instrument of Henry VIII., and his helpless and irresponsible successor.

I have now arrived at the period when Dr. Cranmer stood arraigned for heresy. The reader is already aware that the Archbishop was first tried before Chief Justice Morgan, at Guildhall, found guilty of high treason, and condemned to death. He was then "returned to the Tower authorities to await execution." The Queen subsequently pardoned Cranmer for his treason against her person. She acted, however, as it would seem, with unmerciful duplicity. She saved him from the axe, yet consigned him to the adjudication of another tribunal, which, by a curiously indirect process of law, sent Cranmer to the stake. It would have been far more humane to have handed her prisoner over to the headsman at once. The Queen must have known well what would be the fate of the man whom she had gone through the mockery of pardoning. In fact, the barbarous statute against heretics left no chance of mercy being extended. Cranmer had himself aided in reconstructing, some years previously, the very tribunal which was now summoned for the trial of "a certain man named Thomas Cranmer, some time known in various places in this realm of ours as the Lord Archbishop of Canterbury."

On Saturday, the 7th of September, 1555, Archbishop Cranmer was arraigned before a special commission, held in St. Mary's Church, Oxford. The Bishop of Gloucester presided, assisted by four other prelates. Dr. Cranmer appeared weak and feeble. It is stated that the gaoler would not grant him a seat, so he had to lean upon a staff. His condition at this moment was a disgrace to the authorities, who subsequently shifted the censure from one to another. His clothes were nearly threadbare, and those who remembered the strong and active prelate of a few years before, could scarcely have recognised him now. His jaws were drawn in; his piercing eyes had become glassy and sunk; the pleasant countenance had changed to the woe-attenuated aspect of despair; his long beard white as snow; his head bald; and his whole appearance that of a man in condition of uttermost distress; so that his "veriest enemies seemed moved to pity"—for the moment. At this juncture the Reformers forsook their champion, and "joined in scoffing at the old man who aspired to martyrdom." Such were the words of Daniel Dancer, an eccentric Reformer of those times. The proceedings of the Court commenced by the Proctor reading a long series of charges of heresy against Archbishop Cranmer.

Cranmer replied, that he denied the authority of the Pope altogether. "I have sworn," said he, "never to admit the authority of the Bishop of Rome in England, and I must keep my oath." In another passage he said, "You attribute the *keys* to the Pope, and the *sword* to the King. I say the King hath the keys and the sword."

The substance of Cranmer's elaborate reply was to the effect that at no time did he believe in the principles of the Catholic Church, although he had *repeatedly sworn to those principles with the most open solemnity, and sent men to the stake for not maintaining them.*

The President of the Court informed the Archbishop that the Commissioners represented his Holiness the Pope *in part*, and also King Philip and Queen Mary.

The President is further represented as having remonstrated in a very gentle manner with Cranmer, and then proceeded to address him, at considerable length, upon the "awful nature of the heresies and other crimes" with which he stood charged in the name of his Holiness the Pope, Queen Mary, King Philip, and the whole Catholic community. The address, of four hours' duration, concluded with an exhortation to repentance. The Archbishop seemed deeply moved during the latter part of Dr. Brook's admonition, shedding tears several times; but he soon recovered his bearing, and reiterated his unchangeable hostility to the Papacy. The spectators "became excited at the fashion in which he spoke of the Pope." No Anabaptist could speak with more bitterness and scorn of the Roman Pontiff than Cranmer did on this occasion. Cranmer's replies to the Commissioners and Proctors involved a series of contradictions. He was, however, unaided by counsel, and cross-examined by men who were reputed to be equal to him, if not superior, in a theological joust. Dr. Martyn, the Chief Proctor, cross-questioned him at some length, when the following scene took place:—

"Dr. Martyn: 'What doctrine was taught by you when you condemned Lambert, the Sacramentary, in the King's presence, at Whitehall?'

"Archbishop Cranmer: 'I maintained then the Papists' doctrine.'

"Dr. Martyn: 'That is to say, the Catholic and universal

doctrine of Christ's Church. And now, when King Henry died did you not translate Justus Jonas's book?'

"Archbishop Cranmer: 'I did so.'

"Dr. Martyn: 'Then, there you defended another doctrine touching the Blessed Sacrament, by the same token that you sent to Synne, your printer; that when, as in the first print, there was an affirmative—that is to say, Christ's body really in the Sacrament—you sent then to your printer to put in a 'not,' whereby it came miraculously to pass that Christ's body was clean conveyed out of the Holy Sacrament.'

"Archbishop Cranmer: 'I remember there were two printers of my said book, but where the same 'not' was put in I cannot tell.'

"Dr. Martyn: 'Then from a Lutheran you became a Zwinglian, which is the vilest heresy of all in connection with the Sacrament; and for the same heresy you did help to burn Lambert, the Sacramentary; which you now call the Catholic faith and God's Word?'

"Archbishop Cranmer: 'I grant that then I believed otherwise than I do now, and so I did until my Lord of London, Dr. Ridley, did confer with me, and by sundry persuasions and authorities of doctors showed me quite from my opinion.'

"Dr. Martyn: 'Now, Maister Cranmer, as touching the last part of your oration, you denied that the Pope's Holiness was supreme head of the Church of Christ?'

"Archbishop Cranmer: 'I did so.'

"Dr. Martyn: 'But whom hath Christ here on earth as His Vicar and head of His Church?'

"Archbishop Cranmer: 'Nobody.'

"Dr. Martyn: 'Ah! why told you not King Henry this when you made him Supreme Head? And now nobody is. This is treason against his own person, as you then made him.'

"Archbishop Cranmer: 'I meant not but every king in his own realm and dominion is supreme head; and so was he supreme head of the Church of Christ in England.'

"Dr. Martyn: 'Is this always true? And was it ever so in Christ's Church?'

"Archbishop Cranmer: 'It was so.'

"Dr. Martyn: 'Then what say you of Nero? He was the mightiest prince of the earth after Christ was ascended. Was he head of Christ's Church?'

"Archbishop Cranmer: 'Nero was Peter's head.'

"Dr. Martyn: 'I ask whether Nero was head or no? If he was not, it is false that you said before, that all princes be, and ever were, heads of the Church within their realms?'

"Archbishop Cranmer: 'Why, it is true, for Nero was head of the Church, that is in worldly respects of the temporal bodies of men, of whom the Church consisteth; for so he beheaded Peter and the Apostles. And the Turk, too, is head of the Church in Turkey.'

"Dr. Martyn: 'Then he that beheaded the heads of the Church and crucified the Apostles was head of Christ's Church; and he that was never member of the Church is head of the Church of your *new-found understanding* of God's Word?'

"The Proctor again interrogated Cranmer as to who was supreme head of the Church of England. 'Marry,' said the Archbishop, 'Christ is head of this member, as He is of the whole of the body, of the Universal Church.' 'Why,' quoth Martyn, 'you made King Henry the Eighth supreme head of the Church.' 'Yea,' said the Archbishop, 'of all the people of England, as well ecclesiastical as temporal.' 'And not of the Church?' asked the Proctor. 'No,' said Cranmer, 'for Christ is only head of His Church, and of the faith and religion of the same. The King is head and governor of his people, which are the visible Church.'"*

It does not require much acumen to discover here a shiftiness and inconsistency, a transparency of argument, a tenuity, so to say, of reasoning; a set of distinctions without differences, and a series of "hair-splittings" that,

---

* There are three accounts of the above scene which nearly agree; the official report is to be seen in MS. at the Lambeth Palace Library, No. 1186.

fairly denote the casuistry of Cranmer's theology. In the bygone he had admitted Christ's delegation of the headship of His Church to Peter, who bequeathed it to his successors at Rome: now, with him, Christ was alone the head of the invisible Church, and the monarch the Head of the Visible Church—that is, the people.

Subsequent commentators, following up similar arguments, have gone the length of averring that, according to this proposition of Dr. Cranmer, "Moslem or Pagan monarchs ruling over Christians in all the lands of the earth, must be, in those regions, the heads of the Church of Christ." Of course this is a prothesis not to be ascribed to Cranmer as a belief; but his use of it, in the endeavour to appear consistent, compelled the deduction that his doctrine was illogical, inconsistent, and even unchristian.

Latimer and Ridley underwent a similar examination before the same Commissioners, and for offences of nearly the same nature. On being brought into court, Ridley was uncovered; but when he heard the name of the Pope mentioned, he put on his cap. He was ordered to remove it instantly. "No," said he, "I will not; I do protest against the Bishop of Rome. I will not acknowledge his authority in this realm, for he represents *Lucifer, not Christ*."*

A scene of excitement ensued, and the beadle of the Court was commanded by the President to remove Maister Ridley's cap, when he again resisted.

The judgment of the Court in Ridley's case was to the effect, "that he still continued to be an obstinate and incurable heretic." This judgment, as a matter of course,

---

* Pomeroy states that he heard Ridley use the above words and other strong expressions that escaped his memory.

consigned him to the flames, but no time was named for the execution, as the final decree was expected from Rome.

Latimer next stood forward. He presented, if possible, a more wretched appearance than his friend Cranmer. He had nearly reached his eighty-second year; the withered remains of a once strong, healthy, and energetic man. He was dressed in an old tattered coat broken in the sleeves, a torn handkerchief on his head, with a soiled night-cap over it; his head gear was tied by a leather strap under the chin; a leather belt was round his waist, to which a copy of the New Testament was attached, enclosed in an ivory case, on which was fastened a small silver cross; his spectacles, without a case, hung from his neck; he was half blind, and quite deaf; his teeth were nearly gone; he could scarcely pronounce a word correctly; his once strong voice became faint, yet when excited, he spoke boldly, but with the enthusiasm of a fanatic; he seemed weak and cold, and "shivered like the leaves about to be scattered by the October winds." Such was the condition of Hugh Latimer, once known in England as the poor man's advocate against the encroachments of the wealthy and heartless. Sad times were those, when the law, assuming the forms of equity, demanded the life of such a spectre as Hugh Latimer at the stake fire.*

I cannot help remarking, that several of the officials who made themselves prominent in their action against Cranmer during those trials, became Reformers in the reign of Elizabeth. Dr. Martyn, the Chief Proctor, held office under Elizabeth, and participated in the persecution of his former co-religionists.

---

* State Trials of Queen Mary's Reign; Cotton MS.; Latimer's Remains; John Foxe, "On the Martyrdom of Latimer;" Pomeroy's Chronicle; Thorndale's Memorials; Dodd, vol. i.; Lingard, vol. v.; Froude, vol. vi.

CHAPTER III.

A CHALLENGE TO DR. CRANMER.

SOME months before the trials for heresy, Cranmer, Latimer, and Ridley, were conducted from the Tower (March 10, 1554), to Oxford, and ordered to confer on controverted points with the deputies from the Convocation and the two Universities. The discussion was held for three successive days. Cranmer was hard pressed with passages from the Fathers; Ridley maintained his former high reputation, and Latimer excused himself, on the plea of old age, of disuse of the Latin tongue, and weakness of memory.

In conclusion, Weston, the Moderator, decided in favour of the Catholic party. Two days later, the accused prelates were again called before Dr. Weston, and on their refusal to conform to the olden creed were pronounced "obstinate heretics." *

It is stated that the discussions were by no means fairly conducted, and Cranmer was subjected to many rude interruptions. He asked for more time to consider the questions at issue, and to prepare himself for meeting such learned adversaries as were selected for the occasion. His application was refused. However, unprepared, he made an able display of learning and research.†

---

* State Papers of Mary's reign; Lingard, vol. 5, p. 474-5. Strype's Remains of Cranmer, vol. iv., p. 67.

† Harpsfield, a noted scholar and theologian, "fenced closely," as a spectator writes, "with the Archbishop." John Foxe, in a letter to Anthony Delabarre, states that Cranmer had a triumph over Harpsfield in argument. The reader can draw his own conclusion as to the verdict, here entered by the eccentric John Foxe.

The Moderator, at the conclusion of the inquiry, thanked the Archbishop for the calm manner in which he conducted himself during the disputation.

It has been alleged by some Puritan writers that Cranmer and his two clerical fellow-sufferers were subjected to "privation and insult." Dean Hook may be accepted as a fair historical judge in this matter. "I should infer," remarks the Dean, "that they were not systematically ill-treated. Occasionally a fanatic was in office, or a report came that they were planning their escape,* and they were subjected for a season to annoyance and restraint; but the Government had certainly given orders to the Mayor of Oxford to provide them with good food and raiment. They were not, at all times, prohibited from visiting each other—they were, in fact, associated together."†

Another authority adds that the "three martyrs" constantly ate suppers as well as dinners; that their meals usually cost from three to four shillings; at both meals cheese and pears were the last dish, and that they had wine, of which the price was always threepence, and no more.‡ The imprisoned prelates had the privilege of sending and receiving letters from their relatives and friends. This was very unlike the usage which Gardyner and the other bishops had received from Dr. Cranmer when he consigned them with instant despotism to the Tower, then seizing upon their private property, and refusing them pen,

---

* They could have escaped several times; but men who aspire to martyrdom in any cause, or men who hope to escape prison by a political or class revolution, generally spurn the temptation of a flight, which might consign them to inactive oblivion. Cranmer was certainly of that way of thinking.

† Dean Hook's Archbishops of Canterbury. vol. vii., p. 374.

‡ Dodd, vol. ii., p. 405.

ink and paper—in fact, all communication with their friends. The treatment accorded to political prisoners in the Tower during Edward's reign has been justly described as "barbarous." At the time Cranmer and his companions were under confinement at Oxford (1554-5), provisions were at a famine price, yet the prisoners were well supplied with "good cheer." The following is taken from the book of expenses :—

A large goose, 14d. ; a small pig, 13d. ; a woodcock, 3d. ; two chickens, 4d.; three plovers, 10d. ; half-a-dozen of larks, 3d. ; a dozen of larks and two plovers, 10d. ; breast of veal, 11d. ; a shoulder of mutton, 10d. ; a piece of roasting beef, 10d.

In those times there was an immense consumption of fish in England, especially in London, where the supply was ample. Throughout Cranmer's career he rigidly enforced the rules concerning abstinence from meat on the days commanded by the Church.* Bishop Bonner, once the personal friend of Cranmer, gave an annual fish entertainment to King Henry and the Archbishop of Canterbury. The banquet cost about £6 10s. On one occasion, it being a very cold winter day, the host had a plentiful supply of hot drink for the King and the other guests. The "hot drink was composed of milk, eggs and Irish whiskey." Thorndale, who was one of the party, states that the jovial monarch was much pleased with the liquor and the savoury " belly cheer " provided by his " friend Ned." †

In Lent the Bishop of Winchester gave a fish banquet to the King and the Bishops. Oysters were the special shell fish for the monarch, Bishop Kyte, and the Dean of St.

---

* The reader will find a very interesting passage on the antiquity of the " Lenten Fast" in Collier's Ecclesiastical History, vol. 5, p. 302.

† The King's pet name for Bonner. Henry delighted in Bonner's rustic stories of " Olden Tymes."

Paul's. The love of field sports frequently brought Cranmer and Bonner to the same banquet hall. What a sad fate awaited both of those early friends!

It has been stated that Cranmer gave banquets on Good Fridays, in Edward's reign, in order to show his contempt for the olden creed. I cannot find any reliable authority for this allegation. Ridley gave entertainments on the days of abstinence, and Latimer made himself "odiously prominent" in this violation of ancient usage.

Whilst the trial of Cranmer for heresy was slowly proceeding, the death of a notable man, the early friend and adviser of the Archbishop in the divorce case of Katharine of Aragon, took place. Stephen Gardyner, Bishop of Winchester and Lord Chancellor of England, died on the 16th of October, 1555, at his London Palace in Southwark. Gardyner was one of the clerical judges appointed to investigate Cranmer's case, as to the charge of heresy, but he never attended the sittings of the court, nor in any manner that I can discover, openly participated in its deliberations. Gardyner's last hours are described by Griffin, one of his secretaries, as most edifying. He sent for several persons whom he had wronged in various ways, and humbly sought their forgiveness. Dr. Whyte was the bearer of a message from him to the Queen, of which nothing is known; "but, I think," writes the faithful secretary, that "the message was for reconciliation and peace between the Queen's subjects." A few days before his demise Gardyner said, with tears rolling down his face, "I have sinned with Peter, but have not yet learned to weep as bitterly as that Prince of the Apostles." Three hours before his death he took leave of a few of his old domestics, saying something kind to each of them. His last words were—" I die in peace with all men, and a firm belief in the grand old religion of England. And I pray God may forgive me for the part I have taken in the unjust divorce of the Queen's mother."*

Thus died Cranmer's only real friend—the prelate whom he had so unjustly imprisoned in the Tower for five years.

Portraits of Gardyner, social and political, have nearly all come from Puritan and other sectarian sources. Poynet states that he was "hideously ugly;" and John Bale assured the noisy crowd at Paul's Cross, that he was "a monster of cruelty." The allegations of such men as Poynet and Bale will not be accepted by any reflecting student of history. The personal appearance of Gardyner has also been a subject for discussion. His countenance, it is said, was replete with intellectual powers—still, at times he had an unamiable appearance, and muttered harsh words as he paced his library. When in a passion he looked with scorn at an antagonist; but his mind soon calmed again, and he said something soothing, or rendered a compliment in a gracious manner. His speech was clear and to the purpose. He was far more of the diplomatist than the Churchman. In the arrangement of civil government, especially finance, he held the most advanced views of any English statesman of the reign of Henry VIII.—if permitted liberty of action. As I have remarked, his personal appearance has been often commented upon. He had a large aquiline nose, and piercing eyes, shaded by thick black brows. His clerical costume was always arranged with taste. He carried his prayer-book in a pocket at the right side; from a gold chain encircling his neck was suspended a small cross, ornamented with precious stones. His hospitality was profuse; and, as a host,

---

* The above words have been set down by Thorndale, who was present.

he had no rival in high English society from the days of Buckingham and Wolsey.

Dr. Gardyner's London palace was in the neighbourhood of St. Saviour's Church, Southwark. Winchester House was as large as the palace of Lambeth, and of greater antiquity, having been built early in the twelfth century. It had a magnificent hall, lighted with great bay windows, which were fitted with stained glass of the richest hues. The private chapel was arranged with classic taste. At the above palace Gardyner gave a sumptuous entertainment to Henry VIII. and Anne of Cleves, upon her marriage with the King. Two hundred dishes of "costly devices and subtilties" were served at this banquet. The silver dishes were of enormous size. A royal sturgeon, baked, was served entire. The King, who was a marvellous *gourmand*, complimented Gardyner upon the complete success of his banquet. One of Henry's specialties at table was, that he could not tolerate women eating more than "a few picks;" but Anne of Cleves had a hearty appetite, which quite disgusted the delicate-minded monarch. "Liking the good 'belly cheer' very much," writes Thorndale, "the new Queen cleared plate after plate, which made the King frown divers times." It was at a banquet given by Bishop Gardyner, that King Henry first met the beautiful Catherine Howard, of whose eyes the monarch spoke "in most gracious words, full of admiration and Tudor *tenderness*."

In his private friendship—apart from political considerations—Bishop Gardyner was very sincere and reliable. In religion he was no bigot, as so often alleged by Puritan and party writers. He was treated in an unjust and despotic manner by the Reformers under the Government of Edward VI., when Archbishop Cranmer and the Duke of

Somerset were at the head of affairs in England.* In fact, no public man of his time has been more misrepresented than Stephen Gardyner. In promoting the iniquitous divorce of Queen Katharine, Gardyner aided, unconsciously no doubt, in laying the foundation-stone of the English Reformation, and did more to injure the Church of Rome *in England*, than many of its avowed enemies. The future Reformers, however, evinced their gratitude by attributing the most odious crimes to him. The action of the Reformers against Dr. Gardyner has been looked upon by many of his co-religionists as " retributive justice." Be that as it may, toleration, gratitude, or common honesty, were sentiments utterly ignored by the public men of the reign of the boy-king Edward.

Bishop Gardyner is buried in the ancient Cathedral of Winchester. With the clergy and people of that diocese, his name was long associated with charity and benevolence in every form, and neglected genius always found a friend and a patron in Stephen Gardyner.

A recent writer remarks, " whatever inconsistency, or at least whatever changes of opinion, Gardyner may have shown in after times, he appears to have been throughout the reigns, both of Henry and Edward, the only high ecclesiastic who thoroughly knew his own mind. The mind, the charity, the temper of Gardyner, all were logical."†

---

* For further particulars concerning the imprisonment of Bishop Gardyner, in the reign of Edward VI., I refer the reader to volume ii. of the " Historical Portraits of the Tudor Dynasty," p. 270.

† Hist. of the Church of England, from the Abolition of the Roman Jurisdiction, by the Rev. Canon Dixon, M.A.

CHAPTER IV.

THE ARCHBISHOP DEGRADED.

To return to the heretical investigation. The ceremony of degradation has been ever since a reproach and a scandal to Queen Mary and her Council. It was a triumph over a fallen enemy; a triumph which casts odium and shame upon all concerned. Having been vested as Archbishop of Canterbury at the altar of Christ's Church, Oxford, and the pastoral staff placed in Cranmer's hand, a procession moved out to the church-yard, where a noisy crowd had assembled. The Archbishop was placed kneeling on a low stool, and the vestments were removed one by one, with some coarse observations from Bonner, on the apostasy or marriage of Cranmer. The Archbishop said he should give no trouble. He was compelled to submit by force. He called upon the Almighty God to witness the injustice of the whole proceedings against him. When the pastoral staff was about to be taken from his hand, Cranmer started from his kneeling posture, and seemed to be fired with indignation. Drawing from his sleeve a document, hitherto concealed, he said, " I appeal to the next General Council. In this paper I have comprehended my cause, and the form of it. I desire my appeal to be admitted." Cranmer then handed the document to the Bishop of Ely, and called upon the bystanders to be witnesses of what he had done.

The Bishop of Ely replied: My Lord, our commission is to

proceed against you *omni appellatione remotâ*, and, therefore, we cannot admit it.

"Why then," was Cranmer's reply, "you do me the more wrong, for my case is not that of a private person; the matter is immediate between me and the Pope of Rome, and none other. I hold that no man should be judge in his own cause."

Cranmer's appeal was immediately rejected. "Give me fair play, I ask no more," were his words, uttered in a broken-hearted accent.

In the course of the proceedings, Bonner addressed the spectators in these words:—"This is the man that ever despised the Pope's Holiness, and now is to be judged by the Pope; this is the man who hath pulled down so many churches, and is now come to be judged in a church; this is the man that condemned the Blessed Sacrament of the altar, and is now come to be condemned before that Blessed Sacrament; this is the man that, like Lucifer, sat in the place of Christ upon an altar to judge others, and is now come before an altar to be judged himself."*

The conduct of the populace during the various trials of Cranmer was indecent, and, in some instances, violent; but not worse than that shown at other public condemnations where men were charged with heresy or treason. In the lowest depth a lower deep was found. A barber of "a ruffian appearance" now entered upon the scene in the churchyard, and amidst the laughter of the mob, clipped the thin silver hair off the head of the fallen Archbishop. Cranmer was then commanded to kneel before Bishop Bonner. He obeyed. "Heavy tears ran down his care-worn cheeks;" his spirit was broken; and he seemed to be the

---

* State Trials of Queen Mary's Reign, vol. i., p. 801.

picture of desolation and despair. Bonner "scraped the tips of the fingers that were once anointed as Archbishop of Canterbury."* The threadbare gown of a yeoman was thrown over the unhappy Archbishop's shoulders, and the greasy cap of a ratcatcher,† who stood among the rabble, was rudely pressed upon his head. "You are no longer 'My Lord of,' or '*Your* Grace of, Canterbury,'" was the taunt of Bonner. At this stage of the proceedings Cranmer wept bitterly. His manly courage and dignified bearing had now forsaken him. All was lost.

The excommunicated and degraded prelate was then handed over to the civic authorities, to be finally disposed of at the stake.‡ This was the triumph of revenge, not of justice. If Bishop Gardyner had been alive at this unhappy epoch he would not permit Bonner to outrage the higher feelings of charity and humanity by his conduct. Who can defend such doings? No one with the feelings of a Christian, or the heart of our common manhood. No true Catholic can endorse such behaviour to the fallen, even if he

---

* The ceremony of degradation and excommunication from the Church took place on the 14th of February, 1556.

† To be called a "ratcatcher" in those days was considered by the lower classes of London to be the vilest of reproaches that might be cast upon man. This sentiment existed for centuries. Hoveden and Polydore Vergil speak in scorn of the occupation; and Shakespeare uses the reproach in "Romeo and Juliet," where Tybalt, in a contemptuous tone, to excite the passions of one of the Montagus, says, "Ah, you are a ratcatcher?"

‡ The whole of the proceedings connected with Cranmer's trial are to be found in "Wilkins;" "The State Trials of Mary's Reign;" "Remains of Cranmer," vol. vi.; "Dodd," vol. i.; Strype's "Memorials," vol. i. Dean Hook, in his "Archbishops of Canterbury," vol. vii., gives a "sum up" of the case. The accounts furnished by John Foxe are all of the marvellous type; Speed, Burnet, and Oldmixon follow in the same truthful style of relation.

were convinced that the victim would have acted with similar cruelty had he been the victor. The action of Bonner was utterly unbecoming the dignity of a Church founded in gentleness, consideration, and mercy. There can be no doubt that the Queen entertained a bitter feeling of hatred for the Archbishop; and the "surroundings" of the case prove that Elizabeth shared in her sister's hostility to the man who declared them both to be illegitimate, and then set up a "Pretender" for the throne.

The admirers of Cranmer are not, perhaps, aware of the fact that he ever continued to be the most unpopular prelate in England from the period of his divorce of Queen Katharine. No change of religion influenced the heartfelt hatred the people entertained against him. In Canterbury, for many years Cranmer required the protection of military escorts to save him from the violence of the populace. His ultimate fate gave general satisfaction in London. The women were his unforgiving enemies to the death. For centuries the women of England honoured the memory of Katharine of Aragon; and the name, "Good Queen Kate," became a loving household expression upon the lip of the virtuous and the good. Party writers represent popular sentiment in the opposite light.

CHAPTER V.

THE RECANTATIONS—THE SEQUEL.

At last the final decision arrived from Rome, which was confirmed by the Queen and her Council. After an imprisonment of three years, and having undergone several trials, it was decreed that Archbishop Cranmer should be sent to the stake. When informed that he should die the death of a heretic, he at first appeared horrified, but a ray of hope reached him, and he shortly afterwards made several recantations of faith. In his fifth recantation he anathematized especially the persons of Luther and Zwinglius; *accepted the Pope as the Head of the Church, out of which there was no salvation; acknowledged the "Real Presence" in the Holy Eucharist;* the Seven Sacraments as received by the Church of Rome, and also *Purgatory*. He expressed his penitence for having held or taught otherwise, and he implored the prayers of all faithful Christians, that those whom he had led astray might be brought back to the True Fold.

In the sixth renunciation Cranmer styled himself—

"A blasphemer and a persecutor; that being unable to undo his evil work, he had no hope (he said) save in the example of the thief upon the Cross, who, when other means of reparation were taken away from him, made amends to God with his lips. *He was unworthy of mercy, and he deserved eternal vengeance. He had sinned against King Henry and his wife (Katharine); he was the cause of the divorce from which, as from a seed, had sprung up schism, heresy, and crime; he had opened a window to false doctrines,* of which he had been himself the most pernicious teacher; especially he reflected with *anguish that he had denied the presence of his Maker in the consecrated elements.* He had deceived the living, and had wronged the souls of the dead, by stealing from them their Masses; he prayed the Pope to pardon him; he prayed the King and Queen (Philip and Mary) to pardon him; he prayed God Almighty to pardon him as He had pardoned Mary Magdalene, or to look upon him as from His own cross He had looked upon the thief."*

It has been stated that the above recantation was "drawn up by Cardinal Pole; that Cranmer was induced to sign it;" that "fresh tortures were presented to him by Pole's messengers, and the wearied, timid martyr fell into the trap laid for him by Pole and Bonner." John Strype is also of opinion that this recantation "is in part the composition of Pole." Whatever unworthy schemes Edmund Bonner might concoct, Reginald Pole was incapable of participating in such conduct. Bonner was in awe of the Cardinal, and, at this time, paid particular attention to his commands. It is certain that Pole entertained the very worst opinion of Cranmer, and gave expression to his sentiments in an undignified and uncharitable manner; but, at the same time, he could never descend to adopt the plan of "forced or forged confessions." Burnet is the principal historian who has put forward such serious charges against Pole's honour. Gilbert Burnet's allegations have been wholly disproved by Henry Wharton, an excellent authority. The latest researches, however, prove that the recantation was solely the composition of Cranmer himself. Had any other than himself drawn up the document, is it not most natural that he would

---

* Recantations of Thomas Cranmer, Jenkyns, vol. iv, p. 398; Strype's Memorials of Cranmer; Hook's Archbishops of Canterbury, vol. vii.

have eagerly denounced it? Yet, in his last speech he made no reference whatever to such a transaction.

On Saturday, the 21st of March, 1556, Archbishop Cranmer was led to the stake. The scene, as described by a French priest, was "one of the saddest and most disgraceful spectacles that Christian men could behold." Cranmer made a "long discourse," in which he spoke against the "love of the world, rebellion against the Queen; his feelings on the edge of eternity." He also gave "a wholesome advice to the spectators on the immoral and drunken habits which had got possession of them during the last twenty years. The parents set a bad example to their children, and society was crumbling to pieces. What would be the end?" The Archbishop suddenly paused. All eyes were now fixed upon Cranmer. He was called upon by the civic authorities to make a public declaration of his recent recantations. He addressed the multitude amidst a breathless silence :—

"And now, good people, I come to the great thing that troubleth my conscience more than any other thing that I ever said, or did, in my whole life, and that is the setting abroad of writings contrary to the truth, which *here I now renounce and refuse as things written with my hand contrary to the truth which I thought in my heart, and written for fear of death, to save my life, if it might be; and that is all such bills and papers as I have written and signed with my hand since my degradation, wherein I have written many things untrue, and for as much as my hand offended in writing contrary to my heart, my hand, therefore, shall first be punished, for as I come to the fire, it shall be the first burnt. As for the Pope, I utterly refuse him, as Christ's enemy and Anti-Christ, with all his false doctrines: and as for the Sacrament (Eucharist), I believe as I have taught in my book against the Bishop of Winchester.*" *

---

* Harleian MSS.; Jenkins'; Strype's Memorials; Hook's Archbishops of Canterbury, vol. vii; Froude, vol. vi.

The next scene was that at the stake, which is too horrible to detail. Cranmer met his fate like a stoic, and excited the sympathy of even the hardened bystanders.

The proceedings connected with the trial, condemnation, and execution of Cranmer were conducted with all the indifference to humanity, fair play and equity, characteristic of what at that period was designated "law." The Archbishop was denied counsel; this was a despotic action worthy of the days of Audley and Crumwell. He was clothed as a malefactor in prison vesture, and stood derided and insulted, yet fearless, before a mob who were retained for the occasion. Though he himself had often tried men after the very same fashion, it was not the less wicked that he should be compelled to taste of a similar bitterness of injustice. Equity and humanity not the less condemn the process, whatever might have been the antecedents of the victim. Cranmer's political offences were quite sufficient to seal his doom, in that age; in fact almost in any age. His malfeasance against the Church should have been left for the adjudication of the Supreme Court Above. The Queen's Council should not seek vengeance after the fashion of revolutionary factions, but, in the spirit of the Divine Saviour, pronounce the decree of Heavenly Charity, "*Go thy ways, and sin no more!*" They would then have given a judgment far more fatal to the new tenets of Thomas Cranmer, than would the immolation at the stake of ten thousand "obstinate thinkers."

No man of his era clothed soul and conscience in so many disguises—none embraced more opposite principles than Thomas Cranmer. His demeanour at the stake has won him fame for his wondrous disregard of suffering; but those who have studied the records of his life and actions, look upon his conduct, in the hour of dissolution, as that of a man maddened and desperate from disappointed hope. Indeed, it has been well remarked, and that, too, by a friendly biographer, that the "flames which consumed Thomas Cranmer's body at the stake have cast a false glitter upon his character."*

"He shall be judged by the bloody laws he has himself enacted," was the cry raised by the Council at the time of Thomas Crumwell's impeachment. According to the statute of Henry VIII., those who "relapsed into heresy were to be consumed at the stake *in terrorem*. Archbishop Cranmer was a party to the passing of this barbarous law; and as it was one of his royal master's favourite subjects, it is not improbable that Cranmer drew up the Act himself, aided by Rich, the Solicitor-General—thus perishing, in " legal " shape at least, by the work of his own hands. It is positively affirmed that the execution took place under this cruel Tudor law.

Much ingenuity has been manifested by a certain class of writers, either in denying the crimes of Cranmer, or in excusing them when impossible of denial. The most feeble of all apologies, however, is that which ascribes his actions to " weak-mindedness or timidity." On the contrary, his suppleness of conduct was the result of a self-contained and measured prevision. Dean Hook, remarking upon the Archbishop's bearing when under sentence of death, states that the letters he wrote to the Queen " manifested no want of boldness, nor gave the slightest indication of a wavering mind."† Let the reader reflect on the part Cranmer played, and then draw his own deductions. First, Cranmer had been for seventeen years the confidential adviser of Henry, and was the secret negotiator with German theologians on the divorce question. At the command of the King, he *pro-*

---

* Archbishops of Canterbury, vol. vii.   † *Ibid*, p. 376.

nounced the marriages of three queens to be null and void, and was a party to the judicial murder of two of them. He was an adviser of Henry when the Carthusians were immolated; when Fisher and More were sent to the scaffold; when the Marquis of Exeter and his friends were consigned to the headsman; when the Abbots of Glastonbury, Reading, and Woburn were plundered, hanged and quartered; when the "Pilgrims of Grace" were first deceived and then massacred; when the trees were bent with the corpses of the Northern peasantry; when Lord Darcy and his chivalrous companions perished on the scaffold; when Lady Bullmer was sent to the flames, and the venerable Countess of Salisbury butchered; when his co-partner in the monastic confiscations paid the penalty of an ignominious death; when those who held his own opinions were sent to the stake as heretics; when the Statute of the Six Articles became law; when the rack, the dungeon, the rope, and the axe spread desolation throughout the land; when confiscation or banishment became the lot of those who were the least offensive to the royal will;—still Thomas Cranmer, through all those dark years of violence, blood, and despotism, never sought to allay the fury of his patron, but always enjoyed the tyrant's confidence, even unto the last dread death-scene. And again, having perjured himself as to his dead master's will, for years longer he gave all the weight of his position and talents to promote the schemes of the Duke of Somerset and his colleagues; and then, of the Duke of Northumberland, in perfidy, confiscation legal murders, concocted massacres, and treason. Every conspiracy that was planned by the members of Edward's Council for the destruction of each other received the Archbishop's support, just as soon as he had made himself certain as to which side was the strongest. An ecclesiastic who could have maintained his political position, his liberty, or his life—as the colleague of such men—must, indeed, have been the reverse of "weak." On the contrary, he must have been a thorough "man of the world" in its very worst sense—possessed, it would seem, not only of a remorseless versatility, but a signal power of moulding men and events to his own purposes. Such was Thomas Cranmer, "some time" Archbishop of Canterbury.*

In allusion to Cranmer's recantations, Dean Hook writes:—

"Having conceded much, he evidently became reckless. *He had lost character, and having no character to sustain, he was ready to do anything that might be suggested.*"

The learned Dean continues:—

"It is my business to state historical facts, and not to impute motives. The honesty of a man's own heart may be doubted, when he is continually suspecting corrupt motives in others. I can find no facts to show that there was any insidious attempt to entrap Cranmer into a recantation, and then betray him. Taking the facts as they come before us, all seems to have occurred through a natural sequence of cause and effect."†

John Strype contends that Queen Elizabeth "entertained a high esteem and reverence for the memory of Archbishop Cranmer."‡ This statement is doubtful—very doubtful, indeed. Elizabeth was not the woman to forget a wrong

---

* The student of history will find much valuable matter concerning Cranmer in Dodd, Lingard, Jenkyns, Wilkins, Cox, Pocock, and the MSS. History of Cranmer by Ralph Morrice, which is deposited in the archives of the University of Cambridge. The history written by Morrice must be of peculiar interest, from the fact of his being Cranmer's confidential Secretary for many years. There are many other authorities, all of a conflicting character. The State Papers, and the Records of the times, are the most reliable documents yet known.

† Archbishops of Canterbury, vol. vii., p. 397-404.

‡ Strype's Memorials, vol. i., p. 613.

or an insult, especially in relation to her birth. She felt intensely the nature of Cranmer's judgment against her unfortunate mother, and its consequences to herself. And again, in the action taken by the Archbishop for changing the succession to the House of Dorset. If the projected revolution in favour of Lady Jane Dudley had succeeded, in what position would Elizabeth have been placed? It does not require much reflection to arrive at the conclusion that young Elizabeth's hostility to Cranmer was as deep-rooted as that of her sister Mary. The manifesto is still extant in which Archbishop Cranmer describes "Mary and Elizabeth as bastards, and consequently having *no royal claims* on this realm."

There is almost a general condemnation of Cranmer by Protestant historians for the part he had taken in sending the beautiful Anne Boucher to the stake. Wilkins contends that the Archbishop's address to King Edward has been preserved in a correct form. His exact words were "that Anne Boucher was about to be *deservedly punished.*"* These words undoubtedly signified that the said Anne Boucher was to be *consumed by fire at the stake*, because, as a *Protestant*, she dissented from *the* Protestantism then proclaimed by Archbishop Cranmer *himself*.

Macaulay cannot award the "martyr's crown" to the Archbishop. The brilliant historian writes :—

"Cranmer's martyrdom," it is said, 'redeemed everything.' "It is extraordinary that so much ignorance should exist on this subject. The fact is, that, if a martyr be a man who chooses to die rather than to renounce his opinions, Cranmer was no more a martyr than Dr. Dodd. He died solely because he could not help it. He never retracted his recantation until he found he

---

* Wilkins, vol. iv., p. 44.

had made it in vain. If Queen Mary had suffered him to live, I suspect that he *would have heard Mass again, and received absolution, like a good Catholic, till the accession of Elizabeth, and that he would then have purchased, by another apostacy, the power of burning men better and braver than himself.*" *

The Rev. Dr. Lockock, in his "Studies on the History of the Book of Common Prayer," refers to the Committee convened by Henry VIII., at Windsor Castle, where Archbishop Cranmer was the presiding spirit. The object of this Committee was to "reform and revise the Divine service." The author presents a brief and cautiously framed portrait of Cranmer at that particular period. He writes thus :—

" Of Cranmer many pictures have been given to the world, but probably in no other case have they varied so materially from each other. This variation is due not so much to the bias of the painter, as to the fact that his character *did change in many of its features at different periods of his history.* * * * Cranmer was by no means a man of great genius, or an original thinker, likely to strike out something fresh, but he possessed a good judgment, which would enable him to discriminate between what was new and what was old."

The reverend author adds that :—

" The Crown had its advocate in Cranmer, than whom none could be more attached to the King personally, or more tenacious of his rights and prerogative."

The most conscientious Protestant commentators on Cranmer are far from being satisfied with either his religious or political principles. The latest writer upon the subject is Canon Dixon, the much esteemed Vicar of Hayton, whose two volumes must be read with deep interest by every student of history. I, so far, agree with the "Reviewer" of

---

* Macaulay's Essays.

the *Standard*, in his estimate of the value of the learned Canon's work. Mr. Dixon observes :—

"The virtues and the reputation of Cranmer must not blind us to the tragedy which was acted under his Primacy; nor cause us to forget that he was the slave—first, of Henry and Crumwell, afterwards of Somerset, Paget, and Northumberland: that under him the Church of England *fell from wealth to poverty:* that he offered no resistance to the enormous sacrilege of this and the following reign, from which the Archbishop's *own hands were not altogether clean;* and that nothing was more convenient to the spoilers of the Church than that he should have been the highest of her bishops. In *doctrine he rose from one position to another with the whole rabble of innovators at his heels, until at last he seemed* ready to surrender the Catholicity of the Church to the Sacramentarians."*

In Vol. II. Canon Dixon continues his review of Cranmer in these words :—

"We can discern in Cranmer nothing but the official of the 'new loyalty' (a significant phrase). Of the uncouth jocularity and hidden anguish of a Latimer we should expect no trace in him; but neither is there any indication of *doubt or scruple* concerning the enormous measures that were littering the land with ruins and crowning it with gibbets. He was ever ready to be led; ever willing to trust himself to those who showed the power of leading. His acquiescence was wonderful in *a man of conscience and goodness.*"†

I at once take an exception to the allegation that Thomas Cranmer was "*a man of conscience and goodness.*" The records of his life—his public life—bear testimony to the very opposite conclusion. No amount of special pleading can build up

---

* Canon Dixon's History of the Church of England from the Abolition of the Roman Jurisdiction, vol. i., p. 154-5.

† Ibid, vol. ii., p. 61.

a character for Thomas Cranmer. Quite impossible. All the "facts" point in the opposite direction.

By the part Cranmer had taken in the judicial murder of Anne Boleyn he proved to the world that he was ready to carry out any design of his despotic master. So he declared young Elizabeth, in the most offensive language, to be illegitimate, although for three years the Archbishop daily offered up Mass for the young lady whom he styled the Princess Elizabeth. Of this matter Dean Hook writes:—

"The whole affair is a sad story, from whatever point of view we may regard it; and of Cranmer's conduct in the matter, the less his admirers say, the greater will be their discretion." *

This is a frequent admission. And again Dean Hook writes in reluctant, yet forcible words, upon Cranmer's judgment against the good Queen Katharine:—

"The Archbishop *seems never to have been conscience-stricken* for his conduct in this matter."

The second vol. of a work on Cranmer and his Contemporaries has recently appeared from the pen of a distinguished Anglican divine. The writer observes:—

"A calm review of the Archbishop's character, free from party prejudice, must pronounce upon it a very unfavourable opinion." †

---

* Archbishops of Canterbury, vol. vi., p. 509.
† Reformation of the Church of England, by the Rev. J. H. Blunt. ol. ii., p. 330.

CHAPTER VI.

CLERICS OF THE "NEW LEARNING."

THE "Hot-Gospel" writers, as some of the ultra-Reformers have been styled, estimate Dr. Cranmer and his disciples as a class of men who should rank with the Apostles of Christ and the martyrs of the Primitive Church. But this is the age of inquiry. I must, therefore, briefly enter upon the history of a few of those notable men, and see what claims they have to be set down as apostles or saints. I first present boisterous, good-natured HUGH LATIMER amongst a special group. Latimer's memory has been long cherished by English Churchmen and Dissenters, for his character has "a popular side." How stands the case? During the Primacy of Archbishop Warham, Latimer was cited before Convocation for heretical preaching. He denied the charge of heresy, but admitted that he used "bad language," and was sorry for it. The Convocation condemned him, and he was duly excommunicated. In a short time he recanted his opinions, and was restored to the Church's communion. On this occasion he knelt down before the Convocation, and craved forgiveness in a most abject manner. He again indulged in violent language, but at the request of the King he was once more restored. He now gave a solemn pledge that he would in future obey the laws and observe the decrees of the Church. "Humbly on my knees," he said, "I ask forgiveness, and shall remember you all in my prayers, the only way I have of making restitution to you for the scandals I have caused."* In fact Latimer was continually violating his vows and oaths. He really seems to have had no regard for an oath. The question may fairly be put—" Was he in a sound state of mind ?" Some Protestant writers affirm that Latimer was in " a sound state of mind, but possessed of a violent temper ;" others consider him as " viewing every question in an extreme manner." Carlos Logario, Wolsey's Spanish doctor, states that Latimer informed him that, " when a boy he was thrown from a horse, and fell on his head; and that in after years he felt the effects of it, as he became excited over things that could not trouble any one to a large degree." " He was," writes Logario, " most singular in his mode of doing all things ; apparently out of his wits ; yet he was not so."

Latimer appeared before Primate Warham in 1531, and abjured a second time ; and before King Henry himself at a later period, and made an unreserved submission to the monarch "in all spiritual matters." Lastly, when imprisoned for heresy along with Bishop Shaxton, towards the close of Henry's reign (1546), he abjured a fourth time, to save his life. Thus he dissembled not once, or twice, but for nearly twenty years.

It may be mentioned that the main charge under which Latimer was deprived by Henry VIII., was for an open violation of the Good Friday fast—a custom " not easily chargeable with dangerous superstition." Mr. Froude aptly remarks of a less flagrant violation of the day of abstinence, " that it was *in that* era just as if a bishop of our time were to go *to a theatre on Sunday*—a mere wanton insult to

---

* Wilkins, vol. iii., p. 747. Archbishop of Canterbury, vol. vi., p. 400-1.

general religious feeling." "Latimer's coarseness and profanity" are not left to conjecture, nor to the bias of partisans. He has given ample proofs of them under his own hand in his still extant sermons. It may be pleaded that these faults were those of the age, rather than of the man. I can only answer that those who say so can know very little of contemporary homilists. Latimer was a persecutor too. His name appears as one of the bishops who sat to try John Lambert, who was in 1538 burnt for disbelieving Transubstantiation, which Latimer had himself abandoned in 1529. Nor can it be pleaded that he was forced to be present, having had no share in the matter, for he and Cranmer actually endeavoured to make Lambert recant the very opinions they secretly held themselves. Latimer's signature also appears attached to the death-warrant of Joan Boucher.

Of all the "Smithfield sermons" preached by Latimer—coarse and unfeeling as they were—none were so repellent as that delivered by him against his brother priest, Dr. Forrest. As he was *hanging in chains, roasting over a large fire*, Latimer asked him "whether he would live or die?" "I will die," was the reply, "do your worst upon me. Seven years ago you durst not, for your life, have preached such words as you have now. If an angel came down from the heavens to teach me any other doctrines than those which I learned when a child, and have held during my long life, I would not believe him; no, I would not. *I will stand by the old faith to the death. Take me, cut me to pieces joint from joint; burn, hang, do what you will, I will be true henceforth to the faith of my fathers.*" *

---

* Scaffold Speeches of English Priests, by Roger Bambrick.

Hall and Fox proclaim Dr. Forrest "unpenitent;" that he "put no trust in his Saviour." Edward Hall was well acquainted with Forrest; and, in truth, he could not make such a statement, but John Fox knew little of this high-minded, self-sacrificing man. Perhaps Fox had never seen him. Dr. Forrest's great offence was that of denying the King's supremacy. Mr. Froude says that Father Forrest "went his way through treason and perjury to the stake." But Mr. Froude has not established any case either of perjury or treason against Forrest, unless he wishes to construe loyalty to religion as treason. The King declared it high treason to deny that he was, as he styled himself, the "supreme Head of Christ's Church on earth." Forrest also declared in favour of Queen Katharine. He maintained that Katharine was the King's lawful wife. This declaration on the part of the Queen's Confessor was, perhaps, the most deadly act of treason he could possibly have committed, in Henry's estimation, at a time when the future destiny of Anna Boleyn was under consideration. "The venerable old man," writes Pollino, "who had been Confessor to Queen Katharine, was barbarously used. He was kept two years in a dungeon amongst thieves, murderers, and other persons of infamous character; besides he was cruelly tortured in various ways."

Latimer, in one of his "stake sermons," speaks of a sect styled Donatists. "Those heretics," he says, "went to their execution as they should have gone to some recreation or banquet, or to some belly cheer, or a play."*

Amongst the revolutionary sects of those times the Anabaptists are, perhaps, the least understood by the modern

---

* Latimer's Sermons, p. 160.

Englishman. Blunt, in recurring to the close of Henry's reign, and the troubled times of Edward, is not disposed to estimate the Anabaptists in a high social or religious point of view." "They were," he observes, "becoming dangerous by the contagious rapidity with which their socialist and infidel principles spread among the lower classes."* Although Archbishop Cranmer encouraged some of the Anabaptists of Germany to reside in London, he subsequently considered them to be a class of people who were opposed to every settled form of government. This sect attributed the Sacrament of Baptism to the devil. The Anabaptist sermons were a tissue of shocking blasphemy. The Elector of Hesse, himself an advanced Reformer after a fashion, warned the English monarch against giving any countenance to this Communist sect.† Dean Hook contends that the real charge against them was that, to use a modern term, they were Socialists.‡ Yet, in the estimation of such historians as Fox, Burnet, Oldmixon, Rapin, and other Puritan writers, those people were "*The Valiant Soldiers of Christ*." Did Fox or Burnet believe their own statements to be true? It is impossible to think so.

The origin of the Anabaptists of the sixteenth century is involved in obscurity. They appeared first in Saxony or in Switzerland; but it was not until they had established themselves in Northern Germany that, by their peculiarities and eccentricities, they attracted general attention. Their conduct, based on the most absurd theories, would have led, except for the interposition of the civil power, to the entire disruption of civilised society. They contended that they

---

* Rev. J. H. Blunt's Reformation, vol. i.
† Mosheim ed Stubbs, vol. iii., p. 142.
‡ Archbishops of Canterbury, vol. vii., p. 54.

had as much right as Luther, or any other of the foreign Reformers, to place their own construction upon Holy Scripture, and to bend it to the support of their private judgment. According to their view of revealed truth, they insisted upon a *community of goods and universal equality;* not only titles, but tribute in every form, together with all usury, were denounced as unscriptural; baptism of infants was, in their opinion, an invention of the evil spirit; as all Christians had a right to teach, the appointment of ministers was condemned; Christ being King, *no magistrates were needed;* revelations were still made from God to man, through dreams and visions, vouchsafed to persons who regarded themselves as prophets.*
Immorality in its worst forms prevailed amongst them.

At what time the Anabaptists first appeared in England is not exactly known. Traces of them occur as early as 1536; and in 1538 a royal commission was issued to put them down in England. They were a source of immense mischief in this country, for they refused to yield obedience to the State in any way, so that coercion in a severe form was necessary; but, at the same time, civilization must protest against the stake and its horrors. The English Reformers were greatly exasperated against the Anabaptists, and generally approved of Cranmer's policy in sending them to the flames.† The conduct of the Anabaptists to Cranmer was marked by ingratitude and baseness.

To return to Latimer. Having joined in the rebellion against Queen Mary, he had but little to expect. Six hours' notice was given to him of his arrest; and when the officer

---

* Mosheim, Book 4, sec 3.

† See Archbishops of Canterbury, vol. ix. The Royal archives of Holland contain the most important documents bearing upon the history of the Anabaptists.

arrived at Stamford with the warrant for his capture, he merely stated that the "authorities required the presence of Dr. Latimer in London." The officer further informed him that his orders "were not to arrest him in the usual manner."* So Latimer's escape was actually desired by the Government. But Latimer's fanatical friends cheered him on to play the part of a bravo, or martyr. He went to London, appeared before the Council, where he conducted himself "in a seditious and insolent manner." He was committed to the Tower. Fox and writers of his particular stamp describe Latimer's condition in the Tower as one of wretchedness; "in the winter without fire, or warm clothing, or good food." It is possible that this statement is true, though so attested. The officials at the Tower were then the same men who held office in Edward's reign.

Latimer, in describing the state of society towards the close of the reign of Henry VIII., remarks that "two acres of hemp, sown up and down in England, would not be sufficient to hang the number of thieves who were sent to the hangman to operate upon in the name of justice and law." Latimer was as determined to award the "hemp tie" to the starving author as he was to send a heretic to the stake, assuring him that "the flames which consumed his body were not so cruel in their infliction as what awaited him *in another place.*"

Bishop SHAXTON was as inconsistent as Latimer. He was a man of neither principle nor morality; a coward, a liar, a time server, and an implacable enemy. He had no regard for any religion, and joined the Reformers because he was cast out of the Roman fold. In 1543 he was condemned by

---

* Privy Council Register, MS., Mary's reign.

Archbishop Cranmer to be sent to "the flames as an obstinate heretic." This sentence met with King Henry's entire approbation. A few hours before the immolation Shaxton's courage failed him, and he shrunk from the fiery ordeal, and not only recanted, but preached the sermon at the execution of his former associates—*the very men who received sentence with himself a few days before.* He exhorted the victims at the stake to return to the Catholic Church and their lives would be spared. The Anabaptists were not to be won, and they went to the stake with the wild enthusiasm of fanatics. The English Reformers felt indignant at being thus betrayed by a man who seemed so devoted to the Protestant cause. Shaxton was rewarded with the Mastership of St. Giles Hospital, in Norwich. His career does not end here.

Burnet has an indifferent opinion of Shaxton, whom he describes as "proud and ill-natured." Strype, the contemporary of Burnet, holds a different opinion, and looks on Dr. Shaxton as a model prelate. Shaxton, like many of his contemporaries, must be judged by his actions. From some unknown cause he was reduced to poverty.

JOHN HOOPER, after graduating at Oxford in 1518, became a Cistercian monk, at Gloucester, taking, as a matter of course, the vow of perpetual celibacy. He subsequently left Gloucester, and returned to Oxford, which he was obliged to leave because of his heterodox opinions. When the Bill of the Six Articles became law, he went to Flanders, and thence to Germany, where Bullinger introduced him to a young lady from Burgundy, whom he subsequently married. He was many years the senior of the lady in question.

---

* Ellis, vol. iii., p. 177 ; Collier, vol. ii., p. 212 : Stowe, p. 592 ; State Papers, vol. i., p. 869.

On Hooper's return to England he joined the Duke of Somerset's household. He next commenced preaching in the public thoroughfares, where his "levelling sentiments" made him popular with the Anabaptist democrats. The "upper class" Reformers were displeased with his conduct. The old Conservative party accused him of being "scurrilous and profane in the pulpit." The Reformers deny these charges. His accusers, however, prove at least the charge of scurrility, for even Peter Martyr, a man of extreme views, warned him to be "more guarded and less censorious in his language." The Council of Edward VI. were compelled to silence Hooper for a time for his fanatical sermons and the harshness of his language to those who were opposed to him.* Hooper took an active part in the proceedings against Bonner, and clamoured for his imprisonment. When appointed to the see of Gloucester, Hooper raised strong objections to the use of the episcopal vestments. Ridley, Bucer, and Peter Martyr argued with him in their favour, but all in vain. He held out steadily that the rochet and crozier were "inventions of Antichrist," and that to "wear them was absolute superstition." If he had been convinced by the arguments, or if he had refused a bishopric clogged with the usual conditions, he might be entitled to respect; but he accepted the see and wore the vestments, while declaring them "to be wicked and devilish," and kept up a life-long quarrel with Ridley, who was credited with having had the best of the dispute. "It is not easy," observes a High Churchman of these times, "to stigmatise such conduct too forcibly. If we desired a modern parallel, we should be obliged to invent some wild and improbable hypothesis.

---

* Collier's Ecclesiastical History, vol. v.; Strype's Memorials.

Suppose, for example, that an illiterate and virulent Puritan of our day were to set himself against daily services, especially choral ones, and to write a book to prove that Gothic Church architecture was an invention of the devil to ruin souls, and then, without any previous change of views, were to clutch greedily at the Deanery of a Gothic Cathedral, would not every one, even of his own school, call him a hypocrite? Hooper degraded the episcopal office by following Dr. Cranmer's lead, and consenting to hold his spiritual dignity solely at the King's pleasure. * * * * He had been one of the loudest inveighers against pluralism, and had urged its existence as a main ground for a sweeping reformation. His own first step was to accept the See of Worcester, to be held along with that of Gloucester. He conveyed away the property of his See, of which, of course, he was a mere trustee for life-interest, to the rapacious courtiers to whom he owed his promotion. Of two charges, however, Hooper is to be acquitted. He was no coward, and he was no traitor to Queen Mary, as he steadily refused to join in Cranmer's plots."

Dean Hook does not approve of Hooper's inconsistent policy. "He was," says the Dean, "*pious and obstinate; as ready to be burnt as he was to burn.*" And again, "he was doubtless employed as the spy or public prosecutor in the case of Bonner. This was most shameful conduct." His eccentricity appears to be unaccountable; yet the humblest creature could approach him. Perhaps he was the most honest man amongst the fanatics with whom he was associated.* "The violence of Hooper's language to ignorant and fanatical mobs had often been productive of mischief

---

* Archbishops of Canterbury, vol. vii.

and the conduct of his coadjutor, Peter Martyr, led to the sacrifice of many lives. In Oxfordshire the rope was introduced to give force to the arguments of Martyr, and far and wide among the villages the bodies of the rectors and vicars were dangled from their church towers.*

Many of Hooper's actions were marked by singular kindliness. Every day he gave dinner to a number of destitute people, and dismissed each with "some words of comfort." Unlike many of the leading Reformers, Hooper was as loyal to his legitimate Sovereign as he was faithful to his own newly-formed opinions on religion. In a narrative which he wrote of his conduct, he observes with simple truth:—"When Queen Mary's fortunes were at the worst I rode myself from place to place to win and stay the people for her Highness. And whereas, when another (Lady Jane Dudley) was proclaimed, I preferred our Queen, notwithstanding the proclamations. I sent horses in both shires (Gloucester and Worcester), to serve the Queen in her great danger." The Council, however, and *not* the Queen, should have been condemned by posterity for the barbarous death inflicted upon Hooper. His execution was one of the most revolting scenes that occurred at the "stake" in those calamitous times. The conduct of Lord Chandos,† of Sir Anthony Kingston, and of the Sheriff was indescribably infamous. These men were under no fanatical or bigoted influence, but adapted their principles and conduct to suit every party which gained ascendancy. They were "zealous,

---

* Froude's History of England, vol. v., p. 186.

† Lord Chandos was better known in former years as Sir John Brydges, the Lieutenant of the Tower. He was witness to many revolting scenes on the scaffold and in the dungeon. From such an official Hooper could expect little indulgence or sympathy.

pious Protestants," in Edward's reign; and, upon the accession of Mary, they joined in the "shout of joy" raised by the Parliament—so lately Reformers—in favour of a return to the olden creed. That such cruel crimes as the burning of Hooper and his brethren did not meet with the assent of true Catholics there is no question. Many of the ancient Catholic families of England protested against executions at the stake; the Lord Abbot Feckenham wrote a "warning voice" on the subject to Bonner. The great body of the English nation were opposed to such an outrage upon Civilization and Charity; but the Government were not influenced by the people, and cared little for popular opinion whilst they were backed up by troops—foreign mercenaries. In those evil days political ambition or personal revenge achieved a fatal triumph, not only over the better sentiments of humanity, but in many instances subdued that moral consciousness which Providence has imparted to man to advance his virtue whilst ennobling his nature.

Father Tyrrell, a learned Benedictine, spoke to Bonner in very forcible language of his conduct as a priest; to which the unfeeling prelate replied—"Mind your own business." Griffin, a cleric himself, defends Bonner's conduct in Hooper's case, stating that he was "pushed forward by the personal enemies of that prelate, amongst whom was the Marquis of Winchester, whose flagrant immoralities and scandals Bishop Hooper had often denounced." This is but a poor excuse for Bonner's conduct, who, if he had been swayed by the Divine Charity of that Church of which he was an unworthy member, would have abandoned his cruel crusade, and, in case he could not stop the immolation by fire, take up his crozier and repair to some distant forest scene, where he might mourn over the distractions of his country, and pray for the restoration of peace to the hitherto happy and virtuous people of England. But Dr. Bonner had been too long the political agent of despotic rulers to "mend his ways." So much for the connection then existing between the Church and the State.

It may appear strange that some of the "best defences" made for Bonner have been written by Protestant historians of a recent date. "As a man Bonner was never a zealous persecutor. He seemed sick of his work."* Dean Hook considers the charges against him to be exaggerated; and Mr. Froude looks on him as "a good-natured kind of man." I have already remarked upon Bonner's barbarous conduct in the case of Archbishop Cranmer. As a priest he should never have undertaken such an abhorrent office as that of a judge "in heretic cases." That he could be compelled by a statute of Henry VIII. to appear in such a judicial capacity is, nevertheless, certain. And in Edward VI.'s reign, as the reader is aware, Cranmer and his suffragans held a public court for the trial of heretics, and sent several to the stake under shocking circumstances.† However, the transactions of the reign of the "Boy-King" form a precedent for nothing that was not arbitrary, unjust, and cruel.

The execution of Hooper was one of the worst cases of immolation at stake or scaffold in Mary's reign. Again, I repeat, he was no rebel to his Sovereign like Cranmer and his friends.‡ The trial and execution of Hooper cover all those

---

* Green's History of the English People, vol. ii., p. 260.

† I refer the reader to the second volume (p. 315) of this work for the heresy trials and burnings under Archbishop Cranmer and the Council of King Edward.

‡ State Papers of Queen Mary's reign; Despatches of the French, Spanish, and Venetian Envoys; Strype's Memorials; Collier's Ecclesiastical History, vol. ii.

concerned—whether Civil, Military, or Ecclesiastical—with well-deserved infamy.

It has been remarked, that if the "Reformers had not known how to govern the country, they knew how to die bravely." And die bravely they did.

Dr. ROWLAND TAYLOR, a man of much learning and stainless reputation, was sent to the stake on the day of Hooper's execution. He told the people to be loyal to their Sovereign, and not to hearken to the wicked advice of the German Anabaptists, who were overturning society in London. A most affecting "leave-taking" took place between Taylor and his family. The scene at this sad cremation was revolting; and the conduct of the drunken executioners more resembled that of demons than of human beings. Rowland Taylor died with great fortitude. He was deeply regretted by the Reformers, in fact by every person with whom he was acquainted.

THOMAS BECON, a native of Suffolk, was attached to the party of Dr. Cranmer. He dedicated his Treatise on Fasting to the Archbishop. He was one of the most obsequious men patronized by the government of Edward VI. In Mary's reign he was deprived of his livings, and committed to prison for writing seditious lampoons and pamphlets against the Queen. It is alleged by Puritan writers that his offence was that of "defending the Gospel." This statement will not stand the test of honest inquiry. Under the name of "Theodore Basil" he wrote against his sovereign. His sermons—as some of his gross-minded speeches have been called—were unworthy of the clerical character. In Henry's reign he had to retire to a remote part of the country, lest he might meet the fate of Lambert. He suffered "great privation, cold and misery," says Farlow. In the reign of Elizabeth he became a popular preacher against the Olden Religion. He appeared at St. Paul's Cross to congratulate the people of London upon the accession of Elizabeth. He was as earnest as Latimer in advocating the cause of the poor, but with little effect. Foxe, Pomeroy, Burnet, Strype, and several other writers of the extreme Reformers, are loud in his commendation. It has been stated that he returned to the Catholic religion before his death. There is no foundation for this statement. "In one of his last discourses," writes a contemporary preacher, he said, "thank God I have assisted in overthrowing the corruptions of the Bishop of Rome in this realm." His name ranks amongst the "Valiant Soldiers of Christ" recorded by John Foxe.

ARTHUR BUCKLEY was a member of an ancient family in the Isle of Anglesey. He was educated at Oxford, where he was created Doctor of Common Law. He was consecrated Bishop of Bangor in 1541. Buckley was one of Henry's most pliant agents, and the fact of his being an intimate friend, or associate, of John Bale, at once testifies as to his moral character. Thorndale states that he was married to Rebecca Whitechurch, whom Anthony Woodgate, a Baptist preacher, claimed as *his* wife. Thorndale affirms that he was personally acquainted with the parties. In the reign of Edward VI. Buckley accepted the theological teaching of Dr. Cranmer. There is no record extant of his having acted with "cruelty or harshness" to the members of the faith he had renounced. Some very gross lampoons were written upon Buckley by a Scotch priest named Henry Graham, who subsequently joined the Reformers himself. Godwin, who relates many marvellous tales concerning the Reformers and their antagonists, believes Buckley to have been fonder of "the loaves and fishes" than of preaching the Gospel. "The bishop," writes Godwin, "sold five very curious bells belonging to his own cathedral, and going to the sea-shore to see them shipped for a foreign country, he was immediately struck blind, and so remained all his life."* In Queen Mary's reign he returned to the creed of his fathers, and died in the year 1555, as much despised as Dr. Kitchen, the noted Bishop of Llandaff.

"PAUL BUSH, a handsome young man," writes Simon Fish, "became a student of Oxford about 1512. He received his early education from the Augustine Friars. At a subsequent period he entered himself among the religious styled *Bonshommes*. In after years he received quick promotion; became provincial of the Augustine order; next a royal chaplain, and other preferments." At the dissolution of the monastic houses he facilitated the movements of the inquisitors; enjoyed the friendship of Lord Crumwell, Cranmer and Dr. London. The King was proud of having won over a man of such brilliant talents; his contemporaries declare that he was a man of universal knowledge; a master of Greek, Latin, Hebrew, French, Spanish and Italian; and as a theologian he ranked high. He was a poet of comparative genius, and well skilled in architecture, chemistry, botany and music. "His acquirements," says Baxter, "were most varied; and he had none of that haughty bearing which characterized too many of the clerics of those times." In 1542 Henry VIII.

---

* See Anthony Wood, Athen. Oxon.; Godwin's Annals; Thorndale's Memorials; Dodd's Church History, vol. i.

appointed Dr. Bush to the newly created see of Bristol. Like other Clerical Reformers he married a young wife. " It was my pleasure," writes Phillips—himself a cleric—" to have known Dr. Bush's wife; her name was Clara Ramsay, a native of Dundee—young and handsome; but the elderly man and the lively young lass did not agree as husband and wife." Upon the accession of Queen Mary, Bush resigned his bishopric, returned to his former creed, and separated from his wife and three children, for whom he provided, through the kindness of Abbot Feckenham. Bush then returned to a village within a few miles of Bath, where he died in 1558, almost unknown to his contemporaries.

ROBERT HOLGATE, a monk of the order of Sempringham, became the successor of Archbishop Lee in the diocese of York. Before his consecration Holgate took the following oath of supremacy to Henry VIII. :—

" I, Robert Archbishop of York elect, having now the veil of darkness of the usurped power, authority and jurisdiction of the See of Rome clearly taken from mine eyes, *do utterly testify and declare in my conscience that neither the See nor the Bishop of Rome, nor any foreign potentate, hath, or ought to have, any jurisdiction, power or authority within the realm, neither by God's law, nor by any just law, or any other means.*"

Gardyner, Bonner, Tunstal, Heath, and other prelates subscribed to a similar oath. Kitchen and Ferrars took the same oath at a later period, renouncing the Pope.*

Dr. Whyte considers Holgate as a disciple of Cranmer. Another contemporary (Pomeroy) affirms that Holgate " was a lover of 'good belly cheer' and strong liquor." " It was

---

* See Strype's Cranmer, vol. i., p. 134; State Papers of Edward VI's reign.

bruited that he had a wife and children residing at one of the See houses." "He was a hypocrite, and lived in adultery with the wife of his own gardener. He was a disgrace to the Reformed Church of England, and died in a bad condition, covered with a leprosy of immorality."* Such is the picture drawn of Archbishop Holgate by Hales the preacher, who was himself moral, if not gentle-spoken. Upon the accession of Queen Mary, Holgate was one of the seven bishops superseded by Gardyner at the special command of the Pope.† These prelates were either married or uncanonically appointed, according to Cranmer's "new ordinall." Parker, a Puritan preacher, states that Holgate died happy and contented, was a great searcher of the Scriptures, and abhorred the Bishop of Rome for his tricks to levy money.‡ Father Pemberton makes an opposite statement as to how Holgate ended his days. Collier affirms that Holgate "was not of the most unblemished character. He had betrayed his See, and surrendered many of its most valuable manors to the King. Besides this, he lay under an odious imputation with respect to his marriage." In Edward's reign the Council commanded Dr. Rokesby and two other commissioners to investigate and examine a case in which a man named Norman claimed the Archbishop's wife as his "*own real wife.*"§

Archbishop Holgate was imprisoned in the Tower for eighteen months, and then discharged at the "request of King Philip, who besought the Queen to pardon a great many prisoners."‖ Philip has been always represented as a gloomy

---

* Hale's Sermons on "The Death-bed of Rich Sinners."
† Dodd's "Church History," vol. i.
‡ Parker's "Accounts of the Papists who became Protestant Christians."
§ Council Book, State Papers (domestic) of Edward VI's reign.
‖ See State Papers of Mary's reign.

persecutor, yet we find Strype averring that Philip was not the instigator of any persecution, and often interceded with effect for those who suffered from it, or for the numerous treasons, the punishments for which later writers have confounded with inflictions for so-called "heresy."

Holgate died in 1555, very wealthy. "He was," says Farlow, "a heartless man who had no sympathy for the poor." The "better living" portion of the early Reformers detested him for his immorality; they considered him a fit companion for such a character as John Bale, or Rasper, the hot-gospel preacher of Suffolk. Strype chronicles a list of his effects, which showed that he had laid in a large stock of the good things of this world, which were not, judging from the actions of the man, intended for God's poor.

Here are a few items of Holgate's domestic effects:—

"At Battersea, his chests contained £300 in gold coin; plate gilt, 1600 ozs.; mitre gold, with two pendants set with very fine diamonds and precious stones, &c., weight 125 ozs.; and six gold rings, with emeralds and diamonds. At Cawood he had under lock £900 in gold; silver plate, 760 ozs.; 2500 sheep; an enormous quantity of costly furniture; a chest full of valuable copes and vestments. His household store was also very large; wheat, 200 grs.; malt, 500 ditto; oats, 60 ditto; *wine, five tons*. He had likewise at Cawood, four score of horses. At his other See houses he had a large amount of property, cattle, pigs, crops, fowls, furniture, wines, plate and jewellery." *

In a sermon preached by Dr. Gardyner before King Philip and Cardinal Pole at Paul's Cross, he makes the following allusion to the Archbishops of York and Canterbury:—

"Thus while we desired to have a supreme head among us, it

---

* Strype's Cranmer, vol. i. Collier's Ecclesiastical History, vol. vi., furnish many particulars concerning Holgate.

came to pass that we had no head at all; no, not so much as our two Archbishops. For that, on one side the Queen, being a woman, could not be Head of the Church; and, on the other side, they were both convicted of one crime, and so deposed."*

King Henry, as the "Defender of the Faith," did not seem to know much of what was passing around him.

Archbishop Holgate has been condemned by many Protestant writers of high repute. Burnet, however, whilst allowing that Holgate adopted Cranmer's views of religion, and had been translated from the See of Llandaff to that of York through Cranmer's interest, admits that he was "no credit to the Reformation." Much of the evidence laid before Somerset and Cranmer concerning Holgate is unfit for publication. Morrice is of opinion that the Archbishop very possibly was deceived as to the moral character of Holgate.

ANTHONY DELABARRE was, what might be called now-a-days, a "Scripture-reader." His marvellous relations respecting himself and his friends are not borne out by facts. In the words of his contemporary, Griffin, his "stories were like a large quantity of dust and a few grains of corn together; when the fresh breeze and the light cometh, the dust flieth away, and, lo! there be scarce a grain at all of what was called corn." Delabarre's aspirations for martyrdom in the cause of the "pure Gospel," to use the phrase of the times, had no existence; his austerity and Puritan manners were simulated; he had never been a "saint of the old or the new kalendar;" he was no fanatic—he was a man of the world. He could share in the gross indulgences of the times; he could play at dice; he could drink, and

* Strype's "Cranmer," vol. i., p. 441.

sing the ribald songs which once amused Thomas Crumwell's convivial hours; but perhaps the society of John Poynet extinguished his early virtues, and made him a hypocrite. He was a strange mixture of concealed vice with some of the "goodly parts of nature."* It may be mentioned that Dr. Maitland and Mr. Froude are at issue as to the merits of Delabarre. May they not, like the ancient mathematicians, be contesting about an imponderable quantity? Mr. Froude may rest assured, however, that his estimate will not be sustained if he take the trouble of investigating the facts. Mr. Blunt's latest researches bring us to a genuine conclusion. " Judging," he writes, " from Delabarre's account of himself, he was very unscrupulous, and set no value upon truth, although he talked loudly about *the* truth." † Delabarre did not die at the stake, or on the scaffold, or in a dungeon for " preaching the Gospel," as stated by some Puritan writers. In 1563 he was residing in Oxfordshire, " in easy circumstances," and actually entertained Maister Foxe at his house. What a meeting!!!

According to a recent writer, Anthony Delabarre " was one of the remarkable saints of his time." We are, however, rather advanced in the nineteenth century for reproducing the sayings of John Foxe, or of Baron Munchausen.

ANTHONY KITCHEN, known in some parts as "Tom Dunstan," was appointed Bishop of Llandaff, in May, 1545. His consecration is not to be found in the Register of the date indicated. Kitchen's oaths to Henry VIII., were in

---

* "The tales of Jacob Godfrey," a very rare little black letter book, printed in 1566.

† J. H. Blunt's "Reformation of the Church of England." vol. i., p. 529.

these words:—" I, Anthony Thomas Kitchen, by the *grace of God*, and the pleasure of *my blessed and truly great King*, being now the Bishop elect of Llandaff, and having the vail of darkness removed from my eyes, concerning the usurped power, authority, and jurisdiction of the See of Rome, do now utterly testify and declare before the Almighty God, that the Bishop of Rome has no spiritual authority in this realm, and that no other man save our *blessed King* Henry VIII, *has*, or *should have any authority in guarding God's Church, but the said King Henry and his lawful successors.*"

Kitchen was somewhat of the "Vicar of Bray" type. He was not the original vicar, although his contemporary; but he was, like him, a signal instance of adaptiveness. He was an Abbot in Henry VIII.'s time. The royal conviction of the "Defensor Fidei," about the divorce, convinced the Abbot, who was soon made Bishop of Llandaff. He is said to have made "many valuable suggestions to the King and Thomas Crumwell." In Edward VI.'s time, he was a bishop under Cranmer's system, and when Mary succeeded to the throne, the Bishop of Llandaff *changed again*. How can conscience possibly have given license to such mutations as those of Kitchen and his compeers? A Catholic Bishop in Mary's reign, Kitchen took the oath of supremacy to Elizabeth: he laid his conscience in the highway, and sought the highest bidder. Elizabeth became the purchaser, and Dr. Kitchen was *again* made a bishop, according to the principle propounded by Cranmer. The play upon the bishop's name was not undeserved; and even in the present day the man would not be found guilty of libel for saying, as was then said, that the Bishop of Llandaff was "fonder of *the Kitchen* than of *the Church.*" Mr. Froude describes Kitchen as a man "*whose* character does not bear inspection." The authorities as to this prelate's disrepute, are numerous. *

Mr. Froude remarks that the "Aylmers, the Jewells, and the Grindals were not of the metal of which the martyrs are configured; but they were skilful talkers, and admirable divines. They had conviction enough—though Jewell, at least, had saved his life by apostacy—to be quite willing to persecute their adversaries. They were as little capable as the Roman Catholics of believing that *heaven's gatekeepers*† acknowledged any passport, save in terms of their own theology. On the whole, they were well selected for the work which they had to do." ‡

What worse men could be for a great change in an observance which affected eternal interests? Jewell has been described by a contemporary as the "flower of the reformed bishops," before the art of honest hero-worship had existence. The writer who took the above episcopal photographs, acknowledges the hollowness of his originals; and he will find it difficult to convince the honest reader that immorality and hypocrisy are amongst the fitting attributes of the apostles of a new faith. Bishop Jewell was the author of a well-known work, "The Apology of the Church of England," a work of some ability, but far more remarkable for its suppression of facts, and for the absence of that charity which should characterize a prelate who has been described as "meek and humble of spirit." It is worth observing, now that correct portraits of the reforming bishops are so much

---

* See Strype, Collier, Wharton; Maitland's Essays on the Reformation; Parker and Camden Societies' Papers; Lingard, Turner, and Froude.

† What a profane expression from Mr. Froude!

‡ Froude's "History of England," vol. iii., p. 74-75.

sought after, that Dr. Jewell never signed the Thirty-nine Articles, and was, in fact, one of the nine bishops who disapproved of them. Others, indeed, go so far as to say that he did not believe in them at all.

According to Le Bas, the biographer of Jewell, he became a "clerical Reformer" in 1539, if not before that period; but he "remained judiciously silent as to his change of opinion as long as Henry lived." I find, however, that in 1540 — the year of Thomas Crumwell's fall — Jewell frequently celebrated Mass before the King; and Archbishop Cranmer assured the monarch that Father Jewell was "a very pious priest." Marvellously deceived must Henry have been as to the real characters of Cranmer and of Jewell. Upon the accession of Edward VI., Dr. Jewell, like his friend Archbishop Cranmer, flung off the mask, and denounced the head of the Catholic Church as Anti-Christ. He aided Cranmer during the troubled and despotic reign of the Boy-king. When Edward died he joined in the conspiracy against Queen Mary; but seeing the ill-success of Queen Jane, he deserted her standard, joined the Olden Religion, and signed a most humiliating recantation, which excited the indignation and contempt of Latimer. Jewell seems to have been a coward as well as a traitor. In his new position he did not appear safe: so he suddenly fled to the Continent, where he remained till the accession of Elizabeth. His action in this case might be condemned as mere human weakness, were it not for the hypocrisy of his dying words, wherein he said that his "one great desire in this life had been to be a Protestant martyr, but that he had no opportunity afforded him." This is a wilful perversion of facts, as his contemporaries could affirm. John Jewell, like many men of his time, traded upon a religious sentiment.

ROBERT FERRERS, Bishop of St. David's, who never attained the same rank in popular estimation as the four other prelates who were burnt in Mary's reign, was comparatively innocent of malpractices. It seems, like Hooper, he broke the vow which he had taken as an Austin canon, and married. He made himself unpopular in his diocese, especially to the Cathedral Chapter. In 1551 he was accused of various misdemeanours, by *præmunire*, in a schedule of no less than forty-six articles, the charges in which, as given by Foxe, are simply frivolous. The result of the impeachment was his imprisonment for the costs of the prosecution, and he was still confined at Mary's accession. His chief accusers amongst the clergy were Thomas Young, whom Queen Elizabeth subsequently made Bishop of St. David's and Archbishop of York; and Rowland Meyrick, whom she made Bishop of Bangor, both Reformers of an extreme type. The last-named are guilty, if Ferrers was not, and in either way the promoters of the Reformation gained no credit.

Strype considers Ferrers the victim of the Chapter of the diocese, whose malpractices he sought to put down. Be this as it may, Archbishop Cranmer did not approve of his mode of dealing with the property of the See; and the government so far, believed the charges against him to be well founded. He was committed to prison by his own party. Strype regrets that "the good Archbishop Cranmer was swayed by Ferrers' enemies in this case." But the business-like Dr. Cranmer looked at the matter in its real light—namely, one of fraud; still he delicately hesitated in acting against his friend. He left the new clerical body to deal with their bishop "according to law."* Sutcliff, the apologist of

---

* Strype's Memorials, vol. i.

Ferrers (quoted by Strype), says: "This was a conspiracy of the bishop's enemies against him, and of wicked men who had robbed the Church, lived immoral lives, falsified accounts and records, and committed many other gross abuses." The commentary of John Foxe upon these scandals, perpetrated by men who professed to be Reformers in every sense of the word, is worthy of the man. "These men, knowing how they had wronged the good bishop, came to him before his death, and asked his forgiveness; and he, like a good Christian, forgave them." The Reformers who quarrelled with Ferrers were just the men who were not inclined to forgive their bishop, especially where money was concerned. Strype forms a favourable opinion of Dr. Ferrers' integrity. The Reformers had many private battles over the division of the "loaves and fishes," taken from their Papist neighbours. So the case of unfortunate Ferrers furnished no exception.

NICHOLAS RIDLEY was descended from an ancient family in Northumberland. He was connected with Cambridge for some time, and subsequently travelled in France, and studied at the University of Paris. On his return to England he was appointed chaplain to the King; his next promotion was to the See of Rochester. So he fared in Henry's reign. Ridley was the ablest of the Reforming prelates, and the most implacable and uncompromising denouncer of the religion of his fathers. Ridley procured the Bishopric of London by an act of simony, which was most discreditable. He assigned away four of the richest manors of the See, including Stepney and Hackney, to the King and his courtiers. He was active as a persecutor, and his name was one of those signed to the warrant for burning Van Parris. His theological learning and acuteness far exceeded that of his colleagues. He was a party to the changes introduced in the Second Prayer Book of Edward VI. He knew that they were contrary to the whole order of Christian doctrine; that they were the suggestion of a foreign university; that they would give rise to grave scandals, and could by no possibility do good; and yet, while admitting his dislike to them, he yielded, rather than oppose the worst members of the Council. Had he believed the changes to be doctrinally sound, no charge of this kind could be made against him; but reckoning them as he did to be bad, he stands guilty of betraying the faith, as he held that faith to be."*

Collier supplies a fair character of Ridley:—"His memory and judgments were strong; he was well acquainted with the Fathers and Ecclesiastical antiquities. His life was no less commendable than his learning. He kept a guard upon himself, and spent a great part of his time in prayer. His temper was smooth and obliging, and apt to forget an ill turn; and though he was particularly inclined to serve his relations, yet he would never put them in posts for which they were unqualified, or prefer them beyond their merit. Notwithstanding Ridley's zeal for the Reformation, he was far from approving extremities. . . . . As to Auricular Confession to a priest, *he always looked upon it as a very serviceable usage; that by this expedient, the penitent might be instructed, reproved, or comforted to very significant purposes, as the case should require.*" Here John Foxe, out of an overscrupulous fear of Popery, throws in a condition in his margin, and misrepresents the text. Foxe says: "This confession is to be made by way of asking counsel." There is nothing to this effect to be found in Ridley's letter. In Ridley's note to Bradford, he desires "his assistance *after* his

* Notes on the Reformation Epoch, by the Rev. Dr. Littledale.

martyrdom; and that, when he should come into the other world, he would then pray for those who were left behind and likely to suffer."

In Ridley's letter to Grindal, he complains of the hypocrisy and disorders of Edward's reign, and believes those provocations had brought the present calamities upon them. He laments the insincerity of King Edward's Council; "that they professed the Reformation and countenanced the clergy of that persuasion, for mercenary ends, to enrich themselves with the lands belonging to the Church."*

Foxe records an interview between Queen Mary and Bishop Ridley, in which the latter speaks with greater boldness than any English subject ever used to a Tudor monarch. When retiring—both parties being unconvinced—Ridley, according to the custom of the times, had to drink a goblet of wine to the Queen's prosperity. "Having tasted the liquor he suddenly felt," says Thomas Wharton, the Queen's steward, "that his conscience had smote him." "Surely," he exclaimed, "I have done wrong. I have drunk in this house in which God's word hath been refused. I ought, if I had done my duty, to have shaken the dust off my shoes for a testimony against this house."†

Canon Dixon takes a favourable view of Ridley from the "Reformation standpoint," as some persons contend:—"Nicholas Ridley rose into notice at a very opportune time for the credit of the Reformation. But his temper had a vehemence which sometimes betrayed him into rashness, and in his nature there was something of severity and even hardness. He arrived well, however, when the most honest champions

---

* Collier's Ecclesiastical History, vol. vi., p. 125.

† Foxe, vol. ii., p. 131.

of the Reformation were growing old, lukewarm, or disgusted."*

It was complained by some Reformers of the period that Ridley "went out of his clerical path" to denounce his Sovereign. He preached at St. Paul's Cross, before the Lord Mayor and a numerous congregation. He told the people to remember that both King Henry's daughters were *illegitimate*, and consequently excluded from the succession. He described Queen Mary as "*old, ugly, and filled with Popish ideas.*" He spoke of Elizabeth with scorn, alluding to the miserable scandals respecting her mother. Ridley's sermon made little impression upon the newly created Protestant party, who held in reverence and love the children of Henry VIII. Notwithstanding all Henry's despotism, the mass of the people had a horror of the name of "rebel." They would have had no scruples to hang up such ministers as Crumwell, Audley, or Cranmer; but they considered King Henry's person sacred. A vast body of the Reformers at this time held a similar feeling towards Queen Mary. Lady Jane Dudley was unknown to the people, and her family connections were odious in the eyes of all parties. Those who were best acquainted with Ridley were astonished that his " better judgment became so blinded as to join in the Dudley rebellion."

The private character of Nicholas Ridley was without spot or stain, and, although his religious zeal led him to adopt the banner of the traitor Northumberland, to pardon him would have added to the greatness of the Queen in the hour of her triumph. If the Queen's Council were opposed to "mercy," they ought for the sake of humanity and civilization to have

* History of the Church of England from the Abolition of the Roman Jurisdiction, by the Rev. R. W. Dixon, vol. ii., p. 465.

called in the headsman and dismiss the shocking stake scene. Who can defend such a policy?

HOLBEACH, the predecessor of Ridley in the diocese of Rochester, was translated to Lincoln. He is described by Canon Dixon, a recent Anglican writer, as a man "entirely subservient to the Court; a "promoted monk," who had been the last Prior and the first Dean of Worcester, Latimer's suffragan, with the title of Bishop of Bristol, and had been put forward by Latimer to preach before Henry VIII. His character seems to have been insignificant in itself; but he signalised his advancement to his new See by an act which excited some attention, even in those days of sacrilege. On the day of his institution he signed away all, or nearly all, the estates of Lincoln." Strype states, with reluctance, that this profuse prelate alienated thirty-six rich manors. Canon Dixon thinks that Holbeach was somewhat coerced to do so. No doubt he was; but his questionable character compelled him to accept the proposals of his employers. He did not stop here, for it is accurately recorded, and admitted by such eminent Protestant authorities, as the learned author of the Church of England, Vol. II., p. 465, "that he handed over the episcopal palace in London, of which he had only a life interest." This was, at least, an alienation of a character quite unworthy of a man styled a bishop in "a reformed Christian Church." Holbeach received in return some impropriations, and the Hall of Thornton, which he leased the same year to Sir Edward North. He also scandalously neglected his duty as a prelate, and like Bishop Coxe, and other political Churchmen, his first consideration was the accumulation of wealth; but in this desire he failed. Willis affirms that in his four years of office the city churches all went to rack, and most of them were demolished. Holbeach formed no exception in this neglect of a public duty, especially in the reign of Elizabeth.

It is related that when Dr. Holbeach was advancing to take his throne in the cathedral church, the great tower of the minster confessing the presence of the sacrilegious cleric, "Suddenly trembled, staggered, and fell down." Canon Dixon's commentary on this incident arrives at the conclusion that it was spoken of as "a superstition of the age." Almost in the same passage the reverend gentleman describes the period as "those days of sacrilege."

MILES COVERDALE was an Augustine Friar. Lord Crumwell was one of his early patrons. Coverdale was connected with, and aided in carrying out Somerset's schemes in Edward's reign. He acted as a kind of "military chaplain" to Lord Russell and Anthony Kingston during the massacre of the Devonshire people, who merely took up arms in defence of the rights of conscience. This part of Coverdale's history will not bear much investigation. Many years before the Six Articles were nullified by general infringement, Coverdale took to wife a comely little Devonshire lass. Burnet states that Coverdale was never married; but the evidence of several preachers, who allude to his first and second wife, I consider conclusive. His second wife was a Swede, whom he met at Stockholm, when exiled there in Mary's reign. Coverdale assisted at the consecration of Parker as the "first Protestant Archbishop of Canterbury," but he never received any episcopal appointment from Elizabeth. He had been, in reward I suppose for his services in the Devonshire campaign, made Bishop of Exeter. Upon the accession of Mary he retired to Denmark, where he adopted the extreme Lutheran doctrines propounded by the King of that State. He was very accommodating to Elizabeth and her ministers. Like Calvin, he was in nowise so gloomy in action as in writing. Catharine Parr has recorded a favourable opinion of Coverdale, when she states that "good Maister Coverdale was moral and temperate, but inclined to persecute those who still adhered to Popery." She had, however, been deceived by him in many respects. For instance, Catharine Parr had a particular aversion to married priests, and discharged a chaplain at one time whom she discovered to be a married man. She could not, therefore, have been aware of the fact that Dr. Coverdale had a wife at the very time he was her chaplain and almoner. Poynet, writing to Roger Ascham, describes Coverdale's wife as "young, pretty, and frisky."

Dean Hook contends that high praise is due to Dr. Coverdale for having "presented the Church of England with *the first version of the entire Bible.*" The learned Dean is here labouring under a mistake, which can be contradicted from the very pages of the "Archbishops of Canterbury." The work in question contained many grave errors; and although Dr. Cranmer publicly spoke well of it, he was far from approving of the Bible—as such.* In fact, the work was "a foreign importation." Neither the name of the printer, nor the place where it was printed, was given to the English reader. Whether it was printed at Zurich, Frankfort, Cologne, or the "great Protestant Bible printing town of Antwerp," is very doubtful. Coverdale's Bible professed to be translated out of the Douche and Latin into English. Those who were capable of reading the Scriptures in Latin

---

* Archbishops of Canterbury. vol. vii., p. 139.

rejected this "mass of confused words." Cranmer's opinion in this case must have had some weight, as he was a practised Greek and Latin scholar. Cranmer's private correspondence throws considerable doubt upon the accuracy of Coverdale's Bible; but it did not suit the Archbishop's policy to publicly find fault with it.

Coverdale was no admirer of the men of the "new learning," although he seemed zealous in forwarding their views. When some Reformers spoke of the Holy Eucharist as "Jack in the Box," it is said he denounced their blasphemy.* Nevertheless he persecuted, whenever it was in his power, the members of the Augustinian order; but when his mind, softened by the memories of youth, recurred to its early associations, there were times in which he spoke of the inhabitants of the cloister in the language of charity and love, exclaiming: "The happiest hours I ever spent were in the Priory at Cambridge." His latter days became gloomy and unhappy. It is said that the "cowl, the cross, and the robe of the once austere Augustinian Confessor haunted him by day and by night; he wandered at evening time for hours in his garden, admitting none to disturb the solitude of his meditations." He seemed like a distinguished contemporary, "disappointed in worldly prospects, and uneasy in conscience;" yet he made no outward manifestation of feeling, unless his remarks on the falling of the October leaves, and the mournful cadence of the night wind, be so regarded. "These little incidents," he says, "put me in mind of another world, and I tremble." Miles Coverdale

---

* In Coverdale's Preface to his translation of Calvin's treatise on the "Eucharist," the reader will find this "rebuke," if such it be. In the Parker Society Papers are also to be found some extracts from Coverdale's writings, to which few modern Protestants will attach much importance.

died at the age of eighty-one, and was buried in St. Bartholomew's Church. His evangelical admirers made a search for his remains in 1840. The coffin was discovered, and his bones were transferred to the Church of St. Margaret, London-bridge, where they at present repose.

JOHN POYNET was a distinguished scholar of King's College, University of Cambridge. His mechanical skill first made him known to Henry VIII., to whom he presented "a wonderful dial of his own invention, showing not only the hour of the day, but also the day of the month, the sign of the sun, the planetary hour; yea, the change of the moon, the ebbing and flowing of the sea, with divers other things as strange, to the great wonder of the King, whose commendation he earned at this period." He was soon invited to court, and noticed by the King's favourites. Poynet became a royal chaplain. He appeared at this time to be a very devout clergyman. It has been related by Thorndale "that Poynet agreed with King Henry that heretics should be consigned to the flames," which was the King's favourite punishment.

Strype approaches a very delicate phase of Poynet's reputation when he states that he was "as eminent in preaching as for his other qualifications, being preferred by King Edward for some sermons preached before his Highness."* Let it be remembered that the King was about ten years old at this period—needfully a thoughtful judge of a pulpit discourse. But Edward has been made a perfect wonder by some writers on those marvellous times.

Under Archbishop Cranmer Poynet received rapid promotion. He became Bishop of Rochester, and next of Win-

---

* Strype's Memorials, vol. i., p. 607.

chester. His appointment to the latter See was a flagrant violation of canon and statute law. The bishopric was absolutely sold by Somerset, whilst the lawful prelate, Dr. Gardyner, was committed to the Tower, and detained a prisoner against the statute law of the realm.*

At a subsequent period Poynet joined Wyatt's rebellion; but when he heard of the arrest of that unfortunate young gentleman he fled to Germany, leaving with Sir Thomas Wyatt the comfortless promise of his "prayers for a better fortune."† Maitland, a high authority on the transactions of those times, describes Poynet's exile as "*not that of a persecuted heretic, but as a runaway traitor.*"

There is abundant evidence to prove that Poynet was an immoral man, and a disgrace to the clerical character. Two contemporary documents disinterred by the Camden Society, the "Chronicles of the Grey Friars," and the "Diary of John Machyn," a London citizen who followed the trade of undertaker, prove on independent testimony those events in Poynet's life, and confirm Sander in all except that Poynet was "*wived when he unwived the butcher.*"

Under the year 1551 (Edward VIth's time), we have the following in Machyn's Diary (p. 8), whose words are modernized for the general reader: "The 27th day of July the new Bishop of Winchester was divorced from the butcher's wife with shame enough." In the *Grey-Friars' Chronicle*, the record of Poynet's divorce is set down as follows: "On the 27th of the same month the Bishop of Winchester that was then was divorced from his wife in Paul's, the which was a butcher's wife of Nottingham, and gave her husband

---

* State Papers (Domestic) of Edward VI.'s reign.
† See Stowe's Chronicle; Despatches of the Venetian Ambassador.

a certain money a year during his life, as it was judged by the law."

It was with evident reluctance that Heylin ever wrote a line derogatory to the character of a Reformer, especially one regarded as a leader. Still, he felt compelled to record thus of Poynet, briefly, yet significantly : " John Poynet, a better scholar than *a bishop*, was purposely preferred to the rich bishopric of Winchester, to serve other men's purposes."

The history and traditions of Winchester are also unfavourable to the memory of Poynet.

Dean Hook is not altogether satisfied with the part played by Archbishop Cranmer in placing Poynet over the See of Winchester : " Let us hope, and we may believe, that with this act of gross injustice Cranmer was not concerned. He did not shrink from recourse to measures which would render Gardyner impotent to oppose the Reformation ; but the object of the Council in seizing his bishopric was to divide the spoils among themselves. They appointed Poynet to be the successor of Gardyner, and this was a transaction *which brings disgrace upon the Reformation, not more for the deed itself, than for the manner in which the partisans of Protestantism have defended it.* Poynet was a very learned man, an eloquent and powerful advocate of ultra-Protestantism, yet ever ready to yield when it was his interest to do so. At one time he must have been a consummate hypocrite, for we cannot otherwise account for his having been made chaplain to a man so good, earnest, and upright as Archbishop Cranmer. *Poynet was an immoral and bad man, who was at last so lost to all sense of shame that he lived in open adultery with a butcher's wife,* and was compelled legally to separate by the ecclesiastical courts, and to pay an annuity to the woman's husband. The extent of his profligacy was only known to an interested few when he was appointed to the see of Winchester, until which time he had played the hypocrite's part. That he was, however, an unprincipled man the Council must have known, for he agreed to reserve two thousand marks for himself, and divided the rest of the temporalities among those greedy courtiers whose zeal for the Reformation was of the same character as his own. Such was the man appointed to succeed Dr. Gardyner, who, with all his faults—and they were many—was a stern man, of strict morality, and a man of learning in the law, though not in divinity." *

Burnet denies that Poynet's life was immoral. For making a daring assertion Gilbert Burnet had but one rival—John Foxe. The Poynet scandal was well known to the inhabitants of London in the reign of Edward VI., when some very gross ballads were circulated concerning the "Bishop that robbed the butcher of his wife." Those ballads were issued in Winchester, and throughout Hampshire. Archbishop Cranmer had the bad taste to be present at Poynet's marriage to Maria Simmonds, at Croydon. Dean Hook states that Cranmer was deceived as to Poynet's character about that time. Perhaps so, but then the Archbishop had his clerical spies; besides, the Story Tellers, and the "tattlers about Paul's Cross," according to Thorndale, a contemporary "knew all about Dr. Poynet's gay life" at Bankside. Poynet was popular with the lower classes in London, because he was liberal in spending his money. The poor scholars—an unfortunate class in those times—held him in grateful remembrance. Like John Bale, Poynet should never have been admitted to Holy Orders. A clerical life was not their

---

* Archbishops of Canterbury, vol. vii., p. 244-5.

vocation.* Of Poynet's career in Germany but little is known beyond the fact that he "took to black beer and dice." He died at Strasburg in 1556. It is stated that he was in his forty-first year at the period of his demise; this must be a mistake, for he was not less than fifty at the time set down for his death. Strype states that his remains were attended to the grave by a number of learned men, and the principal citizens of Strasburg.

Poynet was the author of a book in favour of the marriage of the clergy, which was subsequently revised, extended, printed and circulated by Archbishop Parker in the reign of Elizabeth. Strype does not believe that Parker was the editor of this work, which was much read, but does not seem to have had the desired effect, for married clerics in the days of Elizabeth were decidedly unpopular. Wharton doubts if Poynet ever wrote the book in question, although it is generally attributed to him. Henry Wharton may be considered as a good authority on any subject to which he refers.

DR. SCORRY, who succeeded Poynet in the See of Rochester, was a married man for some years previously. Upon the accession of Queen Mary he was deposed, and retired to Germany for a short time. In a few months he returned to England, and abjured his Protestant opinions. He performed public penance at Rochester Cathedral and Paul's Cross for his marriage as a priest, and was restored. At a subsequent period he renounced Catholicity a second time, and became a Protestant. Strype does not consider him "of much account." Farlow states that it was "bruited that

---

* For the details of the career of Bishop Poynet see Strype; Godwin's Annals; Collier's Ecclesiastical History, vol. vii.; Stowe's Chronicle; Thorndale's Memorials; Wharton, Pomeroy, and the Archbishops of Canterbury, vol. vii.

Scorry had two wives alive about the time he was a bishop." Pomeroy contradicts the scandal, which he describes as "a lie concocted by the Papists." It is certain that the more moderate party did not much esteem Dr. Scorry.

DR. REDMAN was another priest who clung to Cranmer in all his shifting policy. He aided the Archbishop in the compilation of the Book of Common Prayer, and was one of the most learned men of his time. He was privately aiding the progress of Reformation principles, whilst celebrating Mass—thereby practising a system of sacrilegious deception and fraud. Some writers allege that he never became a Protestant. His writings prove that he was not of the Papal Church for some time before his death. He held that it was lawful for a priest to marry; but "*not to wife a second time.*"* Although acquainted with such men as Poynet and Bale, his reputation stood far higher than their's, and he enjoyed Dr. Cranmer's friendship till the period of his death in 1551.

RICHARD COXE is described as "a fortunate Country Boy." He was born at Whaddon in Bucks; and, after a struggle, made his way to Eton School, and next to Cambridge University, of which he became a Fellow in 1519, but was removed to Oxford, in 1525, by Cardinal Wolsey. The Cardinal believed at the time that Coxe was "a sincere and devout Catholic." Whilst at Oxford it was discovered that he held Lutheran opinions. He retired suddenly from the University. It was then hinted that he was privately married. He had, however, some influential friends at Court, for he was subsequently made Master of Eton School, Chaplain to Henry VIII., and tutor to Edward Prince of Wales. The

---

* Strype's Memorials, vol. ii., p. 1054.

latter office was a sinecure for some time, the Prince being an infant. In 1541 the King presented Coxe to the Archdeaconry of Ely; several other livings followed; and in 1546 he was appointed Dean of Christ's Church. Upon the death of Henry in 1547, Coxe, who frequently celebrated Mass with great apparent devotion, almost immediately flung off the mask, and joined the party of Somerset and Cranmer. The young King created him his chief almoner; he was also elected Chancellor of the University of Oxford. During Edward's reign he was the most powerful clerical coadjutor Cranmer possessed in England. "Church preferments flowed upon him." He received from his royal pupil a Canonry of Windsor, and the Deanery of Westminster, the last living he held *in commendam* with that of Christ Church.

The name of Richard Coxe holds a place amongst the Clerical Reformers of the days of Edward VI. and Elizabeth. He is described as "a man of considerable learning." His private character "stood high." Like Luther, Coxe protested against the appropriation of Church property for the benefit of the laity. He was consequently unpopular with the recipients of Church lands. He declared that the possessions of the Church were *originally intended* for, and never should have been diverted from, "*the poor, education, hospitality, the sustaining of a learned and virtuous priesthood whose duty should be the instruction of the people and the reclaiming of the fallen.*"

In writing to Sir William Paget, Coxe observes:

"The disposition of colleges, chantries, &c. is now in hand, and ye know (I doubt not) the great lack in this realm of schools, preachers, houses, and livings for impotent or forlorn widows who are poor and miserable; and what lack there shall be utterly intolerable, if there be not a sufficient number of priests established in great circuit and great number. And, howsoever the world beset let them have living honestly, that beggary may drive them not to flattery, *superstition, and old idolatry*. This I speak to you, not distrusting of the King's Highness's goodness on this behalf; but there is *such a number of importunate wolves that be able to devour colleges, chantries, cathedrals, churches, universities, and their lands, and a thousand times as much*. But, for Christ's passion, try to stay for once 'impropriations.' Our posterity will wonder at us."*

Coxe had the courage to write in this spirit in Henry's reign (1545), when the King was confiscating the property of the chantries, and other charitable bequests. When the Prince of Wales became King, in two years later, Coxe was, it is said, dismissed from his office for the liberal principles he inculcated in the mind of his pupil. This statement is very improbable, for upon the death of King Henry Coxe joined Cranmer's party. Although attached to the Reformers, he still continued to denounce the confiscation of the " heritage of the poor." It was stated at the time that Coxe had no objection " to accept of some Church lands himself that were not procured by honourable means." He was very unpopular with the " new territorial lords of the soil."

On the death of the young King, and the accession of Queen Mary, Coxe was one of the first that was committed to prison for the part he had taken in Northumberland's rebellion. After a short time he was discharged. He then retired to Frankfort, where he remained till the accession of Elizabeth. Upon his return he immediately saw Queen Elizabeth and Cecil. He was frequently consulted by the Queen and her Council as to how Popery was to be disposed of, or to use his own words, " stamped out of the land." Neither Elizabeth

---

* R. O. Dom., vol. lxxxiv., N. 4, orig., State Records of **Henry VIII.**

nor Cecil would adopt his cruel suggestions. In the Parliament, which met on the 25th January, 1559, Dr. Coxe preached before the "collective wisdom." He was also amongst the Protestants who challenged the Catholic Bishops to a controversy on the merits of the Olden Creed. In 1560, Dr. Coxe, then sixty years of age, was appointed by Queen Elizabeth to the See of Ely. The Puritan writers describe Coxe as "a wise, pious and learned prelate, who was the terror of the sneaking Papists." The State Papers of Elizabeth's reign, and the records of those times, present Richard Coxe in a very different light.

As Bishop of Ely, in Elizabeth's reign, Coxe became a cruel persecutor of the Catholics of England, and made many suggestions to the Government for the "further persecution of Papists." Sir William Cecil persistently rejected his suggestions."* After a time he was no favourite at the Court of Elizabeth. Another cause of quarrel between the Queen and Coxe was owing to his intemperate language concerning the crucifix and wax-lights used in the royal chapel at Divine Service. The Queen told the bishop that she considered his conduct in this respect an insult to *herself*.

The restless prelate subsequently won an unpleasant notoriety by his many altercations with the Crown. The Queen frequently quarrelled with her bishops; they were compelled by "circumstances" to accept of her theological teaching; but they considered that she had no right to question the "domestic arrangements" of the prelacy. Like her father, Elizabeth would regulate every department of the State." Marriage, under all forms, was disagreeable to the Royal misogamist; the marriage of the "new clergy" was odious to

---

* See Burleigh State Papers, Stevenson's State Papers, and the Hatton Letter Bag.

her; the marriage, and especially "the *re-marriage*, of the Queen's prelates approached to something like sacrilege. Dr. Coxe, when a very old man, became a widower, and, after a while, a certain young lady attracted the episcopal notice. The prelate was in " easy circumstances;" the lady desired a luxurious home, such as the palace of Ely could afford. Coxe explained the difficulty of his position to Cecil, who looked upon the matter as " unseasonable." Cecil was too well acquainted with the Queen's opinions on such matters, so he left Dr. Coxe to his fate.* Perhaps the Bishop, like other prelates, was secretly married at the time. After some further correspondence, and much indignation on the part of the Queen, Bishop Coxe was permitted to retain his young wife. It is stated that some five years were spent " in conjugal happiness," when suddenly the Bishop had a quarrel with the Queen's " Dancing Favorite," the amiable and handsome Christopher Hatton. The courtier in this case desired a portion—" a slice "—off the Bishop's " town garden," now known as Hatton Garden. Dr. Coxe felt justly indignant at the demand, and refused the request, which drew from the Queen her noted letter to the Bishop, so often quoted by historians. In this unqueenly missive of the Head of the Church to *her* Bishop of Ely, Elizabeth says, " proud prelate, if you do not instantly comply *with my wishes, by G.— I will unfrock you.*" The Bishop, acting under the advice of his cautious young wife, who was delighted with the portions of the garden coveted by Hatton, " still stood upon his legitimate rights as a Churchman ;" but Elizabeth, like her father, would not recognize any supposed claims *her* prelates might have upon the Church lands. At first Hatton desired a portion of

---

* The Bishop of Ely's correspondence with Sir William Cecil, Dec. 29, 1569; Froude, vol. ix. p. 379.

the Bishop's garden, but subsequently laid claim to the palace, which then stood in the present Ely-place. At this time it was discovered that Coxe had plentifully helped himself to the "good things of the vineyard." He preached many sermons "in favour of God's poor," but, according to Lord North and other Protestant contemporaries, he did not himself practise what he preached from the pulpit. Lord North, by the command of the Queen, wrote a warning letter to Coxe. I select a few passages from the correspondence which is one of the many illustrations still extant of the servile homage paid to Elizabeth by her courtiers.

"The Queen," writes Lord North, "determines to redress the infinite injuries which of long time *you have offered her subjects.* For which purpose, to be plain with your Lordship, the Queen has given me orders to hearken to my neighbour's griefs, and likewise to prefer those complaints before her Majesty's Privy Council, for that you may be called to answer, and the parties be made satisfied. The Queen has given orders for your coming up (to Court). * * * You shall have a task to judge how well her Highness liketh your loving usage.

"Now, to advise you, my Lord Bishop, I wish you from the bottom of my heart to shake off the yoke of your stubbornness against her Majesty's desires; to lay aside your stiff-necked determination, and to yield yourself to the *known clemency* of her Majesty. This Queen *is our God on earth.* If there be *perfection in flesh and blood, undoubtedly it is in her Majesty;* for she is *slow to revenge and ready to forgive.* She is like her father, King Henry, *of blessed memory,* for if any strive to contend against her, all the princes in Europe cannot make her yield.

"You will say to me that you are determined to leave your bishoprick in her Majesty's hands, to dispose thereof at her good pleasure. * * * Your wife* has also counselled you to be a

---

* The wives of the Bishops, and other clerics, detested and dreaded the Queen. La Motte Fenelon, who knew the Queen personally for eight or ten

Latimer, glorying, as it were, to stand against your *natural Prince*. My Lord Bishop, let not *your wife's shallow experience carry you too far*. You see that to Court you must come.

"The Queen's good favour and grace will be altered from you. Your friends will become strange to you. * * * It will be no pleasure for you to have the Queen and her Council know how wretched you live; how *extremely covetous; how great a grazier; how marvellous a dairyman;* * *how rich a farmer; how great a land-owner*. It will not like you that the world know of *your decayed houses* (churches); *of the lead and brick that you sell from them; of the leases that you pull violently from many; of the copyholds you lawlessly enter into; of the free lands which you wrongfully possess; of the tolls and imposts which you raise; of God's good ministers which you causelessly displace*."

"All this," writes Lord North, "*I am to prove against you,* and I shall be most heartily sorry to put it in execution."

The Queen's *confidential* secretary was the secret friend of Coxe, and concludes his long despatch in these words:—"*Your loving friend,*

(Signed) "ROGER NORTH."

---

years, states in one of his private despatches, "that much of the vicious gossip concerning Queen Elizabeth was circulated by the wives and daughters of Bishops and Deans." Very likely, for Elizabeth treated them with scorn, and was frequently rude to them. Mrs. Parker, for instance, and the wife and daughters of Pilkington, Bishop of Durham, had good reason to complain of the scandalous language used against them by the Queen. But Mrs. Pilkington, like the wives of other clerics, knew how to retaliate upon the Virgin Queen.

* Dr. Lindsay, who filled the See of Kildare in the Anglican Church some fifty-five years ago, kept an immense dairy at Glasnevin, near Dublin, where the milk of a number of cows was sold daily. At the time, the Bishop's dairy was considered a scandal to the Church of England. The dairy, however, rendered great service to the poor of Dublin, who received pure milk for tenpence per gallon. Dr. Lindsay, who was brother-in-law to the Earl of Hardwick, was the last Anglican Bishop of Kildare. He was a most humane and worthy prelate. The palace of the Bishop of Kildare at Glasnevin is now the Bridgetine convent. The Dublin residence of the last Anglican Archbishop of Cashel is another convent, and is now styled Loretto House. What changes!

It is needless to offer any commentary upon this correspondence between the "loving friends." Elizabeth was frequently deceived by her secret agents, when it suited their personal interests.

A few words as to Lord North "the loving friend and accuser" of Dr. Coxe, and the "devoted friend" of Lord Leicester. This North was a contemptible creature—a spy employed by Queen Elizabeth upon her domestics. Perhaps Coxe was not worse than the majority of the Anglican prelates who were hoarding up wealth by dishonest means, oftentimes cheating the working clergy of their miserable incomes, and neglecting the supposed spiritual charge which Parliament gave them. Bad as Coxe has been represented, there were others who acted in a more dishonest manner—for instance, Pilkington of Durham, and Horne of Winchester. There were, however, some honourable exceptions.

Roger North was son to a nobleman of that name, who was connected with the household of Queen Mary. He was set aside by Elizabeth, and died some time later. His son Roger became a Reformer, and received a portion of the confiscated lands and the Charter House from Elizabeth.*

After filling the See of Ely for twenty-one years, Dr. Coxe died in July, 1581, in his eighty-second year. It was bruited at the time that his coffers were filled with golden angels, and his library possessed many volumes of "studied sermons," to which might be added a most fitting text, "*Do as I preach, but not as I practise!*"

Upon the death of Dr. Coxe the Queen made no appointment to the See of Ely for nearly twenty years, and sequestrated the revenues of the diocese, a portion of which she gave

---

* Bearcroft's History of the Charter House.

for some years to "a pretender" to the Crown of Portugal. I must, however, in justice to Elizabeth, state that she was *not* the first sovereign who had seized upon the revenues of the ancient See of Ely. There were bad precedents to be found in the old Catholic times for her action in this case. Henry the First seized on the revenues of Ely, in 1133, and held them till his death in 1135.* The maxim of Henry I was to the effect that no one should violate the law save the sovereign himself. Elizabeth acted on this principle—when convenient.

Another extraordinary action on the part of Elizabeth was her dealings with Archbishop Grindal in the See of Canterbury. The Queen's favourite physician, Dr. Julio, who was also the creature of Lord Leicester, desired to "marry his neighbour's wife," with whom he had formed an illicit intercourse; but when Dr. Grindal was consulted on the matter he at once protested against such a violation of canon law. He commanded his clergy "*not* to marry Julio to his neighbour's wife." The Queen thereupon became indignant at the honest action of her Archbishop of Canterbury. He was at once "sequestered" from his see, and confined to his house by the "Queen's command." Sir Christopher Hatton used all his influence to restore Grindal to his former position, but he appealed in vain. There is no mistake as to the mode of action adopted by the Queen in relation to Julio's projected marriage.†

Dean Hook states that the Queen sequestrated the archbishop's revenues for *five years*, her object being to prevent

---

* Henry I and his grandson Henry II both died in Normandy, and are buried there.

† The correspondence, taken from the original MS. on this subject, is to be seen in the Hatton Letter Bag (State Papers), pp. 52-118.

him holding a convocation. And the Dean adds : " Grindal resigned his see in 1582, on receiving a pension."* It is strange that Dean Hook is silent as to the affair of Dr. Julio and Archbishop Grindal.†

I may remark that Grindal's translation from the See of London to that of York was not considered legal according to canon law, but Queen Elizabeth laughed at " theological lines and distinctions," all which she utterly ignored. Her despotism pressed more heavily against educated Anglican clerics than any other class of Englishmen. " You shall not turn to the right, or to the left, but as I command," were the words frequently used by her Highness to the bishops, who, in turn, bowed obsequiously to her fiat.

HEATON, who succeeded Coxe, after the diocese being sequestrated for twenty years, found the revenues of Ely very much reduced by the conduct of Queen Elizabeth, who helped to enrich men like Sir William Cecil and Lord Leicester from the cathedral lands. The Rev. Canon Luckock, of Ely, in his recently published work on the progress of the " Book of Common Prayer," candidly admits that the "cathedrals presented an appearance of most appalling neglect. The only sign of life among the deans and canons was the principle of self-interest with which the example of the Queen had infected them. They suffered the daily services to cease; the altars to be stripped; *chalices stood on their sideboards; and vestments were slit into gowns and bodices for the wives and children of the priests.*"‡ The clerics here described were the "reformed priests"

---

* Archbishops of Canterbury, vol. x.

† It is a strange incident that both Archbishops Parker and Grindal had to resign the see of Canterbury from blindness.

‡ Rev. Canon Luckock on the Elizabethan Reaction, p. 145.

who took the oath of supremacy to Queen Elizabeth, *as the "supreme head of Christ's Church* on earth."

Archbishop Whitgift, had on several occasions, the courage to warn Elizabeth as to her "sacrilegious spoliation." "Religion," writes Whitgift, "is the foundation and cement of human society; and when the men that serve God's altar shall be exposed to poverty, then religion itself may become an object of scorn to those who have no faith in our reformed Gospel." In another epistle the Queen's favourite primate implores her Highness "to dispose of the Church lands *for the love of Jesus Christ,* as she promised to men, and *vowed to the Almighty God*—that is, *as the donors intended.*" Whitgift's admonition concludes thus: "As you *may expect comfort at the last day,* think over this matter, for monarchs must be judged as well as other people."*

The Queen, however, had no scruples as to her *vows* and oaths to the *Almighty God,* and far less as to the *intentions* of the pious and benevolent donors. So things moved on in this unjust manner for the remaining years of the reign of Elizabeth.

In the face of the above, and many similar cases, a writer of Miss Strickland's integrity describes Queen Elizabeth "as *the nursing Mother of the Church of England.*"

Bishop WEST was succeeded in the diocese of Ely by Dr. GODRICH.† West has been described by his contemporaries as "living in the greatest splendour of any prelate of his time." He kept one hundred and twenty domestics at the Palace of

---

* Whitgift's works, vol. iii.

† In the second volume (pp. 380-1), I have referred to the part taken by Godrich in relation to the Dudley and Wyatt rebellions, and the progress of the Reformation at that time.

Ely. The wages of his servants ranged from 44s. to 100s. per annum. The poor, to the number of two hundred, received "meat and drink daily in a hall set apart for God's poor, who were unfortunate in the race for life." At Christmas, and other festivals of the Church, widows and orphans were always provided for by the bishop's steward.

Bishop West, like Dr. Fisher, was a supporter of Queen Katharine's claims, and consequently lost the royal favour.

WILLIAM BARLOW, a man of low extraction, became one of Thomas Crumwell's agents. Crumwell, after a few brief interviews, understood the man. Barlow afterwards received valuable Church preferment. He became a Canon Regular of St. Augustine's and Prior of Besham. Crumwell introduced him to King Henry, who sent him on a private mission to Scotland, and by his management of affairs there won the entire confidence of his sovereign. He was subsequently created Bishop of St. David's. He was appointed a bishop, no doubt, for some peculiar services rendered to the Crown, which have not transpired. In this respect Barlow was not worse than Gardyner and Bonner, who received their mitres for their conduct in the divorce litigation. The registry of Barlow's consecration is not in existence; and it has been argued by some Catholic writers that he was never regularly inducted as a bishop. Dr. Lingard contends to the contrary. He states that Barlow took his seat in the House of Lords, and in Convocation as the Lord Bishop of St. David's. He was styled by Dr. Gardyner "his brother of St. David's." * * * All that can be said is, that we cannot find any positive registry of his consecration. There is no register to be found concerning Bishop Gardyner, yet it is generally allowed that he was regularly consecrated. In the ninth volume of the Archbishops of Canterbury, Dean Hook enters upon this matter at some length, but proves nothing. All that can be said is, that the registries were lost.

Barlow was one of the Reformers of whom Archbishop Cranmer did not entertain a good opinion. He considered him too jocose, and found him frequently speaking in "an air of ridicule of things sacred and holy." Cranmer had an admirable judgment of men, and was seldom deceived as to the merits of clerics. Barlow was a good scholar for his time, acquainted with Greek, Latin, and Hebrew. Many discreditable transactions have been recorded of him. He "stripped the lead off the palace and sold it, embezzling the price, and letting the palace go to ruin, so that the repairs would have needed twelve years' revenue of the see." The Records of the diocese, the State Papers of Edward's reign, and the correspondence of the leading Reformers of the period, prove Dr. Barlow to have been a very dishonest man, turning everything connected with religion to financial uses. Under Edward VI. he avowed himself a Reformer, and was rewarded with the richer mitre of Bath and Wells, from which he immediately alienated eighteen manors to the Protector Somerset, as the fee for his promotion. Barlow took a chief part in celebrating the Mortuary Masses for the soul of Henry VIII. At this very period he was secretly connected with the wife of a German Anabaptist, who gave him "a sound drubbing" at an inn located in Coventry. Archbishop Cranmer's verdict against Barlow is most severe.

When Queen Mary came to the throne, Barlow immediately recanted, and even wrote "a strong book against the Reformation," whose authenticity Burnet questions, seemingly for no other reason than that such duplicity reflected dishonour on Barlow. When Elizabeth succeeded,

Barlow *recanted again;* and became one of the Queen's clerical utilities. He delivered several addresses at Paul's Cross in favour of the Royal Supremacy "in all matters concerning religion." Barlow persecuted the clergy of his diocese, especially Godshalf and Thomas Stapleton, his prebends (1560), for denying that Elizabeth was the *vicegerent of Christ on earth*.* He persecuted the poor tenants in the neighbourhood of his palace, and took into his own hands the yearly revenue that was long paid to old women who "outlived all their kindred, and were in want." Barlow had, by his wife, Agnes Welleshorne, three daughters, who subsequently married three Reformed priests, who in due time became three Reformed bishops. One of those ladies had the rare distinction of a duplex episcopal espousal—her first husband being a suffragan Bishop, and her second an Archbishop of York.† I further refer to Strype, vol. ii., p. 273, for the charges preferred against Bishop Barlow.

WILLIAM WHITTINGHAM'S mode of reforming the Church did not meet with the approval of the respectable and less fanatical portion of the English Reformers. Upon the death of Edward VI., Whittingham retired to Frankfort, where he quarrelled violently with the Reformers. He visited Strasburg and other places in the interest of the Reformers; he did not, however, succeed in gaining popularity. In grossness and profanity he left John Bale in the shade. In the reign of Elizabeth he was created Dean of Durham. I shall summarise from Anthony Wood an account of the proceedings of this sacrilegious Vandal :—

"As for the works of impiety of which he was guilty while Dean of Durham, they were very many. Most of the priors of

---

* Inedited State Paper (Domestic) Art. 58.
† Godwin's Anecdotes of English Bishops; Anthony Wood, Athen. Oxon.

Durham having been buried in coffins of stone, and some of marble, each coffin covered with a plank of marble, which was laid level with the pavement of the church, he caused them to be plucked up, and ordered them to be used as *troughs for horses and pigs to feed in.* He ordered all the stone and marble ornaments connected with tombs to be removed, and broken up, to make a pavement in his own house. He also defaced all such stones as had any pictures of brass, or other imagery work; or chalice wrought or engraven upon them; he likewise built a wash-house from the material procured in this manner. He could not abide anything in the shape of monuments or architectural beauty that belonged to the old monastic times. Within the cathedral there were two holy water fonts of fine marble, with beautiful workmanship, engraven and bossed with hollow basses, upon the outward sides of the stones. Both of these ancient ornaments, and memorials of the pious simplicity and faith of our ancestors, were placed in the reforming Dean Whittingham's kitchen, and turned to the profane use of *steeping beef and pork to be salted in brine.* The shrine of St. Cuthbert was removed and defaced, so that nothing could be found in the cathedral to remind one of that good and holy man. Several other monuments of historical interest he likewise destroyed. . . . . After many rambles in this world, both beyond and within the seas, and much mischief happening to the Church of England, through his uncharitable Calvinistic preaching, he had at last to submit to the stroke of death. He died in June, 1579, and was buried in the Cathedral of Durham. A handsome monument was erected over his grave by those who had faith in his proceedings. When the Scots invaded England in 1640, they destroyed the monuments in many churches, and having visited Durham Cathedral, they ill-used the monument and rooted up the bones of Whittingham, under the impression that he belonged to the old Popish times." So writes Anthony Wood, who adds, " nothing was left to show where his carkase was lodged." *

---

* Anthony Wood, Athen Oxon, vol. i., p. 194; see also an old book entitled, " The Ancient Rites and Monuments of the Monastical Cathedral Church of Durham," published in London about 1672—a work full of historical interest.

A Puritan commentator has been pleased to assert that I have "done my best to blacken the character of Archbishop Cranmer and the leading Reformers who acted with him." And the reviewer of a noted literary journal alleges that "I manifest a suicidally fierce bias against every person and thing connected with Protestantism; and in favour of every person connected with Catholicism." I protest against this sweeping accusation even on the part of a decided partizan. During the four-and-twenty years I have been connected with English and Foreign Literature I have never wilfully, or otherwise, misrepresented "facts." In Cranmer's case I have merely produced statements drawn from the records of *his actions*. During the reigns of Henry VIII., and his son, Edward VI., I positively affirm that the charges I have preferred against the Archbishop are derived from State Papers, or Protestant authorities of high repute. In the course of my researches I have met with documents which place Cranmer's private and public life in a far worse position. Yet I have hesitated to use such material, and disregarded the suggestions offered for placing it on record. As to Dr. Poynet, he can hardly be made blacker than his actions have painted him; nevertheless, Strype, and writers of his school, have presented him to posterity as "a saint and a God-fearing man." In the preceding pages the reader has seen quite enough of the demerits of Poynet. There is also a concurrence of opinion as to John Bale. No party should *now* feel annoyed at the Truth being revealed. The maxim of the late Dean Hook should be a barrier against sectarian misrepresentation. "The exposure of a lie," writes the Dean, "is the triumph of Truth."

However, I cannot help remarking, that, with a few exceptions, the public men of the "four last reigns" of the Tudor family—whether Catholic or Reformer, had little claim to an honest and honourable reputation. The code of honour which once jealously guarded society had fallen to pieces amidst the indecent scramble for the possession of their "neighbours' goods." The worst feature in connection with the Reformers was an obtrusive assumption of religious sentiment and piety quite opposed to their *actions*. The people were convinced that *they* were *not* the descendants of the hereditary lords of the soil. The Russells, the Cecils, the Dudleys, the Seymours, and the Pagets, were easily traced to a stock far inferior to the hospitable baronial lords, knights, and squires of the olden days of England's chivalry. The "new aristocracy," as they have been styled, were, like many others, retained by King Henry to promote his vast schemes of confiscation. "The new Nobles and Commons," might be described "as *the* gentlemen of no property," who speculated largely upon the enormous seizure of Church and Abbey lands, and next on the results of the Supremacy Statutes, of which some of my critics speak of "as a laudable policy;" but which I consider to be nothing less than plunder.

CHAPTER VII.

CALVIN AND SERVETUS.

As the preceding chapter has had special relation to the Clerics of the "New Learning" in England, I cannot pass over a few of the noted men of Geneva who were in correspondence with the Reformers of this country. The Reformation in Geneva, like that of Scotland, presents many fanatical, and many wicked and disgraceful scenes, which have been chronicled, even by the most partizan writers, upon the Reformation epoch. In a religious and political point of view, Geneva had long held an exceptional position in Europe. Though nominally a fief of the German empire it had, in reality, been governed for centuries by a bishop. In an assembly of the burgesses of Geneva, held in 1420, it was stated that the city had then been more than four centuries under episcopal government—a government which was "sometimes despotic, and sometimes kindly," but always opposed to political reforms. The Church was thoroughly conservative, so that a Lollard or Communistic party had small chance of success in Geneva; nevertheless, their views had been secretly progressing in Switzerland for twenty years before the Reformation. For some years preceding the great German revolution in religion a lack of discipline grew up in the Church of Geneva. The bishop of that See was indolent and neglectful of his duties, and he was subsequently compelled to retire from the See in consequence of his "continued irregularities." There were, however, many zealous and most exemplary priests in the diocese, who publicly denounced the immoral lives of the wealthy, and the drunkenness and violence of the lower classes. The honest clerics were threatened with death. The city was visited by suspended priests from Strasburg and the frontier districts. Those men came, as they alleged, to reform religion. Marvellous that there, as well as here, those who so much needed reform themselves proclaimed their mission to reform religion. The most popular dogma preached by those self-named Reformers was that of divorcing wives. The husbands of old or barren women, on hearing this doctrine advocated, "felt themselves aggrieved;" the divorce process was at hand, and many elderly housewives were quickly supplanted by "frisky young maidens" ranging from sixteen to eighteen years old. The divorce law completely overturned society. The "young stepmothers," and the children over whom they were placed, were in perpetual broils. All the old family ties were snapped asunder. The lower classes became turbulent, immoral, and intemperate. Catholicity had lost its influence in Geneva long before Calvin came upon the scene. The Reformation presented itself in the most fanatical form, giving free scope to license, whilst persecuting its opponents. The men who represented themselves as "refugees from Popish persecution" had been, in too many cases, outlawed from their own country—felons and professional thieves, who quickly corrupted society whilst assuming the mask of piety. The fanatical feeling had caught such a hold of some sections of society, that many men and women became insane. Then the hypocrisy of others was sad to contemplate—in fact religion became a cloak for crime. Of course, there was also a large number of people who were actuated by the most conscientious feelings as to the religious change which they had made. Things were in the condition I have here described, when John Calvin was introduced to the people of Geneva, in 1537, as "a preacher of the Word of God." So wrote his noted disciple, Ferle, to whom I shall have occasion to refer anon.

I shall not inquire into the private history of Calvin, for it will not bear the test of rigid examination. What was the mode adopted by him in Geneva to spread his principles? and what were the results of his teachings in that district? He became "a spiritual scourge," as described by one of his own followers. The respect and submission exacted by John Calvin far exceeded that claimed by other "spiritual Reformers," and was anything but compatible with the meekness and humility inculcated by the Gospel. The most trifling slights or insults, such as most men would have overlooked with contempt, Calvin pursued with vindictive bitterness. The Registers of Geneva abound with instances, which grew more frequent and more severe as his power became more consolidated. His well-known motto—"*moderation is a dangerous thing*," has been often commented upon and condemned, even by Puritans. But Calvin moved forward uncontrolled, no one daring to dispute his authority. He was the John Knox of Geneva. When at Frankfort, he denounced the new English Prayer Book, and his denunciation produced a powerful effect for some time. Although Cranmer corresponded with Calvin, yet he had no personal liking for the man whose dictatorial manner and tyranny he abhorred. There was a wide difference between the social bearing of the English and German Reformers. Let it be remembered that the Reformation in Germany was not supported by a single bishop. None but priests of an inferior class, and those of very questionable morals, joined the standard of Martin Luther. Calvin's Reformation began with a still lower class, whose democratic opinions were fraught with despotism and danger to all Christian interests—despotism and socialism struggling for an ascendancy.

In 1551 we find Bertholier excommunicated by the Consistory because he would not allow that he had done wrong in asserting that he was as good a man as Calvin. Three men, who had laughed during a sermon of Calvin's, were imprisoned for three days, and condemned to ask pardon of the Consistory. Such proceedings were very frequent. In two years (1558-9), 416 despotic cases of imprisonment for "liberty of conscience" are recorded in Geneva. To impugn Calvin's doctrines, or the proceedings of the Consistory, was dangerous to life and liberty.* Dyer affirms that Calvin carried this system to a pitch so blasphemous that he sometimes dared to justify the harshest and most unchristian-like conduct and words by the example of the *Apostles, and even of Christ himself.*† The result was, as might be expected. A Genevese writer, of the Puritan school, states that "those who imagine that Calvin did nothing but good, are immensely mistaken." "I could produce," observes Galiffe, "our registers covered with records of illegitimate children, which were exposed in all parts of the town and country; trials for obscenity; wills, in which fathers and mothers accuse their children not only of errors, but of crimes; agreements before notaries between young women and their lovers, in which the latter, even in the presence of their parents, make a bargain for the support of their dishonoured

---

* See Dyer's Life of Calvin, pp. 143-4.
† Ibid.

offspring. I could instance multitudes of forced marriages, in which the shameful men were conducted from prison to the church; mothers abandoned their children to the hospital, whilst they themselves lived in adultery and shame; husbands abandoned their wives and sought younger women." Morality seems to have been hopelessly shipwrecked in the home of the chief Continental Reformers.*
The writer proceeds:—" Heavy lawsuits between brothers; secret negotiations; *men and women* burnt for witchcraft; sentences of death in frightful numbers; and all these things nurtured by the mystic manna of Calvin."

It is a curious fact, that although Calvin was placed in the receipt of the revenues of a rich parish when only fourteen years of age, he was never admitted to "priest's orders."† His father wished him to study for "jurisprudence;" still he continued, through family interest, to receive the stipend of a parish priest. At a very early age Calvin publicly denounced the Church of Rome, and corresponded with the leading English Reformers, especially the Duke of Somerset, Archbishop Cranmer, and Hugh Latimer.

Calvin's elder brother was a priest, and a very exemplary good man. Calvin's family, with one exception, did not approve of his religious change.

De Thou characterises Calvin as " endowed with a strong and acute understanding, and admirable powers of expression." Davila describes him as a man of great but restless mind; of wonderful eloquence, and of varied and extensive erudition. Calvin's style, both in Latin and French, is remarkable for force, clearness, and facility. His Latin is not marked by unnecessary verbiage, merely for the sake of

---

* Galiffe, tom. iii.
† Melin Court, p. 11.

rounding a period, nor by any affectation of Ciceronian purity, the besetting snare of the writers of that age. If it be truly remarked that the best test of modern Latin is that it should be read with facility and pleasure by a scholar, Calvin's may be pronounced excellent.

The admirable manner in which Calvin used his mother tongue is best testified by several of his learned countrymen. Pasquier remarks that he had "enriched the French language with numberless beautiful turns." The Abbé d'Artigny observes that he knew the turn and genius of the French tongue better than any man of his age.

Bossuet draws a parallel between Calvin and Luther: "Let us then yield to Calvin, since he is so desirous of it, the glory of having written as well as any man of his time; nay, let us even place him, if you will, above Luther; for though Luther had a more lively and original turn of mind, Calvin, although inferior in genius, seemed to carry off the palm by study. In oral discourse Luther triumphed; but Calvin's pen was more correct, especially in Latin; and his style, which was more severe, was also more connected and refined. Both excelled in speaking their native tongue, and each of them possessed an extraordinary vehemence."

John Calvin was of middle stature, of a hale and dark complexion; his eyes, which betokened the sagacity of his intellect, retained their brilliancy to the last. He gave but little time to sleep. His memory was almost incredible, insomuch that he would immediately recognise persons whom he had seen but once, and that after many years previously; and when employed in dictating, he could resume the thread of his discourse without being prompted, after having been interrupted for several hours.*

---

* See Beza's Life of Calvin.

The terms of extravagant eulogy in which several Reformers speak of Calvin are neither consistent with truth nor good taste. Fanaticism and sectarian hate are interwoven with what should be an honest record of the facts which occurred under the clerical dictatorship of Calvin. If we are to judge of him by his "actions," then we must arrive at the conclusion, that no man ever pursued an enemy, or a rival, with such unrelenting malice—such undying hatred, as the reforming apostle of Geneva. Again, I refer to the "actions" of *the* man. Dyer, one of the more recent biographers of Calvin, is impelled, in the face of the records of Geneva, to make the admission that he cherished the "idea of putting Servetus *to death for seven years, and which he effected the moment it was in his power to do so.*"*

I now leave the reader to draw his own conclusions, and introduce to him the case of Michel Servetus, the aspiring rival and victim of John Calvin.

MICHEL SERVETO, or Servetus, was born at Villanueva, in Arragon, in the year 1509. His father was a notary, and his family were of an old and honourable stock.† Young Servetus received his early education in a Dominican Convent. At a later period he studied law at Toulouse. He was far from being popular with the early Continental Reformers, several of whom denounced him as "an unbeliever in any Christian form then practised." His first infidel work was published before he had completed his twenty-second year. The book was condemned both by Catholics and Reformers. In fact, it excited universal indignation, and Quintana procured an imperial edict for

---

* See Dyer's Life of Calvin, p. 536.
† Mosheim's Life of Servetus.

its suppression. The name of Servetus became so unpopular in France, that he had to assume a designation in part resembling the name of his native town.

In 1534 Calvin received a challenge from Servetus to meet him for a religious controversy in Paris. The French Government, at the suggestion of the Archbishop of Paris, prevented the discussion. At this period there was little sympathy in the French capital for the infidel principles put forward by Servetus.

When the works of Servetus could afford him no means of subsistence, he turned to the study of medicine, and entered the Collège des Lombards, from which he was soon ejected for his religious opinions. Still he continued to progress in his new profession.

In 1536 Servetus was considered one of the most rising physicians in France. At Lyons he undertook the occupation of "a corrector of the press," then a most honourable employment.

Many of the personal friends of Servetus besought him to give up his "books on religion." "No," said he, "I will go forward, and conquer."

Servetus has been much misrepresented by the admirers of Calvin, who desired "to make out a case against him." He was several times banished from Geneva by Calvin, and then invited back again; on the last occasion he was "regularly entrapped," as one of his followers alleged. He was immediately arrested, and charged with heresy. The proceedings which followed demonstrate the fanatical malice of Calvin, who claimed a jurisdiction as extensive as that of the Pope. Many of the sectaries fled from his cruel persecution. Dyer declares that one of the "most unjust actions of Calvin's life was that of denying Servetus counsel during his trial."* This was merely adopting the cruel system enforced by Queen Elizabeth. It is a strange fact that much of the Continental popularity enjoyed by Calvin was owing to his spirit of persecution.

No one could defend the errors of Servetus. He was, however, cruelly treated by Calvin, who could never sanction "a rival theologian or doctor." One of the charges against Servetus was, that he "*held the soul to be merely mortal.*" Servetus denied this accusation with horror.† It was, perhaps, one of those assertions for which Calvin was remarkable, for he had little regard for truth. Calvin further alleges that Servetus was ignorant of Greek. This assertion can hardly be credited, for Servetus was one of the most learned men of his time: he had arranged Ptolemy, and written his book on " Syrups "—so it is impossible to believe that he was "ignorant of Greek." He was also one of the most notable Latin scholars that studied at Toulouse in his time, and deeply versed in the literature of the age.

The secret tribunals before whom Servetus was examined decreed that his crimes as a heretic forfeited his life.

On the 27th of October, 1553, Servetus was ordered for execution. Calvin commanded him to retract his "written opinions." Servetus replied, "No, never." The Council of " wise and God-fearing men " pronounced the sentence, which concluded in these words:—

"We condemn you, Michel Servetus, to be bound, and led to the Champel, where you are to be fastened *to a stake and burned alive*, together with your book, as well as the printed one, and the manuscript, till your *body be reduced to ashes; and thus shall you*

---

* See Dyer's Life of Calvin.
† Ibid.

finish your days, to be an example to others who would commit the like crime." *

On hearing this barbarous sentence, Servetus was struck with despair. He supplicated the Council that he might perish by the sword, lest the greatness of his torments should drive him to desperation, and cause him to lose his soul. He protested, that if he had sinned, it had been unwittingly, and that his desire had always been to promote God's glory.† When he found that all his supplications were fruitless,—that he could not move the Council to mercy or pity—then he fell into a stupor, broken at intervals by deep groans and frantic cries for mercy. But Calvin was deaf to his appeal; and the fanatics present reminded him of the "great fire in hell."

A short distance from the city of Geneva rises a gentle but extended eminence, called Champey, or Champel, the place appointed for the execution of Servetus. On an October morning he was led from the prison to undergo his doom. As the procession slowly ascended the hill, the fatal stake appeared in sight, though partly hidden by the oak branches which had been heaped around it, still bearing their autumnal leaves. A crowd of fanatics had gathered round the spot where Servetus was to suffer. Arrived at the summit of the hill, Servetus fell on the earth in an attitude of prayer; and while he lay absorbed in his devotion, Ferel addressed the assembled multitude in these words:—"See," said he, "the power of Satan, when he hath once gotten possession of us. This man (Servetus) is particularly learned, and it may be that he thought he was doing right; but now the Devil hath him fast in hand. Good people, beware lest the same thing happen to yourselves."‡

---

* Mosheim's Life of Servetus; Dyer's Life of Calvin.
† De Morte Serveti, vol. iii., p. 196.
‡ See Kirchhofer; Leben Ferel, vol. ii., p. 119.

When Servetus arose from his devotions, he sobbed and cried, and trembled. The execution was delayed till midday. Then, amidst a mock solemnity, the unhappy man was led to the stake. Before the stake lay a large block of wood on which he was to sit. An iron chain encompassed his body, and held him to the stake; his neck was fastened to it by a strong cord, which encircled it several times. On his head was placed a crown of plaited straw and leaves, strewed with sulphur to assist in suffocating him. At his girdle were suspended both his printed books, and the manuscript which he had sent to Calvin. Servetus implored the executioner to put him quickly out of pain; but the executioner, either from accident or design, had collected a heap of green wood. When the fire was kindled, Servetus uttered a piercing shriek; the crowd fell back with a shudder, followed by a "wailing cry of horror, and many persons fainted away."* A man, more humane than the representatives of Calvin, threw a bundle of faggots into the fire, which roused the flames to instant action; nevertheless, the sufferings of unhappy Servetus lasted for nearly forty minutes.

Just before Servetus expired, an extraordinary amount of energy of mind and body enabled him to exclaim, in a distinct and ringing voice—"*Jesus, thou Son of the Eternal God, have mercy upon me a sinner.*" †

In person Michel Servetus was of middle height, thin and

---

* By the old laws of Geneva the punishment by "fire" for heresy was seldom, if ever, set aside. Dyer, in his Life of Calvin, thus alludes to this statute against heretics:—"The legal labours of Calvin had left that barbarous statute unreformed." But the merciful Father Calvin never believed that the statute in question required any reformation. Thomas Dyer should not forget that Calvin's memorable maxim was—'*Moderation is a dangerous thing.*"

† See De Morte Serveti.

pale; his eyes beaming with thought and intelligence, but tinged with an expression of melancholy, or the gloom of fanaticism. His memory was tenacious, his imagination inexhaustible, his wit great, his industry wonderful; moral and temperate; his desire for learning became an enthusiasm, yet he did not possess sufficient understanding or prudence to use his many advantages wisely. His love of predestination and astrology, and his presumption, led him step by step to the many calamities associated with his restless life. In his last moments, however, he retracted his infidel writings, which, it would appear, never represented his convictions, but were, like those of Arouet, afterwards Voltaire—the "Dead-Sea fruit" of the vanity of mere human learning.*

Calvin boldly avows his share in the proceedings at Geneva, and the immolation of Servetus. He maintains that the punishment of heretics belongs only to those who hold *the true doctrines*—that is, to *himself* and his followers.†

FEREL, the "Protestant Reformer," was born in the year 1489, at Gap, in Dauphiné. He was descended from an old family which had possessions in that province. When a Catholic priest, Ferel vigorously opposed the movements of the early Lutherans. Father Anthony de Lombard relates that he was present when Ferel struck a German physician for having spoken in a "disrespectful manner of the Pope." When a Reformer, his language respecting the Roman Pontiffs was of the grossest character, and often unfit for

---

* "The biographers of Calvin deny that Servetus retracted his writings at the stake. This statement has no foundation in fact. It has also been alleged that Servetus was a friar, but such is a mistake, as he never entered the clerical state. His studies were at first for the civil law.

† See Dyer's Life of Calvin.

repetition. Roger Harrington, an English exile at Strasburg, compared Ferel's "abusive tongue to that of John Bale." It is certain, however, that Ferel was immensely inferior to Bale in learning and genius.

Ferel's history is closely bound up with that of John Calvin; and it has been alleged that many of the arbitrary actions of Calvin were suggested by the former. This statement is doubtful, for Calvin was not the man to listen to dictation, and although he was introduced to the Geneva Reformers by their popular preacher, Ferel, he soon placed himself at the head of the movement. But, at the same time, Ferel became a valuable assistant "where violence took the place of charitable persuasion." Erasmus styled Ferel "a hot-headed Reformer." "I abhor those Evangelists," writes Erasmus, "because it is through them that literature is declining in every place. * * * We have been stunned long enough with the cry of 'Gospel, Gospel, Gospel!' We want *Gospel manners.*" John Bale himself, as the reader is aware, has lamented the injury inflicted upon books, and literature in general, by the "Hot-Gospel" sectaries. The "impetuosity of Ferel, to whom discretion was an utter stranger," led him to attack Erasmus. He was, however, far from being able, either as a writer or speaker, to encounter such a potent antagonist.

Ferel, whose rough eloquence was agreeable to the people of Geneva, gained many followers. The first Protestant sermon ever delivered in that ancient city "against Popery" was delivered by Ferel. On the evening of the sermon the preacher was accompanied home by vast crowds of people, singing psalms along the streets. From the window of his lodging Ferel ordered the crowd to fall on their knees to receive his blessing. They readily obeyed his order.

The biographers of Calvin admit that Ferel was a man of an intolerant and persecuting spirit. Even Thomas Dyer describes the proceedings of Calvin and Ferel in Geneva as the work of "ecclesiastical tyranny."* Ferel was an ordained priest, a Franciscan, and is said to have been a zealous Father of his order for many years.

Ferel lived to be 76 years of age. He was to the close of life the unmitigated enemy of the creed of his fathers, and of all those who professed it.

Several noted Reformers who have been set down as Catholic priests in early life never belonged to the priesthood at any time. John Calvin, for instance, was altogether "a self-constituted apostle," and his conduct partook far more of a political dictator than an *amiable spiritual director*, who came to preach peace and good-will to the erring and the fallen.

My space, and other circumstances, will not permit me to make much further inquiry into the history of the Continental Reformers.

---

* See Thomas Dyer's Life of Calvin, p. 75.

CHAPTER VIII.

QUEEN MARY'S CONSORT.

MR. FROUDE describes King Philip as most unpopular in England, "and that he left behind him no single personal friend." The records of the public and private life of Philip, during the eleven months he resided in England, furnish no incident on which to originate the allegation that he had " forfeited the friendship of all—*even of one personal friend.*"*
It is sad to dwell on Mr. Froude's *facts !*

I now present to the reader a few of the most interesting circumstances in connection with the history of King Philip, his visit to England, and marriage with Queen Mary.

Philip was born on the 21st of May, 1527, at Valladolid. His mother was the Empress Isabel, daughter of Emanuel, King of Portugal, surnamed the Great Isabel. Isabel was an amiable and excellent princess. Under her domestic rule the royal palaces became so many schools of design for the Fine Arts. The ladies of the Court were vieing with one another in producing pictured tapestry and other work to decorate churches, not for Spain alone, but for distant countries. Philip's father, Charles the Fifth, was descended from the Ducal houses of Burgundy and Austria. Both by father and mother Philip could claim descent from Ferdinand and Isabel of Spain. By blood half a Spaniard, by tempera-

---

* In Chapter XII., on " Persecution of Conscience" in England, I shall refer to what part Philip took in those calamitous proceedings.

ment and character he proved wholly so. At the age of sixteen Philip was married to his cousin, Maria of Portugal. In a year subsequent (1544) he became the father of the ill-starred Don Carlos, and in the same year his young wife died.

In 1548, Don Philip first visited the Netherlands. He went thither to receive homage in the various provinces as their future Sovereign, and to exchange oaths of mutual fidelity with the notables of that country. He spent a summer at Brussels, indulging in magnificent entertainments.* Philip was disagreeable to the Italians, and detestable to the Germans. He hated war, and whatever laurels were won in his reign were those of his generals, not his own. His father engaged in great enterprises; Philip would avoid them. The Emperor never recoiled before threats; his son was reserved and cautious; suspicious of all men; almost inclined to sacrifice a realm from hesitation and timidity.† The father had a genius for action; the son a predilection for repose. Charles took all men's opinions, but reserved his judgment, and acted on it—when matured, with irresistible energy. Philip was led by others; was vacillating in forming decisions, and irresolute in executing them when formed. In this respect he sometimes resembled his sister-in-law, Elizabeth. Philip's mental capacity in general was not highly esteemed. He hated to hold conversation, yet he could sit down and write a letter of sixteen pages, stating he had only time to write three. His education was small, in an age when kings and nobles were acquainted with languages; he spoke no language but Spanish, and after some time he had a slender knowledge

---

* Memoirs of King Philip by Cabrera.
† Cabrera, Vol. I.; Luriano, Relazione MS.

of French and Italian. His private character, for a king, in those times, was passing good; nevertheless, he has been described as a shocking profligate.* Philip had, doubtless, many enemies raised up by the convulsions of the Reformation, and we cannot accept as a truth one-half of the charges preferred against him by German and English historians.

Philip resided not more than eleven months in this country, during which period he gave sufficient proof that he did not marry the "half-dying Queen for love." Far from it. While in England, however, the people or the Government had no reason to find fault with him. He spent immense sums within this realm in a few months, and caused hundreds to be released from prison—amongst them some fanatics; others trading upon religion—rebels and socialists of the Lollard type. Poor debtors were also an object of his sympathy. Debt, on the part of the humble, was a great crime in those days of transition. To the members of both Houses of Parliament Philip was profuse in hospitality; and he made presents to the value of £30,000—an immense sum at that epoch. To the Princess Elizabeth he was most kind, and indeed proved himself not only her brother-in-law, but a devoted friend. In subsequent years Elizabeth had the generosity to acknowledge this fact. Through his interest Elizabeth regained her freedom, and was released from the Tower. Before leaving England, Philip made his sister-in-law many costly presents, accompanied by "a most delicate and friendly letter, full of good wishes for her future happiness and prosperity."

If Philip, in the latter part of Elizabeth's reign, sought to deprive her of the crown, he assisted her powerfully in

---

* These statements to some extent rest upon the assertions of such writers as Bradford, Motley, and Froude—all prejudiced.

its obtainment some thirty years before. The State Papers, so ably and impartially calendared by the Rev. Mr. Stephenson, have let in a flood of interesting light upon the events of this period.

"In enumerating the influences," says the Rev. Mr. Stephenson, "which tended to secure the throne to Elizabeth, we must not fail to specify the assistance which she derived from her brother-in-law, Philip of Spain. It was probably more valuable to her than all the others united. We have so long accustomed ourselves to identify Philip's name with everything that is hateful and hostile to England, that it has become difficult for us to believe, without an effort, that at any time he entertained kindly feelings towards our nation. Yet such was the case at the time of which I am writing, and no one knew this better than Elizabeth herself. True, the object which he had in view was neither dignified nor disinterested; but we are stating facts, not analysing motives. When Mary died, Philip did for her sister what no one but himself could have done. The Reformers were afraid of him, and kept quiet. He held in check the great Catholic party, which, but for his controlling power, would certainly have opposed her accession, and possibly would have succeeded. But for him, the more influential of the nobility, the clergy with very few exceptions, and the majority of the landed gentry would have declared against Elizabeth on religious grounds. The Pope, urged on by France, would have pronounced her illegitimate, and therefore incapable of succeeding to the throne; but Philip was now all powerful at Rome, and the Bull of Deprivation was suspended. Of his intervention in favour of Elizabeth we have the fullest and most authentic evidence in his own correspondence preserved at Simancas, and from it we derive the following account of the state of parties in England immediately upon the death of Mary:—

"'Alarmed at the repeated accounts of the dangerous illness of his wife, and anxious to direct the nation in a choice of her successor, Philip despatched to the Court of London his favourite minister, the Count de Feria. The choice was a judicious one, for, of all his agents, Feria was the least likely to alarm the prejudices of the English. He had already spent some time in this country, and having married one of the Queen's maids of honour (Jane Dormer), was regarded as half an Englishman. He understood the manners and prejudices of the country, and had fathomed the intrigues of the several political parties into which the Court was divided. He possessed Philip's entire confidence, and brought with him for his guidance a paper of instructions which the King, with his usual minute attention to business, had drawn up and copied out with his own hand. When Feria reached London on the 9th of November, 1558, Mary's case was hopeless, and she had been informed by her physicians, both English and Spanish, that her days were numbered. The Count was at once admitted to her presence, and found her perfectly conscious, calm, collected, and resigned. She was unable to read her husband's letter, but she listened with attention and interest to the message which accompanied it. Feria had ascertained that a few days previous a deputation from the Parliament had waited upon the Queen, and had reminded her that the great question of the succession to the throne *was yet undecided.* They had gone a step further, and had recommended the claims of the Princess Elizabeth. Mary had offered no objection, but contented herself with expressing the hope that when her sister was upon the throne she would *pay such debts as still remained undischarged, and preserve the Olden Religion of the realm.* Under these circumstances, and anticipating the result which was so near at hand, Feria summoned the Privy Council, and he declared to them his Royal master's anxiety for the quick succession of the Princess Elizabeth. The French, he said, had designs of their own at this juncture, to which Philip *would never lend himself;* they had tried hard to separate him from England, but he would not violate his promises. If Elizabeth were the choice of the English nation, as Philip hoped she would be, he would gladly give her his support, and would join with her in insisting upon the restoration of Calais to the English Crown. Feria's address was so favourably received by the Councillors, that, as soon as the Conference had broken up, he informed his master that Elizabeth's accession might now be regarded as a certainty."

In another despatch Count Feria tells his royal master that he looks upon Elizabeth "as a young woman of much vanity and craft. She evidently admires her father's system of government." * * *

"Nov. 10th, 1558, the Count Feria visited the future Queen of England. She was at that time resident in the house of a private gentleman some thirteen miles from London. She received Feria courteously, though scarcely (he thought) with her usual cordiality. He supped with her, and after supper she conversed with him at considerable length, and without any hesitation. She was already confident of her position, and led him to understand as much. The general turn which he gave to the conversation, and certain special questions and remarks which he introduced into it from time to time, were framed according to the paper of instructions which he had received from the King. The princess admitted, without any hesitation, *the extent of her obligations to Philip; he had always been her friend, she said; nor had he failed her when she was in prison and most needed his protection.* The Count Feria, she added, was not the first of his ministers who had brought her an encouraging message from King Philip, for she had received similar assurances from Diego De Azeredo and Alonzo De Cordova."

The character of Philip, like that of Mary, has been represented in a light more odious than actually false by Puritan writers.

In his private instructions to his son, concerning political matters, Charles the Fifth* inculcated two principles, which subsequently became prominent features in the government

---

* In Brewer's State Papers (1509) are to be seen some interesting relations concerning the boyhood of Charles the Fifth. In the 1st vol. of this work I have referred to the career of Charles as a monarch.

of Philip—namely, to maintain the royal authority with a firm hand, and never to yield to clamour or rebellion. And, next, to uphold the Catholic Church against its numerous enemies—a difficult undertaking. In carrying out these instructions, Philip frequently acted with cruelty and despotism. "Constitutional Government" was a thing he could not tolerate, believing it to be derogatory to the office of a monarch; still he had to listen to the voice of the Cortes. A portion of Philip's subjects changed their religion, and then deemed it a "duty of their conversion" to rebel against their lawful Sovereign. Philip endeavoured to put them down with a strong hand, and, I must add, without mercy or pity. The conduct of Alva was undoubtedly atrocious, but it has often since been far more than rivalled by English Generals and Viceroys in Ireland,* and other "dependencies." In the end, however, those who rebelled against Philip triumphed; they were engaged in an honest struggle for fatherland, but they disgraced their victories by the most shocking barbarities on record.† Yet those "refined cruelties," as a German writer styles them, have been defended on the ground "that it was a work executed against the idolatrous Papists, the enemies of the Lord." Is this the fashion in which history should be written?

Philip's history is of an European character, for his lot was cast in that period when a change of religion took place which overturned all the social and political institutions of Germany, a part of the Netherlands, and our own country also. Of course, Philip had to defend the "dependencies" of Spain, and the question to be entertained is, in what manner did he perform his duty to the Mother Country, and the

---

* See Froude's History of England, Vol. 11, p. 181.
† Motley's History of the Dutch Republic.

revolted provinces. Upon this matter there is, as might be expected, a conflict of opinion, which is unfortunately interwoven with the bitterest sectarian feelings.

Upon the death of his father,* Philip sent an autograph letter to Elizabeth, announcing the fact. The Princess replied in a most gracious and magnanimous manner, overlooking the personal and political enmity with which the illustrious Charles had pursued her, offered a high meed of praise to his qualities as a man, a general, a statesman, and an imperial ruler.

"The happiness I enjoy in being so nearly allied to you, no less than my esteem for your Majesty's signal merit, together with my obligations to you, touch me too sensibly not to make me sympathise with you in your grief for the loss of your illustrious father; but since it behoves me to offer some consolation to you in this your affliction, I cannot do it better than by beseeching you to call to mind that your renowned father thought death so great a happiness that he wished to die to the world before he left it. And it is certain that, as his life has been a compendium of greatness, so also will his death be held in honour to all generations. We ought not to mourn the Emperor Charles as one dead, but rather to regard him as one who shall survive through all future ages; for though his body may be reduced to dust, his name, which is imperishable, can never die. I am employing myself at this time in reading the history of his wars, and his singularly great achievements, his courage and his virtue; that so, by considering the glorious memorials of the father, I may redouble the veneration and esteem in which I hold the son."†

This missive was written but a few days before Queen Mary's death. The amount of sincerity and good feeling

---

* Charles the Fifth was born at Flanders in the year 1500, and was educated by a Dutch priest. He died on the 2nd of September, 1558.

† Leti, Vita de Elizabetha.

which suggested the above letter to her brother-in-law subsequent events amply and strikingly demonstrated.

The Emperor Charles never liked the Jesuits, nor did he even when he became a monk. Amongst the actions which he regretted not having carried out was that of sending Luther to the "flames as the worst of all heretics." The political results of Luther's teaching were disastrous to the interests of the Emperor.

The Escorial, the favourite retreat of Philip, was long the pride of Spain. Los Santos has left on record one of the best accounts of this immense building. The main building, or monastery, he estimates at 744 Castilian feet in length by 588 in breadth. Its greatest height, measured to the central cross above the dome of the great church, is 315 feet. The whole circumference of the Escorial, including the palace, he reckons at 2,984 feet, or near three-fifths of a mile. There were no less than 12,000 doors and windows in the building; the weight of the keys amounted to fifty *arrobas*, or 1,250 pounds. There were 68 fountains playing in the halls and courts. The cost of the whole building amounted to 6,000,000 ducats. The Escorial represented a monastery, a church, and a royal palace. The Escorial continued for a long time as the retreat of royalty, and was in process of time much enlarged.

The contrast between King Philip and his father was sufficiently marked; but the dissimilarity between Philip and *his own son*, Don Carlos—in taste, habits, aspirations, and judgment—was still more signal. It is certain that the Prince was neglected and disliked by his father, of whom he saw little till he reached his fourteenth year. Some writers have suggested insanity as the cause of the Don's extraordinary conduct. Those who had a personal knowledge of the Prince contend that he was "sane enough." It is admitted, however, that he had a violent temper, and was "allowed to do as he pleased." His father looked upon him for several years as "a dangerous lunatic;" but his confessor thought otherwise. A few days before his death, Carlos is said to have made a will, in which he implored his father's pardon and blessing.

King Philip writes thus of his son's death :—" I hope that God has called my poor boy to Himself, that he may be with Him ever more; and that He will grant me His grace, that I may endure this calamity with a Christian heart and patience."

At little more than twenty-three years of age, died Don Carlos, Prince of Asturias. No one of his time came into the world under such brilliant auspices, for he was heir to the noblest empire then in Christendom. The Spaniards, as they hopefully imagined, discerned in his childhood some of the genius of future greatness, looked confidently forward to the day when he should rival the glory of his grandfather, Charles the Fifth. But, it would appear that he had been born under an evil star whose malign influence neutralised the gifts of Fortune. The naturally wild and headstrong temper of Carlos was exasperated by the unkindness and estrangement of his father. Perhaps the marriage of King Philip with Isabel of France, who had been originally intended as the bride of Don Carlos, had some effect upon his mind. He was *present at his father's wedding*, and it is related that he was much grieved at not becoming the husband of the beautiful Isabel. Carlos was fourteen at this period, and Isabel about nineteen. " So attractive was the royal bride," writes a Spanish Grandee, " that no cavalier durst look on her long for fear of losing his heart." Isabel had no love for a cold-hearted man like Philip. She did not see her intended husband till three days before his marriage, and when introduced to the King, she drew back, and then advanced a little towards him; remaining silent, and gazing at the monarch in a searching manner. Philip becoming annoyed, enquired if the Princess "were looking to see if he had many grey hairs in his head." The bride then assumed a more agreeable demeanour, and became apparently pleased. As the daughter of Catherine de Medicis, Isabel was doubtless well instructed in the arts of dissimulation, and must have known that to be candid or outspoken was a dangerous custom to practice at the Spanish Court, at any period. Isabel and Philip seemed to live on good terms, although from such a husband as Philip she could expect little warmth of feeling.

The Spanish Court under Isabel was one of great splendour, yet depressingly deficient in that heartiness which imparted to the hospitality of England an aspect so genial and acceptable to its guests. Isabel *dined alone*, yet she was attended at table by no less than *thirty young ladies of rank*. The Spanish women hated those of France. So the "tall French beauties," to the number of twenty, had to retire to their own country.

Some strange documents were found amongst the papers of Don Carlos, who writes frequently in his correspondence of the "continued unkindness of his father." It seems that he desired to leave Spain privately, asserting that "every step he took he was watched;" he "felt miserable;" he wrote to different persons, "assuring them of his friendship and aid when he became King of Spain;" he did not "forget his old theatrical friends;" "nor the pretty little actress from Granada whom he loved so tenderly;" he speaks frequently in his diary of the "want of money," whereby his desire to relieve the sick and the unfortunate was counteracted. "I have," said Carlos, "great faith in charity; with the ducat in my hand, I whisper to myself 'for the honour and glory of God.'" One paper contained a list of all those persons whom he deemed friendly or hostile to himself. At the head of the former class stood the names of his young stepmother, Queen Isabella, and of his uncle, Don John of Austria—both of whom he mentioned in terms of the warmest affection. On the list of his enemies, "*to be pursued to the death*," were the names of the *King, his father*, the Prince and Princess of Ebeli, Cardinal Espinosa, and the Duke of Alva, whom he mortally hated.*

Of the political or religious struggles going forward in Europe, Don Carlos knew little. "He loved the society of those young nobles who were his ruin; they played at dice and drank till the grey of morning, and then ran through the streets "like so many mad-caps."

The despatches of the Venetian Ambassador are by no means favourable to Carlos. They describe him as being of a reckless, impatient temper, fierce, and even cruel, in his disposition." Badoaro relates when hares and other game were brought to him, he would occasionally amuse himself by *roasting them alive*.†

To account for Carlos's conduct, it is stated that when thirteen years of age he fell headlong down a flight of stairs against a door at the bottom of a passage, and was taken up senseless. The royal surgeon, finding the head injured, "trepanned the patient." In this operation a part of the bone of the skull was removed. It is clear that Carlos

---

* Prescott's Life of Philip the Second, Vol. II.
† Relazione de Badoaro, MS.

was at times labouring under hallucinations; besides, insanity appeared in two or three generations of his family.* Be this as it may, the story of Don Carlos still remains in a cloud, and is one of those Spanish royal mysteries which is likely never to be discovered, or fairly related by historians. In a vast portion of Europe the memory of Philip is still unpopular, and surrounded by the worst prejudice of human nature—namely, sectarian hate. I have seen it chronicled, years back, by some superficial or sectarian historian, that Philip *hanged his son, Don Carlos.* It is true that a Spanish monarch hanged his son for rebellion, and the name of the unfortunate prince was Carlos. But the wretched incident occurred some centuries before Philip the Second was born. The *motive* for this wilful misrepresentation of historical facts is obvious to the reflective reader of the terrible struggles between the Netherlands and King Philip. Upon Queen Elizabeth rests immense censure for the part she took in the Wars of the Netherlands.

Three months had scarcely elapsed from the death of Don Carlos till his young stepmother (Isabel) was consigned to the tomb "amidst dark and terrible rumours;" but those malicious rumours were destitute of any foundation. Isabel's honour at the period of her death was as unsullied as it had been on the day of her nuptial vow to Philip. She had no feeling towards miserable, neglected Carlos, but that of a sympathising humane woman for the imbecile son of her husband by a former marriage.

No foreign princess ever attained in Spain the popularity enjoyed by Queen Isabel for the eight years during which she maintained the irksome position of Queen Consort to

---

* Raumer, Vol. I.

Philip the Second. "Catherine de Medicis," writes Cabrera, the Spanish historian, "had every reason to feel proud of her beautiful and most worthy daughter, who set a noble example to the wives and daughters of our grandees—yea, to all the wives and mothers and maids of Spain." Anne of Austria became the fourth and last wife of Philip. Historians have left us but few particulars of her life and character. Her contemporaries, however, affirm that she was a princess of a very amiable disposition and much given to benevolent actions. She had four sons and a daughter, but all died in early childhood, except the third son, who is known in history as Philip III. The remains of this good Queen are entombed in the Escorial.*

---

* In the 4th volume of this work I shall return to the "last days of King Philip."

[Owing to the brief but serious illness of the author this chapter has been overlooked, and did not occupy its place according to time in the record of King Henry VIII's reign.]

CHAPTER IX.

THE POET SURREY.

No one amongst the victims of Henry VIII. fell more guiltless, or more generally regretted by all whom personal animosity or the spirit of party had not hardened against sentiments of human sympathy, or blinded to the perception of genius, than Henry Howard, Earl of Surrey. His quaint and fanciful songs and graceful sonnets, which served as a model to the most popular poets of the age of Elizabeth, still excite the tender interest of every student of the olden literature of England. Surrey spent a portion of his early years in Italy, then the centre of literature and the Garden of Poetic Inspiration. It is from the return of this accomplished gentleman that we are to date, not only the introduction into our language of the Petrarchian Sonnet, and with it of a tenderness and refinement of sentiment unknown to the ruggedness of our preceding versifiers, but, what is much more, that of the heroic blank verse—a noble measure of which the earliest example exists in Surrey's spirited and faithful version, of one book of the " Æneid." History and tradition have been auspicious to the fame of Surrey; yet it is probable that his early death on the scaffold has imparted a halo to his memory which his actions might not have conferred. As the lover of the "Fayre Geraldyne," he has been placed in the most romantic light by the admirers of the marvellous. It was at the house of the ill-fated Catherine

Howard that the poet is said to have first met Elizabeth Fitzgerald, the heroine of his muse. The love must needs have been on the poet's side only, for the "fair Maiden of the Pale" could not have been more than thirteen years of age when she is stated to have first captivated Surrey. Of course, his enthusiasm for the young lady manifested as much poetic ardour as if she were not existent, or were as a Laura to her Petrarch. How many poets have worshipped fanciful embodiments, and immortalised fictitious divinities! The whole story seems to me but a beautiful fiction—seeing that in plain fact the details of the asserted love passages are full of contradictions, and the "ladye fayre," sad to say, seemed not to have possessed the refined and delicate requirements which deserved the homage of such an intellect; and, again, judged by subsequent events, her love for the poet appears to have been merely imagined. She felt flattered, no doubt, by the sonnets of Surrey, and his stately attentions; but for the benefit of the romantic, may not all the mythic loves of poets be translated in very common-place language? I know that a poet imagines—who, even the most prosaic man of intellect, does not?—an ideal. It might perhaps be more correct to call the myth an idol; but, ideal or eidolon, may not the poet look more to the music of his rhythm than to the charms of his fanciful inspiration? As the sunlight imparted melody to the stern statue of Memnon, and buried Æolia's harp in the granite heart of the Græco-Egyptian Zeus, so Surrey's poems to the "Fayre Geraldyne" may have been but an instance in our cold clime of the imaginative fervour of a lover of the ideal devoting his muse to supposition—imitative of the spiritual devotion of his antecedent idealist, Petrarch, to "Laura,"—who never could be, and never was, *his* Laura —an ideal to whom the "frenzy of fancy" erected the eikōn of imagination at the font of Castalia. However, the lovers of romance in History have had some pleasing thoughts excited by those rhymes, which have had, as not many acknowledge, an effect not unfelt on that wonderful composite—the English tongue. So we may say of Surrey in regard to this his alleged passage of love—

> " Filled with balm, the gale sighs on—
> Though the flowers have sunk to death
> So when the poet's dream is gone,
> His memory lives in music's breath."

I think Anthony Wood is the first author of repute who relates the romantic narrative of "Surrey and Geraldyne's love." Wood quotes Drayton as his authority. It turns out, however, that part of this romance was "borrowed" from a little book written by the eccentric and romantic Tom Nash, and published in 1591. Let it be remembered that the interesting young lady in question was not born till 1528. In this case dates form the nearest clue to facts. "To believe that Surrey could have seen the lovely Geraldyne languishing on a couch, bewailing his absence in all the tenderness of ardent passion; or to give any credit to the story which represents her a prey to jealous doubts and fears, anxiously entreating her lover to guard his heart against the bright eyes and seductive charms of the Italian ladies, and hasten *his* return, that their mutual love might be crowned by a blissful union; when, at that very period, she was only a child in the nursery, and Surrey himself a married man, would betray a credulity altogether irrational."[*] A recent writer contends that Lord Surrey commenced his love narrative of the "Fayre Geraldyne" whilst a prisoner in the Norman Tower, at

---

[*] Nott's Life of Surrey.

Windsor Castle. I cannot accept this statement. It is more likely that Surrey was imprisoned in the Fleet, or the Tower by the river side.

At the "barge procession" from Greenwich to the Tower, on the occasion of Anna Boleyn's coronation, a pale, sad, abstracted-looking gentleman sat beside the Duke of Norfolk in one of the royal barges. The sickly countenance of this young man presented a peculiar contrast with a rich crimson velvet dress, trimmed with miniver, and cap of the same colour, surmounted with a small white feather, and surrounded by a bandeau of rubies. He had small dark eyes, insignificant when bent upon the ground, but brilliant and piercing when raised to encounter the gaze of others; thin compressed lips; a sharp and beardless chin, and a delicate, almost languid appearance.* Such was the poet Surrey, as he appeared at the coronation procession of his unfortunate cousin Anna Boleyn.

Contrasted with the Earl of Surrey, like a rich oil painting with the delicate hues of a miniature, yet aged by care, or concealed sorrows, and wearing on his noble features an aspect of the deepest anxiety, Thomas Wyatt leaned against one of the gorgeous decorations of the royal barge, ever and anon inclining to answer the short and low-breathed communications of his brother poet, Henry, Earl of Surrey. A great friendship existed between Surrey, Rochford, and Wyatt. Roger Ascham writes: "Although very young† at the time of Queen Anna's coronation, I remember the procession on

---

* Amongst her Majesty's Collection of Holbein's pictures is to be seen a magnificent portrait of Henry, Earl of Surrey. The face represents that of an extremely handsome youth of some sixteen years of age. Proud, sad, and lovable; and, may I add, "the most gifted of all the Howards."

† Roger Ascham was about eighteen years of age at the time of Anna's Coronation. He was then a clever student in St. John's College, Cambridge.

the river. I saw Lords Surrey, Rochford, and Tom Wyatt in a royal barge on that day. It was a pleasing sight for scholars to behold the three poets sitting together. Each had his love story, but dare not reveal it. How sad."

Lord Surrey manifested a warm friendship for his brother-in-law, Henry Fitzroy, Duke of Richmond, natural son of Henry VIII. Surrey was fifteen and Richmond twelve years old when they first met at Windsor. Both studied for a time in Paris, and returned together to England. Henry Fitzroy, as Richmond was familiarly styled, was unfortunate in the selection made of his tutors, one of whom introduced him to the society of strolling players, and the "characters" who frequented country fairs and markets. As might have been expected such company led to the loss of morals and health; in fact the boy was permitted to do just as he pleased.* It is supposed that Richmond's marriage was promoted by Anna Boleyn who introduced her cousin Mary Howard to the "bachelor boy." Lady Mary Howard is described as a "peerless gem, a lovely girl of thirteen." Richmond loved her at first sight, and his love was to all appearances returned with fervour. But who could dare introduce the subject to the king? At this time Anna Boleyn's influence with the monarch was immense, and "delicate little Harry Fitzroy" was a favourite with the new queen, so she promoted the marriage which was to strengthen the connection of the House of Norfolk with the throne. Crumwell did not approve of the match, because he dreaded and hated the Howards; but Anna Boleyn, who was always inclined to promote love-matches, procured the King's approval in this case, as well as in that of her cousin Surrey to marry Frances Vere, daughter

---

* In the Second Volume, Chapter X, I have noticed at some length the career of the Duke of Richmond.

of the Earl of Oxford, a lady whose personal advantages were by no means distinguished. Queen Anna took charge of the four affianced lovers at Windsor; they were constantly in her society, but some delay was caused as to the arrival of the Papal brief in the case of Richmond's marriage.

In his "Elegy on Windsor," Lord Surrey describes the meetings of the lovers under the guardianship of the Queen —herself the centre of all attraction and admiration at that period.

> " The large green courts, where we were wont to rove,
>   With eyes cast up unto the Maiden's Tower,*
> And easy sighs, such as folks draw in love,
>   The stately seats, the ladies bright of hue,
> The dances short, long tales of great delight,
>   With words and looks that tigers could but rue,
> Where each of us did plead the other's right."

When Surrey reached his nineteenth year he came to Queen Anna to claim his bride; and Anna gave up to the poet his wife, with one of those short pretty speeches, for which she was so noted. It is stated that they kept their honeymoon for a year; a year of youth and love. Then came a season of gloom and pain, which closed the pastoral of their Windsor life.† It is alleged that Surrey was inconstant to his wife. It is also narrated that she was "loved by him to the end." The Duke of Richmond's delicate health postponed for a time his marriage. Mary Howard and Richmond lived but a very short period of married existence. In the Spring of 1536, this thoughtless

---

* Frances Vere and Mary Howard were lodged in the Maiden Tower, from whose windows they occasionally looked down upon their lovers at play in the tennis court.

† Royal Windsor, vol. III.

youth joined in the conspiracy concocted by Crumwell and the Seymours against Anna Boleyn, who had been his devoted friend for years. The reader is aware that the Duke of Richmond was present at the queen's judicial murder, and conducted himself with an indecent levity of manner which shocked the spectators.

In July, 1536, Lord Surrey lost his young friend the Duke of Richmond. Perhaps this "spoiled and petted child of fortune," was more to be pitied than condemned. From childhood he was brought up in a vitiated atmosphere; all his surroundings were evil, and the "only true boy or man" he had ever known was the noble Surrey. No one seemed to care about "poor little Harry" but his girl-wife, who was two years younger than himself. The grief of the young bride for Richmond's death was intense. For weeks she "indulged in a frantic wail which alarmed her family, and her sorrow seemed to have unsettled her reason."

Harry Fitzroy died at Colleweston, once the property of Margaret of Beaufort. According to the Hardwicke State Papers his death was caused by consumption. It was, however, bruited in well-informed circles about Windsor Castle, where Fitzroy was well known, that his alleged consumption was caused by a quack doctor in the interest of the Seymours.

At the period of Fitzroy's death the king was only two months married to Jane Seymour; yet, even at that time, there were speculations secretly entertained and discussed, as to what might be the *result* if the new queen were to have a daughter—an event which might deprive Jane of the influence which she possessed with the monarch; and, it was further debated by the Seymours that it was very possible the king would endeavour to put into action his long-cherished purpose of creating Fitzroy Prince of Wales. In such a movement the Sovereign might count upon the support of the House of Norfolk. If the project succeeded, the Lady Mary Howard, as the wife of Fitzroy, would advance within a short distance of the throne. The Seymours and their guide, Lord Cromwell, became alarmed. Queen Jane was known to be pregnant at this particular period; and there was, therefore no time to be lost. So Harry Fitzroy was suddenly removed from the scene, and left an unimpeded path to the vaulting ambition of Lord Hertford (Seymour), who detested young Richmond. Dark rumours were afloat as to the cause of the sudden death of the King's cherished son; but those rumours were carefully concealed from the monarch, "who wept bitterly at the loss of the little duke." By what means—foul or fair—Henry Duke of Richmond died, still remains a mystery. Thorndale states that "Edward Seymour and his retainers were the only persons who could unveil the dark surroundings of the case." Another writer upon the mysterious death observes :—" Like to the beginning was the end of that strange life ; out of the shadows he had come, into the shadows he fell back."

It is strange that the "horrible narratives" circulated in Essex, Berkshire and Bucks, concerning the "latter days of the little duke," never reached the royal ear.

In a few weeks subsequent to the death of Richmond, Lord Surrey succeeded in his "earnest appeal" for the remains of his brother-in-law. At Windsor, where he had lived so long, Richmond was denied a grave. This was all done through the intrigues of the Seymours. At Thetford Priory a temporary grave was given to the remains. This incident increased the well-earned hatred of Surrey for Edward Seymour. No other feeling could possibly exist between the loving cousin of unfortunate Anna Boleyn and the brother of that unnatural woman Jane Seymour, who hated "poor little Harry."

Lord Surrey raised a monument in Thetford Priory to the memory of Richmond; and had also a fine portrait of him painted in Lambeth House.

The Duchess of Norfolk described the widow of Richmond "as unnatural in her conduct as a daughter." The Duchess of Norfolk was, however, supposed to be insane, so that her remarks were not heeded.

Lord Crumwell was intriguing for a marriage between Thomas Seymour and the widow of Richmond, but the lady protested against the match. "Marry again!" exclaimed the beautiful young widow, "No; my love lies dead in Thetford Priory. My darling young husband's memory shall be honoured by me to the last hour of my life." Her brother Surrey remonstrated with her; but to no avail. Mary was deaf to him, as she had been to others. A second love appeared to her "unlawful and unholy." "Forget my dear little husband? no, indeed;" were her words to Lord Crumwell.

The Duchess of Richmond suddenly disappeared for some weeks, and was then discovered in the neighbourhood of her husband's grave, which she visited morning and evening.

Burnet and the Puritan writers describe the Duke of Richmond as "very amiable, pious and learned. He was also a staunch friend to the Reformation." The Throcmorton MSS. and other documents place Harry Fitzroy in a very different light. It is absurd for party writers to present this self-willed, vain boy, to posterity as the champion of any religious institution. Harry Fitzroy felt more interest in field sports, or a game of tennis, than in any intellectual exercise, polemical or literary. Of rival theologies he knew nothing—and, if the popular paradox may be pardoned—cared less.

Many years had passed away since the mother of Harry Fitzroy had captivated King Henry by her exquisite voice and elegant style of dancing. Sir John Seymour describes Elizabeth Blount as "one of the most beautiful girls in the realm, when she first appeared at Queen Katharine's Court as one of the maids of honour." In the "Book of Court Payments" for 1513, occurs for one year's wages to Elizabeth Blount the sum of "one hundred shillings." Henry had recourse to the vilest stratagems to decoy this gifted and beautiful woman. Her knightly suitor, Anthony Penrose, suddenly disappeared, and was never heard of more. Elizabeth Blount was subsequently married by the king's "command" to one of his own profligate attendants. Thornton relates that "for many years before her death she gave up her whole time in doing good for the poor and succouring the unfortunate." She outlived King Henry's six wives.

Miss Strickland considers Surrey's love for Elizabeth Fitzgerald to have been of the Petrarchian character, and that the lady believed his addresses to be merely the graceful compliments of a poet. Yet, see how fancy is confronted by facts. At sixteen years old the Fayre Geraldyne whom some of her contemporaries have described as the "most lovely and fascinating lady in England," was married to Sir Anthony Browne, "a lively and romantic bachelor of *sixty-one.*" At twenty it is stated she became a widow; and next entered the service of the Princess Mary. Her second husband was Lord Clinton, who valiantly defended Queen Mary, during Wyatt's rebellion. At this period, and to her death, Lady Clinton was the constant friend of Queen Elizabeth. It has been further contended,—though I cannot trace any authority for it—that Lady Clinton was *married four times.*

The heroine of so many love stories died in 1589, then in a ripe old age.* She was very much beloved by the old families of rank. Her cousin, De Clifford affirms that she "possessed an immense fund of romantic anecdotes. It is stated that a few days before her death Queen Elizabeth visited her; and an affecting "leave-taking took place."

Strange events were passing quickly in those times. The Duke of Norfolk, sagacious, politic and deeply versed in all the secrets and the arts of Courts, saw in a coalition with the Seymours the only expedient for averting the ruin of his princely family. Surrey's scorn of the new nobility of the House of Seymour, and his animosity against the person of its chiefs were not to be overcome by any plea of expediency, or menace of danger. He could not forget that it was at the instance of the Earl of Hertford that he, with some other nobles and gentlemen "had suffered the disgrace of imprisonment for eating meat in Lent;" that when a trifling defeat which he had sustained near Boulogne had caused him to be removed from the government of that town, it was the Earl of Hertford who ultimately profited by his misfortunes in succeeding to the command of the army. Other causes of offence also obtained with Surrey against him; and choosing rather to fall, than cling for support to an enemy at once despised and hated, Surrey braved the anger of his father by an absolute refusal to lend himself to such an alliance. Of this circumstance his enemies availed themselves to instil into the mind of the King a suspicion that Lord Surrey aspired to the hand of the Princess Mary. Surrey's wife was alive at this period. So the accusation had no foundation. They also commented with industrious malice on

---

* The Fayre Geraldyne, on whom so many romantic novels have been written, at home and abroad, was buried in Lincoln Chapel, at Windsor.

his bearing the arms of Edward the Confessor,* to which he was clearly entitled in right of his mother, who was the daughter of Stafford, Duke of Buckingham, but which his more cautious father had ceased to quarter after the attainder of that unfortunate nobleman. The excited mind of Henry in his latter days willingly gave encouragement to every person who wished to destroy life under the pretext of punishing treason. The ruin of Surrey was planned by a combination of men and women who had a personal hatred to one another. So the poet's doom was arranged before the trial was demanded by the Crown. Thorndale states that Surrey was tried before a petty jury at Guildhall, and, after a long investigation of the charges against him, in the Star Chamber style of procedure, was declared guilty of high treason. He made an eloquent and most impressive defence, recurring to the services his family had rendered to the King and the realm—at home and abroad. The narrator adds: " All the loyal spectators who were inside the justice-room, there and then fell a weeping from their devotion to God's truth; and they prayed in a loud voice to the Almighty to save and have mercy on the sowl of Lord Surrey." A summary of Surrey's trial is in the *Baja de Secretis;* also in the MS. State Papers (Domestic) of 1543, are to be seen several of the " early charges" which had been preferred against the noble poet. In Nott's Life of Surrey the extraordinary indictment on which the trial was founded is printed.

Surrey was beheaded at the Tower Hill, on Thursday, the 19th of January, 1547—just nine days before the cruel monarch was himself summoned before the bar of Eternal Justice.

---

* Miss Strickland remarks that Lord Surrey was put to death for a supposed difference *in the painting of the tail of the lion in his crest.*

The body of the Earl of Surrey was first buried in the church of Barking, where it remained till the reign of James the First, when the bones of the poet were removed by one of his kindred to Framlington, in Suffolk, where a tomb was erected to his memory.

The Earl of Surrey ascended the scaffold in the forenoon of what promised to be a distinguished life. All the thought of England, not to mention its sympathy, concentrated around the block placed for the noble victim by the order of a moribund tyrant. No marvel History has only preserved the best traits in the character of Surrey. His life was a mixture of the romantic and the beautiful, and the evil in his brief career was so much overbalanced by the better element, that the name of Surrey presents itself to posterity like a kaleidoscope in which we wish the brightest colours always to prevail.

Terrible times were those when Duchesses and other titled dames of historic lineage appeared as voluntary witnesses against their husbands and their brothers; when the wife sustained the Crown prosecutor, and the mistress confronted her for the defence; when men and women of high social standing were to be found secretly abetting the Star Chamber prosecutors of their nearest and dearest kindred. The picture is almost appalling — almost incredible. Family pride, human sympathy, that generosity of feeling which once characterised the English heart—the higher sentiments of Equity and Charity, all seemed to have been buried in the abyss of annihilation. Truly those were not the days described by the Poet-philosopher, "when Heaven smiled upon Conscience."

CHAPTER X.

ENGLAND DESCRIBED BY FOREIGN CONTEMPORARIES.*

In Loranzo's Despatches from London to the Doge of Venice, many interesting subjects are sketched with brevity and cynical accuracy. This astute diplomatist describes the "nobility, knights and squires, as courteous and kindly to strangers; whilst the people of trade pursuits behave with rudeness and arrogance to foreigners." "They seem," he says, "to think that the profits derived by the foreign merchants from their country is so much taken from them, and they imagine that they can live without foreign intercourse. They do not extend that sympathy to one another which characterises their neighbours beyond the Bordering States. They are sometimes suspicious; but nevertheless, they have good parts."

* * * * * * * * *

"The nobles, with the exception of those who are in the monarch's employment about the Court, do not generally reside in the cities, but in their country mansions, immense houses bearing the names of castles, where they employ a vast number of servants; the consumption of beef, mutton, pork and fowl at those baronial halls, as they are sometimes called, is very large. Wines, beer and ale are in profusion.

"The nobles and squires occupy themselves with hunting of every description, and whatever else can amuse or divert

---

* In the second volume of this work I have referred to Loranzo's flattering description of the English ladies of his time, and the profuse hospitality practised by the upper and middle classes.

them; so that they seem wholly intent on leading a joyous existence, the women being no less sociable than the men. It is customary in London for the women *allowable*, to go without any regard, either alone or accompanied by their husbands or brothers, to houses of public entertainment, and to partake of dinner or supper wherever they please."*

The observant Venetian describes London and York as the two great centres for English commerce. "London," he remarks, "is the most noble both on account of its being the residence of royalty, and because the River Thames runs through it, very much to the convenience and profit of the inhabitants, as it ebbs and flows every six hours, like the sea, seldom causing inundation or any extraordinary floods; and up to London Bridge it is navigable for ships of 400 butts burden, of which a great number arrive from foreign countries with merchandise. London Bridge connects the ancient City with the borough. The bridge is built on solid stone with twenty arches, and a number of shops, curiously arranged, are to be seen on both sides of the said bridge."

The narrator continues:—"On the banks of the river are many large palaces, making a very fine show. The city, however, is much disfigured by the ruins of a multitude of churches and monasteries which, but a few years ago, were

---

* Loranzo is greatly mistaken with regard to respectable women, of any class, frequenting taverns, or public dining-rooms. It was the custom—perhaps for centuries—for country folks of the substantial middle class to visit "London town every summer for a week or more." On those occasions the wives and daughters were lodged at the various inns, where excellent dinners were supplied. The women amused themselves with various little games, of which we know nothing now. The story-tellers, however, frequented the inns, and added to the amusements prepared for travellers. The men generally repaired to the cock-pit, or the bear-baiting. The women of England, like those of Scotland, ruled the domestic circles, and judged by their many good qualities they deserved the confidence reposed in them.

inhabited by friars and nuns. * * * Many privileges have been conceded by the Crown to the London merchants, who are eminent for their commercial enterprise and honourable dealing."

Loranzo draws a gloomy picture of the commercial depression of England at the period of King Edward's death. "The treasury was almost destitute of specie. The taxes of the preceding reign were enormous. Peculation was practised by the higher officials, whilst the subordinate class did not receive the half of their scant pay; and were consequently heavily in debt." The "financial legacy" left by King Edward's Council to their successors put Gardyner's abilities as a financier to the test. Edward's reign was one of wide-spread calamity to the whole nation.*

In another despatch to the Doge of Venice, Loranzo writes :—

"The English do not much delight in either military pursuits or literature. The nobility and gentlemen of minor ranks have no taste for books, so they give little patronage to men who produce works on history or other learned subjects. The nobility, like the people, have no ambition for a military life; but when circumstances or policy bring them into war, they show immense courage and great presence of mind at the approach of danger, and seldom become moved by panic. The English soldiers require to be largely supplied with provisions (beef, bread and beer); so it is evident that they cannot long endure much of the fatigue of a camp life."

Loranzo states that a people so eminently suited as the English were, in those times, for trade and commerce, were not adapted to warlike enterprises. The writer describes the mode of raising an army when some sudden emergency occurs :—

---

* State Papers of Edward VIth's reign.

"A light is placed on the top of a number of huge lanterns fixed on heights in all villages and towns. On the appearance of these signals, the various men (young and brave) muster, and go to the quarters where they are inspected, and if approved of, they become the King's soldiers, and the nation's defenders." * * *

Loranzo states that "the native horses were not good for wars, and there were not many foreign horses then (1553) in England." He next criticises the arms in use, and the military bearing of the "pure-bred" English soldier:—

"The weapons used by the English soldier are a spear, and not having much opportunity for providing themselves with body-armour, they wear for the most part breast-plates with shirts of mail, and a scull-cap and sword. The rest would be footmen, of which they have four classes. The first, which in number and valour far excels the others, are the archers, in whom the sinew of their armies consists; the English being, as it were, by nature most expert bowmen, inasmuch as not only do they practise archery for their pleasure, but also to enable them to serve their King, so that they have often secured victory for the armies of England. The second class consists of infantry, who carry a bill; some of these, when disciplined, would make good soldiers. The other two classes are harquebusiers and pikemen, of which weapons they have very little experience. The English monarch at times hires German soldiers, who generally have experience in war practice."

Loranzo describes the naval force of England in Queen Mary's reign as "a goodly one."

"English sailors are plenty and excellent for the navigation of the Atlantic. There is an abundance of timber for ship-building. * * * They do not use galleys, owing to the strong tide in the ocean. * * * There is a large quantity of good artillery kept in readiness at the Tower, where there is also deposited ammunition of every description that may be required. The courage of the English soldiers and sailors is beyond all suspicion, but the various lieutenants in command are extremely inefficient."

Loranzo adds, that the late Duke of Northumberland was the only man England possessed of any naval or military capacity, for he distinguished himself in both professions.

In those troubled times the Lord Mayor received the Queen at Guildhall, clad in complete steel armour, over which warlike costume he wore the civic robe, and was "attended by the citie aldermen similarly accoutred."

It is very possible that the observant Venetian Envoy was present when the Queen visited Guildhall.

In writing to the Doge, the Envoy speaks of the hospitality dispensed by the Lord Mayor, and the nature of his office. "The Mayor," he says, "keeps a most excellent table with open doors. He spends some four thousand ducats out of his own private purse on hospitality. The Sovereign sometimes makes a knight of the Mayor, of which title the Corporation are very proud. The chief charge of the Mayor is to superintend the victualling department; to arrange the domestic disputes amongst the minor people in trade transactions; between masters and their apprentice boys, servants, and divers others. The Mayor has the custody of the citie by day and by night, and the keys of the said citie are in the possession of the Lord Mayor for the period he is in office."

In the days of the Plantagenets distinguished foreigners left on record their testimony as to the usefulness and hospitality of the municipal bodies of London. At a later period, the grandees who accompanied the Princess Catalina (Katharine) to England, in 1501, were loud in their praise of the hospitality they received from the Lord Mayor of London and his wife. The Mayors of London were always noted for their loyalty to the throne; and several of them won their "spurs" fairly as bannerets, and obtained "pure nobility" by the then truest source of honour—the Sword. In modern times it has been the fashion to speak scornfully of the London Corporate bodies, "who aimed at becoming rich, indulging in good feeding, and ostentatious parade." Be this statement as it may, it is certain that the ancestors of our present municipal guardians were valiant, loyal, humane, and "profusely hospitable to friends and strangers." They were, moreover, generous patrons of learning, which the names of Whittington, De Boleyn, Peacock, Lee, Whyte, Gresham, and many others, sufficiently attest. Sir Thomas Whyte, above alluded to, endowed St. John's College, Oxford, so munificently that he may be considered as its founder.

Loranzo attributes the "sweating sickness" to the bad sanitary condition of the towns and cities. "This terrible disease generally commenced in Wales, and then traversed the whole kingdom. The mortality was immense amongst persons of every condition in life. The people died in a few hours in dreadful torture. During the first three days of this scourge in London upwards of five thousand people died. The shops were closed, and all business suspended for nearly twenty days." A universal terror seized all classes; and, for a while, religious sentiments were respected; the churches were better attended, friends and foes sought forgiveness, and the divine element of Charity triumphed over the demon of sectarian malice.

Notwithstanding the political and sectarian calamities of Queen Mary's reign, there was something done to extend the commerce of the country with foreign nations. Sebastian Cabot, a native of Bristol, was employed by the Queen in arranging commercial relations with Russia, which proved to be highly satisfactory to the interests of England. The ship fitted out for this expedition was the first that ever sailed from England on a commercial speculation to Russia. Jane Dormer states that the idea of this expedition originated with the Queen herself; and that Dr. Gardyner immediately communicated with Cabot, of whom little is known by posterity, although he was an eminent and a good man. His father, who was a Frenchman, rendered service to England in the reign of Henry VII.

In the reign of Henry VIII., Cabot was quite neglected, and almost reduced to poverty. When Somerset came into office he employed him. This incident in the Protector's career redounds to his credit as a financial minister. Somerset granted Cabot a pension of £160 per annum, for "the eminent services he had rendered to English commerce in foreign countries."

Pomeroy states that he saw a most interesting MS. of Cabot's visit to Russia, descriptive of the condition of society in that country. Pomeroy adds:—"To my grief I state that this valuable narrative on the inner life of Russian society was destroyed by a fire in Bristol."

Cabot died in 1556. He was bountiful in aiding poor English sailors, of whom there were a great number then in London.

The total value of the wine entered at the port of London alone, in the January of 1559, for the twelve months preceding, was £64,000. The *retail* price of wine at that period was an average of $7\frac{1}{4}$d. per gallon. The iron trade with Sweden, Russia, and Spain was considerable. At this time the English received their knives, buttons, pins and needles, from the Continent. Sugar and hops were largely imported into this realm in 1560; and one of the "Christmas novelties" of 1559 comprised toys and beautiful dolls from Flanders. Queen Elizabeth delighted in making presents of toys at Christmas to children.

The despatches of Leovanni Michél, published by Friedmann, furnish a new insight into the events of Queen Mary's reign, which will prove of much importance to the Student of History.

CHAPTER XI.

MEN OF THE "NEW AND THE OLD LEARNING."*

WITH the change of religion came a mutation in the order of society; a change of tastes, of habits, a new disposition of wealth, an altered mode of worship, new ideas, new notions; but the heart of the nation did not expand—the sympathy, benevolence, and charity characteristic of England did not enlarge their compass. Out of the transformation were fashioned many fortunate men, the founders of our present great families; and a "sturdy pursy middle class" grew up under the shadow of tall houses in mercantile cities, or "furrowed the land with avaricious industry." Of the former Mr. Froude is not hopeful, and of the latter he writes:—

"The new owners of the soil, the middle class, who had risen to wealth on the demolition of the monasteries, were unwarlike men of business, given merely to sheep-farming and money-making. The peasantry hated them as chief enclosers of the commons. The Crown and the Lords despised them as the creation of a new age, while, as evading in all ways the laws of military tenure, and regarding their estates as a commercial speculation for the building up of their private fortunes, *they were looked upon by Englishmen of the olden order of things as poisonous mushrooms, the unwholesome outcome of the diseases of the age.*"

---

* Under the above title "I have "grouped" a number of notable men who appear in the reign of Henry VIII., Edward VI., Queen Mary, and her sister, Elizabeth.

There is, it may be, an unintentional regret exhibited in the foregoing picture which warrants a belief that the historian considers affairs were not changed for the better by the overthrow of the ancient order of things.

Sir WILLIAM PAGET was the friend and co-conspirator of Somerset;* the friend of Cranmer; the friend of Poynet; the friend of John Bale; the friend of the Dudley family throughout their unprincipled machinations; a loyal subject to King Henry; to young Edward; to Queen Jane; to Queen Mary; the chivalrous supporter of Elizabeth; at one time a zealous Reformer; at another, the persecutor of Reformers; swore allegiance to all parties, and betrayed and deserted them when it suited his purpose.

"One can scarcely recognise," writes Maitland, "the earnest Gospeller, the partizan of Barnes the martyr, in the lively Papist who received again, in Queen Mary's time, the Garter which had been stripped from him as a convicted and confessed scoundrel, and figured as Lord Privy Seal as long as Mary's reign lasted." The "dexterous and fearless Paget," as Mr. Froude styles him, was possessed of considerable talent in conducting diplomacy where "high-bred insolence, petty devices, and deliberate lying were considered necessary to sustain the interests of the Government which he represented."† With all these qualifications for a statesman of the time, neither Cecil nor Walsingham would confide in Paget as a political agent. Nevertheless, he was frequently consulted by Elizabeth and her Council on questions of great

---

* Maitland's "Essays on the Reformation" throw some light on the schemes concocted between Somerset and Paget at the period of Henry's death.

† Paget's Diplomacy for Henry VIII. State Papers, Vol. X., p. 295.

national importance. Mr. Froude considers him "an honest man"; and subsequently observes: "Paget's creed was of the broadest; he hated fanatics; he believed in good order, good government, and a good army, more than in *whitewashed churches*, or in doctrines of justification, however exemplary their exactness." Paget became enriched from the spoils of the Church, and the peculations practised by him as a minister of the Crown. I must pursue the inquiry a little further. Towards the close of Henry's reign Sir William Paget received large grants of Church and Monastic lands. It has been estimated that the Church lands conferred on him were worth £16,000 per annum in 1546—an enormous sum in those days. The See of Lichfield suffered "a good plucking," a portion of its lands having been handed over to Sir William Paget, as a special grant from the King.* The courtiers who surrounded Henry VIII. have been described by their contemporary, Coxe, as "ravenous wolves," and as "men devoid of all honesty, or even common decency." Hallam is rather outspoken in his "Constitutional History." He says:—"Nor did the courtiers and new proprietors content themselves with the escheated wealth of the Church. Almost every bishopric was made to surrender some part of its lands * * * * The bishopric of Lichfield, for instance, lost the chief part of its lands to raise another estate for Sir William Paget." Paget's greed for land was not yet satisfied. He received "further grants." As the reader is aware, he was appointed one of the executors of the King's will, which gave him an opportunity of displaying his talents in peculation. His friend Somerset conferred upon him "another grant"—namely, the town-house of the Bishop of

---

* Records of the Monastic and Church Confiscations in Henry's reign.

Exeter. He was not yet satisfied. The office of Chancellor of the Duchy of Lancaster was next conferred upon him. He here again displayed his "integrity and honour." But let the Boy King—pious Edward—relate the narrative which is entered in his diary.

"The Chancellor of *my* Duchy has confessed how he did, without commission, sell away *my lands and great timber woods;* how he had taken great fines of *my* lands *for his own profit and advantage*, never turning any to *my* use or commodity; and how he had made leases in reversion for more than twenty years."*

The country was aware of this plunder, and the "implicated Council" were obliged to take proceedings in the Star Chamber against their colleague. Paget was fined £6,000, and, on petition, it was reduced to £4,000.† It is very doubtful, however, if the fine was paid. At this period Paget was "a God-fearing Protestant." Upon the accession of Queen Mary, he "saw the error of his way." *He became a Papist again*, and edified the confiding Queen *by his piety*. Not yet satisfied, he "craved *another grant;* and Queen Mary conferred upon him lands in Derbyshire, Leicestershire, and Warwickshire.

Speed attributes to Paget "the suggestion, several times offered to Queen Mary, to put Elizabeth to death."‡ This statement is highly improbable: Paget did not trouble himself in such matters. As to the various plans alleged to be got in motion for the destruction of Elizabeth, they turn out to be the invention of party or sectarian bigots, and nothing more—pure and baseless falsehoods.

---

* See King Edward's Journal.
† "Notes on the Star Chamber of Edward's reign."
‡ John Speed's Chronicles.

Two years after the memorable scene between Lord Hertford and Paget, when standing at the chamber door where the horribly convulsed body of the dead King Henry lay, Paget reminded his friend, then the Protector Somerset, of the solemn oaths they had taken to maintain the monarch's "last testament."* This was a painful remembrance; but as powerful as Somerset then appeared, he left documents amongst his State Papers which prove that he dreaded the "future action" of his perjured co-conspirator, Paget. Sir William Paget was immensely unpopular with all parties in the State.

King Edward was no admirer of Sir William Paget. One of the youthful monarch's objections to him was founded upon the fact that he was "no gentleman born, neither by the father nor the mother's side."† The same objection might have been raised to Cecil and other notable members of the Council. Paget's grandfather was mace-bearer to the Lord Mayor of London. He was also a money-lender in a petty way to the denizens of Bankside. A good beginning.

Paget's whole life has been summed up by a contemporary as "a tissue of dishonesty, ingratitude, treachery, meanness, and falsehood." Such was one specimen of the "Independent Party." What, then, was to be expected from the needy adventurers who adopted and acted on the maxim of Northumberland and Wotton?

The Earl of BEDFORD comes next in my "selected group." Amongst those who became wealthy by the rise and progress of the Reformation none were so remarkable as the Russells

---

* See MS. Domestic, Edward VI., Vol. VIII.; Tytler's Edward and Mary, Vol. I.

† King Edward's Journal.

for their success in obtaining riches and their tenacity in amplifying and retaining them. Mr. Froude's portrait of the chief of that provident ilk in those days does not lack interest. He says :—

"Francis Russell, Earl of Bedford, wss the favourite above all English noblemen with the extreme Reformers. In the late reign (Henry's) he was one of the few of high rank who had not cared to conceal his opinions, and although Queen Mary had not dared to proceed to extremities against him, he had been imprisoned and had been released only to go into voluntary exile. He had travelled into Italy, paying a visit by the way to the refugees at Zurich ; and the Genevans flocked to him afterwards as their surest friend in Elizabeth's Council. In appearance he was a heavy ungainly man, distinguished chiefly by the huge dimensions of his head. When Charles of Austria was a suitor for Elizabeth's hand, and questions were asked of his person, the Earl of Bedford's large head was the comparison made use of in his disparagement; but his expression, like that of Nicholas Bacon, was stern and powerful; the world, as he knew it, was no place for the softer virtues, and those only could play their parts there to good purpose, whose tempers were as hard as the age, and whose intellects had an edge of steel."

The reader has already seen the career of Lord Russell under Somerset. None persecuted their former co-religionists with such intense bitterness as the Russells, whose love for the new religion was sincere in proportion to the wealth its profession obtained them. They hated Popery as they detested poverty, and their veneration of Protestantism about equalled their greed for its worldly benefits. With a few exceptions, this family has always been an exemplification of the superiority, in circumspect hands, of tact over talent. Without genius or mental eminence, their members have made way to the highest offices ; and whilst most others enriched by the plunder of the Church squandered their gains in gaming and licentiousness, this thrifty family clung like leeches to their possessions, augmenting them step by step to a colossal fortune.

"A tried friend" of Lady Morley, writes to her in August, 1585, upon the death of the Earl of Bedford in exulting terms: "The Earl of Bedford is dead, and gone to his Great Master. His son has been murdered by the 'Border Men.'"

The personal likeness of the various members of the Russell family is remarkable. Two centuries ago they were described as "*cunning men with big heads and long purses.*"

ANTHONY BROWNE, whose father had been Master of the Horse to Henry VIII, was created by Queen Mary, Lord Montague, in right of descent by the female line from the ancient house of Neville. In the extraordinary and sudden changes of religion and position, one of his sisters became the wife of Lord John Gray, a Puritan; the other sister was the Countess of Kildare—a pious lady whom the people of Dublin much esteemed. Lord Montague inherited the principles and the fearlessness of the Countess of Salisbury. At the commencement of Elizabeth's reign, Montague was a "leading Catholic," yet he held office under Elizabeth; sometimes he became very pliant to the Council. There were some early associations that should have evoked kindly feelings in the heart of Elizabeth for Anthony Browne.

Lord Montague was the most favoured Catholic with the Protestant party in the reign of Elizabeth. Upon her accession to the throne Elizabeth despatched Montague to Spain as her special ambassador, an action which drew forth a most pleasing and kind letter from Philip to his "dearly beloved sister." This loving epistle to "Golden Eliza" is still extant.

Sir ROGER CHOLMLEY was Chief Justice of the King's Bench under Edward the Sixth. His antecedents were by no means good. He was sometimes engaged by Henry VIII to perform unpopular and illegal actions. He had been one of the commissioners selected to seize upon Wolsey's property; at a later period he was in some way mixed up with the Six Articles, and persecuted the Reformers. He was a Catholic then, or professed to be so, and received his share of the Church confiscation from Henry. In the reign of Edward, Cholmley joined Northumberland, Cranmer, and the other members of the Council, in setting aside the lawful claims of the Princess Mary. He subsequently deserted Lady Jane Dudley, and welcomed Mary to London, as his sovereign. "Queen Mary," says Mr. Foss, "admitted him to her Council." He presided at the trials of several of his former friends, who had become rebels to the Queen, and behaved with the greatest cruelty to those unfortunate men.* Under Elizabeth Cholmley became a pious Protestant, and abhorred Popery."

WILLIAM PAWLET, Marquis of Winchester, was the man who might well be expected to receive bribes, as he profusely did, in the reign of Queen Mary. We have it certified that Renaud, the Spanish Ambassador, for one instance, paid him "fifteen hundred crowns a year for three years."† During Mary's time he acted with the "caution and cunning of the fox," and took example by the fate of Cranmer and Northumberland. He conformed to the olden religion, which he had abandoned in Edward's reign. Foxe states that Winchester was the most active persecutor of the Reformers in Mary's

---

* State Papers of Edward and Mary's reign.
† Grenville State Papers.

reign. The Martyrologist adds:—" No party had faith in his word. He was a Papist or a Reformer when it suited his interests." In 1555, whilst Dr. Gardyner was on public business in Paris, the great seal was for a short time placed in the hands of the Marquis of Winchester; and judging from the Council book, he made ample use of the authority with which he was invested. Writ after writ was issued, stirring up persecution; and letters were directed to the nobility and gentry, inviting them to give their *attendance with their servants at the burning of heretics.** The man who acted in this spirit was *a Protestant in the reign of Edward*, and hunted down all those who professed, but were not permitted to practise, the faith of their fathers. What ingenuous or impartial writer can raise a voice in favour of the Council of Edward VI? Yet volumes have been written in " vindication of their godly works."

Winchester's conduct to Lady Jane Dudley is an additional proof of the prevalent baseness of his character. It is stated by Elizabeth Tylney, the devoted friend of Lady Jane, that when she was brought to the Tower, as Queen, the Marquis of Winchester, who was then just appointed to be her Lord Treasurer, brought her *the* crown,† to try on her head, in order to see how it would fit her; the presence of the crown once more roused the scruples of unfortunate Jane Dudley; but Winchester made a plausible speech, assuring her of the equity of the proceedings, and the service that was rendered to the Protestant cause by her becoming Queen. He would

---

* Sir William Cecil's Diary, quoted Biog. Brit., vol. iii, p. 21-22; Council Book; Archbishops of Canterbury, vol. viii, p. 369.

† This appears to have been the stolen crown, kept with other regalia at the Tower, and not St. Edward's crown, then always given in charge of the Dean and Chapter of Westminster Abbey.

also have another crown made for her husband. Lady Dudley, on this occasion, again protested against her husband being put forward as a king. Young Dudley and his mother (the Duchess of Northumberland), used violence to Lady Jane; in fact, she dreaded *poison from her nearest kindred* if she refused to have her husband crowned as king. In these proceedings Winchester acted entirely in the interest of the Dudley family. In one of her private letters Lady Jane says :—"*I was maltreated by my husband and his mother.*"*

At the period of the proceedings here referred to, Winchester was "the *loyal* and *sworn subject* of Queen Jane." In *ten days* later he deserted her, and took the oath of allegiance to Queen Mary, declaring that he "*was all through her faithful subject.*" He then anathematised the Reformers as heretics and rebels. When preparing for the coronation of Queen Mary, Winchester again visited Jane Dudley, then under sentence of death, and in gross language charged her with having taken from the crown several valuable jewels which were missing. Lady Jane and her husband protested their innocence on bended knees and with uplifted hands; but all in vain. On the pretence of this robbery Winchester confiscated the few remaining jewels and some £300 then in Lady Jane's possession. Of this transaction Queen Mary knew nothing.

On the accession of Elizabeth Winchester avoided the scandal of another sudden change. His Catholicity was *private;* it might have been public, for the Protestant party had no faith in his professions; yet both parties lived on amicable terms with him and courted his society. His hospitality was profuse, and men of the most opposite opinions

---

* Pollino ; Baoardo's Narratives ; Letters of Roger Ascham ; **Queens of England,** vol. v. ; Queen Jane and Queen Mary.

met at his banquet hall, where "hilarity and genuine old English fun abounded." But there were many faces to Winchester's character. For instance, he regarded nothing as sacred but *interest*, and took bribes when offered. Naunton says: "He served four monarchs in as various and changeable seasons, that neither time nor age hath yielded the like precedent." He first held office under Henry VIII., and died in the service of Elizabeth. John Knox notices him under the title of "Shebna the Treasurer," acting like a crafty fox towards King Edward and Mary, but under his outward guise concealing the most malicious treason." "In the last stage of his life," says Nichols, "the Marquis of Winchester rendered himself so agreeable to Queen Elizabeth that she declared, if he were but a young man that there was not a person in her dominions, whom she would so soon take for a husband."

The Marquis of Winchester lived to see 113 descendants, and died as he had journeyed through life, without displaying a sign of conscience. Camden sets down the death of Winchester to have occurred in 1572, aged 97. According to an obituary in Murdin's State Papers, he was 87 years years old when death suddenly visited him. Winchester was descended from an ancient family who were earnestly devoted to the olden religion, the monarchy, and the Constitution—as then understood.

POLYDORE VERGIL, whose real name was Paul Ambrose Pierre Castelli, was a native of Urbino, in Italy. He first came to England on the invitation of his kinsman, Hadrian Castelli, who was appointed Bishop of Bath and Wells. Polydore was appointed to the office of deputy collector of the Pope's "annetes" in England; he also enjoyed the lucrative living of Archdeacon of Wells and Prebendary in

Hertford. He lived more than fifty years in England, where he amassed much wealth. Like Erasmus, Polydore Vergil wrote some sadly sycophantic "dedications" to Henry VIII. Here is a specimen: "You surpass the glory of all the princes who now exist." This was written in 1532, when Henry had begun his warfare against the Church; yet Vergil, though thus writing, sustained the Pope's policy. A man who flatters from selfishness will be as ready to utter deprecatory falsehoods from spite, disappointment, or a mean desire to obtain favour with the enemies of overthrown greatness. Such were Polydore Vergil's motives for his malignant assaults on Wolsey. Vergil enjoyed the friendship of Richard Foxe, Bishop of Winchester, who having a favourable opinion of his learning and judgment, introduced him to Henry VII. as a man competent to write a History of England, which he undertook, the King and his successor placing the public records and other documents of the State at his disposal. Polydore's history is written in Latin, and is brought down to the 30th of Henry VIII. Many distinguished writers have questioned the accuracy of the work, amongst whom were Leland, Bale, Sir Henry Savile, Wharton, and Humphrey Lloyd. Those noted men charge him with ignorance of the affairs of England, and "a wish to magnify to a certain extent the actions of other nations." He is also accused of having destroyed several records, lest there might be any evidence against him of having put forward false statements. He managed however, to render himself extremely unpopular. Educated Englishmen—laymen and clerics—were indignant at their country being caricatured, or cynically criticised by a foreigner who enjoyed lucrative livings in the English Church. At one time Polydore employed two persons for the purpose of writing lampoons on public men with whom he differed.* He was particularly satirical on his own order; indeed, it is difficult to say what party escaped his invective. His conduct to Wolsey proves him to have been a most unworthy and vindictive being. Professor Brewer traces all the falsehoods heaped by subsequent writers on Wolsey to the malicious slanders of Vergil. Even the virtuous Fisher and Sir Thomas More did not escape the indiscriminate venom of his malevolent pen. Henry VIII. professed to entertain a high opinion of Vergil's learning and acuteness, conversing with him for hours upon ancient history. Some of his contemporaries regarded him as "a cunning, miserly man, who always looked to his own interest and those of his relatives."† Dodd states that "if keeping his preferments be a rule to judge of his religion, he went all the lengths of the Court in Henry's reign. But when Edward VI ascended the throne his inclinations appeared otherwise."‡ He resigned his livings to the Crown, and asked permission to retire to Italy. To his petition the young king, or rather his government, returned the following answer:—

"Whereas our trusty and well-beloved friend, Polydore Vergil, hath made suite unto us, that he being born in sunny Italy, and having served our grandfather Henry VII., and our own father Henry VIII., of *blessed memory*, and ourselves, for the space of forty-nine years and more, we now declare, and decree, that the said Polydore Vergil hath our full license and pleasure to depart out of this realm, and to enjoy all the profits and monies which were conferred on him through livings by our grandfather and father. (Signed) EDWARD REX."

---

* Letters of Dr. Francis to Father Longland.

† In Brewer's State Papers some of Polydore's Letters to Wolsey appear. He was always seeking "some favours." Longland relates that he was feared more than respected by Churchmen.

‡ Dodd's "Church History," vol. I., p. 325.

Polydore Vergil lived to be ninety-three years old, and died at Urbino in 1555. He was the last official collector of "Peter's pence" who was recognized by the Government of England. The secular clergy petitioned the King to abolish Peter's Pence.

"PETER'S PENCE," as an annual offering from the people of England to the Pope, was commenced by Ina, King of the West Saxons, about A.D. 720, and continued under all the English Sovereigns down to Henry VIII. Cardinal Garampi states that this voluntary tax may be traced to the days of Offa II., King of the Mercians. Other authorities contend that Peter's Pence was instituted in 855 by Ethelwulf, King of the West Saxons.

Peter's Pence was in a "fluctuating condition" for a long period. Seasons of scarcity, the plague, or the sweating sickness, had an effect upon the collections.* To contribute regularly to Peter's Pence, was a proof of the "devotion entertained for the Pope, as the Vicar of Christ on earth." So wrote Father Paul Bracebridge, a learned monk of the 13th century. In the 13th century England contributed largely to Peter's Pence, and the women of England, like those of Scotland, were in the front rank of the contributors, often selling their jewels to increase the sum sent from certain districts. The mothers sent an offering to Peter's Pence for their "first-born." "The wives and daughters of out-laws and robbers, with sad and hopeful feelings, sold their rings to make an offering, with a fervent prayer that their husbands, fathers or brothers, might see the error of their ways, and return to the holy practices from which they had strayed away." The accounts respecting the mode of collecting Peter's Pence are conflicting. It is alleged by

---

* It is stated that the sum *now* annually collected from Roman Catholics for Peter's Pence amounts to £1,300,750.

some writers that it was "collected by an assessment on towns and villages; and that the poor were exempt." The "poor," however, had a religious feeling, that all might go wrong with them if they did not "contribute their mite towards susstaining Christ's Vicar in Rome." Those old English Catholics of the far-off times were strong in faith. In 1159, the organization for the collection of Peter's Pence in England became complete. In that year Pope Alexander the Third appointed special Legates in England for the purpose of taking charge of this important fund, which was handed over to the Legate by the bishops of the respective dioceses.

A portion of this fund was set aside by the Popes for "the food and lodging of the numerous pilgrims who visited Rome annually, and amongst those pilgrims the most notable, and the most devoted, were of the English nation. The venerable Bede has chronicled many interesting incidents respecting the journeys made to Rome in the 7th and 8th centuries by English men and women—kings, queens, nobles, and princes. The journey was surrounded with dangers, obliged to travel on foot, or at best "upon ill-appointed horses." A large number of English pilgrims were murdered by an Italian banditti in 921. At a later period the Earl of Northumberland and several English bishops were left in a destitute condition by a band of robbers, just as they entered Italy. A "pilgrim Archbishop of Canterbury," and his attendants, were also frozen to death in the Alps. Father Bracebridge relates that the Archbishop's dog was found by his master's side, and after ten days cold and hunger was still alive, but died in a few hours later from exhaustion. These misfortunes did not check the tide of the pious pilgrims.

In process of time a portion of Peter's Pence were appropriated to other purposes, and the Papal Treasury itself received large sums from England, which were bestowed with no niggard hand. The method of collecting was a penny from each family annually, but some persons "sent shillings to the fund." In the fourth year of the reign of Henry III., John Willie, a merchant of London, contributed five pounds to Peter's Pence. In the reign of Henry I., William Wolci, another merchant, subscribed five pounds. Whittington, the munificent Mayor, contributed ten pounds; and in the reign of Edward IV., Willie Caxton, our first English printer, made an offering of seventy shillings to this fund, and ten shillings annually. Caxton's patron, the Marquis of Worcester,* was also a contributor.

A few words as to WILLIE CAXTON, known in the early morning of life as "the little blue-eyed boy who was so constant every morning in his attendance at Mass, and, again, at the call of the Vesper bell." Later on, "the pride of Kent," became the mercer's apprentice, and the Lord Mayor's confidential agent. Like Whittington, he tried his "prentice hand" at various occupations; but the day-dream of his youth, and of maturer years, was the establishment of the printing-press. Aided by the learned Thomas Miling, the Abbot of Westminster, the Marquis of Worcester, and other notable scholars, Caxton commenced the first printing establishment within the walls of Westminster Abbey, in 1471. His star was now in the ascendant, and he became the companion of princes, bishops and nobles. He printed many volumes, amongst the rest "Æsop's Fables;" "Tully's Offices;" the romantic history of King Arthur, which "delighted those who could read." "The Game and Play of Chesse" was the

---

* The Marquis of Worcester was beheaded by Edward IV., upon which Caxton remarked: " Alas! alas; a head has been cut off which contained more knowledge than all the lords' heads in the realm."

first book, according to Leigh, ever printed in England, and became popular with all who love that ancient and scientific game. His "Treatise on the Game of Chesse" was printed in 1474. When the history of "Reynard the Fox" was read by the old fox-hunting squires of those times, they "became transported with delight." Caxton's "Æsop's Fables" is stated to have been the first book that had its pages numbered—a property wanted in a copy of "Willyam Caxton's Recuyel of the Hystoryes of Troye, by Raoul le Feure," described by Phillips. In 1490 he produced a translation of the "Æneid," under the title of "The Boke of Eneydos," incited thereto by the folio edition of "Homer," produced at Florence, in 1488, by Demetrius, and which far excelled all previous efforts of typographic skill. Caxton also produced a book "On Good Manners," which the accomplished Islip commended to many of the nobles and knights of his time for "profitable study"—a useful hint.

Caxton is described by his contemporaries as the "best of sons; a good neighbour; and a loyal subject to the Pope and the King." He was an ingenious artist, as well as a learned man, and ever the friend of the "neglected scholar." Caxton speaks in affectionate terms of his parents. He says:—" I pray most earnestly for my fader and muther's sowles, for they were so good to me, and set me to schole, to learn knowledge of the world's kind; and above all to know of God's Truth, from the teaching of our Holy Mothur the Church."

William Caxton lived to a ripe old age, had abundant means, honoured by his Sovereign, the nobles, and the clergy; and, I may add, that he descended to the grave with the blessings of the poor of both sexes, to whom he had been a munificent benefactor. Civilization suggests many delicate modes of expressing its gratitude. I hope, however, that

England, and those countries which speak its mother-tongue, will enshrine amongst the most precious memorials of the "Bye-gone" the memory of Willie Caxton, who introduced to the people of this great country the noblest art ever invented —an art in which, in all its varied phases, England *now* stands incontestably pre-eminent.

There is to be seen at Windsor Castle a picture of Lord Rivers introducing Caxton and his "first book" to King Edward the Fourth. There is also a picture attached to an MS. in the Library of Lambeth Palace representing the same subject, on another visit to the King, where the noted Duke of Gloucester stands amongst the group. The Queen (Elizabeth of York) and her children surround the throne, and the King is seated in state to "receive little Willie the Printer." The book in which this picture appears was printed in 1477. Henry VIII and Wolsey, both entertained a reverence for the memory of Caxton, and no wonder.

To return to the politicians of the Tudor dynasty. Dr. NICHOLAS WOTTON was another specimen of the pliant and self-adapting politicians of those days. He was ambassador in Paris during part of Henry's reign, and subsequently held office under all the "contending parties." He was engaged in thirteen diplomatic missions from England to foreign Courts. At times Wotton enjoyed the confidence of Cranmer, of Somerset, and of Gardyner. In 1549 he joined Warwick's party against Somerset, and received a Secretaryship of State as his reward. He had been once the ready tool of Somerset. His despatches from Paris, and the Privy Council entries, show that he was almost a stranger to every principle of honour. Somerset must have heartily disliked him. The Reformers professed belief in his honesty, and the Catholic party concurred in their opinion—a pretty good proof of his versatility, if not of his doubtful integrity. Tytler remarks that "it is no easy matter to ascertain what were the real principles, political or religious, held by such a man." Probably the difficulty lies in the fact of there being "no principles to discern."

Two very curious volumes of Wotton's secret correspondence are preserved in the British Museum. Those volumes sufficiently attest the writer's immense knowledge and varied research. Sir William Cecil said he had never known a man possessed of information on so many matters concerning life in every part of Europe. He was also an admirable storyteller, and could adapt himself to the conversational powers of the humbler class of society when dilating upon ghosts and witches—popular topics in those times.

Wotton was one of the few who said a kind word of Anna Boleyn at the time of her fall, and had the courage to visit her in the Tower when her father and professing friends deserted the unfortunate Queen.

It is harsh, perhaps, to be too exacting upon the flexible in perilous times, and in an age abounding in chameleon and unprincipled statesmen.* Wotton caught and changed colour so dexterously that he appears a very Prœteus amongst the mutables. If he did not commit himself in his changings, he deserves credit for his ingenuity. He has been quaintly denominated by one author "the very measure of incongruity;" by another, "a centre of remarkables." So far the description is correct, which states that he adapted himself

---

* In Dr. Brandon's "Anecdotes of Men of Qualitie and Wit," printed in Brussels, A.D. 1560, appear some strange narratives of the public men of Henry VIII.'s reign. Fuller's "Worthies," Lascelles' "Letters," and Mr. Froude's brilliant volumes, all contribute, more or less, to remove the masks worn by Dr. Wotton during his political career.

to every Government, and continued to flourish under every change. The Protector's disgrace only raised him higher under Warwick; Warwick's fall led directly to his promotion under Queen Mary; and her great favour to him appears to have been no barrier to his being thrown into the most difficult and responsible offices by Elizabeth. "*Tempora mutantur, et Wotton mutat cum illis.*"

It is rather curious that Elizabeth should have offered the Primacy to Nicholas Wotton, who then filled the office of Dean of Canterbury; and, as stated by his friends, he refused the great clerical prize.* One of Wotton's contemporaries states that Queen Elizabeth's "motives were good; her object being to conciliate the Papal party, but they spurned the olive branch." The "good Queen Bess," however, never indulged in the policy of the "olive branch." She desired to "divide and conquer." She had faith in no single man—not even in Cecil—for his movements were well watched by her secret spies. As to Wotton's religious sentiments, he was no more a Protestant than Elizabeth herself.

A few words more as to Wotton. An author of the last century presents, what Tytler styles, "a satirical panegyric" on Dr. Wotton:—"This was that rare man that was made for all business—*so dexterous!* This was *he* that was made for all times—*so complying.* This was *he who lived* 'Doctor of both Laws,' and died 'Doctor of both Gospels.'"†

Wotton filled the office of Dean of Canterbury, as well as that of St. Paul's. In 1545 he was appointed a Privy Coun-

---

* Holinshed, p. 1403; Waton's Life of Dr. Wotton; Forbes, p. 112; Haynes, State Papers.

† The Wottons were an ancient stock of squires, remarkable for hospitality "to all classes who were of the goodly and loyal people." The Wottons had also made their mark in the Continental wars.

cillor, and subsequently nominated one of the executors of King Henry's "last testament." In this case Lord Hertford found him a pliant assistant. The Council sent Wotton on a foreign mission, whilst they were "arranging the religious difficulty."

In January, 1566, Dean Wotton died at his house in Warwick Lane. He was 72 years old at the time of his death. A number of persons accompanied his funeral from London to Canterbury. He was buried at the east end of the Cathedral Church of that city, and near the tomb of Edward the "Black Prince."*

Sir EDWARD WOTTON, like his uncle, the Dean of Canterbury, was connected with the diplomatic department, and well known at foreign courts as an astute minister, always faithful to the service of his Sovereign. At a later period Sir Edward Wotton followed up the infamous policy of Throckmorton and Randolph in Scotland.

Amongst the many prisoners discharged from the Tower by Queen Mary was the Rev. JOHN BAPTIST FECKENHAM, a learned Benedictine Monk of Evesham, who was imprisoned by Somerset and Cranmer for "not conforming" at the accession of Edward VI. Queen Mary appointed Feckenham to be one of her chaplains, and Dean of St. Paul's. In a few months later, this distinguished Benedictine Father was elevated to the rank of Lord Abbot of the Royal Monastery of Westminster, recently suppressed by the Protector Somerset. Feckenham, accompanied by fourteen Benedictines, resumed the labours of his order in its ancient shrines; but the times were sadly altered, and the brevity of Mary's reign again consigned to extinction the hopes of the Benedictines.

---

* Lodge's Illustrations of British History, Vol. I.

I have already adverted to the strange and contradictory part enacted by Elizabeth relative to the appointment to the Primatial chair. When the negotiations with Wotton failed, the next cleric named for the See of Canterbury by Elizabeth, to the surprise of the Protestant party, was Feckenham. The story appears almost incredible, were there not vouchers for its authenticity. As the reader is aware, Feckenham was esteemed by all parties.* Even the seditious Anabaptists acknowledged that he was "a man of peace;" they remembered that in Mary's reign he publicly protested against persecution for religious opinions, and was always on the side of mercy and charity. Feckenham was the last Abbot who held a seat in the House of Lords. Camden sums up the character of Feckenham in these words:—"He was a learned and a good man, who deserved well of the poor, and drew unto him the love of his adversaries. He had all the good qualities peculiarly required in the difficult times he lived in; and especially that temper and moderation so commendable in the controversies of life."† A later writer affirms that the Abbot was fixed in the olden religion, without passion or prejudice against the new one. He formed his conduct upon a view of the miseries which are incident to mankind, and gave just allowances to the infirmities of human nature. In a word, his zeal was limited within the bounds of discretion; and in all the parts of a social life, he was disposed to be a friend to all mankind.‡

The Abbot's conduct in relation to Lady Jane Dudley has

---

* In the second volume of this work (Chapter **XXIX**), the reader will find some interesting incidents of the life of Feckenham.
† Camden's Annals, p. 29.
‡ Dodd's Ecclesiastical History, Vol. I., p. 526.

been eulogised even by Puritan writers. He renewed again and again his entreaties with Lords Pembroke and Paget to spare the life of Lady Jane, but his eloquent appeals were made in vain.

Mr. Froude, in describing Feckenham's mission to Lady Jane, says:—"He was a man full of gentleness and tender charity, and felt to the bottom of his soul the errand on which he was despatched; he felt as a Catholic priest, but he felt also as a man."

For Elizabeth herself, in the hour of her trials, the Abbot was likewise an intercessor, and prevented many acts of harshness from being carried out against her.

From the beginning of Elizabeth's reign Feckenham had openly opposed the chief measures of her Government, but it is stated that the Queen thought it possible that, through the offer of preferment, the Abbot could be brought to terms. He remained resolute not to accept the ordinance of the Royal Supremacy. "The failure of these extraordinary negotiations," writes Dean Hook, "brought that conviction to the mind of Elizabeth, at which her Councillors had already arrived, that if her *throne was to stand, she must make common cause with the Protestants.*"*

Men like Cecil, it was plain, would support her on no other terms. So Elizabeth hesitated for awhile, and then became the Sovereign of a party who were bold and unscrupulous as to the means by which they attained their ends.

The question has been often asked, "Was Elizabeth sincere in offering the Primacy to Wotton or Feckenham?" It was alleged that she was "under obligations to Wotton, and desired to pass the compliment." The Queen, however,

---

* Archbishops of Canterbury, Vol. IX.

thoroughly understood the high character of Feckenham, and that he would never consent to become the tool of Cecil. What manifests the duplicity of Elizabeth in this transaction is the fact, that at the very time she was negotiating with the friends of Wotton and Feckenham, Cecil had his arrangements nearly completed to place Mathew Parker in the See of Canterbury. The date of the confidential correspondence between Cecil and Parker leaves little doubt as to the intentions of the Queen.

Abbot Feckenham made a powerful speech in the House of Lords against the revolution which Elizabeth and her Council were making in Church and in State. Only a fragment of Feckenham's brilliant and argumentative discourse has reached posterity. Roger Ascham, who was "concealed in a nook," relates in one of his numerous letters, that the Abbot was listened to "with profound attention by the Lords, because the holiness and goodness of his life commanded the respect of every one, and argued much in favour of Popery for having such a man as its advocate.

The Lord Abbot of Westminster addressed the Peers in these words :—

"My good Lords, in her late Majesty's reign (Mary), your lordships may remember how quiet and governable the people were till revolution cast its seeds amongst them. It was not then the custom for the people to disobey the commands of their Queen. There was then no sacrilegious plundering of God's House; no blasphemous outrages; no trampling the holy sacraments under the feet of wicked men. The real Catholic never dreamed of pulling down the pix, and hang up the knave of clubs in its place. They did not hack and hew and indecently outrage the crucifix in those times. They reverenced the holy season of Lent; they fasted and abstained; and the wicked appeared in the churches filled with tears for their past errors. Where are they to be found now? Alas, in the ale-houses, or some place worse. In the reign of Queen Mary the generality of the people, the nobility and those of the Privy Council, were exemplary for their public devotion. It was the custom for the judges and other public personages, before they undertook the duties of the day, to go to a church or chapel, and beg the protection of God. Now, however, the face of everything is quite changed.* What is the cause?"

Looks were exchanged, and a murmur ran through the House. It was dangerous to express an opinion against the Queen's new policy. But Feckenham stood fearless as the advocate of Truth and Justice.

The Lord Abbot met the fate of the bishops. The Oath of Supremacy was tendered to him "with three day's consideration," but he replied at once, that his " conscience, his honour, and every feeling that was dear to him, demanded the rejection of the oath proposed." He was arrested, and never more recovered his liberty.

There was something vindictive and cruel in consigning the deposed bishops and clerics to the custody of their Puritan successors. The sufferings of Feckenham were not easy to be endured; he was placed as a prisoner with Dr. Horne, the newly appointed Bishop of Winchester, a narrow-minded Puritan, who could not speak respectfully to any one whose religious sentiments were opposed to his own. Feckenham made petition to the Queen, to remove him from the insults that daily awaited him from Horne, his wife, and retainers. What was Feckenham imprisoned for? Why not let him leave the country? First, to rob a man of his private property, and then call on him to swear to a religious faith

---

* Abbot Feckenham's Speech upon the Statute of Uniformity, Bib. Cott. Vesp.

in which he did not believe, was despotism of the Tudor *régime* in its worst phase. Then to be imprisoned for life was a fate that none but the worst statesmen could inflict. All of these transactions have been defended as necessary to "*promote the growth of Protestantism.*" Comment is needless, for the whole of those proceedings impress a black and iniquitous spot upon the reign of Elizabeth; yet her conduct in this respect has been defended by English writers. Here is an extraordinary passage from a recent work:—

"While refusing freedom of worship, Cecil, like his royal mistress, was ready to *concede liberty of conscience.*"

The author again remarks:—

"It was *a far greater gain for humanity when the Queen declared her will to meddle in no way with the consciences of her subjects.*"

The work in which the above passages occur has been extensively read by English Churchmen and Dissenters.*

Feckenham was detained in prison by Elizabeth for *five and twenty years, receiving bad food and every indignity* that it pleased the gaolers of those days to inflict. He died (1585) in one of the dungeons of that gloomy prison, the Castle of Wisbeach, in the Fens.†

Amongst Feckenham's works was a very learned Treatise on the "Holy Eucharist," in reply to Hooper. At the time Dodd wrote his history, this work was still in the "original MS." Bishop Horne assailed the Abbot in a series of letters which place the writer in a very undignified position. But Horne cared not what he wrote "when a Papist's character

---

* Green's History of the English People, vol. ii, p. 292; Ibid, p. 298.

† See Camden; Anthony Wood's Athenæ, vol. I, p. 500; Reyner's Historia Benedictorium; Dodd's "Church History," vol. i, p. 525; Froude, vol. vii Archbishops of Canterbury, vol. ix; Harlow, Pomeroy, and Griffin.

was at stake." Queen Elizabeth was often indignant at his conduct. In the days of his prosperity Feckenham had been a munificent benefactor to the poor of London. He erected public fountains of pure water for the people, and distributed daily the milk of twelve cows amongst the sick and indigent. He also provided food and clothing for thirty orphan girls of "reduced families." His bounty was extended to all irrespective of creed or party.

I may here remark that the venerable "elms" which now stand in Dean's Yard, Westminster Abbey, were planted by Abbot Feckenham. One particular anecdote has been preserved of the good kindly Abbot. When engaged in planting the trees above alluded to, a debate was going on in Parliament respecting the religion of the country, and a messenger having brought word to Feckenham, that the majority were in favour of the Reformation, and that he was planting his elm walk in vain. "Not in vain, I hope," replied Feckenham; "those that come after *me* may, perhaps, be scholars, and lovers of retirement, and whilst walking under the shade of these trees, they *may sometimes think of the olden religion of England, and the last Abbot of this place.*" The fate of John Baptist Feckenham is one of the saddest on the rolls of those days of persecution and injustice.

Maister UNDERHILL, a Worcestershire gentleman, was sent to prison in a cruel and arbitrary manner by Queen Mary's Council. He had been a loyal and chivalrous subject, and when Wyatt advanced against London he at once offered "suit and service" to the Queen. He was a scholar, poet, and musician, but embracing the "new learning," he became a fierce zealot, and was designated as a "Hot-Gospel man." He wrote a narrative of the "sufferings and miraculous escapes of many of the preachers in Mary's reign." The "narrative," itself, is more marvellous than any of the alleged miracles. As Underhill was an acquaintance of John Foxe and Anthony Delabarre, it is probable that those choice experts in invention gave him assistance in his extraordinary production. The original MSS. of Underhill's narrative is in the Harleian Collection at the Museum. Underhill was immensely popular with the fanatical mobs who attended at Paul's Cross, and on whom he expended freely sums of money. He "lived prosperously," we are informed, "much respected, and died at a good old age in the reign of Elizabeth." This is satisfactory to have occurred at an epoch when so many far better men failed in obtaining so comfortable an exit; and when even so many worse men quitted the scene of their machinations under circumstances so very dissimilar.

Queen Mary has been unfairly held accountable for the deeds of some of the worst members of her Council. The persecution of Judge Hales was signally unjust. He was one of those Reformers who refused to be a party to the disinheriting of the late King's daughters. He told Northumberland and Cranmer that they were traitors; that they were acting contrary to the laws of the realm, and reminded the grand juries of their allegiance to their lawful Sovereign. He was misrepresented and maltreated by all parties; but the "Queen's friends" were his enemies. He was illegally committed to the Fleet prison, and in a moment of despair attempted suicide. When the Queen heard of his unmerited sufferings she sent for him and " spoke many words of comfort to him and set him at liberty."* Maister Hales subse-

---

* Martin's "Chronicle," Holingshed; State Papers of Mary's Reign.

quently lost his reason, and in that state put an end to his existence. It is recorded by some Puritan writers that Hales was so tortured and terrified by Queen Mary's gaolers and officials, that when released from prison he came down to Thanington, where, in a fit of despair, he drowned himself in the River Stour. I cannot discover any official record of this statement. Perhaps it is a Foxite "squib." It is certain, however, that he committed suicide, and had been for some years in a very irritable state of mind.

Puritan Writers have published in many works the most extravagant narratives of those few Catholic lawyers and men of station who adhered to their religion in the reign of Edward VI. Amongst this much misrepresented class stands the name of Richard Morgan. Maister Morgan was admitted at Lincoln's Inn in July, 1523, and his call to the Bar 1529. He became Reader to that Society in autumn, 1542—an office which he again filled in autumn, 1546; when he was summoned to take the degree of the coif. The death of King Henry retarded the promotion of Morgan, for the government of Somerset "put aside" every lawyer who would not renounce his religion. Morgan's name occasionally occurs in Plowden's Reports; but he received little or no practice at the bar, indeed, Mr. Foss very candidly admits that, "perhaps his religion operated to the injury of his practice." No doubt it did; and the records of the legal profession in Edward's reign, and the action of the King's Council, account for the injustice inflicted upon the English Bar "for conscience sake." Maister Morgan, like many other professional men was deprived of his liberty for daring to practise the religion of his fathers. He visited the Princess Mary; and when deprived of his own chaplain, he attended her chapel, where he heard Mass on many occasions. He received "warning against the commission of this crime." He persisted again, and again, but in 1551, he was committed to the Fleet as "an incorrigible Papist."* Father Peacock, his old chaplain, died in a putrid dungeon of the Fleet on the day of Maister Morgan's committal. After some time Morgan was released. His professional prospects were nearly ruined; still, like many others, he remained true to his principles. In July, 1553, he was among the first of those who disregarded the Proclamation of Lady Jane Dudley as Queen; he immediately joined the Princess Mary at Kenninghall Castle in Norfolk. He received a warm reception from his Sovereign, and was soon rewarded for his fidelity to the throne. He was raised to the office of Chief Justice of the Common Pleas. The Queen's address to Morgan on his elevation to the bench has been preserved. She enjoined her Chief Justice to minister the law indifferently without respect to persons; always to have a regard to mercy—especially where doubts existed; that everything that could be brought in favour of a prisoner should be received, and fairly considered; and further, that a case between the Queen and one of her people should be decided as it might be between two of her Majesty's subjects"† The Queen always urged upon her judges to act with mercy; but the judges were not inclined to adopt that humane advice. Throckmorton and others had reason to complain that Chief Justice Morgan and his colleagues did not obey the Queen's command. Retaliation and vengeance were maxims of Mary's Council. Let the reader, however, bear in mind that the majority of the men who

---

* State Papers (Domestic) of Queen Mary's Reign; Records of Catholics in the Fleet during the reign of Edward VI.

† The Queen's address to the Judges is to be found amongst the legal records of her reign.

composed that Council were members of the late sanguinary government. They were *then Reformers:* under Mary Tudor they recanted, and sent their late friends to the scaffold and the stake.

It was unfortunate for Morgan that he became Judge at such a troubled time. Almost one of the first cases upon which he had to adjudicate was that of Lady Dudley, her husband, and Archbishop Cranmer, all of whom pleaded guilty. Chief Justice Morgan pronounced sentence of death against all. It is stated by a contemporary that his address to Lady Jane was very feeling, hoping that the royal mercy might be extended to her. It is alleged that he spoke with unusual harshness to Cranmer, describing him as an arch rebel to the Church and State; a man who committed numberless perjuries, and so awfully deceived the late King Henry. The sentence to be burned alive on Tower Hill, passed by Morgan upon Lady Jane, was according to a statute of Henry VIII. against any woman who committed high treason. The reader is aware that Lady Bulmer was the only woman who was sent to the stake under this barbarous law.

Morgan remained Chief Justice for two years after the death of Jane Dudley. He then retired from the bench. Some of his contemporaries state "that he had fits of melancholy, and became unable to discharge the duties of a judge." The popular story was to the effect that he felt such horrible remorse, for having passed sentence of death upon Lady Jane Dudley, that he "cried out she haunted him day and night." It is likewise urged that Morgan had a strong objection to preside at those trials for treason, as he had been once on friendly terms with Lady Jane's family; but his sense of duty to his lawful Sovereign set every other consideration aside.* He was a man of very moderate abilities, irritable and eccentric, yet humane and charitable.

FITZALAN, Earl of ARUNDEL, was a member of the ancient family of Howard, and an adherent of Catholicity. He wished, however, to please all parties, and held office under three English Sovereigns differing outwardly in religion. He is represented as moving in a cloud, suspected of actions which he would not avow; without a conviction; without a purpose; feared by all men, and trusted by none. Although Lodge and Turner have set up a vindication of Lord Arundel, it is impossible to acquit him of treachery to his friend and colleague, Northumberland, whose cause he had sworn to "sustain by shedding his blood for Queen Jane." In this respect, however, he was as trustworthy as the other members of the Council. At forty-two years of age Arundel was the "sympathising friend and concealed lover of Elizabeth" in the Tower, and at forty-seven he openly professed himself as her romantic admirer. Amongst all the lovers of Elizabeth he was the most sincere. Camden, in his Annals, relates that Lord Arundel was the first to introduce the use of coaches into England. He also sustained that celebrated class known in England for centuries as "Story Tellers," who travelled through the country relating marvellous gossip under the name of "news." Anna Boleyn, Mildred Wyatt, Mary, Duchess of Suffolk, and the beautiful Lady Magdalen Dacre, all patronised the Story Tellers who figured in their time.†

---

* See Dugdale's Orig. 118-152; Strype's Cranmer, vol. ii; Queen Jane and Queen Mary; Rymer, p. 334; Dugdale's Chron.; Hollingshed; Machyn's Diary, p. 106.

† In the first volume of this work I have referred to the praise bestowed upon Anna Boleyn by the Story Tellers upon their visit to Dublin.

The MARQUIS of NORTHAMPTON was, perhaps, a Catholic from conviction; but when his interests interposed, he inclined otherwise. He was tried and found guilty of high treason with Northumberland, but pardoned by the Queen. "He delighted," says Lloyd, "in music and poetry; his exercise, war, being a happy composure of the hardest and softest discipline." Some of his contemporaries represent him as "pious, gentle and humane;" others that he "was fierce and cruel in disposition, and a hypocrite in religion;" and again, "indifferently good." The truth is, he was just suited, by his want of worth, to take rank with his fellows of the former or present Council. Later research places Northampton in an odious light. His divorce and second marriage had been one of the great scandals of the reign of Edward VI. His immorality was shocking, and under the cloak of religion he became a detestable hypocrite. Yet some of those eccentric fanatics known as preachers of the "Word" represent him as a saint of the new Gospel—"a man that walked in the ways of the Lord." Such Puritan cant is sadly degrading to the intellect which tolerates it.

WILLIAM HERBERT, Earl of PEMBROKE, was an adventurer, "who rose from a low degree." He was descended from the illegitimate son of a former Earl bearing the above title, and coming early to Court to push his fortune, became an esquire of the Body Guard to Henry VIII. He soon ingratiated himself with the monarch, and obtained from his customary profession towards favourites several offices in Wales, and enormous grants of Abbey lands in some of the southern counties. In the year 1544, in the thirty-seventh year of his age, he procured the King's licence "to retain thirty persons at his will and pleasure, over and above such persons as attended on him, and to give them his livery, badges, and cognizance." The King's marriage with Catherine Parr, his wife's sister, increased his consequence; and Henry, on his death-bed, appointed him one of his executors, and a member of the young King's Council. Pembroke was usefully active, in the beginning of Edward's reign, in keeping down commotions in Wales, and suppressing some which had arisen in Wiltshire and Somersetshire. This service obtained for him the office of Master of the Horse; and that more important service which he afterwards performed at the head of one thousand Welshmen, with whom he took the field, against the "Cornish rebels;" he was likewise rewarded with the Garter, the presidency of the Council for Wales, and a valuable wardenship. He next appears as commander of part of the forces in Picardy and as Governor of Calais, where he found himself strong enough to claim of the Protector (Somerset) as his reward, the titles of Baron Herbert and Earl of Pembroke, which became proximately extinct by the failure of legitimate heirs. The moment his shrewd precision anticipated the fall of Somerset he attached himself to the ascending fortunes of Northumberland. To this aspiring magnate it was an object of rare importance to procure the support of a nobleman who now appeared at the head of three hundred retainers, and whose authority in Wales and the southern counties was equal, or superior, to the hereditary influence of the few powerful and ancient houses then existent. To engage Pembroke, therefore, the more firmly in his interest, Northumberland proposed a marriage between Pembroke's son, Lord Herbert, and Lady Catherine Gray, which was solemnized at the same time as that of the ill-starred union between Lord Guildford Dudley and the Lady Jane, her eldest sister.

No ties of friendship or alliance could permanently engage Pembroke on the losing side; and, though he concurred in the councils which proclaimed Lady Jane's title, it was he who devised a pretext for extricating the members of that Council from the Tower, wherein Northumberland had detained them in order to secure their fidelity. Then Pembroke having assembled the Council in Baynard's Castle, procured their agreement in the proclamation of Mary. By this act he secured the favour of the new Queen, whom he further propitiated by compelling his son to repudiate the innocent and ill-fated Lady Catherine Gray, whose relationship caused her to be regarded at Court with natural antipathy. Mary soon confided to Pembroke the charge of effectually suppressing Wyatt's rebellion, and afterwards constituted him her "captain-general beyond the seas," in which capacity he commanded the English forces at the battle of St. Quentin. As a general of the Royal army, Pembroke crushed Wyatt's rebellion, and his mode of doing so presented a combination of treachery and ruthlessness. He was the chief adviser of all the cruelties in Mary's reign, and his conduct towards unfortunate Jane Dudley covers his name with special infamy. Among the means employed by Pembroke for preserving the good graces of Elizabeth, was that of marrying for his *third wife* the young and beautiful niece of Lord Robert Dudley, and sister to Sir Philip Sidney. This lady was one of the most accomplished women of her age, celebrated, during her life, by the wits and poets whom she patronised, and preserved in the memory of posterity by an epitaph from the pen of "Rare Ben Jonson."*

At the accession of Elizabeth Pembroke was considered one of the ablest generals England possessed. He has been

---

* Aikin's Court of Queen Elizabeth, Vol. I., p. 272.

represented as then "being wealthy, haughty, mean and vindictive." His apparently revived love for the Reformation caused him to be placed on the committee of four to determine on the change of religion. The other members of the committee were Lords Bedford, Northampton, and John Gray. They communicated with Queen Elizabeth and Cecil in private. A "council of divines" also sat in solemn deliberation, but they were the mere mouthpieces of the Queen and her Minister's wishes. It was a strange peculiarity of the period when generals in the army and young political adventurers were taken into conclave to fashion a creed, instead of expatiating on matters more germane to their worldly callings. Pembroke was appointed to office under Elizabeth, to see that the new religion should be "orthodoxically settled and maintained." Mr. Froude draws this picture of the military apostle :—

" The Earl of Pembroke, in the black volume of appropriation, was the most deeply compromised. Pembroke, in Wilts and Somerset, where his new lands lay, was hated for his oppression of the poor, and had much to fear from a Catholic Sovereign, could a Catholic Sovereign obtain the *reality* as well as the *name* of power.* Pembroke (so said Northumberland) had been the first to propose the conspiracy to him, and as Northumberland's designs began to ripen, Pembroke endeavoured to steal from his court."†

There is reason to believe that Lord Pembroke was handsomely rewarded by the Emperor Charles for the services he rendered to the Papal party in Mary's reign.‡ Having.

---

* Is not this statement of Mr. Froude's an acknowledgment that Queen Mary's Council, not herself, deserves the obloquy which has been cast upon her reign?

† Froude's " History of England," Vol. VI.

‡ Grenville Papers, Vol. IV., p. 267.

as has been modernly designated a "wait-a-while," followed all the fantasies of Henry VIII., and obtained from him the lands and revenues of the dissolved nunnery of Wilton, Pembroke professed himself a Protestant under the mature teaching of Edward VI., and one of the first to acknowledge, and then to desert, Queen Jane. Queen Mary, having restored the Abbey of Wilton to the nuns, Lord Pembroke received the abbess and her sisterhood at the gate "cap in hand." When Elizabeth subsequently suppressed the Convent of Wilton, the Earl of Pembroke drove the nuns out of their house *with his horsewhip,* bestowing upon them an appellation which implied their constant breach of the vow of chastity.*

The Earl of Pembroke died in 1570, in the sixty-third year of his age. To the last he retained his high station, with all its emoluments, and never forfeited the favour and friendship of Elizabeth. Like Lord Leicester, his enemies were numerous; but through a well-organised spy system, he was able to crush his antagonists before they had opportunity for action. In an age rendered infamous to all time for the wickedness of its leading men, William Herbert, Earl of Pembroke, stood in the foremost rank of the "battalion of evil."

Shortly after the death of Pembroke, Queen Elizabeth discovered that he had been engaged in a conspiracy with Sir Nicholas Throckmorton, and "other devoted friends," to set her aside, and raise the Queen of Scots to the throne. Throckmorton would have died on the scaffold, if he had not been poisoned by a fig given to him by Lord Leicester. The State Papers disclosing this conspiracy are now attainable.

* Sir James Mackintosh's "History of England." Vol. III., p. 155 : Strype's "Memorials;" Fuller's "Worthies."

The next portrait I present to the reader is that of the DUKE of NORFOLK, representing one of the most illustrious Houses in the realm. The Howard family played a prominent part under the Tudor dynasty. They had originally sprung from a circle of eminent lawyers, who rose to great wealth and honours by their employment under the Crown. The first of this notable Saxon family was a judge under King Edward the First. The descendants of the judge remained wealthy landowners in the Eastern Counties, till early in the fifteenth century they were unexpectedly raised to distinction by the marriage of Sir Robert Howard with a wife, who became heiress of the Houses of Arundel and Norfolk, the Fitz-Alans, and the Mowbrays.* John Howard, the issue of this marriage, was a prominent Yorkist and stood high in the favour of the Plantagenets. He was one of the Councillors of Edward the Fourth, and received from Richard the Third the old dignities of the House of Mowbray, the office of Earl Marshal and the Dukedom of Norfolk. He had, however, hardly risen to these distinguished honours, when he met death at Bosworth Field, gallantly defending the royal standard. He fell from his horse badly wounded within a few yards of King Richard, whom the traditions of Bosworth describe as much affected for his loss. The son of this Duke of Norfolk was taken prisoner towards the close of the Battle of Bosworth, and consigned to the Tower for three years by the victorious Richmond. If the Howards encountered clouds and disaster, much sunshine had also fallen on

---

* Queen Marguerite of France is the ancestress of all our English nobility bearing the proud name of Howard ; the honours of her son, Thomas Plantagenet, Earl-Marshal, were carried into this family by his descendant, Lady Margaret Mowbray marrying Sir Robert Howard. The Howards through Queen Marguerite mingle the blood of St. Lewis with that of the Plantagenets.

their track. The discharged prisoner from the Tower having refused to join in the rising of the Earl of Lincoln, was rewarded by King Henry VII., who restored him to the title of Earl of Surrey. He soon became the most trusted and faithful Councillor of the King. His military abilities were of a high order, and he gave proof of it in his campaigns against the Scots, which soon won back for him the office of Earl-Marshal of England. He likewise commanded at Flodden Field, where fresh laurels secured to him the Dukedom of Norfolk. The son of the hero of Flodden, now Lord Surrey, had already served in Ireland, as Lord Deputy. His coolness and tact had displayed themselves during the revolt against "Benevolences," when his influence alone averted a rising in the Eastern Counties. Since the judicial murder of the wealthy Duke of Buckingham the House of Norfolk stood at the head of the English Nobility. Then again, the King's alliance with Norfolk's niece (Anna Boleyn) brought more power and influence to the Howards. Still, like many other royal favourites and political notables, the House of Norfolk met with more calamities; four members of the family having perished on the scaffold, and others passing a life of sorrow and privation in the dungeons of the Tower. Notwithstanding political inconsistency, and want of patriotism, with a few solitary exceptions, this old stock were always true to the creed of their forefathers.

Thomas, Duke of Norfolk, like many of his order, was a trusted friend and confidant of the King. He made no opposition to the monastic confiscations, and was an active agent in the early divorce proceedings. When Fisher and More publicly denounced the false assumptions of the King, Norfolk proclaimed from his place in the House of Peers, the right of the Monarch to adopt the " Supremacy in Church and State." He did not seem to have formed any idea of what might be the consequence of supporting the policy of the monarch, to whose person he was chivalrously attached. The Duke of Norfolk rendered vast service to the Crown in the course of his long life. As a general, and as an Irish Viceroy, he has left a memory of some distinction. In 1520, when Earl of Surrey, he went to Ireland as Lord Deputy, in which capacity Leland the Irish historian represents him as having acted "with an equity and moderation that disarmed all opposition." I must remark, however, that some Hibernian writers hold a different opinion as to the merits of Lord Surrey. On the other hand it may fairly be stated, that the Celtic race at this period, were very hostile to their English neighbours, who sometimes found conciliation impossible. As a diplomatist Norfolk was less successful; as a general, once at least, signally victorious. At the battle of Flodden Field he was "three times unhorsed," and his life saved by the gallantry of Sir William Sidney. He did the State good service at home and abroad, which was subsequently so appreciated by his ungrateful Sovereign, that he was impeached and condemned to death for assuming heraldic cognizances claimed as the exclusive privilege of royalty. He had many enemies—as all notable men of the time had—amongst the Council and the Reformers. Towards the close of Henry's reign Norfolk was considered the great champion of the Papal, or Catholic party. In a letter to Henry VIII. he defended himself in this guise against the secret whisperings of Cranmer and Hertford:—"I know not," he writes "that I have offended any man, or that any one was offended with me, unless it were such as were angry with me for being *quick* against the Sacramentarians."*

---

* Lord Herbert's Life of Henry VIII, p. 265.

The Sacramentarians were, undoubtedly, a seditious and discontented faction; but Norfolk's opposition to them was on political grounds. The old soldier was not distinguished for Catholic zeal until nearly the close of his long life.

The correspondence of Bullinger occasionally shows the deep-rooted enmity of the leading Reformers towards Norfolk. Let it be remembered that those Reformers were, with few exceptions, rebels; and loyalty to the throne was the great virtue of the illustrious House of Norfolk—loyalty of the most unconditional and chivalrous character. The real and personal enemies of the Duke of Norfolk were men of his own creed, amongst whom was Dr. Gardyner. Their subsequent imprisonment in the Tower, having brought them together, peace and friendship reigned between the former rivals. The King's desire to shed Norfolk's blood was intense. Almost the last words he uttered were, "Let the traitor Norfolk be in the hands of the headsman at six of the clock in the morning."* Four hours preceding that period, as the reader is aware the king preceded his destined victim. The Earl of Hertford and his colleagues of the Council, declined commencing the new reign by the execution of one of the greatest of the King's subjects. Norfolk, however, was retained a close prisoner in the Tower during the whole of Edward's reign. The Reformers made themselves detested by the manner in which they acted as gaolers and judges.

A few days before Henry's death he ordered Sir William Paget to prepare "an allotment of certain lands" belonging to the Duke of Norfolk, to the Members of the Council. By this "deed of transfer" Lord Hertford received £660 per annum, his brother Thomas Seymour £300; William Her-

---

* See Leti; Lord Herbert; Speed, and Pomeroy.

bert £266; Lords Gyle, St. John, Russell, and Sir Anthony Denny, £200 each. The vultures were all dissatisfied with the amount of these grants.*

Norfolk had some claims upon the justice and generosity of Queen Mary, although he had been in former years, the avowed enemy of her mother. When restored by the Queen, Norfolk, in the spirit of the times, retaliated upon his enemies. As Lord High Steward he presided at the trial of his old enemy, John Dudley, Duke of Northumberland, and it seemed a somewhat strange coincidence, that his father, forty-four years previously, took the leading part at the trial of Northumberland's father, who, in company with Empson, was condemned to the scaffold as "a peculator of the public revenue, and for the oppression of the poor in the collection of taxes."

The Duke of Norfolk's antecedents could have won him as little sympathy from the Papal Catholics as from the Reformers. There was scarcely a death by "law or command," which occurred before his own arrest, that he did not sanction as a Minister of the Crown—the execution of the Carthusians, Bishop Fisher, Sir Thomas More, Anna Boleyn, Lady Salisbury, Catherine Howard, and many other notable persons.

The reader has already seen the mode in which Norfolk exercised the "discretion of mercy" in the case of the Pilgrims of Grace.† In Henry's reign Norfolk was the most hostile man in England to the Pope's Supremacy. In one of his letters, he says:—"If I had twenty lives, *I would rather have spent them all than that he should ever have any power in this realm.*"‡ Yet, at the same time Norfolk was opposed to

---

* Extract from the Council Book of the last year of Henry VIII.'s reign.
† See vol. i, p. 481, of the Historical Portraits of the Tudor Dynasty.
‡ State Papers (Domestic); Lord Herbert's Life of Henry VIII.

the Reformation. In Edward's reign Archbishop Cranmer considered Norfolk the greatest and most powerful political enemy the Reformers had amongst the prisoners then in the Tower. If the Duke of Norfolk was opposed to the Reformers in religion, he agreed with them as to the spoliation of monastic property; and, like Sir Thomas Wriothesley, and other influential Catholics, he received his share of the monastic confiscation,—several most valuable manors having been presented to him when enjoying the royal favour. It would be idle to deny that a large number of the Catholic party were just as anxious to plunder the Church as the Reformers; and such a feeling prevailed for centuries amongst the landed proprietors. In subsequent times, however, the "unsatisfied Reformers" seized upon the spoil which Henry conferred on those professing Catholics, fulfilling the adage, "Ill got, ill gone."

A contemporary describes the Duke of Norfolk about the period of Catharine Howard's marriage with King Henry, as tall of stature with a military air, and his expression haughty if not severe; his hair slightly grey, and cut close to the head. His doublet and hose were of scarlet velvet of the most costly description; his surcoat of the same material, but of a darker hue. His buskins were likewise of velvet, crossed by bands and adorned with jewels. He wore a two-handed sword, and a poniard in a gilt sheath dangled at his right hip. From Henry VIII. he received the Order of the Garter, and Francis the First presented him with the Collar of St. Michael. Another writer represents Norfolk as a small man. At no time was magnificence of attire carried to such a pitch as during the first twenty years of the reign of Henry VIII. Large gold chains and girdles decked with gems, were worn by the courtiers who waited on the King at

Greenwich or Hampton Court. Even the pages and other attendants were dressed in rich costume, which frequently attracted the notice of the burghers, and the "lads and lasses of the people's circle." In 1540-1 the Howards of the House of Norfolk were again in the ascendant, for the lovely black eyes and the luxuriant black hair of Catharine Howard, the Duke's niece, had acted like a fairy's wand upon the King's heart—for awhile. And then, came the tragic end of the love scenes.

In Queen Mary's reign the Duke of Norfolk's career was brief but effective. In the eighty-second year of his age, laying aside the warrior, the courtier, the statesman, and the proud baronial lord, Thomas, Duke of Norfolk, retired to the quiet shades of Framlington Castle, where he spent the close of an eventful life in acts of devotion and charity, and died in peace with the world. The character of Norfolk was full of contrast. His ancient lineage placed him above all the nobles of the land. Bearing a descent from Charlemagne down to the Plantagenets—brave as the heroes of antiquity; munificent and princely in social life; haughty to his rivals, and condescending to his inferiors, he was widely popular with a nation who were proud of the fearlessness of its public men, whilst winning the envy of the nobles, and the hatred of an ungrateful King.

WILLIAM CECIL was born in 1520, at Bourne in Lincolnshire. His father Richard Cecil held the office of Master of the Royal Wardrobe to Henry VIII. and was generally known as a zealous Catholic, but, as a politician, he became the obsequious servant of the Court. The father of Richard Cecil was a working tailor. He subsequently kept an inn at Stamford, where he was unsuccessful in trade. He came to

London, and being a fine-looking man, obtained admission to the King's Body Guard. This new position proved to be the turning point in the future prosperity of the Cecil family. The grandson, William, received a university education. He studied for the profession of the law at Gray's Inn. Early in life he was fond of practical jokes. At one time he lost all his furniture and books at the gambling room of a convivial friend. "I am undone," said he; "what shall I do?" He soon, however, thought of an expedient. He bored a hole in the wall which separated his chambers from those of the successful gambler, and at midnight shouted through the passage: "Give me back my property again, or else I will thrash you well; I am poor, do not fleece me; gambling is a great sin, do not cheat your poor friend." The next morning the gambler returned to young Cecil the money and other effects, which he had won from him. Sir Nicholas Bacon has related many of his wild freaks when but eighteen to twenty-two years of age.

In after years William Cecil became one of the most remarkable statesmen in Europe. He first attracted the notice of Henry VIII. by advocating the Spiritual Supremacy of that monarch. At this period Cecil was a very young man; and the fact of his exciting the attention of the King by the expression of certain opinions, was considered a proof that he possessed talent of a high order; besides, he was most pliant, and his principles were—whatever the King desired. At this time he was no favourite with the Seymours; but "circumstances" subsequently brought about an apparent friendship. Upon the accession of Edward VI., Cecil took office under Somerset, and when that Minister was impeached by the Warwick party, he deserted his friend and joined the Government formed by the newly created Duke of Northumberland. Gratitude was not amongst William Cecil's virtues, for he *volunteered* to draw up the articles of impeachment against the Protestant champion of the day; and, let the reader further remember that the "great Reformer" in question was *his benefactor and sincere friend.* When Somerset was informed that Cecil had deserted him, he exclaimed, with tears and sobs, "Ah, my false friend! I thought he was a religious man, I have been deceived." It was a nice matter to discover a religious man connected with Warwick's government.

Between Cranmer and Cecil there existed a private compact to promote the Reformation in Edward's reign.* Cecil at that period was in communication with the German Reformers. He was also the agent through whom Cranmer offered terms to the "wavering secular clergy, to join the English Reformers." When Northumberland attempted to set aside the claims of Mary and Elizabeth to the English throne, Cecil joined him in his treason. The secret correspondence between Cecil and Northumberland, still extant amongst the State Papers of Edward's reign, reads like the despatches of men who were wholly absorbed in religion, but who in reality were engaged in a game of deep deception. They desired to keep the preachers on their side till a convenient opportunity occurred to dispose of them. Northumberland looked upon Cecil as the ablest man amongst the rising school of the Reformation party, and expressed a deep friendship for him. His professions in this case were hollow and treacherous; and Cecil, knowing such, was in daily correspondence with the secret agents of the Princess Mary.

When Lords Winchester, Pembroke, Rich, and Sir William

---

* Strype's Cranmer, vol. i. p. 408; Archbishops of Canterbury. vol. viii. p. 253.

Paget abandoned Lady Jane Dudley's cause, William Cecil imitated their example. He "admired the antiquity of the Olden Religion." Did the Queen believe him?

It has been stated that Cecil merely acted as a witness to some members of Edward's Council, taking the oath of allegiance to Queen Jane; but there is abundant evidence to prove that he had taken the "loyal oath to Queen Jane and the new Protestant Constitution;" and that in *ten days he violated his oath and his honour.** This is "no Popish allegation." William Cecil next appears before Queen Mary at Ipswich, with despatches from the Council; he excuses himself for his treason on the ground of "timidity and want of experience in such matters;" he gives the Queen a list of his "excuses;"† he procures the intercession of the ladies of the Court; and so far satisfies his Sovereign, that she exclaims to Dame Bacon, "Maister Cecil is a very honest man." He kissed the Queen's hand before any member of the new Council appeared before her. Although he expressed his desire to *immediately return to Catholicity*, he received no office in the Government. He however returned to the "faith of his fathers;" "*went to confession and received Holy Communion, and exorted his retainers and relatives to do the same.*" His biographer (Nares) states that he "*confessed himself* in Mary's reign with *great decorum, and heard Mass in Wimbledon Church;*" and for the "better ordering of his spiritual concerns *took a priest into his house.*‡" Dr. Nares, however, in a

---

* See Strype, vol. ii, p. 521; Hayward, p. 327; also the "Secret Movements" of the faithful adherents of Queen Jane; State Papers of Mary's reign.

† To form an estimate of Sir William Cecil's conduct and "probity" at this period, I refer the reader to Tytler's "Edward and Mary," vol. ii., first edition, pp. 169-447.

‡ We are not informed what became of Cecil's confessor when the "penitent" dropped his mask under the protection of Elizabeth.

volume, otherwise devoted to the laudation of Cecil, makes a remarkable admission that "he (Cecil) was not moved by superstition in these proceedings, but by *pure unmixed hypocrisy.*"* Cecil was present in the Commons when a petition to the Pope was agreed upon, praying his Holiness "to receive England again into the bosom of the Church."

Upon this incident the author of the "Queens of England," remarks with some bitterness:—"William Cecil attached himself as a *volunteer agent* on this mission of inviting the Papal Supremacy into this country. Cecil, thus affords an additional instance to the many furnished by history, that leaders of persecutions have been almost invariably renegades.† But the ardent aspirations of this man of *many religions* for office were utterly slighted by Queen Mary, for which he bore her memory a burning grudge."‡

It is odious to contemplate deception when practised in religious matters. Cecil frequently carried his beads and rosary in the presence of the Queen, and assured his royal mistress of his "*devotion to the Virgin Mother.*" In adopting this course he only deceived himself, for the Queen despised a person who simulated religious opinions for gain or favour. She thoroughly understood Cecil; yet, as a politician, she occasionally accepted his services. For instance, he was despatched by the Queen as her "special envoy" to Brussels, to escort Cardinal Pole to London. This mission he discharged *to the entire satisfaction* of the Queen and King Philip.

He endeavoured to cultivate the friendship of Cardinal Pole, who "considered him *a good Catholic and a prudent*

---

* Memoirs of William Cecil Lord Burleigh, by the Rev. Edward Nares, vol. i.

† Macaulay describes a "renegade" as a person who hates with intensified malice those whom he has deceived and betrayed.

‡ "Queens of England." vol. v (first edition), p. 404.

man."* When King Philip arrived at Southampton, Cecil was among the earliest to hail his arrival; when Philip and Mary went to St. Paul's, Cecil sat beside Lord Pembroke, and was, we are informed, "conspicuous for his piety." He lost no opportunity at the time of displaying his devotion to Catholicity. But, remembering events of the previous reign, he should not have embittered the last hours of Latimer and Ridley by his saying—he who had professed himself their friend—that they "were about to die as traitors to their Sovereign." Rodgers, Dance, Paul Rasper, and other Reformers felt themselves betrayed by Cecil. If he did not betray them, he assuredly abandoned and ignored them. Harry Dance exclaimed, "Where is Maister Cecil, now that we are martyrs for the Gospel of Christ? He is waiting on our enemy Cardinal Pole."†

When his old friend Cranmer lay in the Tower, Cecil deserted him; when the trials of the Archbishop took place at Guildhall and at Oxford, he never raised his voice for mercy, because pity in those days was never on the strongest side. When Queen Mary's days were drawing to a close, Cecil was in constant communication with the royal lady who resided at Hatfield, and ready to "salute her as the Protestant champion the moment Mary was dead."‡ Isaac Bannister, an Anabaptist preacher, describes Cecil, in the early part of Elizabeth's reign as "becoming rich by taking his neighbour's goods;" and he adds with bitter truth, that "he went to his half-Popish devotions four times a day, thus endeavouring to make heaven an accomplice in his hypocrisy." Dean Hook contends that Cecil was not a Protestant at this period. What

---

* Letter of Cardinal Pole to the Bishop of Winchester.
† Letters of Harry Dance the Preacher, to Bernard Gilpin.
‡ Lingard, vols. v, vi; "Queens of England," vols. iii. iv.

creed did he really adhere to? The Dean states that he had no connection with the followers of Calvin.* The secret correspondence of Cecil proves that he had little sympathy with the government of Edward VI. He was quite willing to betray his friends, and he acted with consummate baseness to Jane Dudley.

Sir William Cecil received several grants of lands. He secured for himself the greater part of the valuable endowments of the Abbey of Peterborough. He further possessed the best manors in the "Soke."† The means by which he accomplished these transactions would, now-a-days, be justly designated as a swindle, and a robbery of property held in trust for the benefit of the poor for so many centuries.

The gifts and the honours of the Crown did not end here. Cecil was raised to the peerage in 1571, under the title of Lord Burleigh, and the Order of the Garter followed. The public offices and enormous sums spent on the spy system, presented fresh sources of revenue to a minister who was just as dishonest as his Royal mistress.

Again, a statement as to Cecil's "after-life circumstances," is to be found in his own handwriting. "In the whole time (26 years), that I have been labouring for her Majesty, I have not been benefited as much as I was within four years of King Edward."‡ The above statement is incredible. Cecil commenced life with the most limited means for the rank of a gentleman, and he died wealthy. He held office for nearly forty years under Elizabeth; so that he had been the Queen's Treasurer fourteen years longer than the period named, and had ample opportunity of making up for the "years of inaction."

---

* Archbishops of Canterbury, vol. viii, p. 253.
† Records of Elizabeth's Reign: Heylin's History of Queen Elizabeth.
‡ Burleigh State Papers.

The total value of the lands which had passed from the Crown in the reign of Edward VI by *gift*, sale, or exchange, had been something over *one million and a half sterling*. The value of the lands given as *gifts* amounted to £730,000. How much of this sum reached Cecil's private purse, during the four years of his connection with the Boy-King's Government, is now difficult to ascertain. It would appear that young Edward did not know the value of money, or was lavish in expenditure, when the household expenses of the king's palaces rose from £19,000 to £100,000 per annum. Not more than three or four persons connected with Edward's palaces could be called honest; peculation and fraud were to be found from the highest to the lowest office under the State. John Strype printed several extracts from the household expenses of Edward's reign which are full of interest, and exhibit the conduct of the Council in its true light.

It is said that every evil thought which suggested itself to the mind of Elizabeth had its origin with Cecil. In part this statement is correct; and the minister was in many respects a more cold-blooded enemy than his mistress. The Queen in her sudden bursts of passion cried out in her usual masculine manner for the "headsman to perform his office immediately." Her minister would hesitate. "Let us wait awhile longer," was the cool reply. The political victim who had escaped a rapid death from the impetuous queen, was racked by the calculation of her iron adviser, sent to a dark dungeon *filled with rats*, "receiving the worst of food;" sent to another dungeon where the "pinching process" was carried out; "racked again and again;" "becoming half naked for want of clothing;" robbed of every shilling of property, and confined in small cells for ten and fifteen years, and then after suffering indignity and torture, suddenly handed over to the headsman. The secret correspondence with assassins and traitors—especially in the case of the unfortunate Queen of Scots—forms one of the blackest indictments against William Cecil as the minister of Elizabeth.

Edward Hyde, Earl of Clarendon, may be considered a very high Protestant authority as to Cecil's merits as a minister of the Crown. Lord Clarendon writes thus:—" No act of power was ever proposed which Sir William Cecil *did not advance and execute with the utmost vigour. And no man was so great a tyrant in this country.*" Such is the opinion of a most eminent Protestant statesman who had never been guilty of the baseness of betraying his co-religionists like Cecil.

Amongst the Puritan and other fervid and imaginative historians of this country, there has been in a great degree an eulogistic decision upon the policy of Cecil, and an inquest involving a careful suppression of his depotism and cruelty; yet by impartial research truth is now unfolding itself to posterity. At a later period, and in old age, Cecil was still the moving spirit of Elizabeth's Council—the inspirer of her home and of her foreign policy. As I have already remarked, Cecil has been described by Puritan writers as a kind of "heaven-born minister." The secret and undeniable records of his life prove that he was the most unprincipled and unfeeling adviser that ever influenced the state-craft of England. His early correspondence with Lords Moray and Lethington, in relation to the various plots manufactured for the overthrow of the Queen of Scots, and the subsequent schemes in conjunction with Leicester and his familiar spirit, Walsingham, for the long imprisonment and official assassination of Mary Stuart, displays William Cecil's character with revolting truth. Mr. Froude describes

Cecil's policy as in part that of Thomas Crumwell, carrying out the Grand Inquisitor's schemes, without the violence resorted to by the latter.

Can the reader believe that a man holding such a reputation as thus described, could calmly sit down and compose a "prayer for the use of the public?"* The prayer in question was written about the time Cecil was raised to the peerage as Lord Burleigh—a period when the rack was in full swing, the dungeons of the Tower filled with sighs and groans, and the scaffold reeking with the blood of his victims.

For five and thirty years Cecil's handwriting is to be found amongst the State Papers. In the records of Council meetings, the name of Cecil is rarely absent. Hundreds of sheets of paper covered with memoranda are still extant amongst his manuscripts, which show the extent of his labours.

Cecil has found many defenders amongst English historical writers; but Mr. Green, the author of a recent work, extensively read, has adopted a most extraordinary defence of Elizabeth's favourite minister and other prominent personages of his time:—

"It is idle," writes Mr. Green, "to charge Sir William Cecil, or the mass of Englishmen who conformed with him in turn to the religion of Henry, of Edward, of Mary, and of Elizabeth, with *baseness or hypocrisy*. They followed the *accepted doctrine* of the time,—that every realm, *through its rulers, had the sole right of determining* what should be the form of religion within its bounds * * * *. Every English subject was called upon to adjust his *conscience* as well as his conduct, to the *varying policy of the State.*"†

Amongst the secret agents of Sir William Cecil was a man

---

* In Strype's Memorials, vol. iv. p. 262, Lord Burleigh's prayer is printed.
† Green's History of the English People, vol. ii, p. 291.

named William Herle. This despicable varlet performed offices for his employer which others of the same class shrank from. Herle acted as a spy upon the Catholic gentlemen confined in the Marshalsea, whilst at the same time professing "a devoted friendship for several of them as a co-religionist." At a subsequent period Herle travelled in Ireland, Holland, and France, as an English spy. He assumed many disguises—sometimes as a priest, a physician, an artist, or any other which suited the schemes he was engaged in. At Paris he induced several English Catholics to return home, assuring them that they were safe in doing so. Relying upon the friendship and good advice of the supposed priest, a gentleman named Whitlaw, and his Irish friend, Ulick Hurbert de Burgh, came to London, and on the very day of their arrival were arrested by Cecil's agents and placed in the Fleet, where they died of a pestilential prison fever. It is stated that Herle "rendered good service to the cause of the Reformation," and was an *honourable man*. I feel great pleasure in stating that Mr. Froude utterly repudiates Herle's claims to be styled " honourable." This vile creature was also "a secret spy" of Queen Elizabeth's upon the movements of her own confidential minister, Cecil. Elizabeth's good sense taught her to have little faith in politicians, or the love and regard expressed for her by courtiers, and especially by the bishops, who were constantly soliciting favours from her for their relatives and retainers.

Herle possessed "gracious manners," was convivial and witty—to suit circumstances—and winning in the society of unguarded strangers. In Ireland he won the esteem of many honest confiding men. His maxim was that of having "a hand for every worthy, and a heart for no one." In a word, William Herle was a fit instrument for the unscrupulous Walsingham, whether among the Border men, or in those mysterious haunts in Paris, where rebels, traitors, outlaws and mouchards consorted to advance their respective machinations.*

The intelligent and reflective reader can form his own judgment upon the extraordinary propositions advanced by Mr. Green.

Now for a view of Cecil's private life. His character, during a period of licentious living amongst the upper classes of England, stood forth without a blemish. No public man of his time had more enemies; and no statesman of the period did more to provoke the political hatred of mankind, than he; nevertheless, his private reputation, his domestic honour, stood unimpeached. He was a kind and affectionate husband; a man of strict personal morality; a good father, and an indulgent and generous master. All his children were highly gifted, especially his daughters, who were the most learned women England produced during the Elizabethan era. But his eldest son, William, seems to have been "moving in a cloud." He does not appear much, if at all, on the political chessboard of the Home Government. He was known, however, in Paris, and secretly fraternised with, by some of the English and Irish political outlaws who had registered vows of eternal enmity to his father. At a future period the younger son of the great statesman manifested his father's abilities; and has left to posterity an unenviable notoriety under the title of Robert Cecil, Earl of Salisbury.

Sir NICHOLAS BACON was descended from an ancient family in Suffolk. He was a lawyer of some note in the reign of

---

* Anecdotes of an English Spy, by a Borderman. Antwerp, 1601.

Henry VIII. He was brother-in-law to Sir William Cecil, and had been a concealed Reformer for some years, and strongly imbued with Calvinism. At the accession of Elizabeth he was about thirty-six years old; a large corpulent man, with a square massive face, deeply lined, high arched brows, and an aquiline nose—the expression of the whole visage keen, hard, and unsparing. As a politician, Bacon was unknown to Elizabeth, but had been recommended by Cecil. He received a grant from Henry VIII. of three manors, and during Somerset's government he conducted himself with skilful prudence, and gave no offence to any party. In Mary's reign his official position was undisturbed. He appears in a favourable light as depicted by Mr. Froude in his "Elizabethan Worthies." In speaking of her various ministers to La Motte Feneleon, the French Ambassador, Elizabeth said that she had the good fortune to have had in her employment two men possessed of more practical common sense than any others whom she had ever known—namely, William Cecil and Nicholas Bacon. The Queen added with a smile—"But those who had little sense or prudence sometimes pleased me more."* The latter passage would lead to the inference that "golden Eliza," with perhaps a sigh, thought of the days when Dudley or Hatton enjoyed the Royal favour.

Sir Nicholas Bacon held the office of Lord Keeper, or Chancellor, for nearly twenty years. As a judge he gave general satisfaction; and it was remarked, by his contemporaries of all parties, that from the days of Sir Thomas More, justice had never been so well administered in the Court of Chancery. On the bench he was patient and

---

* Letters of La Motte Feneleon.

courteous, and, like Wolsey, he displayed a sympathy for the poor suitor, and always discouraged that spirit of litigation for fostering which the attorneys and lawyers of those times were notorious.

Some time before his death Queen Elizabeth visited Bacon, when she assured him that he had discharged the duties of his office to her "entire satisfaction." After minutely examining his house and domestic arrangements, the Queen remarked, in her usual coarse style, "Verily, my Lord Chancellor, this house is too small, and petty in its furniture, for *my* Chancellor." "No," replied Bacon, "the fault lies at the other side; your Highness has made me far too big for the house."

When we come to examine the "political character" of Bacon, he at once appears to be the unscrupulous instrument of Elizabeth and Cecil. In 1568 the Queen appointed Bacon to preside over the commission which was held at Hampton Court to enquire into the murder of Darnley, and investigate the "casket case." On this occasion he formed a friendship for such men as Moray and Buchanan. At one of the meetings convened for this investigation, Bacon spoke in terms of scorn of Mary Stuart and those nobles and lairds who sustained her legitimate claims in Scotland. The Scots felt that the English Chancellor had offered an insult to their country, and the name of Bacon was long years subsequently execrated by the Scots.

In the English Parliament Sir Nicholas Bacon was also unpopular. He told the Commons that "they should do well to meddle with no matters of State but such as *should be propounded for them.*" The Puritan spirit, was not, however, so easily humbled. Several members brought forward motions about the abuse of the royal prerogative in granting monopolies, and the necessity for settling the succession to the Crown. Several of those "unruly Puritans" were summoned before the Council, when Bacon severely reprimanded them for their temerity; and one member, who persisted in stating that he had a right to express his honest convictions, was carried out of the House, and lodged in the Fleet, where he remained for two years, till death released him from Elizabeth's anger.

At the close of the Session of 1571, Bacon highly extolled the "loyalty and discretion" of the House of Peers.* The Queen was present on this occasion, and she attracted unusual crowds from the fact of her having made her journey to Westminster Abbey for the first time (April 2nd) in a coach, which was drawn by two palfreys covered with crimson velvet, embossed, and embroidered very richly; but this was the only coach in the procession; the Lord Keeper (Bacon), and the Peers, Spiritual and Temporal, were on horseback, magnificently attired. The enthusiasm of the people for Elizabeth was immense; but they preferred seeing "Golden Eliza" on horseback, "she looks so grand," writes Speaker Puckering, who, by the way, was himself heartily despised by the people.

The proceedings of the Session of 1571 did not end without a fresh attack being made on the liberties of the Commons by Sir Nicholas Bacon. The Lord Keeper, in strong language,

---

* Bacon cannot be styled a member of either House of Parliament. When Elizabeth went to open Parliament he was present. He sat upon the woolsack, and delivered an oration in the Queen's name to the members of both Houses. He was not permitted to take part in the Lords' debates, although he sat on the woolsack as their Speaker. This arrangement often led to unpleasant incidents, for Bacon was obliged to listen to attacks upon himself, and remain silent. He sometimes signified his dissent by "a peculiar cough," or playing impatiently with his "walking-stick."

condemned the Commons "for their audacious, arrogant, and presumptuous folly, thus by superfluous speech spending much time in meddling with matters neither pertaining to them nor *within the capacity of their understanding.*"*

The Puritan party in the Commons were rapidly increasing at this time in strength and courage, and the Queen and her Council crushed them whenever an opportunity offered.

It is affirmed that Sir Nicholas Bacon "framed the acts, and gave important suggestions as to the manner in which the Queen of Scots and her adherents were to be disposed of." The noble author of the "English Chancellors" remarks, "that although death saved Bacon from the disgrace of being directly accessary to the death of Mary Stuart, he is chargeable with having strongly supported the policy which finally led to that catastrophe, by urging the continuation of the captivity of the Queen of Scots, and by aiding in the efforts to blacken her reputation; and by contending, that though a captive Sovereign, she ought to be treated as a rebellious subject." What constitutional maxim, or what equitable dictum of international law can be quoted to sustain a procedure like this?

Sir Nicholas Bacon also played a noted part in the prosecution of those who sympathised with the Queen of Scots. Being a Commoner, Bacon could neither act as Lord Steward, nor sit upon the trial of the Duke of Norfolk, who was one of the first who suffered for sympathising with Mary Stuart. Nevertheless, Bacon put the Great Seal to the commission under which this mockery of justice was enacted, and must have superintended and directed the whole proceedings. He is to be considered answerable for such atrocities as depriving

---

* Parliamentary History of Elizabeth's Reign, p. 766.

the noble prisoner of the use of books, and debarring him from all communication with his family and friends; and placing him in a close dungeon in the Tower—giving him *notice of trial only the night before his arraignment;* keeping him in ignorance of the charges against him till he heard the indictment read in court, and resting the case for the Crown on the confessions of witnesses whom the Council had ordered "*to be put to the rack, that they might find a taste thereof.*"* Sir Nicholas Bacon, like his brother-in-law, Cecil, was determined to use every expedient to crush and enslave the believers in a religion which he himself had openly professed in the preceding reign, and had, like Cecil, *partaken of Communion in the Queen's presence;* whilst, at the same time, he was in secret correspondence with the English Reformers at Strasburg, for the overthrow of the religion in whose truth he publicly declared, in the manner above narrated, his solemn conviction. What Puritan advocate can defend such a system of deception and sacrilege?

Elizabeth sometimes consulted Sir Nicholas Bacon as to the treatment of heretics who "continued obstinate thinkers in battling against God's Word." At other times the Queen commanded Bacon to carry out her own views. The Anabaptists were the special objects of her aversion. She writes thus to Nicholas Bacon against the existence of "certain heretics":—

"Those persons have been justly declared heretics, and therefore, as corrupt members, deserve to be cut off from the rest of the flock of Jesus Christ, lest they should corrupt others professing the true Christian faith. We, therefore, according to the

---

* See Statutes of Treason of Elizabeth's Reign, p. 958; Ellis's Royal Letters, Vol. II., p. 261.

regal functions of our office concerning the execution of justice in this special case, require you, our loyal and trusty Councillor, to make out and record our writ of execution for the said heretics.

"(Signed)   ELIZABETH, THE QUEEN."*

Sir Nicholas Bacon, like other public men of his time, suffered in various ways, from the enmity of the Royal favourite. Bacon possessed the negative virtue of hating heartily and holding in supreme contempt the execrable Leicester; nevertheless, he had the prudence to be silent, when the merits of the Queen's "Sweet Robin" were discussed in private society, where the "special gossipper" was happy to retain some thoughtless expression, which was quickly conveyed to Lord Leicester, who was, it is needless to add, universally detested. Of course Bacon won the hatred of Leicester, and he was consequently expelled from the Privy Council. This manifested the power wielded, through a Sovereign's despotic caprice, by a worthless favourite over a public servant. The reasons given for this action on the part of the Queen are not well understood. Some time before his death Bacon was restored to the Council, but he refused to appear again at the Privy Council, or at any other public body, if the Earl of Leicester was present.

The "Keeper" of the Queen's elastic conscience, as well as her Fool, Clod, had to journey "unexpectedly" to the Hereafter. On the 1st of February, 1579, while under the operation of having his hair and beard trimmed, he fell asleep. The barber desisted from his task, and remained silent. Bacon continued to sleep for some time in a current of air, and when he awoke he found himself chilled. To the

---

* State Papers of Elizabeth's Reign; Rymer, Vol. XV., p. 470; Lingard, Vol. V., p. 487.

question, "Why did you suffer me to sleep thus exposed?" the answer was, "I thought it a pity to disturb your nice little sleep." Sir Nicholas replied: "Ah, my good-natured man, by your kindly feeling I lose my life." He was immediately carried to bed, and died in a few days at his residence (Feb. 1579) near Charing Cross, then known as York Place. He was buried in St. Paul's Cathedral.

Bacon's contemporaries, Hayward and Camden, record a very flattering private and public character of Nicholas Bacon. But contemporaneous criticism is to be measured by the characters, opportunities, and principles of the critics, as well as by the circumstances of the times. At a different epoch Nicholas Bacon might have been a passably good man; but, swayed by ambition, led by his surroundings, just as cells multiply in the growing tissues of organized structures, the germs of evil in the nature of Bacon grew and fructified in the torrid glow of an exceptionally corrupt atmosphere. Few good men or women can be pointed at as existing throughout Europe, or England, during the long reign of Elizabeth, of whose statesmen Bacon may be quoted as an average sample, although mistaken encomiasts have sadly injured even *his* reputation, by placing him on the same dark platform with a man inconceivably his superior in all the tortuous arts of deceit, in every want of principle, in every vile and cruel characteristic of an evil and treacherous cunning, which was then called statesmanship—Elizabeth's prime minister, William Cecil.

Sir FRANCIS WALSINGHAM was, perhaps, one of the very worst of the bad men connected with the Council of Elizabeth. For art in corrupting others, and skill in elevating treachery to the dignity of a science; for ability in planning and carrying out forgery, as well as in arranging for the assassination of inconvenient allies or open enemies, Francis Walsingham was vastly superior to his friend William Cecil. Walsingham's hypocrisy was a masterpiece. He is described by his contemporaries as "a man of a cruel and a savage nature." It was evidently a pleasure to him to inflict personal cruelty upon the people who fell into his power. He was known to beat them on the head with his staff. His language to the unfortunate Catholic ladies whom he arrested for attending Mass was most detestable. No matter what outrage he committed upon women of the most stainless character, they had no redress from Queen Elizabeth, who had no sympathy for her own sex at any time.

Much of the barbarous cruelty practised by the Lord Deputies of Elizabeth in Ireland was suggested by Walsingham. There are still extant letters of this baleful minister to Sir Henry Sidney, advising the old policy of the spy-system in its most odious forms. To personate the character of a confessor to a dying prisoner was carried to a demoniac pitch of perfection by Walsingham. He often boasted that he had "improved upon the confessional devices of Thomas Crumwell." Walsingham, like Crumwell, had his peculiarities, but the latter was more "in the rough and ready style" of his royal master. Sir Francis Walsingham had a malignant hatred of Ireland and its Popish people. It has been affirmed by several Protestant writers, that Walsingham had such an intense hatred of Ireland, that "he wished it *to sink into the sea.*" It is, however, in his relations with the Queen of Scots that Walsingham stands forth as the demon of the age. Further on I shall have occasion to return to the history of this man of blood and perjury. He died in April, 1590, and was buried at Old St. Paul's, amidst the deep execrations of the descendants of his numerous victims.

Sir JOHN HARRINGTON, the elder, was originally in the service of Henry VIII., and much in that monarch's confidence. He married Ethelred Maltese, an illegitimate daughter of the King by Joanna Mildred Dobson, and obtained with her a large portion of the confiscated monastic lands. Like several other women, this dame passed off as the daughter of the King's tailor, to whose care she had been committed in childhood. After the death of this illegitimate scion of royalty, Harrington entered into the intrigues of Sir Thomas Seymour. At the time of the scandals concerning the Princess Elizabeth and Sir Thomas Seymour, Harrington was closely examined by the Council of Edward VI. as to the clandestine visits of his master to Elizabeth; but he could neither be induced by promises of reward, nor menaces of the rack, to criminate the young Princess. If any "secret" existed that could impeach the honour of Elizabeth, Sir John Harrington and Blanche Parry "knew all concerning it." Harrington did not, however, deny that Elizabeth was passionately fond of the handsome Thomas Seymour. It was, however, "rather unseasonable," to use the words of Ascham, "to see the daughter of Anna Boleyn forming a romantic love for the brother of the ever to be detested Jane Seymour." All the natural and generous feelings of human nature seem to have been cast aside in those times.

At a later period the Princess Elizabeth took Harrington into her household, where he remained one of her most faithful and attached friends to the close of his life. Harrington's second wife, the beautiful Isabel Markham, was one of

Elizabeth's maids of honour, whom he has sung of in his poetical works as "Sweet Isabel Markham." In "religion," Harrington was as flexible as the times required—"all things to all men," as the wheel of fortune revolved, and men in power unchanged. Queen Elizabeth stood sponsor for the son of this ductile courtier, whom she subsequently playfully styled "Boy-Jack." When a noisy boy, the Queen often boxed young Harrington's ears, and on one special occasion when he smashed her favourite watch,* the only remembrance she possessed of her unfortunate mother. The Queen's quarrels with her godson did not last long, and were followed by kissing and caressing; "Boy-Jack" generally accompanied his godmother in her morning walks in the royal gardens.

The younger Sir John Harrington far transcended his father in the favour of the Queen, as well as in the greedy importunity by which he obtained property. In his letters, some of which he signed himself "Your Grace's saucy Godson," he exceeded Sir Walter Raleigh in avid demands on the Queen's liberality, which was very sensibly manifested by her bestowal upon him of a large portion of "other peoples' lands." *This* Harrington's written portraits of Queen Elizabeth are the most accurate on record.

The convenient marriage of the elder Harrington with the daughter of a discarded leman of his King, reminds me of another instance of Henry's immorality. The life-long friend

---

* This watch was the gift of Anna Boleyn to Margaret Wyatt, at Hever Castle, and many years subsequent it was presented to Queen Elizabeth by the family of Lady Lee, once known as Margaret Wyatt. It was an early memorial of the friendship which existed from childhood between Nan de Boulein—the pet name—and Margaret Wyatt, the Poet's sister,—a noble friendship which continued to the last moment on the scaffold, when the "leave-taking" so affected the Sheriff that he burst into tears. A rare occurrence in those terrible times.

of Anna Boleyn, Margaret Lady Lee, sister of Sir Thomas Wyatt, accompanied Henry's victim to the scaffold scene; yet many who cherish the memory of Lady Lee's courageous devotion, may not know that she, herself, was afterwards the object of Henry's licentiousness, and under circumstances of peculiar baseness, because the subject of his will. The King's conduct in this regard brought shame and grief upon several ancient and honourable families, upon whom no stain had hitherto rested, and added another marked instance of the reckless immorality of the King.* The kinsmen of Lady Lee, however, although deeply wounded and grieved, were compelled to defer to another tribunal the case, which in this world had no chance of justice against the potent profligacy of a remorseless monarch.

It is traditionally believed that Sir Harry Lee, K.G., had had the King for his father, though of course he was the reputed son of old Sir Anthony Lee, of Quarrender, who had married the young and beautiful Margaret Wyatt. Anyhow, since that time, all the Lee baronets and all the Lees, Earls of Lichfield, save the last, were named "Harry"—a custom which came down in the family into the present generation. I have this information from the male representative of the family—the Rev. Dr. Lee, of Lambeth, a learned and most excellent cleric of the Church of England.

Sir WILLIAM COMPTON and Sir GILBERT PICKERING were amongst King Henry's favourites. Those courtiers, accom-

---

* The above may appear incredible to many; nevertheless, I can refer the reader, with confidence, to a description of King Henry's moral life, *one year* after his marriage to the Infanta (1510), when he was only *nineteen years* of age. In vol. I., p. 177, of this work, the curious inquirer will find a satisfactory account of the career pursued by the "young King, who had the reputation of piety and amiable parts."

panied by the Duke of Suffolk and Sir Francis Bryan, joined the royal hunt several days in the week. The nights were spent in gambling and other worse orgies, either in the palace, or in disguise at Bankside, amongst the Swedish lasses imported to that notorious place. Of all the gamblers who were the companions of the King, Sir William Compton was the most successful. He died in 1528, immensely rich. His death-bed is described by Logario, his physician, as a very sad spectacle at the close of a profligate life. With all his faults, Compton was humane and charitable.

That King Henry was a reckless gambler is a fact attested by his courtiers and domestics. In three years he lost many thousand pounds in gambling.* He played at cards, dice, tennis, and some foreign games, not generally known in England. The Comte de Marillac, the French Ambassador, won £200 in one sitting from the King, who always paid such losses very freely.

A few words as to the integrity of officials under the Tudor and Stuart dynasties.† In one of Hugh Latimer's sermons, describing the "corruption in high places," he says, "a good honest man would scorn to take a bribe." In Latimer's time the officials made far more money by "presents" than by the salary paid by the Crown. The reader has seen how openly Thomas Crumwell acted in this respect; but Lord Hertford and his family were the most persistent and unblushing of all officials in plundering the State. In the reigns of Elizabeth, James I., and Charles I., men in

---

* Privy Purse Expenses of the Reign of Henry VIII.
† In the Chapter on "Corruption amongst the Judges," p. 365, in the second volume of this work, I have referred at some length to the venality of the officials of the Crown under the Tudor dynasty.

office became, if possible, more corrupt, and concurrently with being more venal received accessive *douceurs*. From Queen Elizabeth down to the drunken or ignorant Justices Shallow, who administered rural jurisdiction, lawsuits were hastened or delayed by a timely present, whether in golden angels placed under the royal pillow, or in the letter bag of a Chancellor. The Queen's treasurer sometimes found a letter bag full of golden angels, with "a request" written on a slip of paper. When such men as Sir William Cecil received presents from "unknown persons," with "a request," we may not feel any surprise at the "Country Justice" being convicted of receiving a fat goose from one litigant, and a few chickens from another.*

In the preceding volume I have impeached the honour and honesty of English judges, lawyers and attorneys. I reiterate the charge. Of all the corrupt men of those days, "attorneys and lawyers" were the very worst. They were devoid of conscience, as they were of even an apparent manliness of feeling or pity for their unfortunate clients. In truth no body of men ever obtained so many hearty execrations as by contemporary evidence they seemed to have received from their victims. Henry VIII. seemed to believe that it was one of his "privileges" to remove his neighbour's landmark; but the lawyers and attorneys plundered in the name of law; in the name of equity and morality, building up large

---

* Queens of England, Vols. VI. and VII.; Hatton's Letter Bag; Sir John Harrington's Nugæ; Letters of Archbishop Hutton; Burleigh's State Papers; Walsingham's "mode of giving and taking a bribe;" Francis Bacon's "way of managing bribery;" Letters of Archbishop Laud to Strafford on the "evil consequences of officials receiving bribes;" Dr. Varney's Account of People who were "set mad" by Lawyers and Attorneys.—1628. (*A very scarce little* black letter *book*). Lord Campbell's English Chancellors, Vol. II.; Foss's Judges of England, Vol. II.

fortunes upon the ruin of those who were litigious, ignorant or unfortunate in their mode of action.

At Dublin Castle the officials were always notorious for venality; and the character of the lawyers and attorneys for cheating and mercenary conduct was equal to the worst known in London—if not far worse. The Irish Judges not unfrequently fought duels. Lord Norbury appeared upon the bench in a state of drunkenness; and no matter what the merits of a case might be, he invariably charged the jury for the Crown. At one assizes Lord Norbury pronounced sentence of death upon 136 persons, and the death penalty was carried out in 135 instances. Lord Clonmel, and Lord Clare, might rank with Audley, or, later still, have a niche beside the infamous Judge Jefferies, or Scraggs. The conduct of the corrupt Irish Parliament was also adopted both in politics and commercial transactions. The Irish magistrates of the Past were far worse than the English "Justices" of the reign of Elizabeth. Where a Catholic was concerned, in Ulster, the magistrates, in nineteen cases out of twenty, decided against the man who belonged to the proscribed creed. The Orange magistrates of Ireland won an everlasting infamy in those times.

CHAPTER XII.

PERSECUTION OF CONSCIENCE.

"The Divine Law is not of the same nature as that of man, but a law of persuasion and gentleness." Such were the words of a distinguished Pontiff who held the Chair of the Prince of the Apostles within the last century. The indignation aroused in Europe at different periods by the fanaticism and despotic rule of the Turks, unfortunately led to a counter feeling on the part of Christians, which assumed in time a desire to visit with cruel penalties those of their own creed who dissented from the established dogmas of the Church. A false zeal for the supposed interests of Christianity has often led to the worst consequences. Persecution or imprisonment can never be perpetrated by any real followers of the Apostles. The opinions of the great theologians of the Church are on record *against persecution " for conscience sake."*

It has been frequently alleged that the Catholic Church " inculcated and encouraged the persecution of men and women for religious opinions when opposed to those of Rome ; and that the Pontiffs were foremost in using torture." These assertions are unsustained by any authority of repute. In all ages the Papacy was to be heard in denunciation of persecution or oppression of the poor. The military despots of ancient times were but little controlled by the Popes if their vengeance or interests interposed. Not Henry Plantagenet, nor that dramatic Emperor Charles the Fifth, was influenced by the advice of the Pontiffs, unless where it might chance to advance the views of either. It was not for religion, but for territory—not for the dominancy of creed, but from greed and ambition, that the Spanish and French monarchs carried on war with their opponents. There are, moreover, extant in the archives of the Vatican the solemn warnings of the early Pontiffs and Fathers of the Church against the practice of persecuting men for their religious belief. St. Austin says: "*Let us bewail those who go astray; let us endeavour to bring them back to their duty; but never give them room for complaint. For we were not sent to strike, but to instruct, and to reprove with mildness, though with firmness.*" Leo the Fourth once observed that the followers of Christ cannot propagate *His divine law by fire or sword; they must teach as He taught, and be gentle in bringing back stray or wandering sheep to the fold of the Good Shepherd.*" Another Pontiff represents "persecution for religion as the work of false prophets, and the apostles of false doctrines." To teach otherwise, would have been Islamism, not Christianity.

The first person burnt for heresy in England lived in the reign of Henry the Fourth (1401). On this occasion the Convocation of Canterbury condemned William Sautre, the parish priest of St. Osyth (Ositses), London. The Parliament and the King ratified the judgment of the Convocation.*

The Abbé Martyn, writing recently to a distinguished cleric of the Church of England, observed, "that the Catholic Church is not responsible for the faults committed by her children; that she has disavowed all the crimes perpetrated in her name; and that the Church has denounced in the strongest language every abuse of things sacred."

---

* Rymer, Vol. VIII., p. 178.

The aphorism of Madame Roland as to "Liberty" in more modern times might have been with deplorable truth applied at that sad epoch by all who reverenced true religion and respected human brotherhood. Changing one word of the Spartan Girondiste, it may be said of the Reformation period, "*Oh, Religion, what crimes have been committed in thy name!*"

The statute of Henry IV., to which I have just alluded, remained almost a dead letter till the reign of Henry VIII. I have already referred to the sufferers at the stake in the reigns of Henry VIII., Edward VI., and Mary. The Reformers, both in Germany and in England, seem to have had a common desire to consign their opponents to the flames. Beza, in defending Calvin for heterodoxy, and the burning of Servetus, cites Luther, Melancthon, Bullinger, and Capito, in defence of the stake as a punishment for those who dissented from the professors of the dominant religion. The Anabaptist apostles considered fire necessary to the accomplishment of their "justice;" and those who were opposed to them retaliated without pity or mercy.

Bucer, who justly complained of the persecutions for religion in Queen Mary's reign, was a persecutor himself of those who dissented from his views. At Strasburg he denounced Servetus from the pulpit, declaring that "*he was fit to have his entrails torn out.*"* Bucer was fully justified in denouncing the blasphemous principles propounded by Servetus. But when he demanded a death penalty for the "exercise of conscience," he proved himself especially antagonistic to the principles of the Church which he had just abandoned. The English admirers of Bucer, and his denun-

---

* See Dyer's Life of Calvin, p. 299.

ciations of Queen Mary's government, would do well to study his preaching and actions at Strasburg and Geneva. It is a patent fact, that all the leading preachers in Germany advocated religious persecution—their favourite instrument—the stake.

Bullinger has drawn many pictures—real and imaginary—of the "Smithfield stake," yet he persecuted those who held religious opinions opposed to his own. He advocated torture and death by fire as a punishment for some of the Anabaptists, who were undoubtedly the pest of society wherever they settled.

In a letter to Calvin still extant, Bullinger advocates the burning of Servetus. In this letter he writes thus: "What is your honourable Senate of Geneva going to do with that blasphemous wretch Servetus? *If they are wise, and do their duty, they will put him to death, that all the world may herein know that Geneva desires the glory of Christ to be maintained inviolate.*"* What party acted upon this advice?

Servetus, like many other blasphemous fanatics of the period, merely acted upon the "wild license" granted by the leading Reformers, and which was subsequently adopted by many cunning and unprincipled men, who confounded spiritual and temporal matters to promote their own worldly interests. To persecute men for their religious principles was, from first to last, the leading maxim of the English Reformers. Look at the shocking manner in which the unoffending Quakers were treated in England, and in the English colonies. The records of the times establish this fact, in the face of the unblushing narratives called "History." But to come to the sad doings of Queen Mary's reign. The

---

* See Original Letters of Bullinger, published by the Parker Society, Part II., p. 742.

chief blot on that monarch's public career is to be found in the horrible executions for heresy. It is of course small justification of the Queen, or rather of her Council, that "it was the statute law of the land;" that Henry had sent people to the stake for religious opinion, and that Cranmer, Latimer, and Coverdale, representing Edward VI., and the Reformers, did the same. Nor were such examples any excuse for the burnings, rackings, and many other modes of torture, throughout the long and ruthless reign of Elizabeth. A full record of the persecutions by Elizabeth and her ministers on the alleged score of "religion" would fill volumes.* One remark as to Queen Mary. The number of burnings in her reign have been incredibly exaggerated. In this matter the statements of John Foxe are without a parallel in the realms of falsehood, and that they were concurred in by the "Papists" is very "inexact." Even in the corrupt House of Commons of Mary's reign, thirty-seven members seceded in consequence of the persecutions carried on by the Government, and abetted by the House. This small contingent of humanity's phalanx consisted of thirty-four Papal Catholics and three professing Protestants; the leader of the seceders being Serjeant Plowden, a distinguished Catholic jurist, to whom Elizabeth subsequently offered the Chancellorship if he would abjure his religion, to which he is stated to have returned for answer, "No, Madame, not for the wealth of your kingdom." Camden, in speaking of Plowden, observes: "How excellent a medley is made when *honesty*

---

* In June, 1583, Eliza Thacker and John Copping were hanged at Bury St. Edmund's for the crime of "spreading certain books" (miserable little pamphlets) against the "Book of Common Prayer." Those poor creatures were insane, but the Government of Elizabeth rarely drew a line between the "sane and the insane," when the informers or spies of the Crown swore their statements, and received the usual reward.

and *ability* meet in a man of Plowden's profession." A strong proof this remark of the long-standing disrepute of the legal calling.*

"The Marian persecutions," observes Dean Hook, "were generally the result of religious fanaticism; but though religion was the pretext, the persecutions of Henry's reign were those not of the religionist, but of the politician."†

Dean Hook remarks, that at the accession of Queen Mary, the number of educated persons who held Calvinistic, or even Protestant opinions, was comparatively small. And the Dean here makes a candid statement, when he observes:—" If we look to the facts of History, we find, at the commencement of Mary's reign, that there was no desire or intention to deal harshly with the Reformers, whether Protestant or Calvinistic; two years elapsed, after the accession of Mary, before any persons suffered the penalties of the law on account of reputed heresy."

There is one remarkable fact connected with Mary's rule—namely, that the barbarous rack was wholly set aside by the Queen's special orders; but was revived and "carried into full fling" by Elizabeth in a manner to shock the rudest nerves of a heartless gaoler.‡

Stephenson, in his Calendar of the State Papers of 1558-9, relates that the Privy Council of Mary were urging forward the persecution of Reformers, and chided the bishops for their slowness in the work; that even Bonner was subjected

---

* Serjeant Plowden was ancestor of Francis Plowden, whose "History of Ireland" was so true, fearless, and honest, that the author was compelled to go into exile a century ago—a period when truth, even in historical matters, was a very perilous commodity to deal in.

† Archbishops of Canterbury, Vol. VII., p. 54.

‡ See Records of the "Action of the Rack in the Tower during the Reign of Queen Elizabeth."

to their pressure, ordering him in full conclave to "execute certain condemned heretics, and to proceed against others."* As the reader is aware, several members of this very Council had been the ministers of the late King Edward, and upon the accession of Elizabeth became members of her Government; and when she was averse to persecute Catholics, they urged her to do so. The State Records of Elizabeth's reign throw the full light of the present day upon the movements of those dishonest statesmen.

The evidence as to "who were the persecutors," in Mary's reign, is naturally conflicting. Writers of repute, even in the eyes of the educated English reader, affirm that Cardinal Pole was the author of persecution against the Reformers, whilst the Cardinal's denunciation of persecution is on record; and his words were uttered when Pole had the power to persecute, and *did not.* Archbishop Parker declared Reginald Pole to be the "hangman and the scourge of the Church of England." Parker did not reckon courtesy amongst his attributes. He had, however, assumed "many airs" when created Archbishop of Canterbury, which drew upon him the pen of John Bale, who styled him as "a hedge priest, whose servility attracted the notice of Elizabeth."†

Mr. Froude describes Pole in one passage as the author of "all the persecutions;" whilst in another he proclaims the Cardinal's character as "*irreproachable: irreproachable in all*

---

* State Papers of Mary's Reign.

† The Protestants of a later period did not much honour the mortal remains of Archbishop Parker, for we are assured by one of his successors (Laud) that the Puritans broke open the tomb of Parker, and *flung his remains upon a neighbouring dung-hill.* The reader is, of course, aware that the Puritan party sent Archbishop Laud to the scaffold in the reign of Charles the First. Laud was "a worthy little man." His great crime in the eyes of the Puritans was his chivalrous attachment to royalty.

the virtues of the Catholic Church, he walked without spot or stain." Is there any reservation here? Even John Foxe quotes a letter from Bonner to Cardinal Pole, dated December 26, 1556, from which it appears that the Cardinal disapproved of Bonner's proceedings against the Reformers.

Cardinal Pole at one time remarked to Bishop Tunstal — a man who never "persecuted conscience"—"that he (Pole) looked upon persecution for the maintaining of religious convictions, *as the greatest scandal that ever happened to the Christian Church.*" Elizabeth, as the Head of a "Reformed Christian Church," gloried in the most despotic exercise of religious oppression, and her conduct in this respect was a shame and a blot upon the civilization of the age.* In a letter to the Cardinal of Augsburg, Pole wrote :—" *In general lenity is to be preferred to severity. Such ought to show the tenderness of parents, even when they are compelled to punish.*"†

And again, Burnet affirms that Pole "declined all interference with the executions daily taking place." Burnet adds :—" The Cardinal considered the *reformation of mankind was his principal duty*. He censured Gardyner for not relying more on spiritual than temporal agencies. He was known to have rescued from prison several persons who had been condemned to the stake." ‡

Gardyner's long connection with political affairs far more inclined him to use the machinery of arbitrary power, than

---

* See Burnet's History of the Reformation, Vol. II.; also Strype's Memorials; Sir James Macintosh and Sharon Turner both endorse the statements of Burnet and Strype as to Pole in this case.

† State Papers of Elizabeth's Reign; Records of Torture for refusing the Oath of Supremacy.

‡ Pole, Epistle IV, p. 156. Records of persons who were pardoned at the stake. It is an important fact that Foxe, Speed, and Burnet have, with a few exceptions, suppressed those cases.

the benign action of the spiritual influence recommended by Pole. However individuals may have acted, the sentiments of Reginald Pole were those of the vast majority of the prelates and abbots who composed the Council of Trent. Like everything in connection with those unhappy times, the proceedings of the Council of Trent have been maliciously misrepresented by Puritan writers, who could not have any correct knowledge of the character of this august assembly.

John Foxe and Sir Thomas Smythe contend that King Philip was *the author and inciter of " all the cruelties perpetrated against the Reformers."* Sir Thomas Smythe derives his claims to credence on this subject from being closely connected with the movements of the Reformers, and consequently is by no means a trustworthy writer.

Alphonso de Castro, chief chaplain to Philip, denounced the persecution of which his Royal master was accused of being the promoter. De Castro's sermons against burnings made a great impression on the public mind in London, and for six weeks the work of the stake was stayed.* De Castro was especially severe upon Bonner for his part in these persecutions. Bonner's conduct, it must be allowed, was ineffably wrong and wicked. Even if, according to that evil period, his proceedings were to his own mind conscientious, who could defend him *now?* De Castro admitted no excuse for the perpetration of such cruelty *by any one, much less a bishop,* and utterly denounced such proceedings. It is proverbial that "doctors disagree," and to manifest the impartiality with which I desire to issue this work, it must be said, that it is curious to find Lewis Cabrera, *the* Spanish biographer of Philip, praising his King for " carrying out the

---

* State Papers of Mary's Reign ; Correspondence of De Castro with the Spanish Minister at Madrid.

law against the English heretics *by burning them at the stake.*" Did Cabrera know anything of De Castro's memorable sermons ?—or was his information as to Philip's conduct in England derived from some person whose veracity was of the Foxite type ? Cabrera's narrative was what he might desire to see accomplished, for he was a sanguinary persecutor himself. Stephenson's researches point to King Philip as the author of persecution in Mary's reign. The reader has already seen the conduct of the Queen's husband towards the persons who were imprisoned for religious opinion; also the warning given by Renaud to his royal master, to discountenance persecution, and regard the sermons of his chaplain against the punishment of the stake. If the Spanish monarch approved of the horrors of the stake, as so frequently alleged, would the Abbé de Castro have dared to preach against it ? Philip was a man that neither cleric nor statesman could control when he had made up his mind on a certain course.

The charges against Philip have come from most opposite sources, for he was hated by Catholics and Protestants for having defended his " political position," which, as the ruler of Spain, he was bound to assert. Bentivoglio records an answer attributed to the Spanish monarch by some person who desired a death less horrible than the stake for Reformers. "I would," says Philip, " far rather be without the title of a king than to reign over heretics." A crowd of political matters lead to the conclusion that "the uncommunicative " Philip would scarcely speak in this tone to the members of his Council, far less to those outside that grave assembly. Another writer of English history states, "that from the moment of Philip's arrival in England, he exercised an influence over the Government. But, bigot as he was in matters of faith, *his temper was that of a statesman, not a fanatic.*"* Mr. Green here makes a very discriminating distinction as to the character of a monarch who had to deal with " wholesale rebellion and sedition " in the Netherlands.†

In a conversation with De Quadra, the Spanish Ambassador, Elizabeth assured that astute diplomatist, that " *during his master's stay in England, he had been a general benefactor, and had never injured a creature.*" There can be no doubt as to the accuracy of this statement, coming as it does from the secret despatches of the Ambassador. Judging from these despatches, De Quadra enjoyed the confidence of Elizabeth, for she revealed some strange matters to him concerning her own private life.

On one occasion, all the prisoners in England were discharged on condition of taking an oath "to be true to God and the Queen."‡ After a few months the spirit of fanaticism and sectarian hate burst forth again, each party determined to slay their antagonists. At the bottom of these proceedings lay concealed the political ascendancy of the Anabaptists and other Communistic factions. To meet such elements of destruction to social order renewed powers of arbitrary action were unreservedly granted to the magistracy and military authorities—a class of men who were never on the side of mercy or moderation.§ So the persecutions continued till the death of Queen Mary.

Two hundred persons were sent to the stake in three years. Some thirty-six of this number recanted at the place

---

* Green's History of the English People, Vol. II., p. 255.
† See Motley's History of the Rebellions in the Netherlands and the Dutch Republic.
‡ Foxe, Vol. III., p. 660; Strype, Vol. III., p. 307.
§ Rymer, Vol. XV., p. 181-183.

of execution, and held "faggots" for one hour at St. Paul's Cross. This punishment over, the prisoners were considered pardoned, and retired from the scene.

A third party—the *politicians*, the "landless gentry"—used the Reformation movement *solely to promote their own dishonest views, and to "remove their neighbour's landmark."* And, in time, this party became triumphant by means of the most cruel and unjust that ever disgraced a civilised land.

During the sixteenth and seventeenth century, and later still, the Protestant sects in England and Germany openly defended and steadily practised religious persecution.*

And the European Sovereigns for centuries persecuted people for their religious opinions. Charles the Fifth hated Luther for his heresy, and regretted that he had not sent him to the flames when in his dominions. The persecution of the wretched Jews in Spain was long a standing reproach to the Sovereigns of that country. The blasphemously designated "acts of faith" carried out by Ferdinand and Isabel about 1478 are too shocking to describe; yet Queen Isabel was opposed to bull-fights regarded by the Spaniards as "sport."

Some Spanish writers have defended Queen Isabel in relation to her connection with the Inquisition, whilst her dispatches to State officials are to be seen in the archives of Barcelona and Simancas, recommending *torture*. Isabel was no fanatic. During the reign of Louis the Fifteenth, a refugee Quaker was committed to the Bastile; but not tortured after the English fashion of Elizabeth's reign.

---

* See the Public Records and Chronicles of the times. I further refer the reader to Rancke's History of the Reformation in Germany; also Motley on the Dutch Republic, and Prescott's Memoirs of Philip II. of Spain—all Protestant authorities. Mr. Froude likewise protests against the Puritan spirit of persecution.

Those who charge Catholics with the persecutions of Mary's reign should examine the actions of the Reformers in Edward's brief life, and see how far liberty of conscience, or the dealings between man and man for honesty were regarded. The proceedings in Edward's reign stand forth without a parallel in the history of this country. Revolutions, communism, and rebellion in its worst form, presented the general programme of the dominant party whose leading spirits were actuated by the worst motives attributed to Catiline by the Roman orator. The condemnation of them by Burnet and Strype fully proves that the sectaries of Edward's reign must have become the pest of society in England and elsewhere.

In Mary's reign many preachers were imprisoned for the sedition which marked their sermons to the lower classes. John Bradford did not approve of their conduct, although he spoke sedition himself. According to a notable Cambridge Student of History, they were men of "strict and holy lives, but very hot in their opinions and disputations against Popery."* Bradford had much discourse with those men. He was apprehensive that when they left gaol they might do great mischief. Strype admits that "they rose their notions as high as Pelagius did, and that they valued no learning; that the writings and authorities of men of letters they utterly rejected and despised."† The chief of these men was Harry Hart, a "Valiant Soldier of the Lord." Hart wrote a treatise of his opinions, which would tend to subvert all governments. The preachers quarrelled amongst themselves,

---

* Strype's Cranmer, Vol. I.

† Bradford corresponded with Cranmer, Ridley and Latimer on the results of those men's opinions. The correspondence is to be partly found in Strype's Appendix to Cranmer, and Foxe's "Lives of the Martyrs."

and were only unanimous in their desire to overthrow the olden religion. Trew and Abingdon dissented from Harry Dance, and Dance denounced them as "drunkards and hypocrites." Careless, another preacher, held Hart up to the scorn of the people. He said that he had "seduced and beguiled many a simple soul with his foul Pelagian opinions." Hart and Careless agreed on one point—namely, "that there should be no curtailment of 'belly-cheer' in Lent." And Hart was "assured by a holy man that *a young comely wife was a great comfort to a preacher of God's word.*" Pomeroy and Hales relate some unedifying facts of the preachers and their "young spouses." Strype reluctantly admits that the preachers were daily quarrelling and drinking while in prison, and the Marshal of the King's Bench prison "had to separate them in these un-Apostolic contests."* Harry Dance, *alias* "Red Tom," a bricklayer of Whitechapel, was a zealous man amongst the itinerant preachers of Edward's reign. He assembled a large crowd in his garden on Sundays, where he preached upon the "immorality and superstition of the Roman system."† Dance has been represented as "a God-fearing man;" as "moral and temperate;" yet his friend Halcroft calls him "a hypocrite, a drunkard, and a patron of bawds"! Henry Stafford, an assistant preacher, denies that Dance was "a drunkard or a bad man, but he was weak in the flesh,—*two women claimed him as a husband.*" This "weakness in the flesh" was an infirmity to which many of the Reforming priests and preachers were too frequently subject. The system of espionage adopted by Bishop Bonner upon the preachers in Mary's reign had a bad effect upon

---

* In Strype's Cranmer, Vol. I., is printed a long summary of the disputes of the preachers and the antagonistic opinions which they propagated.

† Pomeroy, Hales, and Strype's Memorials.

those who were wavering between the antagonistic creeds. It is also perfectly true that the sermons of those men were filled with sedition and treason, for which they should have been severely punished, but not tortured or sent to the stake. It is likewise certain that many lunatics came upon the scene, and added to the calamities of the times.

The opinion of so distinguished a Protestant historian as Hallam must command the attention of the intelligent and unsectarian thinker of every creed:—

"The difference in persecution between the Catholics and Protestants was only in degree, and in degree there was much less difference than we are apt to believe. *Persecution is the deadly original sin of the Reformed Churches;* that which cools every honest man's zeal for their cause, in proportion as his reading becomes more extensive. The Lutheran princes and people in Germany constantly refused to tolerate the use of the Mass, as an idolatrous service, and this name of idolatry, though adopted in retaliation for that of heresy, answered the same end as the others of exciting animosity and uncharitableness. The Roman Catholic worship was equally proscribed in Germany. Many persons were sent to prison for hearing Mass and similar offences. The Princess Mary (of England) supplicated in vain to have the exercise of her own religion at home, and Charles the Fifth several times interceded in her behalf."*

Here the learned historian points out the many faults of both parties, and their want of charity.

Miss Strickland, writing upon the same subject, says:—

"It is a lamentable trait in human nature that there was not a sect established at the Reformation that did not own as part of their religious duty the horrible necessity of destroying some of their fellow-creatures—*mostly by burning—on account of what they severally termed heretical tenets.*"

---

* Hallam's Con. History, p. 63-64.

The Reformers who were Bishop Gardyner's contemporaries speak far better of him than writers of after times, who looked upon the compilation of "history" as a commercial speculation.

Again, I have to call the reader's attention to the secret despatches of Renaud to the Emperor Charles. Those private letters are completely opposed to the persecuting spirit attributed to Renaud by English historians. The confidential despatches of the ambassador of a great kingdom are the most likely places to find a clue to the real state of affairs. I may, however, remark that the Spanish envoys in those times were the best informed of any amongst the diplomatic body in London as to English politics. They were judiciously selected, and abundantly supplied with money, which, in those days, enabled them to procure information from reliable sources. Renaud, in his secret despatches, relates that he had no less than twelve ladies of rank at one time in his pay. In fact there were few of the "new nobility" that could not be purchased. Simon Renaud, like some of his astute successors in the reign of Elizabeth, was painstaking in sifting to the bottom every narrative presented to him as to the hidden actions of the Queen's Council and their adversaries. Renaud was not the man to be deceived. Amongst other Puritan accusations, it is related that he was "the oracle of the clerical party in England." Yet his despatches prove that he was *not friendly to the secular priests, and censures them frequently and severely for the support they gave to religious persecution in Mary's reign.* Nevertheless, Renaud has been described by the "Hot-Gospel" writers as a monster thirsting for Protestant blood. It is true Renaud's suggestions were to the effect that Jane Dudley should be immediately executed. "Conspirators," he said, " require to be taught that, for the principals in treason, there was but one punishment." * * * And again, the stern envoy remarks :—" The rival Queen *must die, and that quickly.*"*

Lady Jane Dudley's bitterest enemies were to be found in her family connections. Polini states, in a very positive manner, that, during her brief royalty, Jane feared that she " might be made away with by *poison.*" And the assassins named by Polini were her *husband and mother-in-law.*

Those who are well acquainted with the political history of Spain cannot wonder at the sentiments uttered by Renaud with regard to Jane Dudley. I do not believe that he was in the least actuated by any feeling of sectarian malice against Jane. Several of his despatches prove the contrary. He was moved by that dreadful resentment which, on every occasion, makes Spanish statesmen the deadly enemies of a rebel, or a rival to a throne. In no country in Europe has the rebel received less mercy or pity than in Spain. But surely Lady Jane Dudley's case is one of the most exceptional on the records of humanity and equity. It is clear, however, that the sovereigns and statesmen of the sixteenth century did not look upon " mercy " as a virtue.

Ainsworth's " historical " novel of the " Tower of London " furnishes much of the material which has been coined into " history " for Mary's reign, during the last thirty-eight years. It is from such sources " popular opinion " forms its estimate of historical characters. Amongst Ainsworth's notables of Mary's reign, one of the most sanguinary and remorseless stands forth as Simon Renaud. How far he deserves this character, the State Papers of those times, and the despatches

---

* Renaud's Despatches to Charles the Fifth.

of the foreign ambassadors, especially those of Venice, at once decide.*

Renaud's confidential advice to Philip proves that he acted in a very different spirit to that which has been ascribed. He writes in these words to his royal master:—"Above all, *there should be no more of this barbarous precipitancy in putting people to death on account of their religious opinions.* The obstinate must be won from their errors by gentleness and moderate instruction; nothing should be done to *irritate the people against religion.* The Legate (Cardinal Pole) should see that the clergy set a good example to their flocks."† In another despatch Renaud speaks in severe language of the conduct of Bonner; but he considers Gardyner "a man of moderation and good sense; besides he is the only real statesman England possesses at this critical period."‡

Renaud, who reviewed the posture of English affairs " from all points," writes thus to his royal master:—" The English Church should bend to the times, and leave the Pope *to his own fortune."* § Thirlby, Bishop of Norwich, relates that the Emperor Charles did not approve of the conduct of the secular clergy of England. Neither did King Philip. Not much good might be expected from priests who were disciplined and ordained under prelates like Cranmer, Hooper, Latimer, Poynet, Shackleton, and Barlow.

More recent researches at the far-famed Record Office in

---

* Renaud's despatches are in three volumes in the library at Besancon. The most interesting part of those confidential letters are in relation to Queen Mary's Government. The State Papers in question were calendared by Griffet. Lingard and other high authorities bear testimony to the accuracy of Griffet's translations.
† Renaud's Confidential Despatches to King Philip.
‡ Grenville State Papers, Vol. IV.
§ Renaud's Special Despatches to Charles the Fifth.

Simancas, show that Simon Renaud was far *more a Protestant than a Catholic ;* but from his political position he dared not avow his religious opinions. Be this as it may, he has been unjustly misrepresnted by English writers. Let all parties remember the maxim put forth by the late Dean Hook, "*The exposure of a lie is the triumph of Truth.*"

Those who preached and carried out religious persecution were men not under the influence of Christian Charity. They were Politicians—knaves and hypocrites. Scotland under Moray, Knox, and his coadjutors is an illustration of the policy of those evil spirits. It is no justification of the doctrine of persecution to state the real facts of history in regard to the burning of Reformers which took place during Mary's reign, and were repaid five hundred-fold on Catholics during the long reign of Elizabeth, when proscription or death was the doom of all those who rejected the newly-propounded Gospel set forth by the last of the Tudors.

The policy of the Puritans has found many advocates. A sense of equity and truth, which sometimes overcomes sectarian prejudice in England, has placed the Puritans in their true light—judging them by the records of their actions. A recent writer upon the Puritans " in the days of their prosperity and power," states that " Puritanism broke down by the corruption of the Puritans themselves. It was impossible to distinguish between the *saint* and the *hypocrite* as soon as *godliness became profitable.*"* " Honest old Churchman" Pepys, who speaks from a long personal knowledge, describes the Puritans as " profane swearing fellows, and much given to hypocrisy." The Protestant evidence against

---

* See History of the English People, by John Richard Green (M.A.), Vol. III., p. 313.

the Puritans of England and Scotland would fill volumes. Here is an incident that would have startled all parties if it were proposed now-a-days. The Christmas Day of 1644 was kept as a "*solemn fast.*" A proclamation was issued to that effect by both Houses of Parliament, "against the keeping of Christmas in the old superstitious manner of Popery."* The "belly cheer was to be reduced on that day in particular." Several riots were the result of this fanatical freak.

It is an utterly untrue conceit that "burning heretics was solely confined to Queen Mary and the Papists." On the 22nd of June, 1578, two Dutch Anabaptists were sent to the stake by "command" of Elizabeth. John Stowe, the historian, who was present, states that "they died in great horror, with roaring and crying." There is still extant a letter of John Foxe to Elizabeth, protesting against this execution. At another time (1575) the Queen condemned forty-three persons for heresy. The victims in this case were all Dissenters. Yet we are assured by recent writers, that Elizabeth "*never persecuted conscience.*" How any writer can make such statements in the face of the records of those times appears to be a lamentable avoidance of truth.†

Far be it from me to defend persecution for religious opinions, for I have an abhorrence of such proceedings. Charity and Equity demand Liberty of Conscience for all sections of Christians, and the man who is proscribed on the score of religion becomes a slave, whose only hope is in

---

* State Papers of 1644 ; Records of Parliament for the same period.

† The particulars of the above cruelties, inflicted for the honest expression of conscientious opinions, are to be found in the State Papers and Records of Elizabeth's reign ; John Stowe's Chronicle ; Brandt ; Limborch ; Neill, and Collier—all Protestant authorities.

social turmoil or dynastic change. No honest man can be happy that is not free. But then, freedom is not to be understood as "a wild ruffian license" for those revolutionary and dishonest men who have recently disgraced several parts of Europe by horrible assassinations and the destruction of property. Those worthless beings whose life is idleness, and their sole industry incitement to crime, which they have not themselves the courage to commit, should be sought out quickly, and put down by the strong arm of the law. No false sentiment of sympathy should hesitate in stamping out such a terrible-plague spot as Communism, and its remorseless agent—the assassin.

The great battle for "Liberty of Conscience" in this country—the battle of the Reformers against Mary Tudor; of the Catholics against Elizabeth; of the Puritan against Charles the First; of the Independent against the Presbyterian, began at the memorable moment when Sir Thomas More refused to bend, or to deny his religious convictions at the command of that despotic monarch, Henry VIII. Yet, after all, Henry Tudor did not persecute conscience to the cruel and merciless extent pursued by his daughter, Elizabeth.

It is well known that the Quakers, or Society of Friends, were the first community since the Middle Ages who disowned all destructiveness in their religious precepts. How cruelly this peaceable sect has been persecuted the history of this country and of the British Colonies furnishes ample details. Under the government of Oliver Cromwell and Charles II. the Quakers were "penned" by hundreds in gaols—such as the fever dungeons were in those times. The much misrepresented James II. assured the Hon. Mr. Bertie, that he had released *one thousand two hundred and thirty*

Quakers, confined in different English gaols at the time of his accession.*

A few words as to Ireland during the days of persecution and proscription for religious opinions. The penal laws enacted against the Irish Catholics were, if possible, more despotic, cruel, and unnatural than anything devised by John Knox and his followers in Scotland. One of the Irish penal statutes decreed, that if the son of a Catholic became a Protestant, he could *disinherit the father, mother, brothers, and sisters.* A law to encourage the unnatural son to rob and disinherit the father and mother has no precedent in the history of nations—civilised or otherwise. Yet such was one of the statutes enacted for the "growth of Protestantism in Ireland." The late Foundling Hospital in Dublin was instituted for the same purpose; also the Blue Coat School. In 1709, Lord Wharton, then Viceroy of Ireland, introduced and passed a law by which the estates of "Irish Papists should descend *by right to their most distant Protestant relatives.*"†

A Puritan, whose opinions are sufficiently hostile to the Irish and their religion, thus describes the state of the Catholics about the time of Lord Wharton's "experiment in governing," or, as Swift put the problem, "*mis*-governing Ireland." "The Penal Code" (says the author of Political

---

* State Papers of the reign of James II. For a series of shocking as well as revolting revelations as to the *flogging and imprisonment of men and women for their religious opinions,* of the Quaker community, in New England, refer the reader to George Bishop's "History of the Sufferings of the People known in Massachusetts, and other Parts of America, as Quakers." Printed in 1661. This valuable work represents with stern truth the persecutions practised by the Protestant Colonists against Quakers and other Dissenters. The narrative seems incredible, but it is fully authenticated by the records of the Colonies and the papers deposited at the British Museum.

† Records of the Irish Parliament for 1709.

Catholicism), "whatever may have been the causes that produced it, was devised *to extinguish an ancient gentry, to dislocate all the relations of social life, to poison the fountains of domestic peace, to beggar and barbarise the people.* * * * The property of the father was often, by form of law, surrendered to the apostacy of the son. And the houseless priest, too, depended for shelter on the merciful protection of his Protestant neighbour."*

It is impossible to disprove the facts of history with regard to the penal laws enacted against Irish Catholics, or the cruelty with which they were executed. The authorities upon this subject are many and undeniable.† For upwards

---

* There are many noble instances recorded of the spirit in which some Irish Protestants acted towards their Catholic countrymen during the penal laws. In 1813, a barber, named Richard Hill, died in Clonmel, at a very advanced age. During the period when a Catholic could not by law execute a lease for land, the statute was evaded by the Protestant landlord and his Catholic tenant, by having the covenant drawn up and executed in the name of Richard Hill ; and, as I have been informed, at one time leasehold property, to the amount of some thousands, were enjoyed by Catholics through the action of this honest Protestant barber. A volume might be written on the generous conduct of some Irish Protestants during the evil doings inflicted on Ireland by *the English penal laws.* I regret to add that the Catholics, in some instances, were ungrateful to their faithful Protestant friends. The barber died a poor, but an honest man.

† See Statutes of the Irish and English Parliament against Papists ; Records of Dublin Castle ; Carte's Life of Ormonde ; the Correspondence and Evil Deeds of the Irish Viceroys from the reign of Elizabeth down to George II. ; the Plantation of Ulster ; Oliver Cromwell's Campaigns in Ireland ; the Results of the Prince of Orange's Invasion ; Primate Boulter's Life and Times ; Plowden's History of Ireland ; Scully's History of the Irish Penal Laws, and their debasing effects upon the people ; The Rise and Fall of the Irish Nation ; Prendergast's Irish State Papers ; Leckie's recent works upon Ireland ; Daniel O'Connell's Memoir of Ireland ; Musgrave's History of Ireland (an ultra-Protestant work, full of self-gratulatory proofs of my proposition) ; and many other narratives which so fatally manifest the renegade intolerance of the " English civilizers of Ireland—the men who are set down by some writers as having carried the Gospel light to the

of two hundred years the history of the Irish Catholics presented an unbroken course of persecution and debasement. As I have already stated, Plowden, an English lawyer, had to "go into exile," in the reign of George III., for having fearlessly written an honest historical statement as to the condition of Ireland under the various sections of Reformers who represented English interests in that country. It is a stigma and a shame upon the memories of such law-makers, and it is a poor tribute to truth to institute a defence for enactments so unchristian. An illustrious English statesman of the last century describes the penal laws which were enacted "against Irish Papists as a code the most cruel and debasing that ever entered into the perverted imagination of man." A notable Irish judge, within the last twenty years, publicly excused the authors of the penal laws, by stating that "the Protestant party passed those laws *in self-defence*."*
For a general answer to this characteristic assertion of the late Chief Justice Whiteside, I especially desire to refer my readers to the "Tracts on the Popery Laws," by Edmund Burke. And further, History—speaking with the omnipotence of Truth itself—triumphantly contradicts the allegations of the Irish Chief Justice.

Let it be remembered that there had been *no burnings at the stake in Ireland* to be made as an excuse for retaliation. It is needless for me to repeat, that I abhor even the idea of seeming to defend the English burnings in Queen Mary's reign—not her work, but her Councils.

benighted Celts." Much information has been given on the working of the penal laws in England, by a series of contemporary narratives published by Father Morris, under the title of "Troubles of Our Catholic Forefathers."

* Lecture by Lord Chief Justice Whiteside, before the Christian Young Men's Club in Dublin, on the "Life and Times" of Dr. Johnson's "inspired idiot," Oliver Goldsmith.

Upon the accession of George II. the Irish Catholics, who were then both socially and politically in a degraded condition, attempted to lay their case before the new King. The party of persecution became alarmed at such an appeal being made to the monarch. Primate Boulter, one of the most intolerant officials connected with the Church party in Ireland, at once protested against any petition being presented to the Sovereign from "*the rebellious and treacherous Irish Papists.*" The fact of such an address "being proposed by any party in the State," remarked the affrighted prelate, "*is an acknowledgment of the existence of a people whom the British constitution utterly ignores.*"* The Boulter party continued to misrule Ireland, and the English Parliament were quite indifferent as to the consequences. At a subsequent period, the "dapper little King," as George was sometimes styled, unintentionally exclaimed, in relation to the French victory at Fontenoi, "Cursed be the laws that have robbed me of such subjects" (the Irish). Yet the King feared to grant "Liberty of Conscience and Equality" to his Irish Catholic subjects. So England continued to degrade and dishonour herself by upholding a system of tyranny the most cruel and sanguinary ever practised by a civilised nation on a weaker race, for merely seeking the freedom of conscience and the rights of citizenship.

I here quote a passage from Tierney's valuable edition of Dodd's "Ecclesiastical History," which Dean Hook heartily welcomes as the "outpouring of regret for the Past, and a text for Charity amongst all creeds in the Future":—

"As to the number and character," observes the Rev. Mr. Tierney, "of the sufferers in Mary's reign, certain it is that no

---

* Primate Boulter's Political Correspondence, Vol. I.; Despatches of Lord Carteret from Dublin Castle to the English Council at Whitehall.

allowance can relieve the horror, no palliatives can remove the infamy, that must for ever attach to those proceedings. The account of real victims is too great to be affected by any partial deductions. Were the catalogue limited to a few persons, we might perhaps pause to examine the merits of each individual; but when, after the removal of every doubtful or objectionable name, a frightful list of not lower than two hundred remains, we can only turn with horror from the blood-stained page, and be thankful that such things have passed away."

I have now nearly done with this special subject as to Queen Mary's reign, and have freely expressed my opinions upon the religious persecution and proscription in the Past. But I cannot help appealing to the sense of justice of the vast number of readers who have been hitherto misled by prejudice, unconscious, or dishonest writers, to reflect that, in reality, religion had nothing whatever to do with the atrocities of antagonistic interests; that sacred watchwords were abused as the shibboleth of mutual outrage by men who, from the outset, had discarded the commands of the Divine and Merciful Founder of what ought to have been the creed of all—a creed of Charity, Tolerance, and Brotherly Love. Human force should never be used in the cause of religion: God's Truth comes, *Divino afflatu*, from Heaven. To act oppositely is a Mahometan custom, now happily unimitated by Christians.

CHAPTER XIII.

LAST DAYS OF QUEEN MARY.

In the autumn of 1558, the reign of Queen Mary was hastening to a close. Her health had been in a precarious condition for years, and now she was afflicted with "frequent and obstinate maladies." Tears no longer afforded her relief from a depression of spirits, and the repeated loss of blood, caused by "Sangrado" physicians, had rendered her pale, languid and emaciated. The exiles from Geneva, by the number and virulence of their libels, kept her in a constant state of fear and irritation, and, to crown all, came the loss of Calais. "If my breast is opened after death," observed the Queen to her ladies, "you will find the name of Calais written on my heart." It is not generally known that Calais sent two representatives to the English House of Commons. This ancient town had frequently been the hotbed of English sedition. The "King Maker," Warwick, concocted many of his schemes in Calais, for the establishment and overthrow of the Houses of York and Lancaster. Henry the Seventh was likewise aided in his invasion of England by the people of Calais, who "gloried in plots and sedition." In the Cathedral of Calais is to be seen a picture of the Duke of Guise expelling the English garrison from that town. The picture is on a grand scale, the figures being as large as life.

It is said that, during her last illness, Queen Mary edified everyone around her by her gentle manners, her piety, and her resignation to the will of Providence. While on her death-bed the Council were perpetrating the most cruel crimes in the name of religion. Several persons were punished with the pillory for falsely reporting that the Queen was dead. A woman named Alice Driver was committed to the flames by the Marquis of Winchester for heresy. Other punishments of a degrading character were inflicted upon women for the expression of religious opinions. Those women were fanatics, and in some cases dangerous lunatics; but the government took little heed of their victims' condition of mind. When in health, and able to look after public affairs, the Queen was always foremost in her desire to sustain the privileges, the honour, and the happiness of her own sex. Many of the ladies in attendance upon her were the wives and daughters of notable Reformers. Those ladies had no reason to complain of the "rights of conscience" being invaded by their Sovereign. The Cecils, the Bacons, the Herberts and the Grays bear testimony to these simple facts. Such was the state of things whilst the government of the country was in the Queen's hands, although during the reign of her brother the Princess Mary was the victim of the most unmanly and cowardly persecution on account of her religion.

When the royal physicians declared that the Queen's case was hopeless, her Court was quickly deserted. Of this sudden change of feeling she never complained. The sudden admirers of Elizabeth flocked to Hatfield House, where Sir William Cecil was arranging matters to meet the great event expected daily. The hand of death was on the Queen throughout the 16th of November. Still she was composed, and even cheerful. King Philip advised Mary to make the usual legal process of recognizing Elizabeth as her successor; a proposition which Count Feria states, the dying Queen received with satisfaction. The Countess Feria was the medium through whom the royal sisters communicated at this time. Pomeroy, who was a contemporary, states that it was remarked by "many people as very ill-natured and unsisterlike for Elizabeth to absent herself from the death-bed of her sister." Lord Montague "believed that Elizabeth wished, above all things, to see her sister, who had been a mother to her in childhood." "Cecil," writes Montague, "dreaded such a meeting; pledges and vows between the dying and the living might not promote his schemes as to the future. He therefore advised the Princess *not* to go to her sister, and Elizabeth complied with his request." Lord Montague was in a position to learn much of what was passing at Hatfield and St. James's. Judging by the private movements of the Princess Elizabeth about this time, she had no desire to see the Queen. Cecil could throw no obstacles in her way if she had the loving wish for a farewell visit to a dying sister "who had been a mother to her in childhood." Miss Strickland states that, "though much has been asserted to the contrary, the evidences of History prove that Elizabeth was on amicable terms with Queen Mary at the time of her death, and for some months previous to that event." The "positive assertions" of Historians have in too many instances proved untrue. Miss Strickland offers no explanation as to why Elizabeth was absent from the couch of her dying sister, "with whom she was on amicable terms." In fact, all "the surroundings of the case" are most conclusively against Elizabeth in this delicate matter. Her confidential notes to Sir Nicholas Throckmorton—a concealed rebel—during her sister's last illness, further demonstrate the sisterly feeling which moved her "at that exact time."

Noailles, in his secret despatches to the French Court,

draws a melancholy picture of the grief and despondency of Queen Mary for the absence and neglect of Philip. He writes: "She often sat alone for hours, crying and sobbing. She wrote numerous letters to her husband, reproaching him for his conduct to her. And again, in a fit of passion, remarked to her ladye-friend that it would lessen the dignity of the English Queen if she sent such letters to Philip. 'I feel' (she said), however, *as a woman, and a neglected wife, for I loved my husband with enthusiasm.*' Whilst in these gusts of anger she destroyed many of her long epistles to her faithless and cold-hearted husband."

The execution of Lady Jane Dudley (Gray), will long remain a stain upon the memory of Queen Mary. Yet the broken-hearted Queen had her own inner grief—a grief which none save a wife can adequately realise.

On the morning of the execution, Jane wrote the following sentence in one of her prayer-books: "*If my fault deserved punishment, my youth, at least, and my imprudence, were worthy of an excuse. God and posterity will show me favor.*"

Miss Strickland describes Lady Jane as the noblest character of the Tudor lineage.*

Whilst Lady Jane Dudley was confined in the Tower, the Queen issued a special order that the quality and quantity of food provided for her, and her two lady companions, should be "of the description fit for the establishment of a nobleman." The sum paid for the maintenance of Lady Jane and her two domestics was £6 13s. 4d. per week, equal to £27 of our present currency. The Duke of Northumberland's allowance was £6 16s. 8d. per week; and two of his own

---

* In the second volume (p. 471) of the Historical Portraits of the Tudor Dynasty, the reader will find a brief Memoir of Lady Jane Dudley; her speech from, and the scene upon, the scaffold, from an original MS.

servants to attend upon him. Sir John Gates, Sir Thomas Palmer, and the young Dudleys, had smaller sums per week, and each had the attendance of a servant. Bishop Ridley received seventy shillings per week, and the attendance of two servants."* The treatment of political prisoners in the Tower during Mary's reign presents a remarkable contrast with the times of Elizabeth, when the rack was in operation daily, and the gates of the Tower "garnished with the heads of public men."

I now approach the death-scene of Queen Mary. On the night of the 16th of November, 1558, the faithful ladies of her Highness never left her; she slept little. Every half hour one of her chaplains read some pious prayers, concluding with the Litany. At four of the clock on the morning of the 17th, twelve priests celebrated Mass in different apartments of the Palace; about the same period the Queen received *extreme unction*; a few minutes later, Mass was offered up in the royal chamber. The remarkably strong voice of the Queen became faint; yet it was clear and distinct. "Glory, honour, and praise be to the Holy Trinity," were her words, just as the priest approached the temporary altar. After a pause, the Queen said—"The end is now near." She bade her friends a long farewell. She kissed Jane Dormer; and Susan Younge, who had been one of her household for many years. The Queen looked lovingly around upon the group. She spoke no more. Her devoted women were prostrate on the floor; the Mass proceeded. At the raising of the Host, the Queen, clasping her hands, her eyes uplifted to Heaven, expired without a moan.†

---

* MS. quoted in Stephenson's State Papers of Mary's reign.
† The Queen died in the old Palace of St. James, near Whitehall.

When the physician, in a faltering accent said, "the Queen is gone," a moan of sorrow was heard within the Royal chamber, which was quickly taken up by the crowd of faithful domestics who were kneeling at the door. Many of those devoted followers of Mary Tudor were Protestants —current believers—who stood by their Royal mistress to the death, and subsequently vindicated her honour against the slanders of Sir William Cecil's hired traducers.

I must again intrude the name of Cecil in this death-chamber scene. Whilst Sir William Cecil was privately slandering his Sovereign, he appeared regularly in the parish church of Wimbledon, accompanied by his wife, Lady Mildred; and on several occasions "made confession to a pious priest at the said church, and then and there received Holy Communion in the manner and spirit of the Church of Rome, known in divers parts of the world as the Catholic Church."*

The above statement is corroborated by Dr. Nares, one of the biographers of Sir William Cecil. Several of the Reformers connected with Queen Mary's Council went repeatedly to confession and communion at Wimbledon Church. The deluded Queen believed those men to be pious Catholics. In a preceding chapter I have referred to the sincerity of Cecil's Catholicity.

Dr. Whyte, Bishop of Winchester, and Lord Montague were present at the Queen's death.

By her "last will and testament," Queen Mary dealt almost exclusively with benevolent institutions—"benevolence for the love of God—benevolence for the Honour and the Glory of the Blessed Trinity." The poor old soldier was also an object of the Queen's sympathy.

* State Papers of Queen Mary's reign, in the British Museum.

"And forasmuch," she says, "as there is no house or hospital specially ordained and provided for the relief and help of poor and old soldiers—namely, of such as have been hurt or maimed in the wars and service of this realm, the which we think both honour, conscience and charity willeth, should be provided for ; and therefore, my mind and will is, that my executors shall, as shortly as they may after my decease, provide some convenient house within or nigh the suburbs of the city of London, the which house I would have founded and created, being governed with one master and two brethren ; and I will that this hospital be endowed with manors, lands and possessions, to the value of 400 marks yearly."

The Queen recommended that good rules and ordinances should be made for this hospital by her executors ; and "specially I would have them respect the relief, succour, and help of poor, impotent and aged soldiers, chiefly those that be fallen into extreme poverty, and have no pension or other living."

Mary devoted her jewels, and every kind of property, to the payment of her debts by privy seal, and the debts of her father and brother, which seem to have hung very heavily on her mind. She devoted about £2,000 in all to the re-foundation of the convents of Sion, Shene, and the Observants—for works of charity and relief of the poor, and the support of the Savoy hospital. This hospital was founded by Henry VII., and confiscated by his son Henry ; re-established by Mary, and again diverted from the benevolent intentions of the founders by Elizabeth.

One passage in the will is extremely interesting—namely, the Queen's desire to be united in death with her "dearly beloved and virtuous mother, Queen Katharine :"—" And, further I will," she says, "that the body of my most dear and well-beloved mother of happy memory, Queen Katharine, which lieth now buried at Peterborough, shall, within as short a time as conveniently it may after my burial, be removed, brought, and laid nigh the place of my sepulture; in which place I will my executors to cause to be made honourable tombs for a decent memory of us."

The delicate request was never complied with by Elizabeth; in fact every clause of the will was violated. And still the biographers of Elizabeth proclaim her as " *a high-minded and honourable woman.*"

The Queen left a jewel to Philip to keep for " her memory," also various presents to her ladies. Her faithful servants were recommended to the " loving consideration of her successor." Several of the " faithful servants " subsequently *perished from want.*

Queen Mary built the public schools in the University of Oxford, but in a style more suited to her poverty than love of learning. They were afterwards taken down and rebuilt, yet the University remembers her in the list of its benefactors. She likewise granted the establishment on Bennet's Hill, near St. Paul's, to the learned body of heralds, and it is to this day their college.

Fuller says :—" Queen Mary hated to equivocate, and always was what she appeared, without dissembling her judgment or conduct for fear or flattery from any man." Camden remarks that Mary was "a princess never to be sufficiently commended of all men for her pious demeanour and her commiseration towards the poor." " It may be affirmed without contradiction or panegyric," writes Collier, " that the Queen's private life was all along strict and unblemished. Religion was uppermost with her, and she valued her conscience above her crown." Echard avers that " Mary was a woman of strict and severe life, who allowed herself few of those diversions belonging to courts, and was constant at her devotions." A distinguished writer, whose essays some forty years ago excited much attention for their thoughtful research and simple eloquence, without mentioning Elizabeth, draws an unmistakable contrast between the sisters, whilst treating only of Mary. He writes:—" In a word, all was done (in Mary's reign) openly, and by the advice and direction of the legislative power, without any undue interference. She gave no ambiguous answers when questioned about her religion before she ascended the throne; never fomented nor encouraged rebellion; did not amuse the neighbouring princes with sham treaties of marriage; never assisted rebels abroad to rise against their lawful sovereigns; entertained no favourites at court, to the prejudice of her reputation; did not keep the dignities of the Church in her hands for her own convenience; nor invade the revenues of its episcopacy by diminishing their sees, or exchanging their manors for others of inferior value. That she possessed great fortitude is evident from the many attempts that were made to shake her constancy in her faith, both in her father's life-time and that of her brother. To her father, as far as her conscience permitted, she was ever dutiful and respectful; to Edward, she represented that he had neither years, experience, nor as yet authority, to alter the religion of his ancestors. To the bishops and the clergy, who were sent to change her belief, she answered that a year or two before they were of a different opinion as to religion, and she did not know what new lights they had received since, or by what authority they preached their innovations." "The greatest blot on the character of Queen Mary," writes Lingard, " is her long and cruel persecution of the Reformers."*

The rich mass of documents edited by Sir Francis Madden and Mr. Tytler are in direct opposition to the character of Queen Mary as drawn by our English historians. Miss Strickland believes that " Bloody Mary " was a character drawn to suit popular prejudice. The late Canon Kingsley

---

* Lingard, Vol. V., p. 526.

lamented that "our histories were *so overlaid with lies, that it was impossible to arrive at facts.*" Dr. Maitland, a very eminent authority, and an ornament to the Church of England, has frequently warned the student of history, and his readers, that the question of "*authorities is a very grave one indeed.*" Hugo, Blunt, Brewer, and the calendarers of State Papers—foreign and domestic—are unanimous in their verdict against the misrepresentation of "character and facts" to be found in the books so long received as histories of England. Dean Hook is, of course, far from accepting the truthfulness of our old histories concerning Henry VIII., Edward, Mary, and Elizabeth. The Dean, like Maitland, "loved to ramble" amongst State Papers, and, perhaps, more important still, the records of what really occurred in those terrible times. He makes many remarkable statements, in his voluminous works, as to the falsification of some, and the ignorance of other historical writers upon the Tudor dynasty. "The history of the reigns of Edward VI., and of Queen Mary," writes Dean Hook, "*remains to be written.* The materials for such history are many of them at hand, and from the Venetian archives we may expect an increased supply. The Puritan by his hatred of Romanism, and the infidel by his detestation of Christianity, give only *ex parte* statements, and no one has ventured to refute them except Dr. Maitland."*

I agree with Dean Hook, that Queen Mary's Council was composed of some very bad men. The Dean, however, makes frank admissions as to the statesmen who governed under Edward VI., when he says:—"*Worse men than Somerset and Northumberland, Mary's ministers, could scarcely have been, though Somerset has been handed down to us in the character of*

* Archbishops of Canterbury, Vol. VIII., p. (note) 236.

a saint."* In another passage Dean Hook observes.—"The truth is that the Reformation was seriously damaged by the gang of unprincipled men, including Somerset and Northumberland, who had formed the Council of Edward VI."

There is no record extant by which posterity can fairly judge of a tendency to mercy on the part of the Queen's Council. In this respect the ministers followed the policy of their predecessors in office. The Queen's memorable charge to her judges was decidedly in favour of mercy in its most equitable form. A line, however, must be drawn between the actual offenders against the established religion of the country, and those who were up in arms against the Queen's authority as a monarch, and likewise the men who preached sedition and revolution. The words uttered at a far subsequent period by the victim of the triumphant Puritan rebels, are, if possible, more applicable to the great majority of the alleged martyrs of Mary's time. Here are the remarks of Charles I., carefully noted down by that eminent lawyer and statesman, Lord Clarendon:—"*The mask of religion,*" says the King, "*on the face of rebellion will not serve to hide some men's deformities.*" Very true!

Canon Dixon's portrait of Queen Mary when Princess is worthy of consideration, although few English writers seem inclined to do justice to the memory of that unfortunate Princess and her mother:—

"King Henry and his Council were for some time employed in the regulation of the household of Katharine of Arragon and her daughter Mary. Those unhappy ladies were treated with a barbarity which moved the pity of Europe. The repudiated wife of Henry was maintained with a parsimony which almost equalled the destitution into which Wolsey was allowed to fall after his

---

* Archbishops of Canterbury, Vol. VII., p. 322.

political overthrow. Removed from one prescribed residence to another, Queen Katharine's actions spied, her servants harassed; persecuted about the title which she refused to resign; often insulted by the ruffians whom her husband chose to convey his mandates to her, the once joyous and beautiful daughter of Grenada,* languished the remnant of a life of matchless dignity and patience. In the interval between her divorce and her death she beheld her dearest friends perish violently in the rage of the revolution which had cast her from the throne. But her fate seemed almost preferable to that which befell her daughter.

"To describe the particulars of the treatment which Mary Tudor received from her father belongs rather to the censurer or the panegyrist of King Henry than to the Historian of the Church of England; but it may be observed that the sufferings which the Princess Mary underwent developed the nobler qualities of her nature into a sort of morbid intensity. *Her nature was one of strong affection. She let her love go forth whither it was drawn, and had no power to recall it.* When her father made her a nursery-governess to the infant Elizabeth, whom she was to call *princess, but not sister*, neither that menial degradation, nor the insolence of her step-mother (Anna Boleyn), could check the attachment which she formed to her helpless charge. But the great object of her love was her mother. * * * So long as her mother lived, she was inflexible in refusing any concession which would have dishonoured her; maintaining her own legitimacy and her right to the rank of her birth. But that mother had told her to obey the King's commands.

"And after her mother's death, we find the Princess bowing to the threats of Lord Crumwell." †

---

* I refer the reader to Vol. I., pp. 3-12, of the "Historical Portraits of the Tudor Dynasty," for a personal description of the Princess Catalina (Katharine), her public entry into London, her wedding, and "quickly followed" widowhood.

† State Papers of Henry VIII., Vol. I., p. 459; Canon Dixon's History of the Church of England from the Abolition of the Roman Jurisdiction, Vol. I., p. 178.

I cannot omit Mr. Froude's portrait of Queen Mary. The reader, who, by this time, has seen enough of the preceding misrepresentations of history, can now form some idea of what really occurred during Queen Mary's disastrous reign. Mr. Froude writes in these words:—

"No English Sovereign ever ascended the throne with larger popularity than Mary Tudor. The country was eager to atone to her for her mother's injuries, and the instinctive loyalty of the English people towards their natural Sovereign was enhanced by the abortive efforts of Northumberland to rob her of her inheritance. She had reigned little more than five years, and then descended into the grave *amidst curses deeper than the acclamations which had welcomed her accession.*"

In another passage Mr. Froude says:—

"The Queen had lived, up to her accession, *a blameless, and, in many respects, a noble life;* and few men or women have lived less capable of doing knowingly a wrong thing." And, again, Mr. Froude finds " symptoms of hysterical derangement, which leave little room for other feelings than pity."

"She descended into the grave *amidst curses deeper than the acclamations which had welcomed her accession.*"

I have no hesitation in stating that there are no State records, nor even one honest contemporary, to sustain this statement of Mr. Froude. Neither is there any passage to be found in the secret despatches of the foreign ambassadors, *now* open to the Students of History, that can justify the above allegations. Does Mr. Froude hold the Sovereign accountable for the actions of her ministers whilst she was prostrated for two years by an agonising disease. If so, he is guilty of an act of injustice to the memory of Mary Tudor, which is unworthy of any Student of History, because it is cruelly unfair. Mr. Froude admits "the state of imbecility" to which the unfortunate Queen was reduced ; and, further, that she " showed symptoms of *hysterical derangement, which leave little room for other feelings than pity.*" *Pity !* So writes Mr. Froude.

But, notwithstanding the corruption which the national character had undergone, the people of England, of all the conflicting sects then extant, were still possessed of a manly generosity that no sectarian hate could extinguish. To curse a Queen, and a learned woman, under the circumstances attending the long illness and death, so marked by fortitude and Christian sentiment, was a spectacle which the nation, as such, never experienced. Even then, observant men perceived that the misrule of the country was not referable to the impotent Sovereign, but to the execrable ministers who dominated her and the realm.

The social condition of England at the period of the Queen's death comes next for consideration. From many sources I learn that the dwellings of the lower, and many of the middle classes, were very unlike what they had been at the accession of the Queen's father.* The revolution which had swept over the land, dispeopled and destroyed thousands of happy homes. The majority of the houses in Mary's reign were made of timber and clay, or of wattled sticks and mud. The words of honest Hugh Latimer, uttered in Edward's reign, are, if possible, more applicable to that of Queen Mary. He says :—" My dear countrymen and their families have become strangers to good 'belly-cheer.' England has ceased to be the land it was when I was a boy. Then the poorest man had a good feed daily of beef or fish, and if he liked it, a

---

* " Domestic Cleanliness " amongst the better class of people in Queen Mary's reign, was by no means an English characteristic. In Lodge's Illustrations of English History, Vol. I., p. 169, is to be seen an account of the " unclean habits of the nobles of the realm."

stoup of liquor, or some cow's milk. Now, my brethren, *all is changed*. And woe to the wicked men who have robbed the poor of their 'belly-cheer.'"

If the directors of the barbarous Smithfield fires permitted Latimer to live a few years longer, he would have witnessed pestilence and famine in its worst forms.

According to a statistical report of Mary's reign, there were, at her accession, forty thousand families in England who were largely endowed by the confiscated Monastic and Church property, and other lands which had been seized upon by Henry VIII., and the Government of his son, Edward. Upon the accession of Henry, in 1509, the national treasury was filled with chests of gold and silver. In fact, the wealth of the young King was immense. In 1529— scarcely twenty years later—Henry was not only penniless, but overwhelmed with debts, contracted at home and abroad. About this time the idea of the confiscation of Monastic property was entertained by some of Crumwell's clerical retainers. Polydore Vergil, in a letter to Dr. Fox, Bishop of Hertford, states that Crumwell "offered suggestions as to what great issue the property of the Monastic houses might be turned to by the King." It is certain that Wolsey intended to reduce the number of the religious houses; and amalgamated a few of them to promote education at Oxford. It is possible that he consulted Crumwell on the subject. A vast quantity of the Grand Inquisitor's secret papers are yet uncalendared.* In those volumes the plots and schemes for sustaining the policy of the Grand Inquisitor are set down in a most business-like fashion. Crumwell trusted no

---

* There are still some fifty volumes of Thomas Crumwell's secret correspondence and memoranda in the archives of the Record Office and the British Museum.

one about him. He brought his keys to his bed-room, and doubly locked the door. He dreaded the knife of some well-paid assassin. The headsman, however, interposed, and the monarch's desire for vengeance satisfied the hatred of Crumwell's numerous enemies.

At the period of the Queen's death, a fever, which was more destructive than the plague of former years, was depopulating the land. Cardinal Pole could find little fault with the clergy at this period, for they proved to the world by their actions that they had a Divine mission to fulfil, and from the horrors of the pestilential death-bed they shrank not, but went forth full of faith and of hope to meet the "King of Terrors." They discharged their duties to the sick and dying in a manner worthy of the best days of England's Catholicity—worthy of the Observant Fathers, or the heroic Carthusians at the time of the plague. One of my principal authorities for this statement is a distinguished and uncompromising opponent of the Catholic Church, but whose high sense of truth, justice, and charity compelled him to present a true picture of the clergy of England at the period above indicated. Dean Hook states "that the destruction among the clergy—it must be said to their honour—was especially great, and was occasioned by their having to place the ear so close to the mouth of the dying, in order that they might receive their last confession. Prelate and priest, physician and patient, fell alike, and the palace was not more exempt from the insidious entry of the disease than the cottage; two of the medical attendants upon the Queen were among the dying, and nearly half the bishoprics in England were vacant by the death of the diocesans."[*]

Volumes might have been written upon the heroic conduct

---

[*] Archbishops of Canterbury, Vol. VIII., p. 433.

of the English clergy at the various times that foreign pestilence visited this country. In 1348 the "Black Death" made sad havoc throughout the land. In one small district in Norfolk, out of twenty clergymen, sixteen fell victims to this dreadful scourge. The post of danger, however, was quickly filled up by the Benedictines, and others of the Regulars, who were always in the front rank of the Soldiers of the Cross, bearing their well-earned motto—"We labour for the salvation of souls, and the Glory and the Honour of the Great God."

The elements seemed to have likewise combined against the unhappy people of England. Shortly before the demise of Queen Mary, a number of churches were blown down by a fearful hurricane, which added to the misfortunes of the period; men, women and children were dashed against walls and trees, many suffering from broken limbs, others killed. In some parts of the country the rivers overflowed and desolated their immediate neighbourhood, and cattle and crops were carried away by the angry waters. In most cases a pestilence succeeded the famine; in this instance famine was the result, and not the cause. The storms had passed away, and sunshine once more appeared; the crops were ready for the sickle, but were left to rot on the ground, for labourers were not to be found to gather in the harvest; and among the few who crawled into the fields, the majority soon returned to their homes crying out for a confessor; the priests were quickly at the bedside of the dying; and the lamentations of the orphans were to be heard in every cottage home.

Corn and other provisions were at a dreadful famine price * throughout the chief part of Mary's reign, owing, it was said, to a series of inclement years and wet harvests.

---

* See the calculation of the price of corn, throughout four centuries, in Toone's Chronological History.

No friendly hand was raised to aid the people; the rich looked upon them "as a locust pest that should be swept away;" and swept away they were. Pity no longer held a place in the hearts of the well-to-do. This condition of affairs was to be found in every part of the kingdom. In a general point of view, it was the result of many years of misgovernment, heavy taxation, confiscation, despotic laws against the liberty of conscience; and, to crown all, a decline of trade, and the frequent visitation of foreign pestilence in every malignant form.

The abbeys and the convents which had so long succoured the people in times of pestilence or famine were now dismantled; their beneficent inhabitants hunted down, and whatever remained of them were to be seen wandering along the hedges and ditches, "appalling spectres from want and persecution, helpless and homeless."

Many strange omens were noted, and it was said by fanatic Puritans, "that the hand of God was stretched out against the country for re-establishing Popery again." The Catholic party retorted, and pointed to the scenes enacted by the Reformers in Edward's reign. Amongst the omens spoken of was that of the metropolitan river exhibiting so low an ebb that men might stand in the middle of the Thames, and walk from London Bridge to some distance below Billingsgate; the tide did not keep its course, a thing which the very oldest inhabitant had never witnessed.* As already recorded, the worst feeling existed between men of property and the poor. Robbery and assassination became frequent. The highway-

---

* Mackyn's Diary. There were three persons residing at this time (March 1558) in Southwark, whose ages were as follow:—Mary Tyrrell, 116 years old; Abraham Horne, 113; and Charles Hoveden, 110—all possessed of "good sight, and a show of memory of the deeds of other days."

men, who were unusually daring, invaded the public thoroughfares; the city merchants trembled for their accumulations; volunteer constables patrolled the streets of London at night, and having regained portions of the stolen property, "kept it as a remuneration for their *patriotic services.*" The "countrie parts were in a most disordered condition;" the parochial authorities did as they pleased; the roads were out of repair, and weary travellers had to swim or ford the rivers, the bridges over which had fallen into ruin. No nobleman, knight, or squire could travel without a troop of armed retainers. The social condition of the people was something similar to that of Edward's reign; yet they were not oppressed by the Government at this period. The wretched inhabitants looked upon "the new landlords" as the cause of all their misfortunes, and were determined to pursue them to the death. The landed proprietors adopted the old maxim of King Henry and Thomas Crumwell, "*Hang the saucy dogs from the nearest tree.*" Mistrust, hatred, and revenge constituted the social elements of the times, when suddenly, though not unexpectedly, Archbishop Heath, as Lord Chancellor of England, appeared upon the scene to announce to the Lords and Commons assembled, the accession of Elizabeth as Queen Regnant of England.*

In a few weeks another change of scene took place, when the masks were finally removed.

---

* The foreign ambassadors of this dismal period, especially the Venetian envoy, present in their despatches a picture of the misery, anarchy, and party feeling which prevailed in England, as by no means exaggerated. I refer to Stowe, Godwin, Tytler, Strype's Life of Sir Thomas Smythe, Noailles, Michele, Fox, Pomeroy, Burnet, and the State Papers of Mary's reign—all of which, more or less, confirm my statements.

CHAPTER XIV.

DEATH OF CARDINAL POLE.

CARDINAL POLE'S mission was suddenly brought to a close. Being confined to his bed at Lambeth Palace (November 17, 1558), he received intelligence of the demise of Charles the Fifth, and although the conduct of the Emperor had not been always friendly, they had been so often in direct communication with each other, that the Cardinal spoke of the death of the Emperor as that of an old friend. It was with deeper and with more sincere affliction that Pole heard that the condition of the Queen's health was hopeless. He saw that the cause of the Olden Faith was lost in England. This circumstance preyed upon him; his illness increased, yet his mind was clear, though sad, and he made preparation to meet his end. Suddenly, however, an attendant indiscreetly announced to him that the Queen was dead. The scene was most affecting. The Cardinal remained silent for a considerable time. His dear friend Priuli, and the Bishop of St. Asaph (Dr. Goldwell), were watching at his bed-side. He spoke at last, and with some firmness remarked that, "in the midst of so many, and great sorrows, he had most grievously to lament the Queen's death, yet by God's grace he enjoyed a most efficacious remedy by turning to that haven of Divine Providence which, throughout his existence, had ever calmed and consoled him under all public and private afflictions." He spoke with such vigour and readiness that he moved his friends to tears. He continued the conversation, remarking on the parallel between his own life and that of the Queen. He had "sympathised with her in the sorrows of her early life; he had shared in the troubles and anxieties occasioned by her elevation to the throne; they were not to be separated by death." For a quarter of an hour the Cardinal remained calm. Then another paroxysm came on. He ordered that the book containing the prayers said *in transitu* might be kept ready. He received the *Viaticum*, and desired to be brought before the altar, in the Palace chapel. Being unable to stand, he was carried between two of his faithful domestics. At the altar he bowed his head almost to the ground, and with many tears and sobs, repeated the *Confiteor*. He was again free from pain; Vespers were repeated, as usual. Two hours before sunset he heard the *Compline*. The end, he said, was come. He remarked that it was time for the commendatory prayers to be offered. While they were offered he fell asleep. From this sleep he never awoke.*

Reginald Pole survived the Queen twenty-two hours, and died in the fifty-eighth year of his age. According to his own desire, he was buried in St. Thomas's Chapel, in the Cathedral of Canterbury. The most exaggerated reports were circulated as to his great wealth; but it appears that his effects scarcely paid the current debts of the palace.

The moment Elizabeth heard of Pole's death, she sent Lord Rutland and Sir Nicholas Throckmorton to seize upon his effects for the Crown. Elizabeth was only *two days* Queen when she committed this indecent outrage upon the residence where her cousin Reginald lay dead. Amongst Pole's papers were to be seen three letters of Elizabeth's,

---

* The above account is derived from the private letters of two devoted Italian friends of the Cardinal.

acknowledging sums of money he privately sent her, and she expressed her "regard and gratitude to her good cousin."*

Count Feria, in his despatches to King Philip, states that Elizabeth informed him that she "considered Pole to be more of an enemy than a friend to her." And he adds: "The Princess spoke with unusual bitterness of the Cardinal, who was then on his death-bed." Her own letters contradict this statement in a very emphatic manner.

Roger Ascham states that immense distress existed in London, in Mary's reign, amongst householders "who had seen better days." The Cardinal gave large sums of money to relieve the "public distress.† He also caused his cooks to distribute provisions to three hundred people daily. In Canterbury, the milk of ten cows and a quantity of bread was given every morning to the poor, at the expense of Cardinal Pole." Shadwell, a Baptist preacher, states that the Cardinal gave the "belly cheer" as freely to the poor Protestants as he did to the Papists. "I saw him," writes Shadwell, "with his own hands, feed the poor Protestant women and their children. For a proud man of high rank, he was very humble in speaking to the poor; but when he held converse with great lords like the Earl of Pembroke, he was very 'stuck up,' and quite different. Forty years have passed away since I saw Cardinal Pole at Lambeth Palace, surrounded by a crowd of poor women and children. Methinks I see his handsome benevolent face before me still."

---

* See Throckmorton Papers; Letters of Dr. Whyte to Priuli; Goldwell's Correspondence; Lingard, Vol. V.

† In consequence of Pole's small means, and the bankrupt treasury of the English Queen, Pope Julian presented the Cardinal with three thousand ducats on his departure for England. Several of the Roman Cardinals and the French bishops also aided him. All the Catholic countries of Europe sympathised with Pole's mission, and King Philip made him a princely offering in gold.

The extract which I have made from Shadwell's quaint diary is modernized. Shadwell died at Antwerp, in the reign of Elizabeth. He was then eighty-five years old, still in the use of all his faculties. Having been concerned in one of the many plots to rescue the Queen of Scots, he narrowly escaped arrest, and the scaffold.

The contrast in charitable sentiment between the Anabaptist Shadwell and one of Elizabeth's noted prelates is worthy of consideration.

Edwin Sandys, subsequently Archbishop of York, hated Cardinal Pole "in death as he had in life." In a letter from Sandys to Bullinger, written a few weeks subsequent to the death of the Cardinal, he exulted over the change of scene at Lambeth Palace. "We have nothing to fear from Pole *now*, for 'dead men do not bite.'"* This passage requires no commentary; it conveys its own condemnation.

Cardinal Pole's hospitality was on a splendid scale, and, as I have just remarked, his benevolence to the poor, extensive; yet he was soon forgotten, both at Lambeth† and Canterbury. His natural temperament, however, could not descend to the effort of winning popularity. Like the Roman tribune, he had little faith in the professions of the "clamorous crowd," whose shouts have often betrayed even the patriot to forget his disinterestedness, and who would with similar levity acclaim the idol of the day as turn from and abandon him were he the victim of the morrow.

Reginald Pole was acquainted with almost every eminent Churchman, Lawyer and Statesman in Europe. The Univer-

---

* Zurich Letters, Vol. I.

† There remains still to be seen an interesting and well executed portrait of Cardinal Pole in his official robes in the grand dining-hall of Lambeth Palace.

sity of Paris held Pole in high esteem. Speaking of Gasparo Contarini, Pole affirms "that he was ignorant of nothing that the human intellect could by its own powers of investigation discover; and that nothing in him was wanting that the grace of God has revealed to the human soul." In the Venetian State Papers, the name of Cardinal Pole occupies a prominent place.

In the great Venetian library are deposited a number of letters and other important documents, which may form, at some future period, material for a new biography of Reginald Pole, which will place him in a different light from that hitherto set forth by party writers. Both Catholic and Protestant historians have misrepresented Pole's mission to England. The secular clerics, who were his contemporaries, "had no particular regard for the Cardinal." The reason was obvious. A large number of the secular clergy, who were in England at the arrival of Pole, had been for many years under the vacillating and corrupt sway of Cranmer, or prelates who nearly followed his mode of action. Pole was the idol and the hope of the Religious Orders. But the attempt to reconstruct the ancient citadel came too late.

As an illustrious English Catholic, the name of Reginald Pole ranks with that of Sir Thomas More, of whom Mr. Froude writes: "Never was there a grander Christian victory over death than in that last scene lighted with its lambent humour."

CHAPTER XV.

ACCESSION OF ELIZABETH.

THE accession of Elizabeth may be considered the second, and more permanent, establishing of Protestantism in England. At this opening stage of Elizabeth's career as a monarch, I would call the reader's attention to two important questions, first,—the delicate matter of Legitimacy, and next, the religious opinions held by the new Sovereign. English historians are almost silent as to what were the Lady Elizabeth's claims to the throne of this kingdom. If Archbishop Cranmer's divorce of Anna Boleyn from King Henry be considered correct, then Elizabeth had "*no peculiar or hereditary rights.*" And, apart from Cranmer's divorce of Anna Boleyn, let it be remembered, that the clandestine marriage of Elizabeth's father and mother took place *before*, and *not after* the judgment against the validity of Queen Katharine's connubial rights with Henry. Therefore, according to Canon and Civil Law, Elizabeth was undoubtedly illegitimate. The grave questions to be answered are these: "Had Henry VIII. *the power to bequeath the crown to one who was not born* in wedlock?" And next, "Could the Parliament of England legally and constitutionally declare such a bequest *lawful?*" In fact, there is no precedent for Elizabeth's "Royalty" in the constitutional history of European Sovereigns. William of Normandy, although a bastard, held what the sword had won for him, and there was no party in the State powerful enough to overthrow that despotic usurper. Elizabeth, with the farseeing cunning of the Politician, raised a religious war-cry to uphold a throne to which she had no rightful claim. A careful examination of all the public actions of her long reign proves, beyond a doubt, that her Protestantism was that of the Politician, and not the Christian believer. She used the most potent faction to sustain her position as a monarch.

It might be asked—what opinion has the Protestant party formed upon Cranmer's judgment against Anna Boleyn. Was it a Spiritual or a Political decree? or, whatever the King commanded? Posterity have been assured that Elizabeth was a great Protestant heroine—" A Nursing Mother to the Church of England." Therefore, it is necessary to know what were her claims to Legitimacy? or, was she to become the exception to the long roll of English monarchs whose honourable parentage stood unchallenged for centuries?

" Whatever opinion men might entertain of the legitimacy of Elizabeth, she ascended the throne without opposition."* So writes Lingard. A combination of circumstances led to the unopposed succession of Elizabeth. As a matter of course, the " new lords of the soil " were in her favour. Worldly interests, not the merits of creed, were at the bottom of all the intrigues of those times, and of this the reader will see much in the course of the historical inquiry here entered upon.

It is stated, upon the high authority of Camden, that Queen Mary often declared to Elizabeth that the daughter of James the Fifth, of Scotland, was her undoubted heir.† It is certain, however, that Queen Mary subsequently

---

* Lingard, Vol. VI., p. 1.
† See Camden's Introduction.

changed her opinions as to the succession. The matrimonial connection of the young Queen of Scots with France, and the ambitious designs of that country, made the English Queen and her Legitimate supporters hesitate in selecting the wife of a French Prince as Mary's successor. The conduct of France in Queen Mary's reign was selfish, dishonest, and, as a Catholic kingdom, most unjustifiable.

A very remarkable passage bearing upon Cranmer's conduct in relation to *his* divorce of Anna Boleyn, appears in Canon Dixon's " History of the Church of England from the Abolition of the Roman Jurisdiction." " For three years," observes Canon Dixon, " Archbishop Cranmer had been ministering oaths, issuing monitions, bidding prayers, and preaching sermons on behalf of the validity of that marriage and the legitimacy of the offspring born of the said marriage. The whole realm had been convulsed for three years, the Religious Orders had been shamefully persecuted, the new-invented treasons had surrendered liberty in that behalf; the noblest heads in England had rolled on the scaffold in relation to this divorce question; and now Cranmer was commanded to become the instrument of *undoing his own work*. The Archbishop was treated with short ceremony, or open contempt, by men whom he truly felt to be inferior to himself in everything but force and guile. Above all, Cranmer found himself the tool of the unscrupulous layman,* who, though a subject, held a higher office than the Primate. *What was to be the end of the degradation of the realm, and of Archbishop Cranmer himself?"* †

---

* The layman above referred to was Sir Thomas Audley, the Chancellor, and partner in Thomas Crumwell's iniquitous proceedings.

† Canon Dixon's History of the Church of England from the Abolition of the Roman Jurisdiction, Vol. I., p. 387.

Another Anglican cleric writes : "As regards Cranmer's personal character, he was vain, weak, heartless, and arrogant; vain of his position as the great man of Lambeth Palace, and the friend of the Sovereign; weak in servile submission to stronger wills than his own, as well as to flattering tongues and pens; heartless in the ruthless sacrifice of every man or woman, from Queen Katharine downwards, who stood in his way; arrogant to the last degree of insult towards Bishops Gardyner and Day. He was no theologian, as is shown by his dispute at Oxford. Indeed, it is very hard to look upon such a man as Cranmer otherwise than as one at whose door must be laid the guilt of many a slain body and *many a lost soul*."*

The proceedings of those times are scarcely credible, unless where vouched for by State Papers. It is a remarkable fact that the Queen procured an Act from the venal Parliament, recognising her as Sovereign, *without any allusion to her mother's marriage, or Cranmer's judgment against it*. The Statute declares Elizabeth "*to be rightly, lineally, and lawfully descended from the blood-royal of England.*" Sir William Cecil exhibited the possession of characteristic boldness in proposing such a measure to any legislative assembly. † But he thoroughly understood the men who composed the first Parliament of Elizabeth's reign, and their successors likewise.

The results of the Statute in question was soon felt in many directions. A gentleman named Labourne was hanged and quartered at Preston, for stating publicly that Elizabeth was *not* the lawful Queen, but only Elizabeth Boleyn; and

---

* Reformation of the Church of England, by the Rev. J. H. Blunt, Vol. II., p. 330.

† See Statute of Elizabeth for the " Royal recognition."

that Mary Queen of Scotland was the rightful Sovereign of England.*

NOTE.—It is a remarkable proof of the submissiveness of the English nation in those times, when a despotic family, whose claims to the Crown were questioned by the most eminent jurists in Europe, should have been permitted to remain in possession of the monarchy from 1485 down to 1603, a period of 118 years. Henry VII. was proclaimed King upon the field of Bosworth by the army, aided by an artful trick of the victor's kinsman, Sir William Stanley. When Richmond reached London, it was ascertained that an attainder was on the records against him, but the Parliament quickly set it aside. The Parliament of 1484 was remarkable for its thorough dishonesty. In the January of that year they passed an Act against the children of Edward the Fourth, declaring them to be all illegitimate; and also an attainder against Henry Earl of Richmond. These proceedings were taken at the suggestion of the usurper, known as Richard the Third. In a few months later the same Parliament declared Richmond to be the lawful Sovereign of this realm; and the children of Edward the Fourth to be legitimate. For some years preceding the fall of Richard, Henry VII. had been regarded as heir to the House of Lancaster, by the party attached to that aspiring family; yet the title of the House of Lancaster itself to the Crown was generally thought to be very ill-founded; besides, admitting the legality of the claims of the House of Lancaster, Henry was not the true heir to that family. His mother, Margaret, Countess of Richmond, was daughter, and sole heir of the House of Somerset, descended from John of Gaunt,

---

* Letter in Strype's Annals, printed by Parker; Records of Political Executions at Preston.

Duke of Lancaster; but the birth of the first of the Somerset line was well known to have been illegitimate, and consequently set aside. The title of the House of York was the most popular for Henry VII. to claim, through his marriage with the daughter of Edward the Fourth. Henry of Richmond, however, was more ambitious of reigning as the victor of Bosworth Field than as the son-in-law of Edward Plantagenet, or the illegitimate heir of the almost forgotten House of Somerset. The claims of Elizabeth Boleyn to the English Crown were immensely less than those of her grandfather, resting as they solely did, upon the conflicting judgment of Archbishop Cranmer and her father's will, most of whose behests were nullified by Somerset and his Council.*

There are still extant several papers in the handwriting of eminent English jurists on the claims of the Tudor family to the throne. Of course, those documents were carefully concealed till the demise of Elizabeth. The commentaries of learned monks, both in Spain and France, on the "monarchical claims of the House of Tudor," are almost unanimous in their decrees against Henry VII.

Notwithstanding the "political surroundings" of Mary Queen of Scots, she was undoubtedly the legitimate successor of her English cousin, Queen Mary. As I have remarked in Vol. II., p. 475, of this work, the Marquis of Dorset, the father of Jane and Catharine Gray, had a former wife (Lady Catharine Fitzalan), *alive for many years after the birth* of the above ladies, whose mother was the daughter of the Princess Mary,

---

* The reader will find Henry VII.'s claims to the Crown set forth and argued by the following notable authorities: Polydore Vergil; Rymer, tom. vii; Records of the Parliaments of Henry's reign; Coke's Insti.; Bacon in Kennet's Compleat History, p. 579; Hume (folio), Vol. III., p. 2-3; Sharon Turner. Vol. VII., p. 51; Lingard, Vol. IV., p. 262.

sister of Henry VIII., and wife of Charles, Duke of Suffolk. These facts were only known to "a few interested persons at the time." The more the case is investigated, the stronger appear the legal claims of Mary Stuart to the English Crown. Her claims rested upon the fact that she was the granddaughter of the Princess Margaret, the elder sister of Henry VIII., who was legally married to James IV. of Scotland; the issue of that marriage was a son, subsequently known as James V. of Scotland, who, by his second marriage with Mary of Lorraine, left an infant daughter, named Marie, to inherit his kingdom. According to this genealogy, Mary Stuart, the wife of the French Dauphin, stood in the Legitimate line for succession.

Next comes the claimant whom the "political expediency" of party had selected—known by courtesy as the Lady Elizabeth. In the first proclamation issued in Elizabeth's name by Sir William Cecil, he declares the "said Princess to be the *only right heir of blood and lawful succession.*" This was a bold statement to put forward in the face of the public records, and the *facts* with which his contemporaries were all so well acquainted. Courage is a necessary attribute to sustain the assertions of men of no principle. In this respect Cecil was equal to the occasion.

Mr. Froude is silent as to the legitimacy of Elizabeth. He informs his readers that she was the favourite daughter of Henry VIII.[*]

I cannot find Mr. Froude's statement borne out by any State Papers. During his long illness King Henry never sent for Elizabeth. We have, however, satisfactory proof that he had special interviews with his daughter Mary. On one occasion he besought the Princess "to be a mother as well as a sister

---

[*] Froude's History of England, Vol. VII., p. 3.

to her little brother Edward." The King did not name Elizabeth on this occasion, which is another proof that she was not his favourite daughter at that period.* Indeed, Elizabeth was no favourite with her father after the time of her mother's fall. It is true, that when Elizabeth was very young, she was much beloved by Anne of Cleves, who never, as alleged, made her a Protestant. Elizabeth also found favour with her third stepmother (Catharine Howard), who, being cousin-german to Anna Boleyn, took her young relative under her especial protection. On the day when Catharine Howard was publicly announced as the new Queen, she directed that the Princess Elizabeth should be placed opposite to her at table, because she was of her own blood and lineage.† With all the influence Catharine Howard exercised for a time at Court, over the whimsical Monarch, she was not able to prevail on him to repeal the Act of Parliament which described Elizabeth in most offensive words as illegitimate. The Statute in question was founded upon the solemn judgment pronounced by Archbishop Cranmer against the marriage of King Henry with Anna Boleyn. The Act of Parliament passed in June, 1536, against Elizabeth's legitimacy, was set forth at great length. It was *declared high treason in any one to say that the said Elizabeth was legitimate.*

Mr. Froude's impressions with regard to Queen Elizabeth's opinions, religious or worldly, are entitled to some attention. Mr. Froude observes:—

---

* In the second volume of this work (p. 248), I have made a special reference to the scene between the dying monarch and the Princess Mary. The interview in question, when taken in connection with subsequent events, is another proof of the immense deception practised upon the King at this time by Archbishop Cranmer and Lord Hertford, both of whom had taken no less than *twelve oaths*, at different times, "to carry out their Royal master's will, every line of which they afterwards violated.

† See Leti's Elizabeth. Leti is generally considered a trustworthy authority on the transactions of this particular period.

"Circumstances rather than preference had placed her (Elizabeth) originally on the side of the Protestants. Her connexion with them was political, and it was only when she needed their assistance that she acknowledged a *community of creed.* * * * * As Head of the Church, Elizabeth *claimed unrestricted jurisdiction in her own department, and the exclusive initiation of all proposed alterations.*"*

In page 542, Mr. Froude becomes more outspoken in his harsh criticism of a Sovereign, whom Miss Strickland, in a moment of enthusiasm, describes as the "*Nursing Mother of the Church of England.*" "For Protestantism," again writes Mr. Froude, Elizabeth *had never concealed her dislike and contempt.* She hated to acknowledge any fellowship in religion, either with Scots, Dutch, or Huguenots. She represented herself to foreign ambassadors *as a Catholic* in everything, except in allegiance to the Pope."

Although some modern historians may state their belief in the orthodoxy of Elizabeth, and others, their belief in her faith, foreign diplomatists had the caution not to believe overmuch in the frankness of the regal declarations—even though affirmed by adjurations. The Queen *was pious betimes, when not particularly annoyed,* but she was not, it must be admitted, so conveniently and perennially pious as her favourite Minister, Cecil. Elizabeth indited, it is known, some fragmentary prayers,† which possess an edifying tone. The piety is, however, as disjointed as the profession from the practice. I adopt the words of Mr. Froude without dissent—" Elizabeth's *character must be gathered from her actions.*"

When Archbishop Heath and the Council of the late

---

* Froude's History of England. Vol. XII, p. 124; Ibid, Vol. XII., p. 541.
† The prayer in question is printed in Strype's Annals, Vol. IV., p. 440.

Queen waited on Elizabeth at Hatfield, she received them courteously, but replied in a formal and studied discourse. She was "struck with amazement when she considered herself and the dignity to which she had been called. Her shoulders were too weak to support the burden; but it was her duty to submit to the Will of God, and to seek the aid of wise and faithful advisers. For this purpose she would in a few days appoint a new Council. It was her intention to retain several of those who had been inured to public business under her father, brother, and sister; and, if others were not employed, she would have them to believe that it was not through distrust of their ability or will to serve her, but through a wish to avoid that indecision and delay which so often arise from the jarring opinions of a multitude of advisers."*

The speech of the new Queen was well received, for she appeared earnest, and kindly to everyone, "taking leave of the deputation like a private lady."

Two days later (the 20th of November, 1558), Elizabeth held her first Council at Hatfield. The Council was composed of six Protestants and four Catholics. The four Catholics were men not much attached to their religion; and, in a political point of view, vacillating and avaricious, as subsequent circumstances proved. Lord William Howard was the Queen's uncle, Henry Sackville her cousin, the Earl of Arundel the romantic lover of "golden Eliza," and Paulet, Marquis of Winchester. These were the men who represented, or rather misrepresented, the spirit of the Catholics of England in the first administration of Elizabeth. The six Protestants who were destined to play so important a part in the future establishment of a "national religion" were—

---

* Nugæ Antiquæ, Vol. I., p. 66.

William Cecil, Nicholas Bacon, Henry John Parr, Francis Russell, Robert Dudley and Ralph Sadler. Francis Walsingham and Sir Thomas Smith had not at this period returned from their exile.

When the ministers and privy councillors were sworn, the Queen addressed William Cecil in these words :—

"Now, William Cecil, I give you this charge that you shall be of my Privy Council, and content yourself to take pains for me and my realm. This judgment I have of you, that you will not be corrupted by any manner of gift, and that you will be faithful to the State; and that without respect to my private will, you give me that counsel which you think best, and if you shall know anything necessary to be declared to me of secrecy, you shall show it to myself only, and assure yourself I will not fail to keep taciturnly therein, and therefore herewith I charge you."

As true as steel to this ordinance acted Cecil: he could bend; but his recoil against foe, man or woman, was fraught with death. He loved the Queen with fearsome lealty, and was faithful, because she realized his interest and embodied his wishes and ambition.

The Bishops were next presented to the Queen. She would not allow the venerable Archbishop Heath to kneel, on account of his great age. Stretching forth her hand to him to kiss, she said :—

"My very good Archbishop of York, I am happy to see you; and thank you cordially for the large amount of good nature you lately added to your loyalty. Be assured of the continued friendship of your Queen."

Tunstall, Bishop of Durham, and the Lord Abbot of Westminster (Feckenham), were also graciously received. Whyte, Bishop of Winchester, and the other prelates "did homage."

From the period of the accession in November, till January, no political or religious changes of any importance took place.

The coronation of the Queen was surrounded with difficulties. She did not desire to throw off the mask, or be in any way outspoken till she understood the strength of parties. The Reformers were thoroughly united at this juncture; the Papal party were, as usual, divided amongst themselves, each Catholic of position and rank looking only to himself; and the few honest men in their ranks who were courageous enough to express their opinions, soon reached a dungeon in the Tower or the Fleet. The great mass of the people who still adhered to the Olden Religion of England were terror-stricken, half-starved, servile, and debased; they made little opposition to the new religious principles propounded for them. The impassiveness or indifferentism produced by misery and oppression, naturally opened a wide gate for change in an untaught and mingled race, such as then inhabited London. The capital of the kingdom hailed the Queen as the champion of the Reformation. Nothing so resilient as human passion or suffering. The proclamation of a single redemption from even a supposed evil will excite sympathy or interest amongst the masses. The thoughtless are trustful, but doubly confident when they are profusely promised. And so the Elizabethan Government had a difficult task to keep down the fanatical mobs who assembled at Paul's Cross, crying out for "*a Mass priest to kill.*" Many priests received the usual treatment of the mob-law of the time; and, of course, there was no protection. And, sad to say, the actions of those street ruffians were instigated by Reformers who professed to be God-fearing men, amongst whom were Sewell and Sandys.

It is stated that Dr. Oglethorpe was the only bishop present at the Queen's coronation. Soames contends that all the prelates were present, and Dean Hook confirms this statement.* Another chronicler alleges that all the bishops were present, but only one took part in the ceremony. This is unlikely, as such a course would have been considered a personal insult to the Queen. Lingard gives a different account of the coronation. The bishops saw with surprise that Dr. Whyte, the prelate who presided over Winchester, had been imprisoned for his sermon at the funeral of Queen Mary.† Archbishop Heath received a warning to resign the seals of office with the title of Lord Keeper; but that which cleared away every doubt was a proclamation, forbidding the clergy to preach, and ordering the established worship to be observed "until consultation might be had in Parliament by the Queen and the three estates."‡ Alarmed by this proclamation, the bishops assembled in London, and consulted whether they could in conscience officiate at the coronation of a Princess, who, it was probable, would object to some part of the service as "ungodly and superstitious," and who, if she did not refuse to take, certainly meant to violate, that part of the oath which bound the Sovereign to maintain the liberties of the Catholic Church. The question was put, and was unanimously resolved in the negative.§ This unexpected determination of the prelates created considerable embarrassment to the Queen and her Council. Elizabeth attached much importance to the old Catholic ceremony of coronation, whilst her Puritan minister detested everything that in any form resembled Popery. "Friendly messages" were sent from the Queen to the bishops, whose replies were firm, yet most respectful. At length the Bishop

---

* Archbishops of Canterbury, Vol. IX.
† Wilkins Con., Vol. IV., p. 180.
‡ See Strype's Memorials, Vol. III., p. 278-280.
§ Lingard, Vol. VI.; Collier. Vol. VI.

of Carlisle volunteered his services. He, however, stipulated with the Queen that she should subscribe to all the old Catholic oaths and forms; and further to receive Holy Communion in one kind. Under those circumstances, and assisted by some dozen priests, the coronation of Elizabeth took place.

The hour of the Queen's reprisal was postponed. Oglethorpe had reason to regret the part he had taken at the coronation. Commencing to celebrate Mass in the Royal Chapel one morning, the Queen commanded him aloud "*not to elevate the Host in her presence under penalty of her severest displeasure.*" The Bishop replied, most respectfully, that his life was at the Queen's mercy, *but his conscience was his own.* Elizabeth, rising immediately after the Gospel, retired with her attendants.

Dean Hook claims Owen Oglethorpe as a Reformer. This statement is of little importance except so far as historical truth is concerned, for the Bishop of Carlisle proved himself subsequently to be a mean, shuffling personage, always seeking favours from the Court. Dean Hook states " that Dr. Oglethorpe admitted that 'the form and order of religion set forth in the reign of Edward VI. was nearer the practice of the Primitive and Apostolical Church than that which was formerly in England.'"* This alleged opinion of Oglethorpe is something like the learned Dean's theory as to "a *reformed* but not a *new* Church of England."

I have remarked in a preceding chapter, that upon the honest grounds of "Legitimacy" the Catholic party could never accept of Elizabeth as their Sovereign; but the Reformers were not actuated by any sentiment of this kind;

---

* Archbishops of Canterbury, Vol. IX., p. 151.

they required a political agent—bold and unscrupulous—to carry out their views, and in the daughter of Anna Boleyn they found a fitting and most powerful instrument. She nearly stamped the olden religion out of the land; yet to the end of her days she could never be reconciled to the married bishops; indeed, with respect to the clergy generally, the Queen's noted god-son observes, that " *cæteris paribus*, and sometimes *imparibus*, too, she preferred the single man before the married."*

For some time Elizabeth would not allow any irreverent speaking of the "sacrament of the altar;" that is, to enter into discussions respecting the Real Presence. She enjoined the like respectful silence concerning the intercession of saints; she likewise desired to retain the vestments, crucifix, candles, etc., in her private chapel. She laid stress and observance to the holy days of her own adoption; and observed the various fast days of the Catholic Church herself, and compelled the courtiers to do so. Of toleration, or the rights of conscience, she had as little feeling or understanding as any despotic prince or Puritan of her time. It was evident, however, that she had a secret dread of, and aversion to, the Puritan and Republican tendency of the so-called religious bodies who had embraced the teachings of Calvin; and she resolved at all hazards to check the growth of Calvinism in England. The Queen issued a "special command that John Knox was not to enter the realm."†

Notwithstanding the vigilant action of the Queen, Cecil, and Archbishop Parker, the Puritan party were increasing in numbers and in daring. With the self-consciousness of predestinarian pride, they seemed never afraid to give ex-

---

* Harrington's Brief Review.
† In subsequent chapters I shall enter upon the merits of John Knox.

pression to their opinions, however Republican or Puritanical their views.* It now, however, became the policy of Elizabeth to "further amend the Prayer-book of Edward's reign," by giving to it more of a Lutheran tone ; and it was for some time apprehended that she would cause the entire Confession of Augsburg to be received into it. The Queen would permit no "liberty of conscience ;" and the people were compelled to accept the religious system propounded by the Sovereign and her Council, which was one in every way approved of by the new owners of property in land. The reason was obvious.

Miss Aikin remarks, in relation to Elizabeth's vacillation in religion, and the part she assumed between parties, that she "exhibited neither enlargement of mind nor elevation of soul."

---

* See Neal's History of the Puritans in Elizabeth's reign.

CHAPTER XVI.

THE MARIAN BISHOPS.

At the death of Queen Mary the bishops were fully alive to the condition of religious affairs in England; the vacillation exhibited by the prelacy in Henry's reign disappeared, and the episcopacy were ready to "brave the anger of the Sovereign, and the terrors of the dungeon or the scaffold." But this determination came too late. On the 15th of May, 1559, the bishops, fourteen in number, were commanded to appear before Queen Elizabeth at Greenwich Palace. Cecil and Bacon were both present. Her Majesty then informed the prelates that it was her will and pleasure that they should take the new form of oath prescribed for them, or else they should surrender their sees immediately. Dr. Heath, Archbishop of York, was first called upon to take the oath of supremacy. The aged prelate seemed deeply affected, yet he replied in a firm and respectful tone. He told the Queen "to remember what her real duty was, and the policy she was bound to adopt." He admonished her "to follow in the steps of her sister, who had brought back the country to the ancient religion which had flourished in it for so many centuries." He told her to recollect that the see of Rome was the Mother of all Churches; that history and tradition, and the writings of the Fathers, and the great Councils that were held at different times, all proclaimed Rome as the Head of that Church which their Divine Master had founded.

In conclusion, he supplicated the Queen to think well on the course she was about to adopt, and not to be led astray by the politicians who surrounded her, and whose motives were so well demonstrated to the world by their conduct in her brother's reign. "What will be the result to after generations?" exclaimed the Archbishop—"Ah, my good old master, King Henry, would not deny that we are the shepherds of Jesus Christ; but he was deceived on his death-bed."

The members of the Council who were present seemed somewhat ruffled, and the Queen felt annoyed at the allusions to her father; but her Majesty soon regained her firmness, and proceeded to tell the bishops what mind she was in concerning them:—"My Lord Archbishop, I will consider you in the words of Joshua—'I and my realm will serve the Lord God.' My sister could not bind the realm, nor bind those who should come after her to submit to a usurped authority. My Lords, *I take those who maintain here the Bishop of Rome and his ambitious pretences to be enemies to God and to me as the Sovereign ruler of this realm.*"*

The Queen delivered this address in tone and gesture most emphatic. The bishops were ordered to retire from the royal presence, the Queen's "pleasure being that they should be allowed twenty-one days to re-consider their position, and the demands made by the Crown." With one exception (Dr. Kichen) they remained firm to the faith of their fathers. When the time for "further consideration" elapsed, the bishops declined the oath. They were immediately arrested after the fashion of common malefactors, and committed to the worst

---

* I have met with several versions of the scene between the Queen and the bishops. I select one given by Farlow, a very intelligent preacher, whose father was present. I am indebted for the above to a clergyman of the diocese of Lincoln, whose valuable MSS. and black-letter books I have been most kindly permitted to examine.

dungeons in the Tower and the Fleet. They "were compelled to pay for their own food, whilst they were left without a shilling to do so," writes Farlow; "but some kind-hearted people made up a purse for the deposed bishops and sent it to them, and the 'good givers' were *nearly all Protestants*, but not of the same mind as Maister Cecil."

The news of this sudden change in the religious affairs of England created considerable excitement on the Continent, and the name of the English Queen was quickly associated with all the shocking gossip once detailed of her mother, and for which there was little foundation.

At this early period of her reign the name of Elizabeth become hated in Paris, Vienna, Rome, Madrid, and other great cities.

After a time, the name of Queen Elizabeth was universally detested in Ireland. And no marvel, for the Queen's deputies and generals were, with few exceptions, men only noted for cruelty and dishonesty.

CUTHBERT TONSTAL, Bishop of Durham, met with a striking reverse of fortune. In early life he enjoyed the friendship of Sir Thomas More, Richard Foxe, Bishop of Winchester, Bishop Fisher, Archbishop Warham, and other eminent scholars and divines. More states that "the world had not then anything more learned or prudent, or better, than Cuthbert Tonstal." Archbishop Warham was one of his immediate patrons. In a letter from Warham to Cardinal Wolsey, he speaks of Tonstal, on his promotion to the see of Durham, in terms of eulogy, and describes him as a man of "learning, virtue, and goodness."[*] Camden, writing at a later period, presents Tonstal to posterity as "an able nego-

---

[*] MS. Correspondence of Warham and Wolsey.

ciator, and a most exquisite master of all critical learning." A high compliment from such an eminent authority. In 1541, Tonstal assisted Dr. Heath, then Bishop of Worcester, in a revised edition of the Bible. He was a noted Greek scholar at thirty years of age, and well versed in ancient history. His private character was without reproach. All Protestant writers agree that he was moral, amiable, and benevolent. Unfortunately for his reputation as a priest, he became a courtier. He advocated the divorce of Katherine of Arragon. He took the oath of supremacy to the King; he was silent when Lord Crumwell and Dr. London issued their monastic reports. In 1535 Tonstal wrote to Reginald Pole, denouncing the Pope for not "quickly agreeing to the assumptions of the English King." He preached at Paul's Cross against the spiritual power of the Pope in England. He described Clement VII. in very uncourteous language as " a disturber of the peace of Europe." Father Peto and the Remonstrant Friars answered him from the pulpit in fearless contradiction, for they cared not for the favour or the power of the King. Notwithstanding the warnings he received, Dr. Tonstal still adhered to the policy of King Henry and Thomas Crumwell. Tonstal's letters to Reginald Pole prove that he was completely in the King's interest.* It is stated that he was in favour of the marriage of the clergy.† There is no reliable evidence for this allegation. It is pretty clear, however, that he never violated his vows as a priest. According to Dean Hook, he did not believe in Catholicity, and made some such statements to Parker. In Mary's reign, it is stated that Tonstal shielded his nephew,

---

* M.S., Chap. VI., p. 375.
† See Collier's Ecclesiastical History, Vol. VI., p. 293.

Bernard Gilpin, and enabled him to hold a lucrative living.*
Gilpin was a prominent character in Edward's reign, and it
does not appear that he did anything to mitigate the sufferings of his uncle whilst unjustly imprisoned for so many
years in the Tower. Dean Hook contends that all the
deposed prelates were treated with kindness by Sir William
Cecil and the Queen. The conduct of the Reformers to
Tonstal was marked by peculiar baseness. Upon the death
of King Henry he was deposed from his see, stripped of his
private property, and committed to the Tower during Edward's
reign. Being released from prison, on the accession of Mary,
he never actively remembered his former wrongs; he never
persecuted, and in his broad diocese no man suffered for his
belief. When Elizabeth felt herself established on the
throne, she deprived him not only of his episcopal revenues,
of which he had been a munificent dispenser, but of his
private fortune and personal liberty. The early associations
that existed between Elizabeth and Cuthbert Tonstal place
the Queen's conduct to him in a specially unamiable light.
He was the prelate who had baptized her at Greenwich
Palace, and was also one of her godfathers. For many years
previous to his deprivation he was in the habit of sending
her presents on her natal day, accompanied by some "pretty
lines," breathing good wishes for his god-daughter. Although
the incarceration of this aged prelate may seem not harsh to
some minds, as it presented the distinction of his being
merely remitted to the "honourable custody of Archbishop
Parker," the confiscation of his private property was not
perhaps half so annoying to Tonstal as the choice of his
imprisonment. *Choice* is not the word, for the bitter irony
of Cecil may be seen in the apparent leniency of its destina-

---

* Archbishops of Canterbury, Vol. IX.

tion. No two men were more opposite in character than Tonstal and Parker.* As a virtuous prelate, acting up to the dictates of his creed, Tonstal obeyed the law as it was constituted, without adopting the motives of its enactment; he stirred up no strife against the constituted order of things, however he might regret its causes and lament its effects.

Until the reign of Henry VIII., many of the legal functionaries were clerics; and the offices of the Exchequer were for a long period filled by priests, to the dissatisfaction of the laity. Dr. Tonstal held the office of Master of the Rolls for six years. He was not alone a great canon and civil law judge, but an eminent diplomatist, who discharged several political missions to the satisfaction of the King. Henry's high opinion of Dr. Tonstal induced him to appoint that prelate as one of the executors of the "royal will." At a subsequent period Tonstal denounced Somerset for violating the King's will. For his honesty Tonstal was committed to the Fleet by the Council of King Edward.

"It was the destiny of Cuthbert Tonstal," writes a recent biographer, "to live in the reign of every one of the Tudor family; to witness the beginning and almost the end of the Reformation. The character of Tonstal was solid and prudent; his countenance, refined though florid, expressed benevolence and intelligence; his learning, which recommended him to the favourable notice of Erasmus, had gained him a reputation beyond the shores of England. For some

---

* Aikin's Court of Elizabeth, and Neal's History of the Puritans, will, to some extent, enable the reader to judge of Archbishop Parker's merits as a prelate. In Dean Hook's Archbishops of Canterbury, Dr. Parker is represented as a *saint;* but the records of his actions prove him to have been the very opposite. He persecuted his former co-religionists without pity or remorse. He was the active co-partner of Sir William Cecil in his measures of penal proscription; and that fact requires no further comment.

years he was regarded as the leader of the constitutional party among the Churchmen, a position which he enjoyed so long as moderation, dignity, and integrity were sufficient to maintain it. But he failed to show the energy of a leader as the troubles of the times increased."*

Dr. Tonstal did not long survive the loss of his honours. He died at Lambeth Palace, November 18, 1559. Dean Hook alleges that he died a Reformer, having "made many admissions as to his errors." There is no record extant of "any admissions."

Maurice Chauncey states that it was bruited at St. Omers that "an unpleasant altercation took place between Dr. Parker and his wife, as to whether Tonstal should be allowed to have the visits of a Catholic priest at the time of his last illness." Father Davern, an Irish Dominican, then in concealment in London, "heard it stated that one of the chaplains of the Spanish ambassador was permitted by the Queen to attend Tonstal; that Parker and his wife were compelled to give way." It is certain that other bishops were not permitted "the benefit of clergy," thus placing them on a level with murderers or outlaws, who were, by the barbarous laws of Henry and Edward's reign, denied the rights of all religious consolation at the hour of death.

Dr. Tonstal was a member of an ancient family, his father being Sir Thomas Tonstal, and his mother of the honoured name of Neville—a name long associated with all that was chivalrous, brave, and generous in the realm.

Dr. WHYTE became Gardyner's successor in the See of Winchester. He was the first prelate whom Elizabeth

---

* History of the Church of England from the Abolition of the Roman Jurisdiction, by R. Dixon, A.M., Vol. I.

deposed. On descending from the pulpit after preaching the funeral sermon of Queen Mary, Elizabeth ordered his arrest, and he remained in the Tower till his health was totally prostrated. He was subsequently released, and permitted to reside at the house of his sister, where he died in 1561. Camden states that, although allowed to live with his relative, he was prevented from practising his religion. Camden may be considered a good authority on this matter; yet another contemporary alleges that during the imprisonment of Dr. Heath, Archbishop of York, the Queen ordered every facility to be rendered him in the practice of his religious duties. Dr. Whyte is described by an Oxford professor " as an eminent scholar, a pleasing poet, an able theologian, an eloquent preacher, a prelate of primitive behaviour, and altogether a worthy good man." Sir William Cecil has left on record his own " private opinion " of the Bishop of Winchester. "He was," writes Cecil, " sincere, candid, honest, and hospitable; very attentive to the duties of his see, and charitable to God's poor." If Dr. Whyte deserved this character—which he did fully—why did Sir William Cecil advise such treatment towards him ? The fact is, virtue was the very worst recommendation for prelatical prosperity in the days of Cecil and his royal mistress.

Dodd affirms that few men received such rapid promotion in Henry's reign as Dr. BONNER. He was indebted for his promotion to his kinsman, Lord Crumwell. Within a fortnight Bonner was installed Bishop of Hereford, and transferred to the see of London. He was expediently grateful: he spoke and acted with the court; advocated the divorce of Katharine of Arragon; supported the King's supremacy, and the dissolution of the monastic houses. In later days came the revulsion. After the death of Henry, Bishop Bonner became conscious of the mischief he had done to the Church in the reign of his "good old master." During the brief rule of Somerset and his colleagues, Bonner was committed to the Tower, where he was kept in close confinement, not permitted the "use of pen, ink, or paper, and no fire." Cranmer was censured for this cruelty.

When Bonner was called upon by Lord Hertford to take the oath of supremacy, he at once refused to do so; and that refusal may be considered the best action of his mischievous life.* Bonner was no coward.

Lingard states that it is doubtful whether Bonner deserved all the odium which has been heaped upon him. The Council commanded; the bishop obeyed. Foxe and Strype admit in favour of Bonner, that "as the law stood, he could not refuse to hear those heresy appeals as they were sent forward by the Council." Dodd is likewise favourable to Bonner, believing that he was compelled by the government to pronounce judgment in the heresy cases. As a priest, however, it was the duty of Bonner to have nothing to do with the sacrifice of human life. It is only justice to Bonner to state, that he was "severely rebuked by the Council for not acting with expedition in case of some obstinate heretics." But he should have remembered that his first duty was to God, and taken a warning from the memorable sermon of De Castro, the Spanish friar, already quoted. De Castro pronounced "*persecution, or burning at the stake, as contrary to the principles laid down by our Divine Lord; it was not by severity, but by mildness,* that

---

* See Dodd's "Church History," Vol. I. Bonner's private despatches from Rome to Lord Crumwell place him in the worst light. His conduct as a diplomatic agent in France was not approved of by Francis I. (Foreign State Papers, Vol. VII.)

men were to be brought into the fold of Christ; and it was the *duty of the bishops not to seek the death, but to instruct the ignorant who had wandered from the paths of righteousness."* Such clerics as Bonner have done irreparable injury to religion.

Canon Dixon's portrait of Bonner's early life is not favourable to his reputation as a cleric. He was a thorough man of the world, and was consequently suited to become one of King Henry's agents in the iniquitous divorce litigation of Queen Katharine. Whilst engaged in the early intrigues upon this question, Bonner visited France, Italy, Denmark and Germany. He was also engaged in several diplomatic intrigues; and his violent manner sometimes called forth complaints from Francis I. and Charles V. Bonner's conduct towards Clement VII. was disgraceful; and Gardyner was equally insolent. The rebuke of the Pontiff was almost prophetic. A quarrel of a most undignified nature occurred between Gardyner and Bonner whilst both were "on the King's business in Paris." Gardyner gave the lie to his reverend colleague in the most offensive manner; and received in return the foulest language that might have been used by the Cambridge students in the reckless days of the Dolphin Inn.* At the period of these unedifying quarrels between Bonner and Gardyner, the Monastic Inquisitors were carrying out their sacrilegious robbery in England, whilst Bonner and Gardyner never raised their voice to protest against such proceedings.

Dr. Bonner is described by a recent Anglican writer, as "a clerical judge who had never been a very zealous persecutor, and was sick of his work."† Bonner's ambition for office

---

* Crumwell and Wriothesley, State Papers, Vol. VIII.
† Green's History of the English People, Vol. II., p. 260.

helped him on to an unenviable notoriety in the eyes of posterity, who have, in too many instances, adopted the reckless assertions of such writers as Foxe, Speed, and Burnet. Bonner's conduct to the Head of his own Church, in Henry's reign, might tend to enlist the sympathy of Puritan writers in his favour, for at that period he did far more to promote the Reformation than to uphold Catholicity in Mary's reign. Bishop Horne acted in a shameful and vindictive spirit to Bonner.

NICHOLAS HEATH, the deposed Archbishop of York, was descended from the Heaths of Aspley, near Tamworth, where the family held estates for several generations.

Hepworth Dixon adopts the statement of John Strype, who affirms that young Nicholas Heath was maintained at college by Anna Boleyn, her father, and brother.* The inference to be drawn from this assertion is, that, as his patrons were *Protestant*, he soon favoured the " new learning, then being advanced in a cautious and clandestine manner." In 1519 Heath took the degree of B.A. at Christ College, Cambridge, and that of M.A. in 1521. In 1519 Anna Boleyn was in France, and had been there for some years. Her Catholicity was as unquestionable at that period as it may well have been when she was under the instruction of her clerical uncles. Her brother George, too, was a boy at the time indicated by Strype, and in fact had no means of aiding Maister Heath to pay his college fees. Anna Boleyn's " allowance for clothes, &c.," was very small. And further, I believe that up to the time mentioned, she had never seen Heath the student.

I think I have made the question as to the religious

---

* Strype's Memorials, Vol. I., p. 279.

principles of the Boleyn family perfectly clear in the first volume of this work.

In 1531 Nicholas Heath received Holy Orders, and in eight years subsequently he was consecrated Bishop of Rochester, and, at a later period, translated to the See of Worcester, where he remained till the accession of Edward VI.

Upon Queen Mary's accession to the throne, she released Dr. Heath, then in the Tower. In 1555 Heath was consecrated Archbishop of York. The death of Dr. Gardyner opened a fresh field for the display of his talents, when he became Lord Chancellor of England. In that capacity he signed the warrant for the execution of his "late persecutor," Thomas Cranmer.*

It is stated that Dr. Heath felt horrified at signing the fatal document, being of opinion that a Churchman should have "no concern whatever with the shedding of human blood." But unfortunately, there were many, and recent precedents, for such a proceeding.†

Hayward, a contemporary historian, writing of the changes upon the accession of Elizabeth, observes:—" Amongst these Dr. Heath was removed from being Lord Chancellor of England, a man most eminent, and of generous simplicity; who esteemed everything privately unlawful which was not publicly beneficial and good. But as it is no new thing for merchants to break down, for sailors to be drowned, for

---

* The warrant is still extant, signed "Nicholas Heath, Lord Chancellor of England." It has been stated that Gardyner never signed a death-warrant. As Chancellor, he signed for the Queen in several cases of treason.

† Dr. Cranmer, who never filled the office of Chancellor, placed his name as "Regent of the Realm" to the warrant for the execution of Sir Thomas Seymour; and, at a later period, at the suggestion of Lord Warwick, whom he feared and hated, the Archbishop consented, in a similar manner, to the execution of his own patron, friend, and brother Reformer, Somerset.

soldiers to be slain, so it is not for men in authority to fall."*

Another writer, of Calvinistic tendencies, remarks :—" Dr. Heath's career, though not marked by any striking events, was most honourable to his character, and ought to make his memory revered by all denominations of Christians."† All historians, excepting the Puritan writers, agree in their commendations of Dr. Heath."‡

It is contended that Elizabeth and her Council ordered Heath to be "punished" in order to discover some Popish plots, but this statement is not correct.

In the year 1561 Dr. Heath was again removed to the Tower, to undergo "an examination as to some fresh Popish plot." The scheme, however, failed, owing to the sudden death of a witness. About this time the newly-created Archbishop of York "felt indignant" at the idea of any other man daring to call himself "an Archbishop." So Dr. Heath was "duly cited," and excommunicated as "a Popish pretender."§

Foss, a high Protestant authority, exonerates Archbishop Heath from any participation in the "stake fires" which were in operation during his Chancellorship.

Dr. Heath was, perhaps, more fortunate than many of his clerical brethren. After a time Queen Elizabeth permitted him to retire to a private residence at Chobham, in Surrey. In this quiet retreat he resided for a few years, pursuing with devotion the sacred studies to which he had been so long and so ardently attached.

---

* Hayward's Annals of Elizabeth's Reign, p. 13.
† See Lord Campbell's English Chancellors, Vol. II., p. 81.
‡ See Godwin ; De Preasul ; Anthony Wood ; Burnet ; Hayward ; Dodd ; Lingard ; Strickland's Queens of England, Vol. V. (first edition).
§ Machyn's Diary, p. 238.

Archbishop Heath died in the year 1579, and was buried in the chancel of the parish church of Chobham. Such was the end of the eventful life of the last Catholic Archbishop of York, and Lord Chancellor of England.

THOMAS THIRLBY was a native of Cambridge, and in time received his education at Trinity Hall. He became eminent in Civil Law. He received Holy Orders, and was "generally considered to be a prudent and respectable priest." His introduction to Henry VIII. soon led to his promotion. In 1534 he was appointed to the Archdeaconry of Ely; and in a few months subsequent his royal patron made him Dean of the Chapel Royal. The new Bishopric of Westminster was next conferred on him. This See was dissolved in the reign of Edward VI., Thirlby having agreed to the terms proposed by Somerset's Council. Upon the accession of Queen Mary, Thirlby was in high favour at Court, and was again translated to the See of Norwich. Queen Mary sent him to Rome on a special mission, to represent to the Pope the state of religion in England at that period. His Protestant contemporaries speak of Thirlby as a man opposed to religious persecution, nevertheless he sent three men to the stake for heresy.[*] It may be stated that the Council "pushed forward those cases," which is very possible. It is certain that, as one of Cranmer's clerical judges, he shed tears in pronouncing one of the decrees against his former friend.

Thirlby was considered one of the most munificent benefactors to the diocese of Ely. He also added to the endowments of Jesus College, in Cambridge, which was first founded by Bishop Alcock. In the beginning of Elizabeth's reign she employed Thirlby in diplomatic missions to France and Scot-

---

[*] Records of the Cathedral of Ely, p. 191.

land, which, it is stated, met with the Queen's "entire approval." When his presence was required in his diocese, Sir William Cecil, by "the Queen's command," called on him to take the Oath of Supremacy to her Highness in all things concerning religion. Thirlby at once refused, and was committed to the Tower. He was next handed over to the custody of Archbishop Parker, who retained him a close prisoner for nearly ten years. The scrupulous Queen retained his private property.

When entering the Tower, he had on his person gold to the amount of 500 French crowns. The usual search having been gone through, the Lieutenant of the Tower remarked on his having "so large a sum on his person, coming there as a prisoner." Thirlby replied with a smile, "I love to have my friends about me, not knowing what fare I may meet with in this place." He died in 1570.

The accounts as to how the Marian bishops fared under the rule of Elizabeth are contradictory. Ratclyffe states that "every degradation was heaped upon them by the bishop-gaolers and their wives—a class of women who specially denounced the olden bishops for their celibacy." And again, Dr. Ratclyffe says :—" As far as public opinion dared express itself in Elizabeth's reign, there was a general disapproval of making the deposed bishops the prisoners of the 'new prelates.'" Ratclyffe was a Protestant physician well known in the social circles of the period.

To commit the bishops to the worst dungeons in the Tower would not have been so painful and humiliating as that of being placed in the custody of the men who had just taken possession of their dioceses. What feeling could the deposed prelates experience towards their gaolers? This degrading and cruel action was done for the purpose of debasing the bishops. The motives are clear enough. "The bishops conformed more or less to the new order of things," observes Dean Hook, "but Dr. Whyte and Dr. Watson could not conscientiously submit. Watson was at first committed to the custody of Grindal, the new Bishop of London, and afterwards to that of Coxe, Bishop of Ely. Instead, however, of meeting courteous treatment with courtesy, Dr. Watson was found 'preaching against the State,' and it was deemed necessary to place him under closer restraint."* Wisbech Castle became his next prison. Here he remained *twenty-four years*, and died in 1584. Dean Hook is very emphatic in his statement as to a change of sentiment in the Catholic bishops; but he produces no authority for his allegation. If they conformed in any way, Elizabeth would have been glad to retain them, if it were only for an incitement to win others; for she heartily detested the Puritan element amongst her new bishops.

Neither Horne, Barlow, Coxe, Jewel, or Grindal† enjoyed her confidence; they were forced on her by circumstances.

A pamphleteer of those times states that when party feeling ran high—when did it not?—"*occasional instances of harshness* must have occurred."‡ This admission on the part of Sir William Cecil's secretary (Camden) allows a wide margin for the persecutors of this age.

---

* Archbishops of Canterbury, Vol. IX.; Godwin, p. 361.

† Grindal is a characteristic specimen of the clerical gaolers of the time. He was one of John Foxe's correspondents in framing the marvellous history of the "martyrs." Grindal's whole nature was impregnated with the hatred of his Catholic countrymen. Both in the diocese of London and Canterbury he was the instigator of persecution against Catholics. Liberty of conscience was a sentiment he could not understand, yet he was a tolerant instrument in comparison with Horne, Jewel, and Coxe, and, I may add, Whitgift and Hutton, in the latter years of Elizabeth.

‡ Printed in Somers's Tracts, Vol. I., p. 193.

Dr. DAY, Bishop of Chichester, desired to remain "on friendly terms" with the Court party, but the Queen desired unconditional submission to her commands in Church and State. A learned Anglican divine states that Day was more courageous in holding his opinions than Bishop Thirlby. When King Henry issued letters for the conversion of altars into tables, Dr. Day refused to enforce the order in his diocese; and, being threatened with deprivation, he pleaded vigorously for the rights of conscience. Finding, however, his efforts to be unsuccessful, he expressed his final decision in terms which command the respect of every person, save the ungracious Puritans. "I account," said he, "*it to be a less evil to suffer the body to perish than to destroy the immortal soul. I would rather lose all that I ever had in this world than act against the convictions of my conscience.*" Dr. Day was committed to the Fleet prison for daring to make the above declaration of an honest man. So he shared the fate of the other prelates, whose long imprisonment and confiscation of property are amongst the worst deeds of Elizabeth and her Council.

In closing this brief reference to the Marian bishops, I beg to place before the reader a few observations upon the much misrepresented "executions at the stake," in Henry's reign, for heresy. It has been boldly asserted by Foxe, Speed, and the Puritan writers of subsequent times, that the people who were sent to the stake in Henry's reign suffered at the "instigation of the bishops and clergy." Canon Dixon is one of the latest writers upon the history of those sad times; and he may be considered a high authority, truthful and honourable in his mode of relation. Canon Dixon observes: —"The reader will by this time have perceived that the clergy had wonderfully little to do with the proceedings

under the Six Articles. *The King desired those religious persecutions, and they commenced and ended at his command."* *
Canon Dixon does not seem to approve of the "theological patchwork" of King Henry and Archbishop Cranmer. "To substitute the conceptions of a single age for the determinations of all antiquity was perilous." So writes Canon Dixon.

The following is an abridged copy of the Six Articles which caused so much angry discussion in Henry's reign :—

First.—That in the Most Blessed Sacrament of the Altar, by the strength and efficacy of Christ's mighty word (it being spoken by the priest) is present *really*, under the form of bread and wine, the *natural Body and Blood of our Saviour, Jesus Christ*, conceived of the Blessed Virgin Mary. And that, after the consecration, there remaineth no substance of *bread* or *wine*, nor any other substance but the substance of *Christ, God and man.*

Secondly.—That communion in both kinds is not necessary *ad salutem*, by the law of God, to all persons; and that it is to be believed, and not doubted of, but that in the Flesh, under the form of bread, is the very Blood; and with the Blood, under the form of wine, is the very Flesh; as well apart, as though they were both together.

Thirdly.—That priests, after the order of priesthood received, as afore, *may not marry by the law of God.*

Fourthly.—That vows of chastity, or widowhood, by man or woman, made to God Almighty advisedly, ought to be observed by the law of God; and that it exempteth them from other liberties of Christian people, which, without that, they might enjoy.

Fifthly.—That it is meet and necessary that *private Masses* be continued and admitted *in this the King's English Church and Congregation*, as whereby good Christian people, ordering themselves accordingly, do receive both godly and goodly consolations and benefits; and is agreeable also to God's law.

---

* Canon Dixon's History of the Church of England from the Abolition of the Roman Jurisdiction, Vol. II., p. 404.

Sixthly.—That auricular confession *is expedient and necesary* to be *retained, and continued, used and frequented, in the Church of God.**

The whole Act, which, in the original draft, was somewhat long, was ordered to be read in all churches and chapels by the clergy *once in every three months.* In this royal proclamation, for it is nothing less, the religion of the country is described as the "*King's English Church* and Congregation," is a proof that the prelates and clergy, as a body, did not, nor could not, sanction the King to be styled "*Head of the Church.*" The Six Articles evidently originated with the King, aided by Crumwell and Cranmer; yet we are assured that Archbishop Cranmer argued for *three days against* the Bill in the House of Peers. This statement is contradicted by the diary of a Peer who was present; and it is further proved by the records of Parliament, that on the appearance of the King *himself* in the House of Peers, where he made a speech —an illegal essay, of course—in favour of the Six Articles, Cranmer immediately rose, and after congratulating *his* Sovereign on *his* devotion to the principles of *the* Church, declared that he was "*confounded by the wisdom, learning, and powerful arguments of the King.*" The facts are very plain that Cranmer and Lord Crumwell dare not oppose the passing of the Six Articles. "The whole affair," writes Canon Dixon, "proceeded from the King, the Court, the Parliament, and *not* from the Bishops or the Church."†

After rehearsing the Six Articles in a strain of slavish loyalty, the Statute proceeded to enact "pain of death by way of burning," with loss of goods, as in the case of high treason

---

* The Six Articles are arranged as above in the Act 31st of King Henry VIII., c. 14.

† Canon Dixon's History of the Church of England from the Abolition of the Roman Jurisdiction, Vol. II., p. 124 (note).

against all persons convicted of speaking against the first of them. No abjuration was allowed to excuse the offender. The loss of goods and imprisonment, at the King's pleasure, were the penalties attached to the first offence against any of the other Five Articles. The punishment awarded for a second offence was the death of a felon *without benefit of clergy*. In fact, the King detested heretics (Protestants) quite as much as the down-trodden monks, for whose blood he thirsted, and whose homes he had laid desolate ; and, at the same moment, plundered, without pity or remorse, the heritage of the poor. Let the reader never forget the confiscation of the lands bequeathed for the support of *one hundred and ten hospitals*. Humanity stands appalled at this instance of the King's rapacity.

For years King Henry had been issuing proclamations which had been obeyed by the people in a slavish manner. Those proclamations were upon all matters, from the price of corn, to the distillation of ale ; and, as a matter of course, something concerning the heretics. The proclamations invariably contained a threat of heavy penalties upon all those who disobeyed the despotic and dishonest demands of the monarch.

CHAPTER XVII.

CHANGE OF RELIGION IN ENGLAND.

THE Queen and Sir William Cecil having summoned a Parliament, and by a very strange process, quite at variance with the old constitutional system, obtained a majority in their interest, soon gave indications of their desire to follow up the policy of Somerset and the Reformers of Edward's reign. If these Reformers had only evinced a regard for the rights of property, their "spiritual labours," as Fuller has put the matter, "would have left a very different impression on the minds of posterity." It seemed in the nature of the times as fitting cause and effect that a denunciation of Popery should be followed by the spoliation of the denounced. These "confiscations," as they are judicially termed, were conceived and enacted on often the flimsiest pretexts. What was commonly styled "the law," was one of the greatest outrages upon equity that despotism could adopt. The system of enormous fines for disobeying of the Queen's "spiritual commands" was another cause of just complaint; yet such actions are defended by writers of those times on the grounds of "expediency, and to promote the Gospel Truth." To comment upon such a defence of flagrant plunder would be an insult to common honesty between man and man. Religion is brought forward to cast a shield around the actions of thieves. If the highwayman of remote times had few scruples, he never blasphemed religion by demanding his neighbour's purse in the name of the God of Justice and Charity.

At the accession of Elizabeth the Catholics were in a large majority in every county in England, excepting Middlesex and Kent.* The authorities on this question are quite conclusive. It has been often stated that "the whole country cried out for an immediate change of religion." This assertion is contradicted by the records of the times. Three-fourths of the population, a third of the Privy Council, and a very large minority of the lay Peers, were opposed to any alteration of the national religion.†

In the Parliament of 1559, Elizabeth was prepared to "unsettle" the religion of the country, and, in the words of John Bale, " to dash Popery to the winds." The laws passed in Mary's reign for sustaining the Catholic faith were repealed by Elizabeth, and the Acts of Henry VIII., in derogation of the Papal authority, and of Edward VI., in favour of the "Reformed service," as it was then styled, was revived. Let it, however, be remembered, that the Parliament who revived those statutes was mostly composed of the men who had set aside Protestantism in Mary's reign. It was then enacted by this partial and interested assembly that the Book of Common Prayer, with certain additions and emendations, should alone be used by the priests in all churches, under the penalties *of forfeiture, deprivation, and death;* that the spiritual authority of every foreign prelate within the realm should be utterly abolished; that the jurisdiction necessary for the correction of errors, heresies, schisms, and abuses should be incorporated with the privileges of the Crown, which should also possess the power of delegating such

---

* Domestic MSS., Elizabeth, Vol. I. ; Froude, Vol. VII.

† Lingard, Vol. VI. ; also State Papers of Elizabeth's Reign.

jurisdiction to any person or persons whatsoever, at the pleasure of the Queen. It was likewise enacted that the penalty of asserting the Papal authority should ascend, on the repetition of the offence, from the forfeiture of real and personal property to *perpetual imprisonment, and from perpetual imprisonment to death,* such death as was inflicted in cases of high treason; and that all clerics taking orders, or those in possession of livings, all magistrates and inferior officers having fees or wages from the Crown, all laymen suing out the livery of their lands, or about to do homage to the Queen, should, under pain of deprivation and incapacity, take an oath declaring her Highness to be *the supreme Governor in all ecclesiastical and spiritual things, or causes, as well as temporal,* and renouncing all foreign spiritual jurisdiction within the realm.*

On the part of the clergy and prelates, the bills submitted to Parliament were vigorously but hopelessly opposed. The Convocation presented to the House of Lords a declaration of its belief in the Real Presence, Transubstantiation, the Sacrifice of the Mass, and the supremacy of the Pope—with a protestation that, to decide on doctrine, sacraments, and discipline, belonged not to any lay assemblage, but to the lawful pastors of the Church. Both Universities subscribed to the Confession put forward by the Convocation; and the bishops were unanimous in speaking and voting against those innovations of the Queen and her advisers.†

---

* See Statutes of the Realm; Foxe, Vol. III.; Burnet, Vol. II.; Strype's Memorials, Vol. I.; Lingard, Vol. VI.

† See Wilkins' Con., p. 179; The Speeches of the Archbishop of York and the Bishop of Chester may be seen in "Strype's Memorials." The Spanish ambassador encouraged the English prelates in their opposition to Elizabeth, assuring them that his Royal master would sustain them " in the good cause." Notwithstanding his promises, Philip left the bishops to the

Dean Hook contends that the secular clergy were nearly all in favour of the Reformation, but the Regulars were the men who offered "some opposition." These statements are made in opposition to a number of well-authenticated facts. In the Dean's attempt to prove that the Seculars were always some kind of "masked Protestants," he observes:—"The Secular clergy had for centuries murmured at the Papal usurpations; and we may *infer* from the legislation of Synods and Councils, that they submitted with reluctance to the imposition of ceremonies which seemed, during every century, to increase. From this charge, the Regulars are, of course, excluded. The Regulars were called the Pope's Militia. * * * The Seculars were generally in favour of the royal supremacy; and although many of them were not sufficiently learned or well informed to appreciate to its full extent the merits of those changes which had taken place in our formularies, yet they acquiesced in the mandates of their ecclesiastical superiors, when they were *backed by the authority of the Sovereign.*"* Dean Hook produces no authority to sustain his statements. He says, "We may infer" so-and-so. This can never be an accepted mode of writing History, where the character of a large body of men is at stake. Surely we cannot, with any show of fair play, judge of them by "inference"? The Dean sets down the Seculars at 10,000, and "supposes" that 9,800 took the oath of supremacy to Elizabeth. I believe there is no accurate account of the number who seceded. Some Catholic writers put down 1,500; but that is not correct, for they

mercies of Elizabeth. It is true that Gonzalez brought over 60,000 gold crowns to sustain the Catholic cause. A large portion of this money was seized upon by the Government.

* Archbishops of Canterbury, Vol. IX.

might be counted by thousands. The character of the Seculars who took the oath of supremacy has been highly extolled. Further on I shall return to the history of the Seculars who took the Oath of Supremacy to Elizabeth.

In another chapter Dean Hook represents the clerics who had taken the Oath of Supremacy "as much divided in religious opinions, and not likely to act in harmony with the bishops. Two-thirds of them were Anglo-Catholics—that is, Catholics who were opposed to the Pope, though still more hostile to Calvin."*

I question the accuracy of this statement. In Henry's reign the majority of the Seculars, and a large number of the bishops—amongst whom were Gardyner, Bonner, and Tonstal —"reneagued," to use an old expressive word, the Pope's Supremacy, and accepted the King as "*the* Supreme Vicar on earth." But the death of Henry, and the policy adopted by Cranmer and Hertford, soon convinced them that a great change of religious observance was meant. Having given way in the first instance, they were unable to retrace their steps. *Nulla vestigia retrorsum* in a matter of eternal interest like this. They could never undo the evil they had done to the ancient Church. Those whom Dean Hook calls Anglo-Catholics in the early part of Elizabeth's reign were priests who had married, and consequently could not remain in the Catholic Church, and having families they were compelled to join the " new fold."

The Spanish Ambassador in Mary's reign has drawn a sad picture of the Seculars who had just returned to the Olden Church, after having served in that of Cranmer and Somerset. "The orthodox clergy," he remarks, "are still unreformed.

---

* See Archbishops of Canterbury, Vol. IX.

Their scandalous conduct accords ill with the offices to which they are called."* The priests who took the Oath of Supremacy in the reign of Elizabeth verified, to a lamentable extent, the saying of the Anglican satirist, that "a bad Papist makes a worse Protestant." According to the testimony of such acknowledged Protestant authorities as Burnet, Wharton, Mackintosh, Macaulay and Froude, the Elizabethan clergy were notoriously ignorant, apathetic, drunken, and immoral.

The Queen's Council (now we see) ordered "a public discussion on the religious questions agitating the Christian mind." Five bishops and three doctors of divinity on one side, and eight Reformers on the other. Sir Nicholas Bacon and Dr. Heath presided. The whole affair was one of those devices arranged by Cecil to create a stronger sectarian feeling than any already in existence. The conduct of Sir Nicholas Bacon in this affair was that of an undisguised partizan. Such discussions seldom end in "convincing" either party.

This "religious conference," however, was suddenly brought to a close. The Bishops of Winchester and Lincoln were committed to the Tower for not, by a condition consequent, though unknown to them, taking the Oath of Supremacy, and adopting the tenets of a "religion which was secretly arranged," in the reign of Henry, by men who, at that same period, had solemnly sworn allegiance to the Papal Church. I have had frequent occasions to allude to this incident.

The Bishop of Lichfield was fined 500 marks; other prelates were fined from 500 marks down to £40. Every

---

* See Granville State Papers. Vol. IV., p. 395.

action of the Queen and her Council at this time was in violation of all statute law and constitutional usage. It was a despotism, unworthy of a civilised nation to tolerate. If there is any circumstance that can consecrate insurrection, it is the uprise of a people to defend the religious principles which had been cherished and maintained by their forefathers for more than one thousand years. To manacle liberty of conscience is a crime against Civilization. Yet, for this policy, for this mode of rule, Elizabeth and her advisers have been immortalised by a succession of English historians.

The Council having created a system of terror throughout the land, the labour in Parliament was easily performed, and the nascent representative system was extinguished. The bill for instituting the new Book of Common Prayer was read a third time in the House of Lords, and passed by a majority of three—nine spiritual and nine temporal peers voting against the adoption of the new Prayer Book.* Dr. Kitchen proclaimed his adhesion to the new order of things, and consequently supported the Bill. Amongst the nine Temporal Peers who opposed the Queen on this occasion appear the names of Lords Rich and Winchester—worthies to whom I have already alluded.† At a later period Rich professed Protestantism, but is reported to have "recanted" that profession at the approach of death. He was equally zealous in supporting, at either side, the opposing parties, whenever his own interests might be promoted.‡

The next important action taken by the Queen was to provide a hierarchy for her new Church. For this purpose

---

* The bill was drawn up by Cecil and Parker.
† D'Ewes, p. 28 ; Lingard, Vol. VI., p. 16.
‡ Foss's Judges of England, Vols. V., VI.

she sent for the deposed prelates and required them to conform and take the Oath of Supremacy. On their refusal, they were finally deprived of their sees and committed to close confinement; the same fate awaited their brethren in the country districts. In a few months the bishoprics were filled with the exiled Hot-Gospel men from Geneva, Basle, and Frankfort. Mathew Parker was appointed Metropolitan; and from this versatile prelate the Catholics could expect nothing but oppression. The legality of Parker's consecration has been long a question for discussion. According to Cranmer's canon-law code, laid down to advise King Henry, the very fact of the monarch "laying his hand on some certain priest, with the intention of making him a bishop," that moment he became a Right Reverend Father in God. Elizabeth did not follow Cranmer's ruling in such case, but commanded "men to consecrate" who are described as canonically incompetent. It is not unlikely that Parker had more faith in the Queen's "command" to take up the pastoral staff of Canterbury than in the consecration ceremony performed by such prelates as Barlow, Scorey, Coverdale, and Kitchen.* According to canon-law, one of the four prelates should have been an archbishop. The Queen, of course, acting "as Christ's Vicar on earth," dispensed with the obligation of canon law. Dean Hook states his opinion that the ceremony was quite correct; and proves it to be so—at least to his own satisfaction. But it is now, indeed, a question of little import whether Elizabeth or Dr. Kitchen placed the pastoral staff in the hands of Mathew Parker, as the *first* Protestant Archbishop of Canterbury.

---

* Dr. Bale was summoned to attend the consecration, but he did not obey the "royal command." It is scarcely possible that the Queen was not aware of the bad reputation of this cleric.

In March, 1560, the Elizabethan bishops were placed in charge of their respective dioceses.

In general the Oath of Supremacy was refused by the deans, prebendaries, archdeacons, and the leading members of the Universities, who sacrificed their offices and emoluments, and in many cases their personal liberty, at the dictates of conscience.* The country presented a strange spectacle at this period. The bishops were all confined, and in some cases denied "the use of pen, ink, or paper;" and others not permitted the use of their own Breviary, being commanded to study the "new books of prayer." Of course they refused to receive a State-framed cultus for the olden belief. Dean Hook contends that they were all well treated, and merely committed to the custody of gentlemen appointed by the Queen. Again, the Dean gives no authority for this statement. I feel certain, however, that Dean Hook would not wilfully place before his readers an erroneous record of what occurred. Yet it is probable he has reposed too much confidence in documents said to have been written by the "new bishops," who in some cases desired that their actions might appear in a more excusable light before posterity. From such men as Horne, Coxe, or Parker, the deposed prelacy could expect little consideration, or even the slightest respect. Dean Hook admits what might be their fate if Bishop Horne had his wishes gratified.†

The new bishops and their clergy did not act in harmony. The prelates complained of the neglect of many clerics, and the morals of others; scenes of recrimination followed, which were *not* edifying. Cecil and the Queen were not yet satisfied

---

* See Statute of Realm, IV; Strype's Memorials; Lingard, Vol. VI.; Froude, Vol. VII.

† Archbishops of Canterbury, Vol. IX.

with their work. Some of the clergy were said "to be still Papists in their hearts;" others "incorrigible Puritans, who despised crowned heads." Of the latter class Mr. Froude remarks that "perhaps they were the only people who honestly believed in, or worshiped God." The clergy, who were miserably paid, became loud in their denunciation of the tyranny and pride of the bishops, who looked more to the interests of their large families than to the welfare of the diocese. These charges had become most obviously true; and in the twenty-fourth of Elizabeth's reign the state of the new ecclesiasticism achieved a perfect scandal. "The spiritual sheep-walk was sadly neglected, and in a state of disorder; the shepherds—high and low—only looked to their own worldly interests." A lamentable state of things, but merely the result of a political patchwork of all that had been sacred and holy in the land.

Elizabeth generally acted with some courtesy to the Peers; but, from beginning to end, she treated her Bishops with contempt. In the eighth year of her reign, the Queen gave a remarkable instance of her gross conduct to the newly-created prelates. Turning sharply upon Archbishop Grindal and Pilkington of the See of Durham, her Highness said :— "And you, *doctors*,* make long prayers about this matter (the royal marriage). One of you dared to say, in times past, that *I, and my sister Mary, were bastards; and you still continue to interfere in what does not concern you.* Go home and mend your own lives, and set an honest example in your families. The Lords in Parliament should have taught you to know your places; but if they have forgotten their duty, *I will not forget mine.* Did I so choose I might make *the*

* When the Queen desired to become personally offensive to the bishops, they were styled "*doctors.*"

impertinence of the whole set of you, an excuse to withdraw my promise to marry; but for the realm's sake I am now resolved that *I will marry; and I will take a husband that will not be to the taste of some of you.* I have not married hitherto out of consideration for *you;* but it shall be done *now,* and you who have been so urgent with me will find the effects of it *to your cost.* Think you the prince who will be my consort will *feel himself safe with such as you, who thus dare to thwart and cross your natural Queen."*

Sir William Cecil calmed down Elizabeth's stormy passion, and, further, undermined the prospect of an alliance with the Archduke Charles.

Parker and his suffragans did not agree upon many matters besides religious teaching. The Archbishop wished to curtail the expenses attendant on visitations, which pressed heavily on the poorer clergy, and the bishops protested against this "innovation on their ancient social usages." They were quickly informed that they had "no rights but what the Queen had recently pleased to confer upon them." So Dr. Parker compelled his right reverend brethren to act on his instructions.† The arrangement was for the social good of the clergy whose revenue had been much reduced by the "clippings" of the Tudors. Visitations were, in a religious and social point of view, very differently managed in the old Catholic days, when the whole parish came forth to meet their bishop, and tents were erected to entertain some hundreds of people.‡

It was enacted by the Parliament of 1559, that the Queen

---

* MSS. of Elizabeth's Reign ; Froude, Vol. VIII.
† Archbishops of Canterbury, Vol. IX., p. 422.
‡ Thorndale's "Account of Countrie Visitations ; " "History of Cathedrals of the Foundation."

and her Council could delegate their authority to commissioners, who were to investigate " all heretical opinions and practices—in fact to punish all persons who dissented in any mode or manner, either in religion or political thinking, or acting in any way opposed to the Sovereign Lady and her Council; or opposed to anything whatsoever that her Highness may dislike either in religion or social things."* On this foundation was erected the famous High Commission Court, in which Laud and Strafford figured so prominently as advisers of the Crown in the reign of Charles I. From the period of the establishment of this Court, its proceedings assumed a character of arbitrary action utterly incompatible with the security and weal of the subject, and hostile to the ancient charters of the country. The High Commission Court was established on the despotic principles of the Spanish Inquisition, and in some respects was more cruel and less logical and considerate.†

Between Elizabeth and the House of Commons no mutual feeling of good will existed. Despite the Queen's despotic action, the Puritan element was in the ascendant. The Puritans possessed undoubted courage, and on many occasions Sir William Cecil was compelled to modify his plans to obtain their assent. He was, it would seem, a Puritan himself, but dared not avow it. Whilst the Queen sanctioned the persecution of Catholics, the Catholics were the only people on whom she placed any reliance. Catholics were her confidential friends, and, to their discredit be it said, her secret spies. In the worst days of her father he seldom ordered the arrest of members for giving utterance to their opinions in the Commons. Elizabeth frequently ordered the

* History of Parliament; State Papers of Elizabeth's Reign.
† Rymer, Vol. XVI., p. 291-297.

arrest of Puritan members, and construed her own imperious commands into a law. She seemed determined to govern the Commons as if it was a debating society of riotous boys.*

In 1563 sermons were preached by Dean Nowell at St. Paul's, and by Provost Day at Westminster Abbey; the subject of these discourses was the "*propriety of killing the caged wolves*†—then in confinement—*with the least possible delay.*" Mr. Froude turns aside with horror from the sermons of these men, and writes :—" It is *mournful to remember that Nowell was the author of the English Church Catechism in its present form.*"‡

I must remind the reader that Nowell was one of those secular priests who some five years previously took the Oath of Supremacy to Elizabeth. Dean Hook presents those men as stainless and God-fearing; " they had long renounced the Supremacy of the Pope in secret ;" but yet they had acknowledged Henry Tudor to be their spiritual chief pastor; next, a conceited self-willed boy was the " Head ;" and to crown all, they swore fealty to a handsome capricious young woman as the " Vice-gerent of Christ." This is a puzzling question for Dean Hook's readers to explain.

Dean Hook prints a list of bishops, priests, and laymen, who were committed to the custody of Archbishop Parker. According to this statement they were all kindly treated,§ but the "undetected letters," and other documents preserved

---

* See Domestic MSS. ; Froude's History of England, Vol. VIII., p. 323.

† " Caged wolves " was the name given to the Catholic prelates confined in the Marshalsea and Wisbech Castle.

‡ Queen Elizabeth withheld her sanction to the Catechism in question. See Strype's Annals, Vol. I., p. 525 ; Chunton's Life of Nowell ; Cardwell's Documentary Annals, Vol. I., p. 300 ; Burleigh MSS., Vol. IX. ; Froude, Vol. VII., p. 479.

§ Archbishops of Canterbury, Vol. IX.

in several old families in Norfolk and Cumberland, present a very different picture of the haughty Mathew Parker as a clerical gaoler.

Dean Hook charges the "Regulars" with a conspiracy to assassinate Queen Elizabeth. Here are the words of the Dean:—" Among the 'Regulars,' to their eternal disgrace it must be recorded, were found too many who, coming from foreign parts, were only prevented, by lack of opportunity, from becoming the assassins of Queen Elizabeth."*

Speed, Oldmixon, or writers of that school, could not indict a more baseless statement. The few clerics belonging to the "Regulars," who were in England during the reign of Elizabeth, were men of the highest character. Anthony Wood, and other Protestant writers, bear testimony to this fact. Does Dean Hook forget that Walsingham and Cecil employed a well-trained band of "experts in forging and concocting plots," which *incidents* cover the statesmen named with consistent infamy. There is a mass of State Papers at the present moment which can furnish material for a "black book" as damaging as that of Nicholas Throckmorton, or his disciple, Thomas Randolph.

Sir William Cecil's attempted defence of Elizabeth's persecuting policy to the English Catholics is set down in a pamphlet under the title of "Execution of Justice in England, *not* for Religion, but for Treason." The records of the times furnish the most satisfying contradiction of Cecil's book, which is a wondrous perversion of facts, and quite unworthy of any man holding the high position occupied by Sir William Cecil. The secret correspondence of Cecil, urging on persecution of conscience and the plunder of his

---

* See Archbishops of Canterbury, Vol. IX., p. 124.

neighbour's property, is a powerful evidence against his statements; and the most crushing proofs are to be found *in his own handwriting*. I call the reader's attention to one most deplorable instance of religious persecution with which Cecil was more or less connected. It is the case of a young English gentleman who refused to take the Oath of Supremacy to Elizabeth. He was confined in Tutbury Castle, when the Queen of Scots was a prisoner in that "House of Solitude." This tragic narrative is related in Labanoff, Vol. VI., p. 160; and also in the 7th volume of "The Queens of Scotland." The latter work is the most accessible.

The Catholic party seemed divided as to whether they should adopt a course of "political expediency," and acknowledge Elizabeth as their lawful Sovereign, or fall back upon the time-honoured canon-law, which sustained Legitimacy in all its purity. If the latter course were adopted, then Mary Stuart would have been the lawful heiress to the English Crown. Hence the origin of the continued hatred of Elizabeth to her cousin, the Queen of Scots. Here is an instance of the divided opinion of the prelacy following upon the considerations raised by the facts just premised. In Caron's *Remonstratio Hibernorum* will be found a declaration, signed by a majority of the deposed bishops and abbots of England and Ireland, soon after the Bull of Pope Pius V., declaring that, "notwithstanding that Bull, or any other Bull that might be issued, they held Elizabeth to be *the lawful Queen of England*."* Caron refers for collateral proof to Lord Burleigh, in his work entitled "Executions for Treason."†

If a constitutional history of the monarchy were permitted

---

* Caron's work was published in 1665—the fifth year of Charles II.

† This book is to be found at the British Museum; also at the University of Oxford.

to be the guide of the Parliament and the country, the claims of Queen Elizabeth could never have been entertained. Maintained they were, however, notwithstanding Dr. Cranmer's contradictory judgments—sustained by faction, by interest, by party, and, in great part, by prejudice. It was the age of what the German philosopher designated that of "vielseitikheit," or many-sidedness,—presenting an exchange of religious belief in order to gain the support of the Reformers, who held the confiscated property of three-fourths of the English Catholics. In our present notion of constitutional law, Elizabeth was *not* the legitimate Sovereign of England.

As to the "religion" of Queen Elizabeth, by the most careful examination, the most rigid perusal and poring over every document and book of doings and sayings, records, State and otherwise, I never could ascertain that Elizabeth *had* a religion.

I cannot close this chapter without submitting to my Protestant friends a few of the opinions placed upon record by distinguished clerical and lay Catholics, as to what has been described as "the mental reservation of a Popish Conscience." In relation to killing Protestant Kings, Gother, a learned divine, says :—

"As for the king-killing doctrine, or murder of princes excommunicated for heresy, it is universally admitted in the Catholic Church, and *expressly so* declared in the Council of Constance, that such a doctrine, or doctrines, are *impious and execrable, being contrary to the known laws of God, and nature.*

"It is also a *fundamental truth in our religion that no power on earth can license men to lie, to forswear, or perjure themselves;* to massacre their neighbours, or destroy their native country, on pretence of promoting *the* Catholic cause of religion."*

---

* Gother's opinions on the above questions were annexed to a work printed in 1682.

I may remark that Gother was much esteemed by religious Protestants, and his writings have been quoted by several distinguished Anglican bishops.*

Innocent III. writes :—" We will not judge of the King's grief; it is the King who is to judge." * * * * His Holiness then cites the authorities of ten Popes holding the same opinions; also of General and Provincial Councils of various States, and likewise of the Fathers of the Church.†
The same Pontiff declares, in one of his memorable decrees, " that any attempt on the life of a King or Prince, under the pretext of promoting the Catholic religion, *is a most horrible and detestable crime, which no political circumstance, or oppression, could for one moment countenance.*"

This decretal of Innocent III. is one of high authenticity, as it recognises the monarch to be " paramount in temporals, and that the sense is clear and the words precise."‡

Lord Stafford, in his scaffold speech, on the 29th of December, 1680, said :—

" I have no reason to be ashamed of my religion ; for it teaches nothing but the right worship of God—*obedience to the King, and due subordination to the temporal laws of the kingdom.* * * * *

---

* Dr. Law, an Englishman, who filled an Irish See (of Elphin), some eighty-six years ago, in one of his pastoral charges, observed :—" The Roman Catholics in my diocese are numerous. I feel certain that I cannot induce them to become Protestants. I wish, therefore, to make them *good Roman Catholics;* and, as a step towards that end, I put into their hands the works of Gother, a most eminent and pious divine of their own Church." I may add, that Dr. Law lived in peace and harmony with his Catholic neighbours, by whom he was very much beloved. I believe this good prelate was brother to that eminent judge, Lord Ellenborough.

† "La Grandeur de nos Rois et de leur Souveraine Puissance." This decretal was printed in Spain in 1576.

‡ "La Grandeur de nos Rois et de leur Souveraine Puissance." As above.

And, whereas it has been so much and so often objected, that the Church holds that Sovereign princes, excommunicated by the Pope, may, by their subjects, be deposed or murdered : As to the murder of princes, I have been taught, *as a matter of faith*, in the Catholic Church, that such a doctrine *is diabolical, horrid, detestable, and contrary to the law of God, nature, and nations.* * * * *
" I do here, on my conscience, declare that it is my true and real judgment, that the same doctrine of deposing Kings is contrary to the fundamental laws of this kingdom, injurious to the Sovereign powers, and consequently, in me, would be, or in any other of his Majesty's subjects, impious and damnable."*

---

* The opinion of different generations becomes conflicting upon the most important questions. Walter Eustace, brother of Lord Baltinglass, and a zealous Catholic, being examined before the Irish Council, in 1583, expressed the very opposite opinion to Lord Stafford, in relation to the obedience due to a Protestant monarch. Eustace was, however, an unreflecting enthusiast, just as the Puritans were enthusiasts, with this exception, that *he* would not, in that unenlightened age, commit murder in the name of God.

CHAPTER XVIII.

ELIZABETH AND HER SUITORS.

WHEN ten years old, Elizabeth's father sought to espouse her to a Portuguese prince, but the scheme "fell through."* At a later period (1545) there was a proposal from the English king to Charles the Fifth to unite Elizabeth to Don Philip of Spain. This negotiation was "seriously entertained" at first, and then declined.

I now approach the history of the suitors of Elizabeth, as the Queen of England, a relation which is not without some interest, and is a puzzle to the reader as to what were her real sentiments concerning the marriage state.†

Naturally there were many foreign princes and native subjects, whose ambition aspired for the prize of becoming the husband of Elizabeth. Of foreign princes, the first, and the most important of all, was Philip of Spain. Count de Feria received his royal master's instructions to make a proposal in his name within two months after the accession of Elizabeth. The English queen was highly flattered, but perplexed. She was not unmindful of her former obligations to King Philip, who was her earnest friend during the troubled reign of her sister. With Philip as her husband, she could have defied the claims of Mary Stuart and her French allies. On the other hand, the confidential advisers of Elizabeth reminded her of her former disapproval of the

---

* Marivac's Despatches. † Camden's Annals.

marriage between Philip and her sister Mary. Cecil and his colleagues raised a "cloud of objections," and the religious element was potently organized against it. The Queen replied to the ambassador that, if she had made up her mind to marry, she would prefer her dear kinsman, King Philip, to any other prince. At the second audience with Count Feria, the Queen declined the match altogether, on account of the impediment arising from Philip's former marriage with her sister Mary.* Still the opponents of the proposed union were apprehensive of the result. The Protestant party in Parliament, in order to show their hostility to the projected match, called loudly on the Council to bring forward measures for the abolition of Catholic worship, and to compel, by penal enactments, the "use of the new creed." The conduct of the Government, and the violence of the Protestant party, led King Philip to withdraw the negotiations. Philip next sought Isabel of France, who accepted his proposal. When the announcement was made to Elizabeth of the matrimonial success of Philip in France, she "cried, and affected to be much hurt." She asked the ambassador "why was his royal master in such a hurry; could he not wait for four short months, and not take an evasive answer for a positive refusal?" She again spoke in eulogy of King Philip, and, although Robert Dudley was within sight at the moment, Elizabeth assured Feria that she would long remember the associations which once existed between herself and Philip, adding, with a gracious smile, "*I hope your royal master and I shall always continue on terms of friendship. He was kind to me when I really needed a friend. I do not forget the past.*" The next prince who sought the hand of the English queen

---

* Count Feria's Secret Despatches to King Philip, 1559.

was the Archduke Charles of Austria, son of the Emperor Ferdinand, and cousin to Philip. The high connections of this prince promised equal support against the rivalry of Francis and Mary of Scots. To the person, talents and acquirements of the Archduke no objection could be adduced; but his religion opposed, if not in the opinion of Elizabeth, at least in that of her Council, an insuperable obstacle to the suit of the Archduke. The Queen's vanity was much flattered by the proposal of this elegant prince, of whom she had heard so much romantic gossip. It was generally understood that the Archduke had resolved to visit his intended bride under an assumed character. Elizabeth is reported to have said, "that of all the illustrious marriages that had been offered to her, there was not one greater, or that she approved of more, than that of the Archduke Charles."* In the foreign courts an idea prevailed that the marriage was actually concluded, and that the English queen "was immensely in love with her husband."

Correspondents, like Nicholas Throckmorton, amused the Queen and her ladies with such trifling stories; but Elizabeth delighted in romance and love gossip, although it is very doubtful if such sentiments found an echo in her heart.

The Emperor Ferdinand, however, desired a settlement of the matter at once. He would not be trifled with by the intrigues of Cecil. Although the Emperor was induced to withdraw his first demand of a church for the celebration of the Catholic service in London; though he consented that his son Charles should, on occasions of ceremony, attend the Queen to the Protestant worship; still he insisted that the Archduke should possess a private chapel for his own use

---

* Queens of England, Vol. IV., p. 181.

and that of his Catholic family. To this it was replied that the laws of the realm allowed of no other than the newly established liturgy. And it was further stated by Sir William Cecil that "the Queen's royal conscience forbade her to connive at the celebration of an idolatrous worship." The young prince and his family received this communication with indignation. The Emperor sent a special envoy to the English queen to demand an explanation and a positive answer. Elizabeth coolly replied she had, "*on reflection, no desire to marry, but to live and die a virgin.*" *

This was another of Cecil's intrigues in which he triumphed over his strong-minded mistress.

During the marriage negotiations De Quadra, the newly appointed Spanish ambassador, informs King Philip that Queen Elizabeth "was not sincere in dealing with the proposals of marriage offered to her upon the part of the Archduke Charles." And he adds, "that the peers, the majority of whom were *then* Catholic, might offer the crown to the Archduke, and marry him to Lady Catharine Gray." †

De Quadra was much mistaken at the juncture as to the probable action of the Catholic nobles. Besides, there was scarcely a man amongst them who could plot and intrigue against Sir William Cecil. His spies were everywhere, violating the privacy and honour of domestic life. Husband and wife, sons and daughters, were in turn the unconscious agents of Cecil's debasing schemes of action, which struck at the very foundation of private friendship and the integrity which should exist in all proper conditions of society.

Just as the Austrian ambassador was retiring from the scene, "full of indignation" at the fashion in which his royal

---

* Queens of England, Vol. IV.
† De Quadra's Correspondence with Philip, Nov. 15, 1559.

master had been treated, the Duke of Finland arrived in London to solicit the hand of the Queen for his brother, Eric, King of Sweden.* The Duke of Finland was received with royal honours, and, like the envoys of other suitors, flattered with delusive hopes. To Elizabeth he paid the most effusive attentions. He also sought to win the goodwill of the Queen's favourites by his affability and presents. As he went to court, he scattered "small bags of money amongst the needy crowds who occupied the streets, saying he gave them silver, but the King, his royal brother, would give them gold."

"The Swede, and Charles the son of the Emperor Ferdinand," observes Bishop Jewel, "are courting at a most marvellous rate. But the Swede is most in earnest, for he promises mountains of silver in case of success. The lady (Elizabeth), however, is probably thinking of an alliance nearer home."† The Duke of Finland, on this occasion, thought to supplant his royal brother in the Queen's affections, but Elizabeth cared little for either. Finland presented a ring worth five thousand crowns to the Queen, who at once, with great dignity, declined the gift.

On the ground of religion, the Queen and her Council could have had no objection to handsome King Eric, for he was as Protestant as they desired. But the private and public character of the man quickly dismissed his suit from all consideration by the English Queen. The Duke of Finland was recalled by his brother, who sent eighteen piebald horses

---

* Eric was, next to Henry VIII., the greatest Church plunderer in Europe. Like Henry, he confiscated the small income then in the possession of hospitals for the poor in Sweden. His immorality was revolting. In a note on Vol. VII., p. 96, of Mr. Froude's History of England, he describes Eric, King of Sweden, "*as the greatest ruffian among the crowned heads of Europe.*"

† Zurich Letters, printed by the Parker Society.

and several chests of bullion, with an intimation that he would "quickly follow in person to lay his *heart at the feet of the Virgin Queen.*"* Elizabeth had no objection to the presents: indeed, there are many cases on record where she accepted presents from the prisoners of her arbitrary will.† But, to relieve herself from the expense and embarrassment of a visit from King Eric, she requested him, for his own sake, to postpone his journey to England till the time when she could make up her mind to enter into married life.

So the proposed match was abandoned, and Eric married one of his own subjects—a woman of humble life, but far superior in beauty to the English Queen, and repaid his choice by the sincerity of her attachment.

I cannot pass over this romantic incident in the life of a prince whose whole career was full of adventure and ended so sadly. A "beauty of humble degree," called "Kate the Nut-girl," with whom King Eric became passionately in love, from seeing her occasionally selling nuts on the public streets of Stockholm. Having found the virtue of the humble maid impregnable, a sudden change came over the spirit of the King's dream, and the licentious Eric raised the Nut-girl to the position of his Queen, in which rank she proved herself to be a model of conjugal tenderness, and with a heart full of sympathy for the poor and the unfortunate. When reverse of fortune overtook her husband, being dethroned, and subsequently murdered by his brother, the "Nut-girl" proved to be the noblest of wives. In after years

---

* See Holinshed; also Nichols' Progresses; and Lingard, Vol. VI.

† When Mary Queen of Scots was confined at Tutbury Castle, she sent costly dresses and magnificent embroidery to Elizabeth, which the latter very freely accepted, whilst she kept her predestined victim in close confinement.

Queen Elizabeth often recurred to the tragic story of King Eric and "faithful Kate," as she sometimes styled her former rival.

Jealousy of the power of Eric had induced the King of Denmark to set up a rival suitor in the person of his nephew, Adolphus, Duke of Holstein. This prince was young and handsome, and, for a brief period, charmed "Golden Eliza." On his arrival he was received with honour, and treated with marked attention. The ladies of the Court believed that the Queen was "quite in love with him." Peyto, writing to Sir Nicholas Throckmorton, assures him that the young prince loved the Queen, and she warmly returned his passion for her. Throckmorton thoroughly understood the secret feelings of his Royal mistress, and he often had the courage to tell her so. Elizabeth and Holstein were constantly together—for a while. She created him a Knight of the Garter, and granted him a pension for life; yet, with all her seeming love for this young prince, she could not be induced to take him for her husband.* What part did Cecil take in this "love-match?" Most probably he was in favour of it, whilst, through the agency of his female spies, he caused matters to take an opposite turn.

While Charles, Eric and Adolphus openly contended for the hand, or rather the crown, of Elizabeth, they were secretly opposed by a rival whose pretensions were the more formidable as they received the united support of the secretary (Cecil) and of the secretary's wife.† This rival was the Earl of Arran,‡ whose "zeal for the glory of God had been stimulated with the hope of an earthly reward in the marriage of Queen

---

* Camden, Vol. I., p. 69.   † Forbes, Vol. I., p. 443.

‡ See Letters from Maitland, Melville, and Arran, in Haynes, 359, 362, 363; Keith, 154; Lingard, Vol. VI.

Elizabeth." During the war of the Reformation Lord Arran had displayed a courage and constancy exhibited by none of his associates. To the deputies of the Scottish Convention, who urged Arran's suit, Elizabeth replied that she was "*content with her maiden state*, and that God had given her *no inclination for marriage.*

The Earl of Arran was "affronted at this disappointment," and, we are informed, he fell into a melancholy which ended in the loss of his reason.

From foreign princes I may turn to those among the Queen's own subjects, who, prompted by their hopes, or deceived by her fascinating smiles, flattered themselves with the expectation of espousing her. The first of these notables was Sir William Pickering. He could not boast of noble blood, nor had he exercised any higher charge than that of a mission to some of the petty princes of Germany. But the beauty of his person, his address, and his taste for the polite arts, attracted the notice of the Queen; and so lavish was she of her attention to this unexpected favourite that for some weeks he was considered by the courtiers as her future husband. The courtship of Pickering, however, suddenly came to an end, and he was soon forgotten.

If disparity of age could have been compensated by political experience and nobility of descent, Henry Fitzalan, Earl of Arundel, and Premier Earl of England, had a better claim to royal notice than Pickering.* For some years Arundel persevered in his suit, to the "disquietude of his conscience and the disparagement of his fortune." He was by persuasion a Catholic, but, to please the Queen, he voted in favour of the change of religion; yet he never openly

---

* In the chapter entitled " Men of the New and the Old Learning," I have referred to Lord Arundel.

joined the Reformers. Both parties looked upon him with "some degree of suspicion." The Earl of Arundel possessed considerable estates, but involved himself in debt, by expensive presents, and by entertainments given to his Sovereign, whom he almost worshipped. When at length he could no longer subserve the Queen's whims, promote her political intrigues, or minister to her amusements, Elizabeth cast off the most faithful of all her suitors, and treated him not only with coldness, but permanently with asperity. In 1566 Lord Arundel felt the weight of the Queen's displeasure for his participation in the scheme for marrying the Duke of Norfolk to the Queen of Scots; and from that time till his death, in February, 1580, he was almost always confined to his house by an order from the Queen's Council. So much for being a lover under the last of the Tudors.

Anon I shall introduce to the reader the rival—the successful rival—for a time, of Lord Arundel, in the handsome and youthful person of Robert Dudley, popularly known as "Golden Eliza's Sweet Robin."

CHAPTER XIX.

THE ROYAL FAVOURITE.

BEFORE the death of Queen Mary the Dudley family regained a portion of their former honours. The dowager Duchess, through interest with King Philip, procured the "restoration in blood of her remaining children." The dukedom had been, "in way of law," formally estreated. Robert Dudley, who subsequently played so notable a part at the Court of Elizabeth, became, upon his release from the Tower, a favourite with Philip and Mary. He was the confidential agent who carried all messages from the Queen to her husband during the absence of the latter from England. Having completely won Mary's confidence, she appointed him Master of the Ordnance.

Dudley's personal graces and elegant accomplishments were sufficiently striking to dazzle the eye and charm the heart of Elizabeth.* There are several stories related as to how Dudley first became acquainted with Elizabeth, but perhaps the most correct one is that she first knew him at her sister's Court, where, as just stated, he was much regarded, although he had been a rebel a few months previously. In this memoir, it is with reluctance I am compelled to make a few references to the scandals that have been chronicled concerning the Queen and Robert

---

* Aikin's Court of Elizabeth, Vol. I., p. 240.

Dudley. The country undoubtedly believed that there were good grounds for the reports in circulation.

In the fifth year of Elizabeth's reign she granted Robert Dudley the castle and manor of Kenilworth and Astel Grove, the lordships and manors of Denbigh and Chirk, with other lands and possessions, together with a special license for transporting cloth, which license he sold to some merchant.* He was appointed Master of the Horse, with a fee of one hundred marks a year; and, to the astonishment of the nobility and the people, this favourite, or lover of the Queen, was created a Knight of the Garter, and soon afterwards Constable of Windsor Castle. Leicester was installed in his honours with great state at Westminster Abbey. The Queen, in her chair of state, personally invested her "own sweet Robin" with the new robes of his dignities as he knelt before her. The Queen seemed delighted on this occasion, and did not conceal her admiration for the man, when she tickled him under the chin, and then, turning to the Scotch ambassador, Melville, she inquired how he liked the new Earl; and was he not the kind of man a young maiden could love?—adding, with a coquettish smile, "I will never marry, but remain a Virgin Queen."†

The private and public character of Robert Dudley has been almost universally condemned by historians of every creed and shade of opinion. In religious matters he held the accommodating opinions of the Dudleys. In Edward's reign he was a Reformer; when Mary succeeded, and Jane Grey was vanquished, he seemed a zealous Catholic; upon the accession of Elizabeth he once more changed sides. He recanted *three times*, and, according to the De Quadra

---

* The Sydney Papers.   † Sir James Melville's Letters.

despatches, he was prepared to enter the lists as a champion of Catholicity if his Royal mistress thought proper to become reconciled to the Court of Rome.

De Quadra, the Spanish Minister who was, perhaps, one of the keenest judges of men in his time, has left on record his opinion as to the character of Robert Dudley. In a letter to Count Feria, dated March 7th, 1560, he says :—

"Lord Robert Dudley is the worst young man I ever encountered. He is heartless, spiritless, treacherous and false. There is not a man in England who does not cry 'out upon him' as the Queen's ruin."*

When that picture was drawn, Robert Dudley was six and twenty years of age, but looked some five years younger, and this was the period when the enthusiastic infatuation of the "Golden Eliza" for the handsome varlet was at its highest.

To the astonishment of the country, the Queen conferred the title of Earl of Leicester upon the "married man" whom the voice of scandal pointed to as the lover of her Highness. No man in the Court of Elizabeth could have better known the subject of the foregoing description than Thomas Radclyffe, Earl of Sussex. Although grand chamberlain, he often quarrelled with Dudley; he nearly as often made peace for him with the Queen; besides, he was aware of the "projected relationship," and, being the Queen's cousin, he was prudently silent.

At a period when the "Royal Favourite" became universally detested, and the scandals connecting his name with the private life of Elizabeth was upon every lip, the Queen's Council made a public declaration to the effect that everything that had recently been written and spoken against Lord Robert Dudley, known as the Earl of Leicester, were

---

* De Quadra's Despatches to Count Feria.

"the pure inventions of some vile person," and they declared "*in their sincere consciences* that the Earl of Leicester *rendered wondrous service to the country; that they believed in the sincerity of his religious professions, and all the faithful dealings he had made towards her Highness the Queen; and of his goodness, loyalty and truth, they had long and true experience.*"

The above statement came from Sir William Cecil, whose secret correspondence and other papers supply sufficient material to lay bare the true character of Robert Dudley. Yet, *before* the Queen, *before* the people of England, William Cecil was the bosom friend of Robert Dudley. Yet both hated each other, though their interests made them apparent friends.

There are documents still extant, in the handwriting of Dudley and Cecil, concerning a proposition for the assassination of the unfortunate Queen of Scots, which at once present the real character of those ministers of Elizabeth. The reader is aware of the cruel readiness with which Dudley subsequently wrote from Holland to suggest "*the sure but silent operation of poison.*"* He went so far as to send over one of his *chaplains — a discreet divine —* to convince the "tender-hearted and scrupulous" Francis Walsingham, of the "lawfulness" of the means he proposed for destroying the Royal prisoner then pining in Fotheringay Castle.

In May, 1559, De Quadra despatches an account of the state of affairs in England and Ireland to his royal master:—

"Of the Archduke Charles her Highness (Elizabeth) affects to know nothing; but she declared 'never to marry a man who

---

* See Camden's Elizabeth, in White-Kennett, p. 519; Miss Strickland's Queens of England, Vol. IV., p. 513.

would *sit all day by the fireside.* When she married, it should be some one who could *ride, hunt, and fight.'* * * * * The Irish Chiefs have communicated with me. They humbly request your Majesty to receive them as your subjects. *You have but to say the word, and Ireland is yours in devotion and love."*

The Irish chieftains were profuse in chivalrous pledges, but whether from accident, inability, or destiny, they never fulfilled their promises.

In October, 1559, De Quadra writes more freely to his friend Count Feria. "It is," he observes, "the devil's own business here."

The Catholics were far from being] as united and patriotic as the Spanish ambassador was led to believe. The English Catholics of this time were a cold, selfish people, and, above all, they did not desire to fraternise with their Irish co-religionists, whom they looked upon as a conquered race. The Irish on this occasion came forward with a wild enthusiasm to defend their religion, regardless of every sacrifice. The contrast between the "defenders of the faith" in England and Ireland was striking. De Quadra had a great admiration for the Irish Catholics; "but," said he, "I regret they are so *wild and indiscreet. They are, however, as brave and as good-natured as if they were Spaniards.* Their history has been a sad one. Will they ever become united? I fear not. We all sympathise with the brave warm-hearted Irish, who are so devoted to our holy religion."*

About Christmas, 1559, De Quadra sent one of his lively missives to Count Feria:—

"*This woman* (Elizabeth), is possessed *with a hundred thousand devils; and yet she pretends to me that she would like to be a nun, and live in a cell, and tell her beads from*

---

* The Bishop of Aquila's Correspondence with Shane O'Neill.

morning till night. What does she mean ?—or can any one control her ? I believe not."

To return to the Dudley scandal, sufficient evidence remains that the sentiments of Sir William Cecil respecting the Queen's behaviour to Dudley coincided with those of his friend ; and that fears for her reputation gave additional urgency about this period (1560) to those pleadings in favour of matrimony which her Council were doomed to press upon her attention so often, and so much in vain. But a circumstance occurred soon after which totally changed the nature of their apprehensions respecting her future conduct; and rendered her anticipated choice of a husband no longer an object of hope and joy, but of general dissatisfaction and alarm.

Just when the whispered scandal of the Court had apprized Dudley how obvious to all beholders the partiality of his Sovereign had become ; just when her rejection of the proposals of so many foreign princes had confirmed the suspicion that her heart had "given itself at home ;" just, in short, when everything conspired to sanction hopes which under any other circumstances would have appeared no less visionary than presumptuous; at the very juncture most favourable to his ambition, but most perilous to his reputation, Lord Robert Dudley lost his wife, and by a fate equally sudden and mysterious. This unfortunate lady had been sent by her husband, under the conduct of Sir Richard Verney, one of his retainers—but for what reason, or under what pretext, does not appear—to Cumnor House, in Berkshire ; a solitary mansion inhabited by Anthony Foster, also a dependent of Dudley's and bound to him by particular obligations. Here she soon after met with her death ; and Verney and Foster, who appear to have been alone in the house with her, gave out that it *happened by an accidental fall down stairs.* But this account, from various causes, gained so little credit in the neighbourhood, that reports of the most sinister import were quickly propagated. These discourses soon reached the ears of Thomas Lever, a Prebendary of Coventry, and a very conscientious person, who immediately addressed to the Secretaries of State an earnest letter, still extant, " Beseeching them to cause strict inquiry to be made into the case, as it was commonly believed that the lady had been murdered * * * *." The popular voice, which was ever hostile to Dudley, continued to accuse him as the "contriver of his wife's fate."* Sir William Cecil, in a secret memorandum, drawn up some years later, gave his reasons for opposing a marriage between the Queen and Lord Leicester. If the union took place Cecil was determined to resign office.

Whether the thorough investigation of Lady Dudley's death was evaded by the artifices of her husband, or whether his enemies, finding it impracticable to bring the crime home to him, judged it more advisable to drop the inquiry, certain it is that the Queen was never brought in any manner to take cognisance of the affair, and that Dudley continued to enjoy her friendship, or, as the ladies of the Court would have it, HER LOVE.

Lord Robert Dudley was married to the beautiful Amy, daughter of Sir John Robsart, when in his nineteenth year. The ceremony was performed in the presence of young King Edward, who notes it in his diary. The Court gossip of the time would have the marriage a love match. It turned out, however, to have been a most unhappy union. Upon the

---

* Aikin's " Court of Elizabeth," Vol. I., p. 291-2.

accession of Elizabeth, Dudley spent his time at Court, and in constant attendance on " golden Eliza," by whom he was " passionately caressed," to the astonishment of her ladies. It is worthy of remark that his broken-hearted wife was never invited to Court, or in any way noticed by the Queen. Lady Dudley's reputation was above reproach. She occupied her time for years in doing good offices for the poor, and fostering orphans. She was as much beloved as her husband was despised. According to her brother's statement, Lady Dudley had a presentiment, during the last two years of her life, that she would meet " a sudden and violent end."

In every circle, from the peer to the peasant, Dudley was an object of scorn or hatred. The popular saying in London was to the effect that the " Royal Favourite " was the son of a duke, the brother of a king, the grandson of a knight, the nephew of an esquire who robbed a church of a golden chalice, and the great-grandson of a carpenter; that the *carpenter was the only honest man in the whole family, and the only one who died in his bed.**

The excitement on the Continent respecting the " accident " by which Lady Dudley lost her life, was very great. Sir Nicholas Throckmorton, the English ambassador in Paris, writing to Sir William Cecil on the subject, remarks:— " I know not where to turn, or what countenance to bear. I would rather perish with honesty than live with shame."†

I cannot help here remarking that subsequent events proved that, notwithstanding this flourish of sentiment, Nicholas

---

* A tradition once existed in Warwickshire that Lord Leicester did not die on "his bed," but "went roving through the house for hours in great agony, then sat down on a stair, gave a scream, and expired." No reliance can be placed on such narratives.

† Hardwicke State Papers, Vol. I., p. 121.

Throckmorton was a man possessed of neither "honesty nor shame, as subsequent actions proved."

Elizabeth's conduct, on many occasions, involved singular contradictions. In reply to the first address presented to her by Parliament, she declared that, from a *religious feeling*, she never intended marrying. At the conclusion of her oration, her Highness drew from her finger the coronation ring, and, showing it to the Commons, told them that— "when she received that ring she had solemnly bound herself in marriage to the realm, and that it would be quite sufficient for the memorial of her name, and for her glory, if, when she died, an inscription were engraved on a marble tomb, saying—'*Here lieth Elizabeth, which reigned a Virgin, and died a Virgin.*'"*

At this time the Queen was twenty-five years of age, and in the face of the above declaration, was secretly pledged to marry Lord Dudley, and, at the same period, she "entertained proposals" from several others, both at home and abroad. In after years she affected to throw a certain air of romance around her love story.

I refer the reader to Sir Christopher Hatton's "mysterious love epistles" to Elizabeth, written about 1573, when she had attained her fortieth year. At this time her admiration for Hatton was well known; she boasted of it to her ladies; and was enthusiastic in speaking of the beauty of his person. Hatton's letters place the honour of the Queen as a woman in an unpleasant light. That great delver in historic lore, Sir Harris Nicolas, expresses a strong opinion as to the impropriety of her Highness in receiving a correspondence like that of

---

* Grafton's Chronicle; Holinshed, Vol. II.; Renaud's Despatches; Miss Strickland's "Queens of England," Vol. IV.

Hatton's.* The Queen, however, expressed her resentment at the warmth of his correspondence, and she did so in very emphatic words.

It is difficult to separate the deeds of a minister from the action or assent of a Sovereign—especially when the monarch is absolute, and the subordinate not only an adviser but a lover. Perhaps the most villainous act of a life of wickedness was committed about 1583-4, by the Earl of Leicester. Although the scaffold streamed with blood, and the demon of hate and destruction banquetted on daily horrors, the treatment of Edward Arden startled mankind by its peculiar atrocity. This fine old English squire, the cousin of Shakespeare's mother, had, like a spirited yeoman, refused to don the livery of Leicester, and to " do suit and service " at his Castle of Kenilworth in one of those displays of his ill-gotten wealth in which he was so fond of indulging. Arden had the misfortune of having a son-in-law named Somerville, who chanced to be a Catholic, but was known to be insane. The lunatic had threatened in one of his paroxysms that he would murder every Protestant in England, and the Queen as their head. This access of madness supplied a ready pretext to the mindful vengeance of Leicester. Arden, his wife, daughters, sisters, and a priest named Hall, were arrested and thrown into prison. The two men were subjected to the torture of the rack ; Arden was then carried to the gallows, and Father Hall was permitted a brief but painful existence with half-broken limbs. Somerville, the lunatic, was strangled in his cell at Newgate ; the ladies were enlarged—but as beggars, for Leicester had parcelled out all the lands and goods of Edward Arden amongst his dependents.†

---

* Memoirs of Sir Christopher Hatton, calendared from the State Papers, by Sir Harris Nicolas, pp. 25-28.

† See Camden ; Dugdale ; Bishop Goodman ; Howell's State Trials ; Lingard, Vol. VI. ; Miss Strickland's " Queens of England," Vol. IV.

In this much-vaunted reign the sacrifice of human life was appalling; and the absence of all moral and divine restrictions of conscience more melancholy still. Scaffolds streamed with blood; the pestilential gaols were crowded with victims, the greater number of whom died of fever or famine, unpitied and unrecorded, save in the annals of private families. In November, 1577, the Attorney-General was commanded by the Queen to examine Thomas Sherwood *on the rack*, and orders were given to place him *in the dungeon among the rats*.

Leicester was anxious to lower the bishops in the eyes of the people in order to please the Puritans; whilst such prelates as Parker and Whitgift thought that the right way to raise the Prelacy in the popular estimation was to keep a stately appearance, and to dispense hospitality on a large scale. At a later period, when Whitgift became Archbishop of Canterbury, he entered the cathedral city attended by one thousand horse, and one hundred servants in magnificent livery.* The bishops, of course, did not like the "Royal Favourite," though they paid him the most obsequious homage. The reasons were obvious. Perhaps, like Christopher Hatton with the Bishop of Ely, Dudley desired "a few acres" from some bishop's highly cultivated domain. With a large section of the Puritans Leicester was popular merely for the contempt and scorn he cast upon the bishops, whom they hated. There was no real bond of sympathy between Leicester and the Puritans. They believed the Royal Favourite to "have been in reality a Papist." They were, however, much mistaken in that respect.

Gilbert Talbot's description of the Queen's Court during the Leicester scandals in some measure bears out all that

---

* Archbishops of Canterbury, Vol. IX.

has been reported:—" My Lord of Leicester is very much with her Highness, and she shows him the same great, good affection she was wont; of late, he has endeavoured to please her more than heretofore. There are two sisters now in the Court that are very far in love with him, as they long have been—my Lady Sheffield and Frances Howard. They (striving who shall love him the best) are at great wars with each other, and the Queen thinketh not well of them, and not the better of him; for this reason there are spies over him. My Lord of Oxford is lately grown into great credit, for the Queen's Highness delighteth more in his person, his dancing, and his valiantness, than any other. I think the Earl of Sussex doth back him all he can, and were it not for his (Oxford's) fickle head, he would pass all of them shortly. My Lady Burleigh has declared herself, as it were, jealous. [My Lady Burleigh's daughter had married Oxford, who used her cruelly; she was, probably, jealous of the Queen's coquetries with her daughter's husband.] The Queen has been not a little offended with her, but now she is reconciled. At all these love matters my Lord Treasurer, Burleigh, winketh, and will not meddle any way."*

Carte is of opinion that Lady Dudley's death " was occasioned *not* by accident, but by violence."† Of Dudley he says:—" He had great vices, and no sense of honour or religion." Echard, like other Puritan writers, feels reluctance in approaching any investigation of Dudley's character; but, nevertheless, he makes a few admissions:—" Robert Dudley lived without any religion towards God, or fidelity to man. * * * He had all the tyranny, insolence, and aspiring

---

* Gilbert Talbot was son to the Earl of Shrewsbury, one of the cruel gaolers of Mary Queen of Scots.

† Carte's History of England, Vol. III., p. 416.

ambition of the worst of favourites; and all the luxury, treachery, and most abominable villanies of the worst of men; Queen Elizabeth, with all her virtues and goodness, was scarcely able to secure herself from being made infamous and unfortunate by the monstrous wickedness of this Earl of Leicester."*

Lloyd affirms that the amount of "treasure possessed by Lord Leicester was vast, his gains uncountable; all passages to preferment being in his hands, at home and abroad. He was seldom reconciled to the Queen, when they quarrelled, under £5,000, nor to a subject under £500." A contemporary says of him, in incongruous words:—" Every one respected, feared, and loved him." Hume concurs in the general censure passed upon Dudley. "He possessed," observes Hume, "all those exterior qualities which naturally arrest the attention of women; he was very handsome in person, had a polite address, and an insinuating behaviour. By means of these accomplishments he had been able to blind even the penetration of the Queen, and to conceal from her the many defects, or rather odious vices, which marked his character. He was mean, proud, insolent, sordid, and ambitious, without that integrity which characterises honour, without that generosity for which men of rank and education in those days were so often remarkable. He neither possessed pity nor humanity. Attendant on his bad qualities he was a man of poor abilities and less courage, and wholly unfit for the high offices with which he was honoured by his Sovereign." Mr. Froude sums up:—" Of Robert Dudley's qualities so little can be said to his advantage that were not the thing so common, one would wonder which of them attracted such a

---

* Echard's History of England, Vol. II., p. 384.

woman as Elizabeth. If the Queen had a man's nature, Robert Dudley combined in himself the worst qualities of both sexes; without courage, without talent, without virtue, he was the handsome, soft, polished, and attentive minion of the Court."*

The name of Elizabeth has long been pronounced with reverence and love by the English people. Results have inverted causes in the vision of the unreflecting, and consequences have been accepted with too ready faith in utter oblivion of motives. If this be true of Elizabeth as a Politician, may it not be also true of her as a Woman? De Foy, the French ambassador, like other foreign ministers, bears testimony to the outspoken passion of Elizabeth for Dudley: "Why, monsieur, I cannot *live without seeing him every day*. He is like my lap-dog; so soon as he is seen anywhere the people say I am at hand, and whenever I am seen, it may be said that he is there also."† De Foy is "most positive" that Elizabeth promised, in the presence of witnesses, to marry "her own Sweet Robin." To the great mortification of the Queen's Council, Leicester was in the habit of boasting to foreign ambassadors of the "immense influence he exercised upon her Highness." It is well known, however, that he never influenced her to do a good action for anyone; but, on the contrary, his interest at Court was used for malicious purposes. How unlike Hatton or Essex!

In almost every relation of life there is a striking contrast between Lord Leicester and his nephew Philip Sidney. Even Sir Thomas Naunton, a zealous partisan of Dudley,

---

* A very fine miniature of the Earl of Leicester is in the possession of the Duke of Buccleuch. It is inscribed with the name of Lord Leicester, and the date of his death, 1588.

† De Foy's Despatches to the French Government.

hesitates to say much in his praise ; and what he does venture in the way of eulogy is but the expression of a presumption to which any well-acted deceit can give birth. The De Quadra correspondence, and the records of the man's actions, furnish the best refutation of these silly statements, which are so detrimental to the cause of historical truth. The Sydney Papers, Camden, Goodman, Dugdale, Howel's "State Trials," Lingard and Froude, have long since given an honest verdict against the reputation of Leicester.

Birch, in his Memoirs of Elizabeth and her Ministers, writes thus of Lord Leicester :—" He was most obnoxious in his private character ; and suspected on good grounds of the most shocking crimes, which he affected to conceal under high pretensions to piety."

It must have been with regret, and influenced by a high sense of truth, that Thomas Birch admitted so much regarding Leicester, for he was a noted adulator of Elizabeth and her ministers. What might not this cleric have said, had he known, as we do now, that, along with all his other execrable faults, Leicester was *a rank Atheist ?**

---

* In the fourth volume of this work will appear the " last days " of the Earl of Leicester.

CHAPTER XX.

DIPLOMATIC REVELATIONS.

DE QUADRA, writing to King Phillip, in September, 1560, gives, on the authority of Sir William Cecil, amply confirmed by independent testimony, sufficient proof of Elizabeth's knowledge of some dark deeds at Cumnor Hall.

"After many protestations and entreaties that I would keep secret what he (Cecil) was about to tell me, he said that the Queen was going on so strangely that he would immediately withdraw from her service. It was a bad sailor, he said, who did not make for the port when he saw a storm coming. . . . He perceived the most manifest ruin impending over the Queen through her intimacy with Lord Robert Dudley. Dudley had made himself master of the business of the State, and of the person of the Queen, to the extreme injury of the realm, with the intention of marrying her Highness. She was *shutting herself up in the palace to the peril of her health and life.* That the realm would tolerate the marriage, he said, he did not believe. He was, therefore, determined to retire into the country, although he supposed they would send him to the Tower before they would let him go. He implored me, for the love of God, to remonstrate with the Queen, to persuade her not to throw herself utterly away; and to remember what she owed to herself and to her subjects. . . . Of Lord Robert, Cecil twice said he would be better in Paradise than here." The Ambassador continued: "Last of all, Cecil stated that there was some rumour of *destroying Lord Robert's wife.* It was given out that she was very ill; but she was not ill at all, but was very well, and *taking care not to be poisoned.*"

"The day after this conversation the Queen, on her return from hunting, told me that Lord Robert's wife was dead, or nearly so, and begged me to say nothing about it.* Assuredly it is a matter full of shame and infamy. Nevertheless, I do not feel sure her Highness will marry Dudley, or, indeed, that she will marry at all. She wants resolution to take any decided step. Sir William Cecil states that she wishes to act like her father.

"These quarrels amongst themselves and Cecil's retirement from office will do no harm to the good cause. We could not have to do with any one worse than he has been."

De Quadra then goes on to discuss the chances of a French interference on behalf of Lord Huntingdon, and ends his letter with this simple and significant sentence, " Since this was written the death of Lord Robert's wife has been given out publicly. The Queen said, in Italian, 'They say she has broken her neck.' It seems she fell down a staircase."

From the above, the reader may form some idea of the secret intrigues which existed between Elizabeth and Dudley. Court affairs must have been in a sad state when Sir William Cecil deemed it, as it may appear, a duty to unbosom his feelings to such an astute diplomatist as De Quadra. Many will naturally discredit such statements as those of the Spanish envoy, but there are the very best reasons for giving entire credence to the letters of De Quadra to his Royal master.

---

* Miss Strickland, who is undoubtedly a high authority, "cannot credit this scandal"; she states that "Amy Robsart was in her grave two years before the accession of Elizabeth." If that were the case, the accidental death must have occurred in Mary's reign; but an overwhelming mass of evidence fastens the transaction upon the early part of Elizabeth's accession. Cecil's objection to the marriage with Dudley; the excitement on the Continent; Throckmorton's confidential letters; the denunciations from the English pulpits against Dudley and the Queen; and the scenes from the De Quadra correspondence, make the case, if possible, stronger. Miss Strickland has evidently fallen into an error, and one of the few which are to be found in her interesting and valuable history.

Mr. Froude, who, whilst admitting De Quadra's abilities, writes of him otherwise in no friendly mood, gives valuable and sterling evidence to the trustworthiness of this distinguished diplomatist. "I think it likely," observes Mr. Froude, "that the Spanish ambassadors in those times possessed sources of information which the representatives of foreign States are usually without. I think that no deception could be long practised upon them by either party in the Council which would not have been betrayed by the other, and in no instance where their statements can be tested by other criteria have I found them to have been seriously mistaken."*

In January, 1561, De Quadra wrote another confidential letter to his Royal master. This secret despatch details thoroughly the deceitful policy of Elizabeth. With all her duplicity and cunning, the Queen could scarcely conceal the enthusiasm of her love for Robert Dudley. Was the Sovereign Lady sincere on this occasion? A difficult question to solve. The astute De Quadra, seated in his quiet mansion in the Strand, writes in this fashion to King Phillip :—

"There came lately to me Sir Henry Sydney, who is married to Lord Robert's sister,—a high-spirited, noble sort of person, and one of the best men the Queen has about her Court. After speaking generally on ordinary matters, he came to the affairs of his brother-in-law, and the substance of his words to me was this: 'The marriage is now in everybody's mouth,' he said, ' and the Queen, I must be aware, was very anxious for it. He was surprised that I had not advised your Majesty to use the opportunity to gain Lord Robert's goodwill. Your Majesty would find Lord Robert *as ready to obey you and do you service as one of your own vassals, with more to the same purpose.*'

"I replied that all which I had heard about the business was of such a character that I had not ventured to write two lines on

---

* Simancas MSS., translated by J. A. Froude.

the subject to your Majesty. Neither the Queen nor Lord Robert had spoken to me about it, and it was of no more importance to your Majesty to gain the goodwill of English sovereigns than it was for them to gain your Majesty's. Your Majesty could not divine the Queen's wishes, and she had shown so little inclination to follow your advice when you had offered it hitherto, that you could not be expected to volunteer your opinion.

"He (Sydney) admitted this. He is evidently well acquainted with what had passed, and is not too prejudiced to see the truth. But he added, that if I could be satisfied about Lady Dudley's death, he thought I could not object to informing your Majesty of what he had said. The Queen and Lord Robert *were lovers*, but they *intended honest marriage, and nothing wrong had taken place between them* which could *not be set right* with your Majesty's help. As to Lady Dudley's death, he said that he had examined carefully into the circumstances, and he was satisfied that it had been accidental, although he admitted that people thought differently.

"If this was true, I replied, things were not so bad as I had believed. Had Lady Dudley been murdered, God and man would have punished so abominable a crime. Lord Robert, however, would find it difficult to persuade the world of his innocence.

"He (Sydney) stated *that there was scarcely a party or person who did not believe that there had been foul play. The preachers in their pulpits spoke of it*, not sparing even *the honour* of the Queen; and this, he said, had brought her to consider whether she could not *restore order in the realm in these matters of religion. She was anxious to do it; and Lord Robert, to his own knowledge, would be ready to assist.*

"I answered that your Majesty would gladly see religion restored in England, as everywhere else; but it was not a thing to be mixed up with the concerns of this world. Whether married or wishing to be married, if the Queen was a Christian woman, she would regard religion as between God and herself.

"He (Sydney) said that I spoke truly, and, though ill-informed in such matters, he was satisfied that religion in this country was *in a deplorable condition*, and that it was imperatively necessary to take steps to reform it. He assured me, *on his solemn oath, that the Queen and Lord Robert were determined to restore the religion by way of the General Council.* He then went on to press me to write to your Majesty to forward the affair in such a form that Lord Robert should receive the prize at which he aims at your Majesty's hands.

"I reminded him of what had passed between me and Lady Sydney in the affairs of the Archduke Carlos, and how the Queen had deceived both her and myself. I said I could not write unless I received instructions from the Queen herself. In that case it would become my duty, and I would do it with pleasure.

"He said the Queen could not begin the subject with me, but I might assure myself she waited for nothing but your Majesty's consent to conclude the marriage. In the meantime Lord Robert would speak with me, and would desire me to communicate to your Majesty what I should hear from him. He would offer your Majesty his services to the extent of his power, in whatever you would be pleased to command; and, especially, he would be ready *to assist in restoring the religion—seeing clearly that it ought to be done, and that it was this which has separated England from your Majesty, and forfeited your protection.*

"I said again, that *religion ought not to be complicated with matters of this kind.* If Lord Robert desired me to communicate with your Majesty on the subject, I would make no difficulty; but I thought that his conscience should be motive sufficient when the course to be taken was so plain. If he desired to obtain your Majesty's good opinion, so much the more improper it seemed to me that he should stipulate for conditions.

"Sydney then asked whether I thought it would be well for the Queen to send a special minister to your Majesty to satisfy you on the point where your Majesty might look for fuller explanation as to what you were to expect both from herself and from him. The ambassador resident in Spain was a confirmed heretic, and not a person, therefore, whom the Queen could trust in a matter which concerned religion.

* * * * *

"I said I would think it over, and I would tell Lord Robert as soon as I had heard what he had to say. Sydney himself, I imagine, desires to go to Spain. He is a cousin of the Countess de Feria, and would like to see her.

"This was the end of our conversation. I now wait till Sydney brings Lord Robert Dudley to me.

"I have related to your Majesty exactly what passed between us. For some days I suspected that the Queen had something to communicate."

In a few weeks subsequent to the scenes between Sir Henry Sydney and the Spanish Ambassador, Lord Robert Dudley had an interview with De Quadra; but, as the latter had received no reply to his despatches, the question was not discussed. In his next letter to King Philip, De Quadra describes an interview with Elizabeth on the marriage question. The cautious diplomatist addresses his Royal master thus:—

"I informed the English Queen that she must be aware of your Majesty's desire to see her married. It was rumoured (said playfully the adaptable envoy) that she was seriously thinking of it, and I could not but tell her what pleasure the report had given me. Should she wish to consult your Majesty, I would use my diligence in communicating her wishes to you; and if I could not at that time be more precise, it was because my commission did not allow me.

"The Queen replied, with much circumlocution, that she would make me her ghostly father, and I should hear her confession. . . . It came to this—*she was no angel:* she could not deny that she had a strong regard for the *many excellent qualities* she saw in Lord Robert Dudley. She had not, indeed, resolved to marry him, or any one; only every day she felt more and more the want of a husband. She thought her own people would like to see her married to an Englishman. She next asked me what your Majesty would think if she married one of her own household, as the Duchess of Suffolk had done, and the Duchess of Somerset, whom she used to laugh at. To these questions I replied that I had formed no opinion, and had never spoken to your Majesty upon the matter; but if she directed me what to say, I would write to you and seek your advice. I further added, that, marry whom she may, your Majesty would be pleased to hear it; and, again, your Majesty was well aware of the *high character which was borne by Lord Robert Dudley.*

"With an air of much satisfaction, the Queen said she would speak to me in *confidence;* and in the meanwhile she would promise to do nothing without your Majesty's sanction. She evidently wished that I should say more; but I refrained, from fear of making a mistake, and because she is—*what we know her to be.* As there is danger, however, that, carried away by passion as she is, she may fly into some opposite extravagance, I would not, therefore, leave her without hope.

* * * * *

On the following day Lord Robert Dudley again visited De Quadra. He assured his Excellency that her Highness the Queen was quite delighted with her recent interview. She was but hesitating out of timidity; if he would but press her a little further, she would give way. Dudley then describes his own feelings:—

"For himself he could assure his Excellency (De Quadra) *that he would be Spanish, heart and soul. And, as to religion, not only should England send representatives to Trent, but, if necessary, he would attend the Council in person.*"

Robert Dudley at the Council of Trent! Such "an appearance" would accomplish the greatest marvel and the greatest scandal of the sixteenth century.

De Quadra smiled, and gave a searching look at the young man who would aspire to the position of a theologian. The wily diplomatist questioned the honesty of purpose which characterised the above professions on the part of a man who had earned a reputation in many English circles for Protestant zeal and piety, whilst his real character was that of the most noted profligate the country possessed, and added to this evil reputation was made a credible impeachment *for the murder of his own wife.*

De Quadra resumed the discourse. He said his Royal master would be happy to accept of Lord Robert Dudley's services; but, with respect to the Queen's return to the Catholic Church, *it must be a matter of conscience rather than a condition: it must not be said that Spain had made a bargain to recover England to orthodoxy."*

A fair consideration of these letters, whatever attempts may be made to explain them away, leaves an impression which the sequel will confirm, that Elizabeth's interest in the Reformation was eclipsed for an interval by her interest in Lord Robert Dudley.

Mr. Froude observes: " Stung by the reproaches of the Protestant preachers, which in her heart she knew to be deserved, she was tempted to forsake a cause to which, *in its theological aspect, she never was devoted.* If Philip would secure her the support of his friends in making a husband of the miserable son of the apostate* Northumberland, she was half ready to

---

* In what sense does Mr. Froude pronounce this base man as an *apostate?* As the reader is aware, when Earl of Warwick, upon the accession of Edward VI., he joined with Somerset in setting aside the religion of his fathers, to which he had sworn allegiance in the presence of King Henry VIII. Upon the death of Henry he commenced a series of revolutionary schemes; sent his friend Somerset to the block; created himself Duke of Northumberland; changed the royal succession: and finally perished upon the scaffold as a rebel, declaring in the most emphatic manner to the multitude, that he had been for sixteen years propagating a religious system in which he had never believed. And *then,* he *returned,* to use his own words, to the " grand old religion of his fathers." Mr. Froude may fairly apply the strongest epithet to this " Papist in disguise," who was doing the work of the Reformers, but he cannot style him an *apostate.*

undo her work, and throw the weight of the Crown once more on the Catholic side. Self-willed, self-confident, and utterly fearless, refusing to believe in her lover's infamy, and exasperated at the accusations which she might have wilfully considered undeserved, she could easily conceal from herself the nature of the act which she was contemplating; and the palace clique might have kept her blind to the true feelings of the country. De Quadra's story has *not the air of an invention.* It is, however, incredible that Sir Henry Sydney would have ventured to make a communication of such a character unless he had believed himself to have the Queen's sanction. This was the real secret of Elizabeth's position."*

Sir Henry Sydney knew his Royal mistress well. He was a sensible man, practical, far-seeing, and honest—honest, perhaps, as far as circumstances permitted. He was, like his kinsmen, the Dudleys, a political believer in the new creed, by which his fortune became improved. Elizabeth had immense confidence in him, styling him, at times, as "honest Harry." He was secretly consulted by his Royal mistress upon matters of which Cecil knew nothing. Considering all the "surroundings" of the extraordinary interviews with the Spanish Ambassador, I can arrive at no other conclusion but that Sir Henry Sydney was an "accredited agent" from his Sovereign, and that Lord Robert Dudley spoke more directly in the Queen's name.

De Quadra presents another scene (June 1561), in which he gives a likely reason for much of the hesitation and inconsistency exhibited by Elizabeth, and the pressure exercised by Sir William Cecil. Few monarchs, even the strongest minded, have been without an adviser, who, managing to

---

* J. A. Froude's History of England, Vol. VII., p. 314

render himself indispensable, has become the tyrant of his Sovereign. Cecil was one of these, although, of course, he never pretended dictation. He ruled by bending, and swayed Elizabeth by the fears he excited, and the belief he raised that he and his assistants could alone protect her from the cause of her apprehensions.

De Quadra writes thus to his Sovereign of the "little scene" on the river between the Queen and her lover :—

"In the afternoon we were in a barge, watching the games on the river. The Queen was alone with Lord Robert and myself on the poop when they began to talk nonsense, and went so far, that Lord Robert at last said, as I was on the spot, there was no reason why they should not be married, if the Queen pleased. Her Highness said that perhaps I did not understand sufficient English. * * * I let them trifle on in this way for a time, and then I said gravely to them both, that if they would be governed by me, they would shake off the tyranny of those men who were oppressing the realm and themselves likewise. By taking such a course, they would value religion and good order, and then they might marry when they pleased. *And gladly would I be the priest to unite them.* * * * With your Majesty (Philip) at her side Queen Elizabeth might defy danger. At present it seemed she could marry no one who displeased Sir William Cecil and his friends in the Council.

For a time Sir Nicholas Throckmorton had much influence with Elizabeth, but he never understood her character with that critical nicety which enabled Cecil to control her actions.

The answer to De Quadra's confidential correspondence arrived in due time. Philip doubted the sincerity of Elizabeth with regard to the proposition made in her name by Sir Henry Sidney. He required a declaration in her own hand, and signed with her name, that she wished to be reconciled to the Church. She must release the bishops and others who were in the Tower at that moment for refusing the Oath of Supremacy; she must allow her Catholic subjects to use their own services freely till the decision of the proposed Council. If she would satisfy Philip on these points, she might assure herself that his Majesty, and the English Catholics too, would promote her marriage with Lord Robert Dudley.* Mr. Froude does not approve of the policy pursued by Elizabeth at this juncture. "It was," he observes, "a misfortune of Elizabeth's stratagems that she deceived her friends as well as her enemies."

When Sir William Cecil was made acquainted with the contemplated changes, De Quadra saw that the Queen was not in earnest, and that Dudley was deceiving himself. If the Nuncio was received by the Queen, then there was some evidence that she was sincere; if she acted in the opposite spirit, Cecil triumphed. The Reformers became alarmed. "Were the Popish bishops to be released? Impossible." To satisfy his supporters Cecil had instituted a general search for "Popish conventicles." Sir Edward Waldegrave, one of the late Queen's Council, had Mass celebrated in his house. He was sent, with his wife, the priest, and the congregation to the Tower.† When this outrage upon Civil and Religious Liberty took place, Elizabeth was boasting to foreigners of the large amount of religious toleration enjoyed by her subjects. In fact the Queen was far more attached to her own love of power and authority than to any particular form of religion.

The Bishop of London (Grindal) was foremost in the persecutions carried on in the second and third years of Elizabeth's reign. He applied to the Lord Chief Justice

---

* King Philip's Correspondence with De Quadra.
† Domestic MSS., Rolles House.

Catlin to learn what the law was in the case of Sir Edward Waldegrave, and the Chief Justice replied, that it was an offence for which no provision had been made. " Then the law must be amended," said the bishop, in a very disappointed mood. Grindal was most vindictive where Catholics or Puritans were concerned.

Sir William Cecil, writing to Sir Nicholas Throckmorton, states that he thought it " necessary to check the Papists by at once punishing the Mass-mongers."*

Sir Henry Sydney suddenly received orders from the Government to repair to his Presidency in Wales. Before leaving London he visited De Quadra, and assured him of the treachery which had been enacted in " certain high quarters." The Queen had changed her mind, and would act like a woman, and the censure might fall upon himself, or perhaps it would affect Dudley.† The end of this entangled scheme was the rejection of the Nuncio, and the increased proscription of the Catholic party.

The interesting correspondence of De Quadra was suddenly brought to a close on the 20th of August, 1563. He died of the plague at his residence in the Strand. His last words to his chaplain and secretaries were :—" I am grieved to end my services at a moment when I hoped to be of use to the Catholic cause in England." After a pause he continued :— " I can do no more, but the faith which is within me gives the powerful assurance that Peter's Ship will never sink."

What a man might have done who had opened the mental cabinet of Sir William Cecil, and scanned the dark adyta within, will now ever remain a mystery. He certainly did not live long enough for his Royal master's advantage, and

---

* Conway MSS. ; Froude's " History of England," Vol. VII.
† Froude's " History of England," Vol. VII., p. 248.

Philip in him lost a heart leal through good and evil. Mr. Froude offers a tribute to the memory of the great diplomatic agent of Spain :—" He was brave as a Spaniard should be— brave with the double courage of an Ignatius and a Cortez. He was perfectly free from selfish and ignoble desires, and loyal with an absolute fealty to his creed and his King."

Lord Leicester renewed his propositions to the successor of De Quadra, Guzman de Silva, assuring the Ambassador, that if he was married to the Queen, he would engage to mitigate the sufferings of the Catholics. By this time the Spanish minister understood the character of the man, and consequently paid no attention to his alleged plot to overturn the newly-established religion of the country.

Mr. Froude has been the first to publish the above remarkable documents in full, and his translation is an admirable one. What a strange coincidence, that after the lapse of three centuries, O'Donnell, Duke of Tetuan—a descendant of that " Red Hugh " who was driven from Ireland by the arms of Elizabeth—should have had it in his power to open up the secret records in the archives of Simancas,* to enable the reader of English history to learn the true character of the arch-enemy of O'Donnell's creed and race.

---

* Simancas, a strong State fortress about eight miles from the city of Valladolid.

CHAPTER XXI.

1561—THE SOCIAL AND RELIGIOUS ASPECT OF ENGLAND.

IN July, 1561, under Sir William Cecil's directions, "letters went round the southern and western counties of England, desiring the magistrates to send in reports on the working of the laws which affected the daily life of the people; on the wages' statutes, and acts of approval; the tillage and pasture lands, the act for the maintenance of archery, and generally on the condition of the population." A trusted agent of Sir William Cecil was commissioned privately to follow the circulars, and observe how far the magistrates reported the truth, or were doing their duty; and though the reports are lost, the chief Commissioner's private letters to Cecil remain, with Mr. Tyldsley's opinion on the character of the English gentry. "If that opinion was correct," writes Mr. Froude, "the change of creed had not improved them." The report says:—"For tillage it were plain sacrilege to interfere with it, the offenders being all gentlemen of the richer sort; while the ale-houses—the *very stock and stay of thieves and vagabonds—were supported by them for the worst of motives*. The peers had the privilege of importing wine *free of duty for the consumption of their household*. By their patents they were able to extend the right to others under shelter of their name; and the tavern keepers were ' my lord's servants,' or, ' my masters ;' yea, and had such kind of licenses, and ' license of license,' to them and their deputies and assignees that it was some danger to meddle with them." The intention of the exemption, it was alleged, " had to do with the encouragement of hospitality in the houses of the country squires."

Times were changing, and the *old-fashioned open house for which England was so long noted was no longer the rule*. Without "abolishing the wine-privilege," the Council restricted the quantity which each nobleman was allowed to import. *Dukes and archbishops* were allowed ten pipes annually; marquises, nine pipes; earls, viscounts, barons and bishops, six, seven and eight pipes of wine.*

The magistrates of "high and low degree did little to put the law in force." The lower classes were dreadfully oppressed by the *new proprietary*. The summary eviction of the small tenants, and cruel treatment they received, caused *a widespread feeling of revenge against the lords of the soil*. People in trade were extortioners and usurers, and generally put the law at defiance. * * * *

The reports are not favourable to the condition of religion or morality in the fourth year of Elizabeth, when the priests of the secular order and their Puritan bishops were safely installed in their offices. I quote the report, with Mr. Froude's commentary :—

" The constitution of the Church offended the Puritans; the Catholics were as yet *unreconciled to the forms which had been retained to conciliate them*. * * * * *Self interest was interwoven with all religion*. The bishops and the higher clergy were the first to set an example of evil.

" The friends of the Church of England," writes Mr. Froude, " must acknowledge with sorrow that, within two years of its establishment, the prelates were alienating the estates in which they possessed *but a life interest*, granting long leases and *taking fines for their own advantage*."

---

* See Domestic MSS. of Elizabeth's reign, Vol. XX.

The Council sorely rebuked them for these dishonest proceedings. Not a voice was raised in defence of the bishops.*

The marriage of the priests was a point on which the Reformers were frequently divided, and peculiarly sensitive; *in fact, with few exceptions, they quite agreed with the Papal Catholics on this subject.*

It is related, upon high authority, that the frequent surnames of Clark, Parsons, Archdeacon, Dean, Prior, Abbot, Bishop, Friar and Monk are memorials of the stigma affixed by English prejudice on the children of the *first married* representatives of the clerical orders.† "And though married priests were tolerated, the system was generally disapproved, and disapproved especially in members of cathedrals and collegiate bodies, who occupied the houses, and retained the form of the religious orders. While, therefore, canons and prebends were *entitled* to take wives *if they could not do without them;* they would have done better had they taken every advantage of their liberty."

"To the Anglo-Catholic," remarks Mr. Froude, "as well as the Papal Catholic, a married priest was a scandal, and a married cathedral dignitary an abomination." ‡

Such was popular opinion in the reign of Elizabeth, and the Queen was emphatic in endorsing the sentiment. Notwithstanding, the married priests multiplied, and the spiritual flocks were completely neglected. The Queen and her Council soon found the difficulty of governing a multitude who were no longer under the influence of religious feeling.

There is still extant a proclamation issued by the Queen for "expelling wives" out of colleges. It is in the handwriting of Sir William Cecil, and runs thus :—

---

* See Articles for the Bishops' Obligations, 1560, Domestic MSS., Elizabeth.
† J. A. Froude's History of England, Vol. VII., p. 464.   ‡ Ibid.

"For the avoiding of such offences as were daily conceived by the presence of families, of *wives and children* within colleges, contrary to the ancient and comely order of the same, the Queen's Highness forbade deans and canons to have their *wives* residing with them within the cathedral closes, under pain of forfeiting their promotions. Cathedrals and colleges had been founded to keep societies of learned men professing study and prayer, and the rooms intended for students were not to be sacrificed to *women and their children*."*

The Church dignitaries treated the Queen's injunction as the country gentlemen treated the statutes. Deans and canons, by the rules of their foundation, were directed to dine and keep hospitality in their common hall. Those among them who had married broke up into their separate houses, where, in spite of the Queen, they maintained their families. The unmarried "*tabled abroad at the ale houses.*" The singing men of the choirs became the prebends' private servants, "having the Church stipend for their wages." "*The cathedral plate adorned the prebendal side-boards and dinner tables. The organ-pipes were melted into dishes for their kitchens; the organ-frames were carved into bedsteads, where the wives reposed beside their reverend lords; while the copes and vestments were coveted for their gilded embroidery, and were slit into gowns and bodices.*† Having children to provide for, and only a life-interest in their revenues, the chapters, like the bishops, cut down their woods, and worked their fines, their leases, their escheats and wardships for the benefit of their own generation. Sharing their annual plunder, they ate and drank and enjoyed themselves while

---

* Domestic MSS., Elizabeth, Vol. XIX.

† Mr. Pocock, F.S.A., has published a work full of sad memories on the fate of the magnificent vestments of the English Church furniture, ornaments, &c. In many cases the vestments were sold to strolling players.

their opportunity remained. * * * The priests decked their wives so finely for the stuff and fashion of their garments, 'as none were so fine and trim.'" By her dress and her gait in the streets, "the *priest's wife was known from a hundred other women;*" while in the congregations and in the cathedrals they were distinguished by placing themselves above all others the most ancient and honourable in their cities; "being the Church—as the priests' wives termed it—*their own Church;* and the said wives did call and take all things belonging to *their* Church and corporation as *their* own ; as *their* houses, *their* gates, *their* porters, *their* servants, *their* tenants, *their* manors, *their* lordships, *their* woods, *their* corn."*

Nothing could exceed the insolence of those wives belonging to the *elderly secular* priests so much lauded by Dean Hook for having taken the oath of supremacy to a young woman scarcely thirty years of age! A strange proceeding altogether! Mr. Froude fully admits and confirms the reports as to the condition of religion under the *reformed* bishops and priests in the third year of Elizabeth's reign. He states:— "While the *shepherds* were thus dividing the fleeces, the *sheep were perishing.*" In many dioceses in England a third of the parishes were left without a clergyman, resident or non-resident. There were in the diocese of Norwich (1561), *eighty parishes where there was no cure of souls ; in the Archdeaconry of Norfolk one hundred and eighty parishes ; in the Archdeaconry of Suffolk one hundred and thirty parishes* were almost, or entirely, in the same condition.† In some few of these churches an occasional curate attended on Sundays. In most of them the voices of the priests were silent in the

---

* Complaints against the Dean and Chapter of Worcester, Domestic MSS., Elizabeth, Vol. XXVIII.

† Strype's "Annals of the Reformation," Vol. I.

desolate aisles. The children grew up unbaptized; the dead buried their dead. At St. Helen's, in the Isle of Wight, the parish church had been built upon the shore, for the convenience of vessels lying at anchor. The Dean and Chapter of Windsor were the patrons, and the benefice was about the wealthiest in their gift; but the church was in ruin, through which the *wind and rain made free passage*. The parishioners were fain to bury their corpses themselves.* The narrator gives a sad picture of the " spiritual destitution " of the Isle of Wight. * * * *

" It breedeth," said Elizabeth in a remonstrance which she addressed to Archbishop Parker, " no small offence and scandal to see and consider upon the one part the curiosity and cost bestowed by all sorts of men upon their private houses; and on the other part the unclean and negligent order and spare keeping of the Houses of Prayer, by permitting open decays and ruins of coverings of walls and windows, and by appointing *unmeet and unseemly tables with foul cloths, for the communion of the Sacrament*, and generally leaving the place of prayer desolate of all cleanliness and of meet ornament for such a place, whereby it might be known a place provided for Divine Service."†

In the reign of Elizabeth the foreign element was just as " ungodly and dishonest " as the Germans, patronised by Archbishop Cranmer in the days of Edward VI. Mr. Froude is again outspoken as to the impolicy of encouraging those " foreign saints." " Nor again," he observes, " were the Protestant foreigners who had taken refuge in England any

---

* Domestic MSS. of Elizabeth's reign; Froude's History of England, Vol. VII.

† The Queen to the Archbishop of Canterbury, 1560; Domestic MSS., Vol. XV.

special credit to the Reformation. These 'exiled saints' were described by the Bishop of London as marvellous *colluvies* of evil persons, for the most part *facinorosi clerici et sectarii.*" Between prelates reprimanded by the Council for fraudulent administration of their estates, chapters bent on justifying Cranmer's opinion of such bodies—that they were good vianders, and good for nothing else; and a clergy among whom the only men who had any fear of God were the unmanageable and dangerous Puritans, the Church of England was doing little to make the Queen or the country enamoured of it. Torn up as it had been by the very roots, and but lately replanted, its hanging boughs and drooping foliage showed that as yet it had taken no root in the soil, and there seemed too strong a likelihood that, notwithstanding its ingenious framework and comprehensive formulæ, it would wither utterly away.*

"Our religion is so abused," wrote Lord Sussex to Cecil, in 1562, "that the Papists rejoice; the neuters do not dislike change, and the few zealous professors lament the lack of purity. The people without discipline, utterly devoid of religion, come to Divine Service as to a May-game; the ministers for disability and greediness be had in contempt; and the wise fear more the impiety of the licentious professors than the superstition of the erroneous Papists. God hold his hand over us that our lack of religious hearts do not breed in the meantime his wrath and revenge upon us."†

"Covetousness and impiety" were not the only impediments to a genuine acceptance of the "reformed religion."

---

* Froude's History of England, Vol. VII., p. 468.
† Sussex to Cecil, July 22, 1562; from Chester, Irish MSS., Rolls House; Froude, Vol. VII., p. 468.

The submission of the clergy to the change was no proof of their cordial reception of it. The majority were interested only in their benefices, which they retained and neglected. A great many continued Catholics in disguise, and remained at their posts, scarcely concealing, if concealing at all, their inner creed, and were supported in open contumacy by the neighbouring noblemen and gentlemen.

In a general visitation in July, 1561, the clergy were required to take the oath of allegiance. The Bishop of Carlisle reported that thirteen or fourteen of his rectors and vicars refused to appear, while in many churches in his diocese Mass continued to be said, under the countenance and open protection of Lord Dacres; and the priests of his diocese generally he described as wicked "imps of Antichrist," "ignorant, stubborn, and, past measure, false and subtle." Fear only, he said, would make them obedient, and Lord Cumberland and Lord Dacres would not allow him to meddle with them.*

The marches of Wales were as contumacious as the border of Scotland. In August of the same year "the Popish justices" of Hereford commanded the observance of St. Laurence's Day as a holy-day. On the eve no butcher in the town ventured to sell meat: on the day itself "no Gospeller durst work in his occupation or open his shop." A party of recusant priests from Devonshire were received in state by the magistrates, carried through the streets in procession, and so "feasted and magnified, as Christ himself could not have been more reverentially entertained." †

---

* The Bishop of Carlisle to Cecil; Domestic MSS.; Froude, Vol. VII., p. 469.

† Bishop of Hereford to Cecil; Domestic MSS.; Froude, Vol. VII.

In September, 1561, Bishop Jewell, going to Oxford, reported the Fellows of the Colleges so "malignant that if he had proceeded peremptorily as he might he would not have left two in any one of them." And here it was not a peer or a magistrate that Jewell feared, but one higher than both, for the Colleges appealed to the Queen against him, and Jewell could but entreat Cecil, with many anxious misgivings, to stand by him. He could but protest humbly that he was only acting for God's glory.*

The Bishop of Winchester found his people "obstinately grovelling in superstition and Popery, lacking not priests to inculcate the same daily in their heads"; and himself so unable to provide ministers to teach them that he petitioned for permission to unite his parishes and throw two or three into one. †

Another report of the same visitation states that the Bishop of Durham called a clergyman before him to take the Oath of Supremacy. The clergyman said out before a crowd, "who were much rejoiced at his doings," "that neither temporal man nor woman could have power in spiritual matters, but only the Pope of Rome"; and the lay authorities would not allow the bishop to punish men who had but expressed their own feelings. More than one member of the Council of York had refused the oath, and yet had remained in office; the rest took courage when they saw those that refused their allegiance not only unpunished, but held in authority and estimation. ‡

In 1562 the Bishop of Carlisle once more complained

---

* Jewell to Cecil; Domestic MSS.
† Domestic MSS., Froude, Vol. VII., p. 470.
‡ Domestic MSS.

that, between Lord Dacres and the Earls of Cumberland and Westmoreland, "God's glorious gospel could not take place in the counties under their rule." The "few Protestants durst not be known for fear of a shrewd turn; and the lords and magistrates looked through their fingers while the law was openly defied. The court was full of wishings and wagers for the alteration of religion."†

The condition of the Catholics at this time was one of thorough slavery, for they dared not practise their religion, under heavy penalties, imprisonment, the rack, and next—the scaffold. The spy system was practised to a fearful extent. The Ambassadors, the members of the Government, the Bishops, the Peers and Commoners were "in turn watching one another."

De Quadra had spies amongst Cecil's household, and, in return, the ambassador was betrayed by one of his own secretaries. The Queen had two persons in her pay who watched all the private movements of her Prime Minister. Cecil, however, was a match for the secret fencing of his antagonists, for he had a host of persons always at hand ready to swear to whatever was required by the Council. This was an improvement upon the tactics used by the Government of Edward VI. As much as Elizabeth admired Robert Dudley, she placed a Catholic gentleman named Blount to report upon his private movements. Judging of Blount by his actions, and the vile instrument he became in the hands of the Queen, he fell little short of Robert Dudley in all that constitutes worthlessness in man.

Sir William Cecil, who laboured in vain to reform the

---

* Domestic MSS., Vol. XXI.; Froude, Vol. VII., p. 471.

bishops and clergy of the Anglican Church, informed the Queen that the Church could not " progress in spiritualities whilst the bishops shamefully neglected their duties." Cecil charged the Bishop of Lichfield with making (ordaining) seventy priests in one day *for moneyed considerations*. "Some were *tailors*, some *stonemasons*, and others *craftsmen*." "I am sure," he says, "the greatest part of them are not able to keep decent houses." *

It is from the wild harangues of such illiterate men that Puritanism gained strength, and, at a later period, sacreligiously trampled under foot the time-honoured monarchy of the realm.

A few words as to the Elizabethan coin. Towards the close of 1560 Elizabeth completed her great monetary reform in England—a commercial change which was much required. The Queen strictly forbade melting or trafficking with the coin in any way—a precaution the more necessary inasmuch as the silver was better and purer in England during her reign than it had been the last two hundred years, and exceeded in value the standard of that of any other nation of Europe in her time.†

The reformation of the currency extended to Ireland, and was joyously received by all parties in that country. The commercial classes, and the farmers, who suffered much from the base coin of Henry VIII. and Edward VI., rejoiced at the new issue. "Bonfires were set ablazing on the hills," and the Queen's health was pledged by many who had been hitherto her mortal foes.

---

* MS. Domestic, Feb. 27, 1585; Notes of Conversation between the Queen and Cecil on Church matters.

† Camden's Annals.

Several ballads were written on the "great change in money." Here is a specimen :—

"Let bonfires shine in every place,
And ring the bells apace,
And pray that long may live her Grace
To be the good Queen of Ireland.

The gold and silver, which was so base
That no man could endure it scarce,
Is now new coined with her own face,
And made to go current in Ireland."*

When the Queen visited the Mint at the Tower, she coined certain pieces of gold with her own hand, and gave them away to those about her.

The gold coins of Elizabeth are really beautiful; they were sovereigns, half-sovereigns or *rials*—the latter word being a corruption from royals; nobles, double-nobles, angels, half-angels, pieces of an angel, crowns and half-crowns. One pound of gold was coined into twenty-four sovereigns, or thirty-six nominal pounds, for the value of the sovereign was thirty shillings, the value of the royal fifteen shillings, and that of the angel ten. On the sovereign appeared the majestic profile portrait of Elizabeth, in armour and ruff, her hair dishevelled and flowing over her bosom and shoulders. The lovers of the picturesque and graceful must regret the want of taste which induced the Tudor sovereigns to set aside the elegant garland-shaped diadem of the Saxon and Plantagenet monarchs of England for the double-arched royal cap, which so completely conceals the contour of a finely-shaped head and the beauty of the hair.

Queen Elizabeth's silver money comprised crowns, half-crowns, shillings, sixpences, groats, three-pences, two pennies,

---

* Simon's Essay on Irish Coins.

half-pennies and farthings. There was no copper money coined before the reign of James I.

Amongst the many interesting matters Elizabeth stated her desire to carry out in her reign was that of a "History of Money" in various parts of Europe, from the beginning of the eighth century. Several learned antiquarians volunteered their assistance for the work; but they died off in time, till the Queen perhaps thought herself too old to proceed with such a weary search as the "History of Money" would involve; so her promises on this branch of literature fell through, like many of those fair and hopeful pledges she had made at Cambridge.

CHAPTER XXII.

QUEEN ELIZABETH'S FOREIGN POLICY.

THE foreign policy of Elizabeth was the most tortuous which a supposed necessity could impel any monarch to pursue. To weaken by division, alarm by suspicion—to deceive kings and betray peoples—was the unprincipled course adopted in the foreign policy of Elizabeth, for with her lay the blame of accepting as well as inspiring the counsels of Sir William Cecil. She even paltered in this regard with the faith which constituted her power. Honesty recoils at her conduct to the Scotch Protestants in 1559, to the French Huguenots in 1562; and all integrity revolts at her treating with Moray in 1565—evolving a policy at once ungenerous and false. In these "extern circumstances," as her foreign affairs have been vaguely described, Elizabeth manifested a vacillation, which only hesitated between degrees of evil, and sinned even in the mode of sinning—a double baseness. She would first help with money doled out with parsimony; when confronted with the fact of her partial subsidy of insurrection, she would summon God and all things sacred to attest that she had rendered no aid at all. But afterwards, if peace came into question, she intervened to make its consummation of some advantage to herself.

Cecil, in one notable instance, stands clear of complicity in the crooked policy of his Queen. His rapid signing of the

Treaty of Edinburgh deprived Elizabeth of the profits of deceit in the case of the Scotch Protestants, but no one has cleared him of the dishonour respecting the Huguenots, nor relieved the Queen's memory from the horrors of the plague at Havre, the sacrifice of the oppressed Huguenots, and the loss of their insufficient vindicators. But perhaps of all her "secular" actions of policy, her conduct in 1565, with regard to Scotland, leaves the deepest stain upon her honour. She instigated Moray, Chatelherault, Glencairn, Kirkaldy, and others to rebel against the Queen of Scots; made promises never fulfilled; withheld the few hundred men who might have assured them success—permitted them to be driven across the Border; placed them in mock incarceration as rebels, but soon sent them back when the way to successful treason had been made more smooth by external artifice and domestic crime. Historians have told how Queen Elizabeth aided the Low Countries, but have spared the comment that her assistance was the result of fear and personal revenge. In Motley's revelations on the progress of revolution and treason in the Netherlands, the conduct of Cecil and his Royal mistress stand forth in the darkest colours. The secret correspondence carried on by Cecil with rebels, and their Sovereigns, at the very same time, proves beyond question, that there was no wickedness he was not capable of enacting, provided always, that the light of day could not discover it to the world. Time has, however, revealed to posterity the terrible pictures of the Past.

In August, 1559, Elizabeth, writing to the Queen Regent of Scotland, disclaimed all connection with the Scottish rebels; yet the very next day the English Queen and her Minister, William Cecil, despatched Ralph Sadler with three thousand pounds (in gold), to the Northern Border, to be distributed amongst the rebels.* Upon the division of the money the "saints" quarrelled amongst themselves, as they considered the sum forwarded "too small for a divide," although the money had been borrowed from the Dutch Jews by Gresham, the English financial agent, at 14 per cent. On this occasion Elizabeth instructed Sadler to "treat in all secresy, with any manner of persons in Scotland, for the union of the realms." To have this proposition entertained, however, required "more money;" and in due time another "bag of gold arrived." The astute Sadler had to play a cross game, but he was always equal to the occasion. Elizabeth referred him for "further instructions" to Sir William Cecil. The "letter of instruction" from Cecil to Sadler in this case is full of intrigue and treacherous insinuation. Sadler was to create feuds between all parties, especially the French and the supporters of the Catholic cause. The emissary discharged his mission to the satisfaction of Cecil and his Sovereign. His "suggestions" were those of a cold-blooded assassin; and, more shocking still, was his custom of invoking the name of the Holy Trinity in documents concerning the direct or indirect commission of deeds of darkness.† It is curious to ascertain from the "secret instructions" of Cecil to Sadler, that the former did not approve of Lord James Stuart at that period.‡ He thought better of the Hamiltons. "You shall," writes Cecil, "do well to explore the *truth*, whether the Lord James do mean any

---

* See Ralph Sadler's] Secret Correspondence with Sir William Cecil; Scottish State Papers; Froude, Vol. VII.; Lingard, Vol. VI.

† Scottish MSS., Rolls House; Lingard, Vol. VI.; Froude, Vol. VII.

‡ The reader must remember that James Stuart had been early in life the ordained Prior of St. Andrew's. He was the illegitimate son of the King of Scots. In the subsequent chapters in relation to Mary Queen of Scots, the history of this apostate monk will frequently occur.

enterprise towards the Crown of Scotland for himself; and if he do, and the Duke of Hamilton be found very cold in his own cause, it shall not be amiss to let the Lord James follow his own desire therein."* * * * * Lord James was to be supported to a certain extent, and then abandoned. About the same time Throckmorton, the English ambassador in Paris, assured Cecil " that there was a party in Scotland who secretly desired to place Lord James Stuart on the throne of that country ; and that he himself did, by all means aspire thereunto."†

Cecil and his royal Mistress were frequently embarrassed by the fanatical conduct of the Scotch Reformers, who were turbulent, rebellious, and rapacious; and the more money they received from England, the larger became their demands. Cecil, who was no friend of anything good, did not, however, admire anything fanatical or communistic, knowing too well the difficulty of governing elements derived from such sources, although they were in the main part of his own creation. The " Scottish difficulty " now proved far greater than anything he experienced in England. The avid impecuniosity of the felonious Scotch " nobility " was a bitter pill to Cecil. No " pious movement " could progress in Scotland without English gold; and then the violence of the preachers, and the fanaticism of the " new congregations " were running too fast for the quiet calculating Cecil, whose plans for crushing the Olden Creed could not coincide, in consequence of its tardiness, with the sharp and rapid procedure of the Reformers beyond the Border counties.

Here is a specimen of how Elizabeth's agents acted towards

---

* Apud Chalmers, Vol. II., p. 410.
† See Forbes, Vol. I., p. 180.

the ambassadors of foreign countries, especially Spain. In June, 1562, Borghese, one of the secretaries attached to De Quadra, the Spanish envoy, became a spy and a traitor to his Royal master, Philip. It also happened that the Spanish ambassador had several of Cecil's chief clerks in his pay, and from this source ascertained the treachery of Borghese. A few days later, the Spanish courier was waylaid at Gadshill, and stripped of his despatches. Two of the notorious Cobham family, disguised as highwaymen, were the perpetrators of this stroke of "State policy." In due time the "highway servants" of Elizabeth lodged the Spanish secret despatches in the hands of Sir William Cecil.* On the following day Sir George Chamberlain and several others were lodged in the Tower. Commentary on this transaction is unnecessary.

I have again to recur to the policy of Elizabeth at the early stages of her diplomatic action. In June, 1559, De Quadra, the Spanish ambassador, calls his Royal master's attention to the mischievous manner in which Elizabeth was then proceeding. De Quadra writes: "If the Queen of England can spread the poison and set your Majesty's Low Countries on fire *she will do it without remorse.*" In another passage he remarks: "*I have my spies about the Queen's person . . . . I know every word that she says.*"

In the July of the same year Philip wrote from Brussels to De Quadra, to remonstrate with Elizabeth as to the evil consequences of her "intermeddling" in the affairs of other countries. "You shall tell her," wrote Philip, "that by what she is doing she is disturbing my affairs as well as her own; and that, if she do not change her

---

* State Papers of Elizabeth, 1562.

proceedings, I shall have to consider what it will be necessary for me to do. I cannot suffer the peace of these Estates to be endangered by her caprices. I see plainly how it may end."

This is a direct and important proof, from a monarch who felt it, of Elizabeth's tendency to meddle in the affairs of her neighbours. She began her interference in the very earliest period of her reign; and was ever active in her annoyance of both France and Spain, with whose princes she coquetted, and whose subjects she disturbed. Twenty-nine years passed from the writing of the above letter to the season of the Spanish Armada; and age brought not wisdom to either Elizabeth or Philip.

Writing from London, in the June of 1560, to the Spanish minister in Madrid, De Quadra says:—"It has become too plain that neither menace can terrify the Queen, nor kindness win her confidence. I employ a tone with her, therefore, in which I can point out her mistakes, and show her the mischief which may arise from her chimerical policy, without driving her into a passion. I do not blame her. I lay the fault upon her advisers. I have told her that, at the beginning of her reign, she ought to have strengthened herself with a prudent marriage: she should have looked for alliances abroad; she should have attended to her revenues, and engaged officers to train her soldiers in the art of war. . . . . Her object in pressing matters to extremity has been to divide us from France. * * * The Queen is now aware that she cannot light up a Continental war again; but she still hopes to expel the French from the 'Island' (Scotland), and to unite the realms; and, until she is undeceived on this point also, she will never confess the truth. Her conviction is that the Low Countries will not endure to be at war with

England, and that his Majesty, for his own sake, will be forced to continue her friend."*

The above was written by an acute observer of Elizabeth's foreign policy when she had been not two years upon the throne. "As years wore on she bettered not:" and even so, it is a great pity that the prominent figure of the group should have all the shortcomings or wrong doings of the subordinates laid to her charge; yet, as the highest point of an edifice retains longest the parting glories of the sun, so is it more liable to be stricken by the thunderbolt. So the misdeeds of the reign of Elizabeth survive to her dishonour, whilst the memory of many of her statesmen remain in the shade.

---

* De Quadra's secret Despatches to the Foreign Minister of Spain (Simancas State Papers).

CHAPTER XXIII.

THE RESULTS OF "ROYAL PROGRESSES."

IF a great indictment can be preferred against Queen Elizabeth, much can also be said in her favour, to which I willingly give a place in these pages.

In one of her early summer tours through England, Queen Elizabeth visited Northamptonshire. This incident might furnish material for the painter, the poet, or the minstrel. The Queen had a desire to see the ancient Castle of Fotheringay, so long associated with "Royalty in misfortune." Little did the Queen then think upon the future of this gloomy and ill-fated fortress, that subsequently linked her own name with one of the darkest and most deliberate judicial murders on record? This fortress was erected by a remote ancestor of Elizabeth—namely, Edmund of Langley, son of King Edward III., and founder of the House of York. By the direction of this warlike baron the keep was built in the likeness of a fetter-lock, the well-known cognizance of that ancient family. In the windows the same symbol, with its attendant falcon, was repeatedly and conspicuously emblazoned. From Edmund of Langley it descended to his son, Edward Duke of York, who was slain at the battle of Agincourt. The castle next descended to his nephew, son of the decapitated Earl of Cambridge; to that Richard who fell at Wakefield in the attempt to assert the title to the crown which the victorious arms of his son, Edward IV., subsequently won. Richard III., and several other notable scourges, were either born in Fotheringay Castle or had lived there at various times. Edward IV. had some famous hunting parties in the vicinity of Fotheringay, which were often attended by five or six hundred horsemen, and one hundred dogs.

In a collegiate church adjoining Fotheringay were deposited the remains of Edward and Richard, Dukes of York, and of the once beautiful Cecily, wife to the latter, who survived to behold so many bloody deeds of which her children were the perpetrators or the victims. Queen Elizabeth, having visited the Castle, next appeared at the tombs of her ancestors. She cried, on beholding the ruins of those once magnificent memorials, affectionately raised by the living to the memory of the dead. The college and lands to which those tombs were somewhat attached were seized upon in the reign of Edward VI., by Lord Warwick. Elizabeth ordered new monuments to be erected; but her "commands" were ill-obeyed. A complaint she might have often made.

It is stated that James I., in after years, "levelled Fotheringay Castle to the earth, one stone not left upon another of the prison-house where his mother was beheaded." This is a mistake. King James received rent from one of the Fitzwilliam family for the Castle and grounds of Fotheringay. King James actually visited the Castle, and made minute inquiry as to the apartments occupied by his mother. The Castle was subsequently taken down to procure building materials for another residence, but not at the suggestion of King James.

It is worthy of remark that about the time of Elizabeth's visit to Fotheringay her future victim, the Queen of Scots, was a prisoner in Lochleven Castle, with the infamous Lady Douglas as her gaoler.

In 1563 a terrible plague raged in London, which carried off nearly twelve hundred persons weekly. Every person possessed of any means retired from the city. Parliament held its sittings at Hertford Castle, and many members repaired to distant parts of the country to avoid the infection. The Queen took up her abode at Windsor, where she remained in privacy for some months, and was daily engaged in classic studies, especially Greek. During the plague the Queen quite exhausted her private purse in relieving widows and orphans, who became numerous from the dreadful scourge which had just visited the country.

The employment of fire-arms had not as yet (1559) consigned to disuse either the defensive armour or the weapons of offence of the Middle Ages. The military arrays of that time amused the eye of the spectator with a rich variety of accoutrements far more picturesque in detail, and probably more striking even in general effect, than that magnificent uniformity which at a modern review dazzles but soon satiates the sight. Of the fourteen hundred men whom the metropolis sent forth on one occasion, eight hundred, armed in fine corselets, bore the long Moorish pike; two hundred were halberdiers, wearing a different kind of armour, called almain rivets; the gunners, or musketeers, were equipped in shirts of mail, with "morions or steel caps." The Queen, surrounded by a brilliant Court, beheld all their evolutions from a gallery over the park-gate at Greenwich, from which her Highness addressed some gracious words to the crowd, who "looked up at her in such a loving manner."

On another occasion the Queen's Pensioners were appointed "to run with the spear"; and this animating exhibition was accompanied with such circumstances of romantic decoration as delighted the fancy of Elizabeth.*

The Queen caused a banqueting-house to be erected in Greenwich Park. The building was made with fir poles, and "decked with birch branches and all manner of flowers, both of the field and the garden, as roses, sun-flowers, lavender, marigold, and all manner of stewing-herbs and rushes." Tents were also set up for the Royal Household, and a place was prepared for the tilters. After the exercises were over, the Queen gave a supper in the banqueting-house, succeeded by a masque. Then followed great casting of fire and shooting of guns till midnight.

The band of Gentlemen Pensioners, the boast and ornament of the Court of Elizabeth, was probably the most elegant assembly of gentlemen in Europe. It was entirely composed of the flower of the nobility and gentry.† To be admitted to serve in its ranks was, during the whole of the reign of Elizabeth, regarded as a distinction worthy the ambition of young men of the highest families and most brilliant prospects. Sir John Holles, afterwards Earl of Clare, was accustomed to say that while he was a Pensioner to Queen Elizabeth he did not know *a worse man* in the whole band than himself. He was then in the possession of an inheritance of £4,000 per annum—a large property in those times. It is painful to dwell upon the fact that those wealthy men, after a time, became remarkable for servility and baseness, entering into every petty intrigue about the Court, and then betraying their friends. Amongst the most servile creatures in attendance

---

* Collins's Historical Collections.

† Sir Christopher Hatton, the Queen's dancing favourite, was admitted a member of the Band of Gentlemen Pensioners when only a few months at Court. His elegant personal appearance left him for a time without a rival.

upon Elizabeth was the wealthy Earl of Derby. The Queen had her spies at Court; so had Walsingham and Cecil. Such a system must have destroyed every honourable and confiding feeling. The author of the "Court of Elizabeth" affirms that this taint infected, with a few honourable exceptions, the entire Court of Elizabeth.

On the 17th July, 1560, the Queen set out on the first of those "Royal Progresses," as her touring has been styled. In her intercourse with the people on those occasions the Politician was always present, but artfully concealed. She sought to unite political utilities with the gratification of her taste for magnificence, and especially for admiration. If the burgher, the peasant, or the dealer, could possibly become Politicians, the Queen would give them a very different reception. An earnest and constant desire to win popularity was her special design from the period of her brother's reign. She had evidently studied the character of the English people with thorough acuteness. She appeared before them as the warm-hearted, well-intentioned young woman. And, again, she was most facile of approach; private persons and magistrates, farmers and their wives, the peasant women and their children, all came joyfully and without any fear to make known to her their domestic troubles. She often "rated" bad husbands, and caused reconciliations. The quantity of money and clothes she gave away on those occasions was immense. The Queen, however, went on her "country journeys" "well stocked," and made the local magnates pay a goodly portion of the expenses. The lower classes thought the Queen had the power of a magician, or some wonderful fairy, to comply with their requests. She assured " a group of women on one occasion that she was only a human being, like themselves; that she had little to bestow, save good advice, which was cheerfully given to all who sought it."

During her journeys through the country the Queen took with her own hand, and read the petitions of the humblest rustics, who seemed to have had much confidence in her advice. She frequently assured them that she would *herself* inquire into the nature of their complaints. There was one particular feature which marked those interviews between the monarch and her subjects. The Queen was never seen angry with the most unreasonable requests, or the uncourtly mode of approaching her. The traditions of the times represent the endearing manner in which the Queen spoke to the rustic children whom she met along the roads; and young women always received motherly advice from her. Sir William Cecil was far from approving of the "interviews" which the Queen so largely granted to the rustic classes. Nothing tended more to the Queen's popularity with the people—middle and lower order—than the facility and condescension with which Elizabeth received all that came to her palaces; and the hospitality was profuse. A certain Irish chieftain caused to be emblazoned upon his gates, " Let no honest man that is hungry pass this way." The same might fairly be said of Elizabeth's mansions—as far as the hostess was *personally* concerned. It is probable that the title of " good Queen Bess " had its real origin in the early traditions coming from the rural classes, who were so delighted with the Queen's "free and easy" mode of speaking to them concerning their social affairs.

In the fourth volume of this work I shall again recur to Elizabeth and her " Progresses " through the country.

CHAPTER XXIV.

THE REFORMATION IN SCOTLAND.

SCOTLAND played a remarkable part in the sixteenth century, for in that century the "Evangelism of the North" assumed its wildest aspect, and presented a marked contrast with that of England. The English Reformation was an affair of State policy and violent coercion. The State was, throughout, its mainstay—its very life and soul. The supremacy despotism made the monarch the Head of the Church. In Scotland the Reformation proceeded from the lower and middle classes, who were no credit to any creed, being immoral, superstitious, needy, grasping and dishonest. The nobles and chiefs also enacted a prominent part in the Reformation movement. The Campbells, the Douglasses, the Kennedys, the Erskines, and many others, were in "search of land or movable valuables." M'Crie, the biographer of John Knox, makes many astounding admissions as to the motives of the Scottish lords in promoting the Reformation in their own country. Speaking of what occurred in 1540, M'Crie says:—"It has often been alleged that the desire of sharing in the rich spoils of the Popish Church, together with the intrigues of the Court of England, encouraged the Scottish nobles on the side of the Reformation. It is reasonable to think that at a later period this was so far true." Sir James Macintosh admits this statement to be correct. Of the character and motives of the upper classes in this overturning of religion, of law, order, and common honesty, as hitherto understood between man and man, I shall have much to relate in the subsequent chapters upon the history of Mary Queen of Scots.

"During the first half of the sixteenth century," writes Archbishop Spalding, "the Catholic Church in Scotland seems to have been in a most unhappy condition. The same causes which had contributed to the relaxation of discipline, and the increase of abuses in other places, had operated in Scotland with still greater force. * * * The creatures of the monarch were frequently forced into the vacant bishoprics and benefices. After this fashion King James V. had provided for his illegitimate children by making them abbots and priors of Holyrood House, Kelso, Melrose, Coldinghame and St. Andrew's. The lives of men who were thus intruded by the civil power into the high places of the Church were often openly scandalous."*

The King's "illegitimates," and those of the nobles—who were numerous enough—were the first to hail the Reformation. The ecclesiastical patronage exercised by the Crown and the nobles was disastrous to all purity of faith. Bishops and abbots rivalled the first nobility in magnificence, and preceded them in honours; they were Privy Councillors and Lords of Session, as well as Peers of Parliament, and had long engrossed the principal offices of State. A vacant bishopric or abbey called forth powerful competitors, who contended for it as for a principality or petty kingdom; it was obtained by similar arts, and not unfrequently taken possession of by the same weapons. Inferior benefices were openly put up to sale, or bestowed on the illiterate and

---

* Archbishop Spalding's History of the Protestant Reformation, Vol. II., p. 226.

unworthy minions of courtiers.* The vices of the higher Scottish clergy, originating chiefly in this fruitful source, greatly facilitated the success of the Reformation.†

JOHN KNOX was a notable man amongst the Scottish Reformers, and the most impartial portrait which can be laid before the reader of his character is to be found in the records of his actions, and the dark deeds of which he boasts so frequently in his correspondence. All his actions prove Knox to have been a thorough revolutionist, fiercer than John Calvin, and more indomitable than Luther. This "man of Ice," as Knox has been described by some of his contemporaries, was born in Scotland, about 1505. He was of obscure parentage, his mother being a "milk-maid" at the baronial mansion of the Earl of Cassilis. Through the interest of the Cassilis family, it is stated, Knox became a student for the priesthood at the University of St. Andrew's, where he was well conducted, and had the reputation of being a pious youth. He was, however, rude in manner, and sometimes received censure for his continued desire to violate the discipline of the College. He was ordained a priest in 1530.‡ In some years later he secretly embraced the Reformation, but did not publicly proclaim his Protestant principles till 1542.§ During the seven years he remained in the Catholic Church he celebrated Mass almost daily, whilst, at the same time, turning it into ridicule to his confidential friends in Geneva and Strasbourg.

In 1546 Knox was taken prisoner by the French army, which had just stormed the Castle of St. Andrew's. The

---

* M'Crie, p. 145.
† Archbishop Spalding on the Reformation in Scotland, Vol. II., p. 227.
‡ See M'Crie's Life of John Knox.
§ Ibid.

French General sent him as a prisoner to France, where he was detained for two years as "a revolutionary and seditious character, who desired to set man against man." Knox received his liberty from the French Government through the "repeated intercessions" of young King Edward VI.* Upon his return to Scotland Knox remained for some time in seclusion, and then suddenly repaired to England, where he resided for several years as "a travelling missioner" to Somerset and his party. Cranmer gave the "rustic apostle," as Knox was sometimes styled, "a cordial reception;" yet the Archbishop was far from approving of his violent mode of action.

In 1550 Knox married Marjery Bowes, at Berwick. Upon the death of his wife, he was soon "on the look-out," as George Douglas relates, "for a comely young virgin *to wife*." His second wife was Margaret Stuart, daughter of Lord Ochiltree. He was fifty-nine years of age at this time, and his bride, it is affirmed, was sixteen, some say eighteen years old. Nicol Burne, and other Kirk men, are very positive in stating that Knox fascinated or bewitched Margaret Stuart by "glamour." The real facts of the case were, however, that the young lady was a fanatic, and became a perfect slave to her tyrannical, gross-minded old husband. Nothing, in fact, more clearly establishes the nature of John Knox than his brutal treatment of this sadly deluded young woman. Upon the death of Knox his widow became the wife of another bad husband in the person of Andrew Kerr, one of the dagger-men at the assassination of Rizzio. This arrant bravo had been engaged in several murders; yet, strange as it may appear, he ranked high amongst the "Kirk saints!"

---

* See Tytler's Edward and Mary, Vol. I., p. 295.

Knox became a man of much importance with a section of the English Reformers in the reign of Edward VI. The bishops of that period openly fraternised with him, and employed him in important offices of trust, even consulting with the rustic Reformer in regard to doctrines and the new Prayer Book, and this, notwithstanding his undisguised hostility to episcopacy.*

To judge from multiplied examples of the fact, John Knox seems to have made it a general rule, to fly whenever danger threatened his person. If naturally courageous, as alleged, he was certainly boldest where there was least peril. He fled from England in 1554—a few months after the accession of Queen Mary. In Geneva he was violent in his language, and frequently insulted his brother Reformers.

At Frankfort-on-the-Maine, Knox participated in the quarrel which had sprung up between the Episcopal and Calvinistic sections of a Church recently established in that city by the English Protestant refugees. M'Crie gives a long account of this quarrel amongst the English Protestant refugees, in which John Knox seems to have got the worst of it. Dr. Cox, his opponent, remained in possession of the field, and Knox returned to Geneva.†

After an absence of two years on the Continent, Knox returned to Berwick in 1555. In a few weeks subsequent he entered Scotland again, but did not preach in public. He lectured in private houses for the "downfall of the Synagogue of Satan," the name he applied to the Catholic Church. In July, 1556, Knox had to retire again from Scotland on account of the violence of his language. He next appeared at Geneva, where he remained for some years. He was

---

* See M'Crie's Life of John Knox, p. 61.
† Ibid.

certainly much honoured in Geneva, and upon his final departure for Scotland was presented with the freedom of that ancient city. About this period (1559) the "Lords of the Congregation" were ready to take up arms for the establishment of the new Kirk.

In the preceding volume I have commented upon the part taken by Knox in the assassination of Cardinal Beaton. The Cardinal was not a prudent man. He urged strong repressive measures against the Reformers, and demanded the "execution of the law against heretics." Walter Milne, a priest, eighty years of age, was arrested and soon after committed to the flames, with three others. Archbishop Spalding remarks: —"This was as unfortunate as it was lamentable." But all parties seemed to think that their opinions could only be advanced by personal persecution. Rejecting all conciliation, and not even waiting for the result of the Council, the Lords of the Congregation, led by Knox, held a meeting at Perth, on the 11th of May, 1559. M'Crie, the biographer of John Knox, gives a narrative of what occurred, and attempts to defend the action of his hero.

"Knox," writes M'Crie, "remained at Perth, and preached a sermon in which he exposed the idolatry of the Mass, and of image-worship. The sermon being ended, the audience quietly dismissed; a few idle persons only loitered in the church. An imprudent priest, wishing either to try the disposition of the people, or to show his contempt of the doctrine which had been just delivered, uncovered a rich altar-piece decorated with images, and prepared to celebrate Mass. A boy having uttered some expressions of disapprobation, was struck by the priest. He retaliated by throwing a stone at the aggressor, which, falling on the altar, broke one of the images. This operated like a signal upon the people present, who had taken part with the boy; and in the course of a few minutes the altar, images, and all the ornaments of the church, were torn down and trampled under foot. The noise soon collected a mob, who, finding no employment in the church, by a sudden and irresistible impulse, flew upon the monasteries; nor could they be restrained by the authority of the magistrates and the persuasions of the preachers—who assembled as soon as they heard of the riot—until the houses of the Grey and Black Friars, with the costly edifice of the Carthusian monks, were laid in ruins. It is said that none of the 'gentlemen or sober part of the congregation' were concerned in this *unpremeditated* tumult. It was wholly confined to the ' baser inhabitants,' or, as John Knox himself describes them, the ' rascal multitude.' "*

This was not the first, as it did not prove to be the last, of those exhibitions by which the Scottish Reformers signalised their fanatical ferocity of temper. The burning and pillage of churches and monasteries is complained of in the acts of the Council of Edinburgh, which was dissolved before John Knox returned to his native country.†

With the Bible in one hand, and far more earthly instruments in the other, Knox and his disciples marched through Scotland proclaiming the principles of Calvin in their worst and most reckless form. They acted in the spirit of the Vandal, burning time-honoured churches and monasteries, with all the noble monuments of art and learning which they contained. This mission of violence has been defended by M'Crie and others in the defence of Knox and his followers. Who raised the storm at Perth, which, it is said, the preachers and magistrates could not calm? Who but John Knox

---

* M'Crie's Life of Knox, p. 182.
† See Wilkins, Conc., Vol. IV., p. 208.

aroused the "rascal multitude" to do their sacrilegious work? This was but the beginning of the calamities which followed.

When Knox heard of the premature death of Queen Mary's first husband (Francis), he openly expressed his *joy and thankfulness to God for the occurrence, which he viewed as " a righteous judgment on idolatry."*

Mr. Froude's estimate of Knox differs from most historians' of the "past and the present." He describes "the man of peace" thus: "John Knox was no narrow fanatic, who, in a world in which God's grace was *equally visible in a thousand creeds*, could see truth and goodness nowhere but in his own formula. He was a large, noble, generous man, with a shrewd perception of actual fact, who found himself face to face with a system of hideous iniquity."

Contemporary evidence cannot be discarded without cause. Queen Elizabeth must have known what manner of man Knox was far better than Mr. Froude. Sir William Cecil, in a letter to Ralph Sadler, assures him that there was no man so abhorred by Elizabeth as the "*gross-minded Scotch preacher John Knox.*"

Whilst Elizabeth's diplomatic agents in Scotland publicly applauded Knox and the preachers, they secretly wrote to Cecil and the Council in a very different spirit. Randolph, in a letter to Cecil (1559), states that the Scotch preachers "have little learning, and no charitable bearing." Of Knox the observant Randolph writes thus:—Maister John Knox is more vehement than decent or learned. . . "On Sunday Knox gave the cross and the candle such a wipe that those as learned as himself wished him to have held his tongue." *

---

* Sir Thomas Randolph's secret despatches to Sir William Cecil.

The reader is aware that Archbishop Parker and Queen Elizabeth, had an utter abhorrence of Knox.

A French writer, who was hostile to Mary Stuart, describes John Knox as the 'Savonarola of Edinburgh.' "Knox," writes Lamartine, "stood alone between the Throne and the Parliament as a fourth power, representing '*sacred sedition*'—a power which claimed a place side by side with the other powers of the State; a man the more to be feared by the Queen because his *virtue*, so to speak, was a kind of fanatical conscience."

It is a remarkable fact, that when Knox was expelled from Frankfort, it was at the suggestion of such notable English Reformers as Jewell, Coxe, and Sandys, all of whom became bishops in the reign of Elizabeth. John Knox having used unbecoming language of Queen Mary, in the presence of the above Reformers, and although they were exiled by their Sovereign, still, with a feeling worthy of Englishmen, they resented the insult. John Knox and a few fanatics who favoured his proceedings were ordered to leave Frankfort "within three days." Several of the leading English Reformers denounced Knox as "a mad fanatic." It is certain that he caused much ill-will in Frankfort. His friends—Lords Moray and Lethington, evil as they were—spoke in very forcible language against his unchristian denunciations of those who adhered to the Olden Creed. "Such a policy," writes Lethington, "is perfect tyranny."

With reluctance and contempt, I allude to John Knox's work entitled "The First Blast of the Trumpet Against the Monstrous Regiment (Government) of Women." This book was denounced, not only in England but on the Continent. It was an insult of the grossest character to women of cultivated minds; and a still greater outrage to the Royal ladies then so prominent in Europe for their learning and "knowledge of governing." The work in question bears striking evidence of being the production of a foul-mouthed unmanly fanatic. Queen Elizabeth was justly indignant at the sentiments and bearing of Knox, and, "with a mightie big oath, swore that he should never enter her realm again." Nevertheless, he continued to be one of her *paid agents for disturbing Scotland down to the very day of his death*.* The Church party in England were loud in their protest against the publication of Knox's scurrilous *brochure*. Dr. Aylmer, wrote a pamphlet in reply to Knox, styled "A Harbour for Faithful and True Subjects Against the Late Blown Blast Concerning the Government of Women." This reply was a very able answer to Knox for his attack upon Queens—in fact, upon educated, thoughtful women, for daring to think, or do anything in the State save enduring the bondage of domestic slavery, as did the unhappy wife of Knox. Queen Elizabeth was so pleased with Aylmer's book that she raised him from the Archdeaconry of Lincoln to the Bishopric of London. I cannot help regretting that the "Defence of Queens" was not written by a more honourable and worthy man than Dr. Aylmer subsequently proved. Aylmer's letters on other subjects, seem to have thoroughly disgusted the monarch and Sir Christopher Hatton. Sir Harris Nicolas, our great antiquarian historian, describes Aylmer as "a Court sycophant." And I may add that the clergy of the diocese of London almost unanimously pronounced him to be "a spiritual tyrant, whom they could never conciliate."

Before I close this chapter I must refer to the days of Edward VI. In the early part of the "Boy-King's" reign, John Knox, although no subject of England, demanded the

---

* See State Papers of England and Scotland of Elizabeth's reign.

execution of the English bishops. He called upon the Duke of Somerset to send to the scaffold, or the stake, Bonner, Gardyner, and Tunstal. Knox writes in this fashion:—" The Popish bishops *might have been justly put to death for nonconformity.*"* In the Constitution of the Church of Scotland, which was drawn up under the influence of Knox, to celebrate Mass, or to hear it celebrated, was made a capital offence.† Similar statutes were enacted by Elizabeth, and cruelly put in force.

* John Knox's "Admonition to the Faithful in England."
† Froude's History of England, Vol. V., p. 444.

CHAPTER XXV.

MARY OF LORRAINE.

THE widow of James V. of Scotland was in many respects well qualified to fill the office of successor to the Duke of Chatelherault as Regent. She possessed a calm judgment; good, though not brilliant, natural traits; manners which without losing their dignity were feminine and engaging; and so intimate a knowledge of the character of the people over whom she ruled, that, if left to herself, there was every prospect of her managing affairs with wisdom and success. Although of a different religion, she had so entirely gained the affections of the Protestant party that their support was one chief cause of her success.* As the Knox party had not yet entered upon the scene, the government of the country moved on for a time in peace and harmony. Frazer Tytler remarks that the assumption of the Regency by Mary of Lorraine was viewed with equal satisfaction by the clergy, the nobility, and the people. Of this period Mr. Froude remarks, that the "Catholic party acted with moderation." Such were the cheering prospects of Scotland in 1554.

Mary of Lorraine is described by her contemporaries as "one of the loveliest and most fascinating princesses in Europe." She took as much delight in music as her late consort, James V. had done, and kept up a fine band and a choir of vocalists, among whom there were five eminent

---

* Frazer Tytler's History of Scotland, Vol. V., p. 17, 18.

Italians. As Queen of Scotland, her hospitality was on a profuse scale of splendour; and the revenues derived from her extensive estates in France prevented her from calling upon the poor treasury of Scotland for support. Her charity, unseen to the world, was delicate, thoughtful, humane, and almost unbounded. The Reformers could not find fault with the "young Papist Queen" in this respect, for, like the good Samaritan of old, she never inquired from the destitute or the fallen at what shrine they prayed. They were the work of their Divine Creator, and her sympathy was extended to them in the hour of distress. The Queen Regent had, as well from prudence as humanity, protected the Reformers from persecution. In the crisis through which Europe was passing, it was almost impossible to hold the balance evenly between the contending parties. Such was the general belief in the integrity of the Queen that, in an age of unexampled intolerance her enemies reproached her not. She appointed several of her own countrymen to positions of trust and emolument; but upon learning that public opinion disapproved of those foreign appointments, she sent the new officials home to their country, recompensing them from her own private funds. She endeavoured to moderate the animosities of the rival factions—a circumstance which, at first sight, promised to strengthen the Catholics, but which had the contrary effect. The accession of Mary Tudor to the English throne, and the persecutions which followed, caused many Protestants to take refuge in Scotland, where, under the mild rule of Mary of Lorraine, they were allowed to live in peace. The English exiles returned the kindness of the Scotch Regent by attempting to raise a cry against the Olden Religion of Scotland. In this course they were successful, under the direction of a preacher named John Wilcock, a native of Ayr, who had been some years previously a Franciscan friar.

On the 24th of April, 1558, Mary Stuart was married to the Dauphin of France, in pursuance of the treaty which had been concluded two years before. This event opened new prospects to the ambitious House of Guise. The most prominent members of that family were Francis, Duke of Guise, and his brother the Cardinal—the one the most distinguished soldier, and the other the most ambitious statesman of France. The Duke of Guise's triumphant defence of Metz against the Emperor Charles V., and, still more, his recent capture of Calais from the English, in whose hands it had remained for two hundred years, rendered the Duke of Guise at this time the most popular man in France; while his brother, though personally less popular, exercised considerable influence at the Court of Henry II. It was at the instigation of these ambitious men that Mary Queen of Scots and her husband assumed, on the accession of Elizabeth, the arms of England in addition to those of Scotland and France. Elizabeth and her ministers rightly interpreted the action of Mary Stuart as that of raising a question as to the legitimacy of her English cousin. To this circumstance we may, in part, trace the commencement of that bitter feeling which sprang up between the two Queens, and which led to such disastrous results.

While the princes of Lorraine were indulging in " glorious dreams of the future," their sister Mary became aware that a crisis was fast approaching in Scotland. From the toleration with which she had all along treated the Protestant party, we may conclude that it was her object to effect eventually a compromise between the two religions; but the arbitrary counsels of her French advisers on the one hand, and the fanatical spirit of the Scotch Reformers on the other, rendered all such efforts unavailing. The Regent (Mary of Lorraine) experienced, in short, the fate of all who attempt, in time of revolution, to conciliate contending factions. She lost the confidence, for a time, of both.

It had long been the custom in Scotland, when men were about to embark in any dangerous enterprise, to sign a " band," or bond, by which they obliged themselves to stand by each other at the hazard of their lives.* The reader is aware that, at the instigation of John Knox, who was then at Geneva, the Protestant leaders formed themselves into a league for the maintenance and the extension of their faith, under the name of the " Congregation of the Lord"; while on their opponents they bestowed the far less deserved appellation of the " Congregation of Satan." There can be no doubt that, from the time of the formation of this league, it was the intention of John Knox and his followers to attempt to establish their " newly organised creed by force and violence." The parties to this " bond " declared that they would " continuously apply their whole power, their substance, and their lives in maintaining their doctrines." And, again, they solemnly vowed that " they would stake their lives against Satan, and all who troubled the aforesaid congregation." †

Mr. Hosack remarks that the religious movement of 1560 was marked by all the excesses which invariably accompany popular commotions.

---

* Matthew Paris relates that it was the custom of the men of Galloway in his time, and derived from the remotest period, before engaging in any dangerous enterprise, to pledge themselves in blood, drawn from their own veins, to stand by each other to the death.

† See Keith. Vol. I., p. 154.

The "Bloody Covenant," subscribed by the leading Scotch Reformers, was very naturally regarded by the Catholics as a declaration of war against them by the Reformers. The persecution of Protestants, which had been abandoned since the death of Cardinal Beaton, was now renewed. The attempt, as it proved, was highly impolitic, and tended only to widen the breach between the opposing parties. The victim selected for punishment was a priest named Michel Mill, who had for some years openly professed the doctrines of the Reformation. He was condemned to the stake as a heretic. He died with unshaken fortitude. Mill was the last victim of Catholic persecution in Scotland. Then commenced the fulfilment of the "Bloody Bond." The Regent appealed to the Reformers to uphold her in her efforts to put down bloodshed and anarchy, and reminded them of the liberal spirit in which she had acted towards them on all occasions. The past was quickly forgotten by the leading Reformers, and the Lords of the Congregation soon bade defiance to Mary of Lorraine. About this time the Queen Regent was charged by Knox, and the Puritan writers who advocated his policy, with various acts of dissimulation and falsehood. "It was necessary," writes Mr. Hosack, "for the Protestant leaders to justify their rebellion, and we require better evidence of the truth of these charges than the unsupported testimony of the unscrupulous enemies of the Queen."

It is worthy of remark, that in none of their numerous public documents do the Reformers accuse the Queen Regent of a breach of faith in any manner. Even their noted Act of Deprivation, which enumerates their charges against her, is silent on this point.

While matters were in this state, Knox returned to Scotland. The zeal, the energy, and the dauntless spirit of that remarkable man were well known to the Reformers of every class. From the time of his arrival he seems, by common consent, to have assumed the direction of the religious revolution which was impending. Knox reached Edinburgh in the beginning of May, 1559. On the 11th of the same month, in defiance of the prohibition of the Queen Regent and the Council, he preached at Perth, and on that occasion he denounced the Olden Creed of Scotland in language too gross to be repeated here. He roused the popular feeling to a pitch of frenzy. The people ran through the streets crying out " for a priest or a nun, that they might kill them. Old men and old women were knocked down, and trampled to death. The churches were defaced and profaned, and the ancient monasteries of the city laid in ruins." In a few days subsequently Knox, accompanied by his disciples and an infuriated mob, proceeded through the adjoining counties of Fife, Stirling and the Lothians, at that period the most prosperous and populous in Scotland. Wherever Knox appeared, the same scenes of violence and bloodshed announced his presence and proclaimed his power. In the course of a few weeks innumerable religious edifices, including the metropolitan Cathedral of St. Andrew's and the Abbey of Scone, where from time immemorial the Kings of Scotland had been crowned, were either irreparably damaged or levelled with the ground. " The great Reformer," writes Mr. Hosack, " might boast with Attila, that *desolation followed on his track whichever way he turned.*"

In the midst of these dismal scenes, the " Congregation " was alarmed by the intelligence that Mary Stuart, their Queen, had unexpectedly become Queen Consort of France. In the end of June her father-in-law, Henry II., was accidentally killed at a tournament, in Paris, and the amiable but feeble Francis succeeded to the crown. By this event, the Princes of Lorraine acquired for a time the sole direction of affairs in France. During the life-time of Henry, the great services and the high character of the Constable, Montmorency, induced the monarch, on many occasions, to prefer his moderate counsels to those of his ambitious rivals. But the unbounded influence which the young Queen possessed over her husband Francis, and the deference which she naturally paid to her uncles, the Cardinal, and the Duke of Guise, enabled them easily to triumph over every competitor for power. Catherine de Medicis hated her daughter-in-law, and plotted against her. Mary Stuart, young as she was, dexterously intrigued against Catherine. All those proceedings were productive of infinite evil. Mary Stuart stood by the old Catholic party, many of whom were corrupt and vacillating. Catherine's Catholicity was political: so she would sacrifice the Reformers at the very moment she made private compact with them. Upon the whole, Catherine de Medicis was a base and an unprincipled woman.

The alliance which had been so eagerly courted by the Scots, in their anxiety to defeat the policy of Henry VIII., had now resulted in the union of the crowns of Scotland and France. The anticipations of those who had planned and carried out this project were signally disappointed.*

The prospect of fresh dangers to the Reformation in Scotland roused John Knox to renewed exertion. It had become evident that a collision between the rival parties was now inevitable. Knox proclaimed his undying hatred to Popery. He told the "people to die like men or live victorious." The

---

* Mary Stuart and her Accusers, Vol. I.

vast majority of the people were on his side; and that they entertained a blind unreasoning hatred against the Olden Religion is beyond doubt. The Queen Regent offered the Knox party a complete amnesty for their rebellion, provided they would put a stop to the "Vandal destruction of the religious houses"; and further, that they would prevent their preachers from publicly exciting the people. In the disturbed state into which the country had been thrown, it is hardly necessary to say that the first condition would have been worthless and impracticable without the last; but both were peremptorily rejected.* "The Lords and the whole brethren," with Knox at their head, "refused the propositions made to them, declaring, that the fear of no mortal creature should cause them to betray the verity known and professed; neither should they suffer idolatry to be maintained."†

The Queen Regent finding it impossible to deal with the Knox party, retired to the fortress of Dunbar, at that time the strongest in Scotland. A detachment of one thousand soldiers soon afterwards arrived from France, with assurances of more men, arms, and ammunition. At this period (1559) the insurgents occupied the capital, but Leith, the fort of Edinburgh, was still in the hands of the Royalists, and the Regent employed her French officers in strengthening its walls. The Reformers protested against the Queen making this necessary plan of defence. The Queen Regent's reply was expressive of the dangers by which she was surrounded. "Like as a small bird still pursued," writes Mary of Lorraine, "will provide some nest, so her Majesty could do

---

* See Hosack's Mary Queen of Scots and her Accusers.
† John Knox to Anna Lock. This letter is to be found in the Record Office.

no less but provide some sure retreat for herself and her company."*

The insurgent lords now resolved upon a very extraordinary step. On the 21st of October they met under the presidency of Lord Ruthven, who proposed to them the following question :—

" Whether she (the Queen Regent), that so contemptuously refused the most humble request of the rightful counsellors of the realm, being but a Regent, whose pretences threatened the bondage of the whole commonwealth, ought to be suffered so tyranically to domineer over them ?" †

Much difference of opinion having been expressed, it was resolved that the preachers should be heard upon the subject. John Wilcock and Knox unhesitatingly declared that, under the circumstances, the Regent might be lawfully deprived of her authority. This opinion, expressed in the most emphatic language, appears to have speedily overcome the scruples of the Lords of the Congregation, for the members present forthwith agreed, without a dissentient voice, that the Queen Regent should be deposed. An Instrument, which they termed an Act of Deprivation, was drawn up and proclaimed at the Market Cross of Edinburgh on the same day.‡

The Earl of Arran, eldest son of the Duke of Chatelherault, had embraced the Reformation while he was serving in the Scottish Guard in France; and, according to Keith and other writers in the interest of the Scotch Reformers, he made his escape from that country with difficulty. On his arrival in England he was abundantly supplied with money. He was also granted a private audience by Elizabeth at Hampton

---

* See Keith, Vol. I., p. 229.
† Proceedings of the "Lords of the Congregation."
‡ See Keith, Vol. I., p. 234.

Court. What passed on that occasion is unknown; but the Lords of the Congregation, with the special forethought of their country, had previously arrived at the conclusion that the surest way to establish Protestantism in Britain was to marry the Earl of Arran to the then young Queen of England. Their own Sovereign might then be deposed, as they had unlawfully set aside her mother from the Regency. "It was," writes Mr. Hosack, "a bold, and to all appearances, not an impracticable scheme; but there were serious obstacles in the way, as the Congregation afterwards discovered." This marriage scheme was, it is said, first suggested to Sir Nicholas Throckmorton, in Paris, and by Alexander Whitelaw, an emissary of the Congregation. Throckmorton gave him a letter to Cecil, in which the following passage occurs:— " Sandy proposed a marriage between the Queen and the Earl of Arran, *the chief upholder of God's religion.*" Throckmorton adds, referring further to Whitelaw :—" This bearer is very religious, and therefore *you must let him see as little sin in England as you may.* He seemeth to be very willing to work and do what he can to induce Scotland to forsake utterly the French amity, and be united to England." Nicholas Throckmorton continues to impress upon Cecil the fact, that advances of money to the "*saints is highly necessary to promote God's Truth, and the glory of the Gospel.*" "The Queen's purse," writes the conscientious and pious Throckmorton, "*must be open, for fair words will not serve.*" *

---

* Despatches of Sir Nicholas Throckmorton in the Record Office. Amongst the State Papers are likewise to be seen the MSS. records containing the names and signatures of upwards of two hundred Scotch barons, chiefs and lairds, who had secretly received bribes from Henry VIII. and Elizabeth, for aiding in the extinction of their nationality. Amongst the most prominent in this list stand forth the names of the noted houses of Douglas, Lord Cassillis, the Earl of Lennox, with his coadjutor, Tom Bishop, to whom I have alluded in the second volume of this work.

A few words as to the Earl of Arran. This nobleman, "so promising," was willing to join in any scheme which led to personal advantage. The vigour, the high resolve, the ability and self-command, requisite in the leader of a party composed of unruly Scots, were wanting in Lord Arran. He was vain, passionate, and capricious. His plans were adopted without due consideration, and, upon the first approach of difficulty, abandoned with precipitation. Those who sought Arran as a political tool, to promote their own selfish views, were, for a time, unaware of the real character of the man. To deceive one another was the maxim of the Kirk politicians—in fact, of all the contending parties in those times.

The Lords of the Congregation proceeded to attack Leith, which by this time had been carefully fortified by its French garrison. They soon, however, discovered that the capture of this ancient town was an enterprise in which they could not succeed. All their attacks were speedily repulsed, and, instead of taking Leith, they were themselves, in the course of a few weeks, driven from Edinburgh, which was once more occupied by the troops of the Regent. Previous to this event, an incident occurred highly characteristic of the manners of the age. Elizabeth instructed her political agent (Sadler) at Berwick to transmit a large sum of money to the Lords of the Congregation, whose treasury was exhausted at this period. Cockburn, of Ormiston, was entrusted with the treasure. All went safe, till Cockburn was within a few miles of Haddington, and the night being dark, he was suddenly attacked by another Puritan champion, who carried off the boxes containing the English gold. It is curious that the "highway robber" in this case was the Earl of Bothwell, at that period about twenty-four years of age, and though an outspoken enemy to Catholicity, he was a chivalrous adherent to the Queen Regent. Early next day Bothwell's Castle was attacked by the troops of the Lords of the Congregation, to recover their bribe. Bothwell had barely time to escape, having mounted " a horse without saddle, boots, or spurs." The money was carefully concealed, and, of course, never " realized." To the demand of the Lords of the Congregation, that " he should return the money," Bothwell replied by sending a " cartel of defiance"* to the Earl of Arran; but Arran prudently declined having any altercation with so daring a character as Bothwell, who was dreaded alike both by Catholic and Protestant. He was, however, the idol of the " Border Men," the outlaws, and all those who lived upon a kind of free quarters. Those classes were numerous, and, like Bothwell himself, almost unconscious of danger; they clung to one another with a kind of chivalrous devotion.

On the discomfiture of the Lords of the Congregation at Leith, they retired to Stirling, where they resolved to seek the aid of Queen Elizabeth. William Maitland, of Lethington, a member of an ancient family, a man of talent and address, " who served and betrayed all parties in their turn," and who, notwithstanding, continued to be courted by all until the day of his death, was the person selected to proceed to London on this mission of treason. He had acted as Secretary to Mary of Lorraine down to the period when she retreated to Dunbar; but, with characteristic inconstancy and treachery, he went over to the enemies of the Queen Regent. In a few weeks subsequent he appeared in London, and received a cordial reception from Sir William Cecil, who was always "gracious in manner to Scotch traitors and rebels till they had carried out his schemes." He desired to

---

* Sir Thomas Randolph's Secret Despatches ; Sadler's Letters to Cecil.

aid the Scotch Reformers, and at the same time to appear neutral. He could not, however, but regard the Lords of the Congregation, "notwithstanding all their piety," to be rebels. To support them openly against their lawful Sovereign was a dangerous precedent, which might, at no distant time, be turned against the Queen of England.*

Sir Nicholas Bacon was of opinion that the English Queen should continue to "assist the Scotch rebels in secret," but that open rupture with France should be avoided, as England "was not then in a condition for war."†

About this time (1560), France made extensive preparations to equip an army of twenty thousand men, to sustain the rights of young Queen Mary in Scotland. The English Council were not idle; they sent a fleet to the Firth of Forth, which arrived in safety. The French fleet, for the same destination, encountered most tempestuous weather; they were driven back with the loss of many ships, a vast quantity of arms and provisions, and three thousand soldiers. Only two vessels reached the Firth of Forth in safety, where they were immediately attacked and taken, after a desperate fight of several hours.

A large English force, under the command of Lord Grey,‡ came to the aid of the Lords of the Congregation, but were defeated through the bravery of the Queen's troops; and, I

---

* In reply to one of the many letters addressed to Cecil by the Lords of the Congregation, seeking for money. he called their attention to the quantity of gold, silver and jewels, to be procured in the churches, chapels and abbeys throughout Scotland. This hint was unnecessary, for the Scotch Reformers acted with more promptness than Lord Crumwell and his inquisitors in such matters.

† State Papers Harl. MSS. (1559); Henry Killigrew's Secret Despatches to Queen Elizabeth; Tytler, Vol. V.

‡ Lord Grey was the brother of the Marquis of Dorset, executed for high treason in Queen Mary's reign. It is strange that Elizabeth should have given a military command to this nobleman, for she detested the very name of Grey.

might add, the incompetency of Lord Grey. This nobleman has been described as "a coward and a tyrant. He was hated by the soldiers." Twice he narrowly escaped assassination.

An incident occurred during the last illness of Mary of Lorraine, which places Lord Grey in a painful light. The malady under which the Queen was suffering assumed the form of dropsy, and the royal patient applied to the commander of the garrison at Leith to send her a surgeon; but the letter was intercepted by Lord Grey, who, after reading it, committed the note to the flames. We are told by Knox that when it was held to the fire, it was found to contain some private message to the French ambassador.* One of the recent biographers of Mary of Lorraine repudiates this statement of Knox. He contends that Lord Grey never made such an allegation, nor was it asserted by "any camp followers." It was "a premeditated and malicious lie put forward by John Knox."

The Foreign Policy of Elizabeth, at this early stage of her reign, was one of intrigue and treachery. She fomented secret internal discord in every country from which she apprehended danger to her own. But, notwithstanding all her powers of mendacity, she rarely succeeded in deceiving anyone except her friends, or those who had the misfortune to place confidence in her honour as a monarch.

I now approach another crisis in the political affairs of Scotland. At the close of May, 1560, Mary of Lorraine, the deposed Queen Regent of Scotland, was prostrated upon her death-bed. Her last days were most edifying. On the morning of the 10th of June, the Queen sought an interview with the Lords of the Congregation. She desired to die in peace with all parties. A deputation from the Lords of the Congregation,

---

* Knox's History of the Scottish Reformation, p. 246.

headed by the leading spirit of the party, Lord James, waited upon the Queen at Edinburgh Castle. Upon entering her chamber, they were welcomed by the dying Princess with a kindness and cordiality which even moved this iron-hearted Puritan section of the Congregation. She expressed her grief for the distracted state of the nation, and advised them to send both the French and the English forces out of the kingdom. The Queen reminded them of the allegiance they all owed to her daughter Mary, who was their lawful Sovereign. Being raised in the bed, after a long pause, the Royal lady contrived to add many endearing expressions, and with tears asked pardon of all whom she had in any way offended, declaring that she herself freely forgave the injuries she had received, and trusted that they should all meet with the same forgiveness at the judgment seat of Jesus Christ. Then, with an expression full of sweetness, though her countenance was pallid and emaciated, she embraced and kissed the nobles one by one, extending her hand to those of inferior rank who stood by, as a token of dying charity. Lord James, and Argyle seemed intensely affected, especially the former, whose hand the Queen grasped, and gazing at him for a moment, in a faint utterance exclaimed: "Do not forget my darling daughter, Marie. You should feel different towards her from any other subject. Remember the Past." Lord James sobbed and cried, and "was led from the room almost fainting."

Frazer Tytler remarks: "It was impossible that so much love, so gently and unaffectedly expressed, should fail to move those to whom it was addressed. The hardy barons, who had lately opposed the Queen with the bitterest rancour, were dissolved in tears."* Tears were shed in profusion on

---

* See Tytler, Vol. V., p. 122.

this occasion; but they were quickly dried, and soon forgotten.

Yet the Lords of the Congregation were guilty of an ungenerous insult to the dying Queen, by demanding that she should receive a visit from Wilcock, one of the most rabid amongst the Scotch preachers.* The Royal lady complied with the request; and Wilcock soon appeared at her dying couch, and made a violent harangue against her religion. The Queen replied: " I am convinced of the Divine origin of *my religion;* it is that faith which the Apostles preached after the ascension of our Lord. *Go thy ways. Let me die in peace.*" Pressing a crucifix to her lips, Mary of Lorraine spoke no more.

"Thus died," writes Mr. Hosack, "amidst the tears of her enemies, the best and the wisest woman of her age." Knox alone sought, by means of the most loathsome slanders, to vilify the character of this excellent princess; and it was, doubtless, *at his instigation that the rites of Christian burial were denied to Mary of Lorraine in Scotland.* In Knox's history, he asserts that the Queen was the mistress of Cardinal Beaton; and again, he contends that the Cardinal *was the father of Mary Queen of Scots.* In another passage of his book Knox insinuates that the Queen was on terms of criminal intimacy with D'Oysell.†

---

* Wilcock had been a Scotch Franciscan Friar, and, to use his own words, he "suddenly discovered that he was on the wrong path, so he abandoned Popery." He became Puritan chaplain to the Marquis of Dorset about the time that nobleman was elevated to the Dukedom of Suffolk by Northumberland. Wilcock was connected with rebellious plots both at home and abroad. He indulged in the foulest invective against those who refused to adopt his Calvinistic principles. Such were his views of "Liberty of Conscience." He was a perfect incendiary against life and property in the Scotch towns. Nevertheless, he ranks amongst the "most worthy Saints of the Kirk."

† See Mary Queen of Scots and her Accusers, Vol. I., p. 49.

Laing, another Scotch historian, has added to the slanders of Knox upon the stainless reputation of Mary of Lorraine. Other writers, however, of the Kirk school, have been honourable exceptions to Knox and his admirers.

Leslie describes the Queen as "a noble, wise, and honourable princess; a chaste and modest woman whose widowhood was passed with great honour."

Holinshed and his contemporaries bear testimony to the "universal grief and lamentation of the people of Scotland for the death of Mary of Lorraine." And Miss Strickland, in her highly interesting work, "The Queens of Scotland," passes a high tribute to the memory of this slandered and much-injured lady. "The Queen's last farewell with her enemies," writes Agnes Strickland, "was an incident which, for Christian meekness and charity, has no parallel in history."*

Mr. Froude, in an affected tone of pity, but in reality something akin to contempt, speaks of the disasters amidst which the Queen-widow closed her life. "She received the sacrament of the Catholic Church from her confessor, who was an abandoned profligate." If the chaplain in question were an "abandoned profligate," Mary of Lorraine would not permit him to approach the altar of her chapel. When I seek for Mr. Froude's authorities to sustain this most improbable and scandalous assertion, I find that it rests upon the statements of John Knox and Thomas Randolph; both branded with deliberate perjury at that very period.

The burial of the Queen was deferred from the 12th of June till the 19th of October, 1560, when the coffin was privately conveyed to France.† According to the "Diurnal

---

* Miss Strickland's Queens of Scotland, Vol. II., p. 266.
† Calderwood, Vol. I., p. 421.

of Occurrents," the funeral did not take place till the 16th of March following (1561).

Mary of Lorraine was interred in the Benedictine Abbey at Rheims, of which her younger sister, Renée de Lorraine, was Abbess. Henry VIII. was once a suitor for this princess; but she rejected his proposal with indignation. "A faithful few" of the Scots attended Mary's funeral; and amongst that "faithful few" were several of the Scotch Puritans, "who," says Adam Ramsay, "on seeing the Queen's coffin, shed many big tears for her who had been a liberal benefactor to all parties in times of distress or domestic sorrow."

I regret that I cannot afford sufficient space to go more into the history of the relations which existed between Mary of Lorraine and the Reformers of Scotland. I respectfully, however, refer the reader to a few authorities upon the subject:—See Lindsay of Pitscottie; Buchanan; Frazer Tytler, Vol. V.; Keith; Ralph Sadler's State Papers on Scotland; Lord Herries' History of the "Royal Maries" of Scotland, edited by Pitcairne; State Papers of Scotland of the days of Mary of Lorraine; The Maitland Club, Vol. IV.; the Hamilton State Papers; Diurnal of Occurrents in Scotland; Calderwood, Vol. I.; Bannatyne's Memorials; Royal Compotus, kept by Kirkaldy of Grange; Archbishop Spottiswood's History of Scotland.

CHAPTER XXVI.

THE FAMILIES OF DE CLIFFORD AND HOLLES.

GEORGE DE CLIFFORD, third Earl of Cumberland, was one of the remarkable characters of the reign of Elizabeth. His family were also of a notable class. The race of De Clifford takes its origin from William Duke of Normandy; in a later age its blood was mingled with that of the Plantagenets, by the marriage of the seventh Lord de Clifford with a daughter of the celebrated Hotspur. Notwithstanding this alliance with the House of York, two successive Lords de Clifford were slain in the civil wars fighting under the Lancastrian banner. It was to the younger of these, whose sanguinary disposition gained him the surname of the "Butcher," that the barbarous murder of the young Earl of Rutland was generally imputed. A well-founded dread of the vengeance of the Yorkists caused his widow to conceal his son and heir under the lowly disguise of a shepherd-boy, in which condition he grew up among the fells of Westmoreland totally illiterate, and probably unaware of his origin. At the end of five-and-twenty years, the restoration of the line of Lancaster, in the person of Henry VII., restored to Lord de Clifford the name, rank, and large possessions of his ancestors; but the peasant noble preferred through life that rustic obscurity in which his character had been formed and his habits fixed, to the splendour of a court or the intrigues of politicians. Upon the approach of the battle of Flodden Field, De Clifford came forward at the head of five hundred of his tenantry, "well-mounted, brave, and enthusiastic in the cause of England and its King." The "peasant lord" fought bravely at Flodden, for which he received the thanks of his Sovereign. King Henry was the idol of his English subjects at this period, and for many years later.

The son of the "peasant earl" was very different from his father, who was deservedly beloved by his tenants and neighbours. This nobleman attracted the attention of Henry VIII., who created him Earl of Cumberland, and made for his heir an alliance with the King's niece, Eleanor Brandon, the daughter of Mary Tudor by the Duke of Suffolk.* This latter union brought ruinous expenses upon Lord Cumberland. By a second marriage Cumberland became the father of George De Clifford, who subsequently appeared as a noted personage in Elizabeth's reign. The death of his parent, whilst the heir was yet a child, brought George Clifford under the wardship of Queen Elizabeth; and by her command he was sent to pursue his studies at Peterhouse, Cambridge, under Dr. Whitgift, where he was educated as a Protestant, contrary to the special command of his father's "last testament"; but Elizabeth had little scruple in violating the injunctions of the dying, especially in reference to a subject. Under Whitgift, young Cumberland continued for some time. He applied himself to mathematics, a study most attractive to the bent of his genius. He also showed some talent for nautical pursuits. In a few years he "entered upon the road to fashionable life," which, in the reign of Elizabeth, was one

---

* Lord Cumberland had one daughter by Lady Eleanor Brandon, who subsequently married the Earl of Derby. In the fourth volume of this work the reader will find chronicled the fate of this unfortunate lady.

of profuse expenditure, dissipation, and license. His fortune was rapidly reduced; but his ardour for adventure suggested many schemes for bettering his condition. With "secret aid from the Queen, or some one who hated the Spaniards," in 1586, he fitted out three ships to cruise in the Spanish waters and plunder the settlements of Spain. In these adventures the titled buccaneer realised much treasure, which was as quickly squandered on his return to England as it had been recklessly obtained. At this period the plundering of Spanish ships at sea was "regarded with high favour in England," and especially by the Queen herself." * Lord Cumberland's expeditions became a scourge to Spain, and excited, in return, a deadly animosity. In reward for those felonious services, the Queen granted him her Royal Commission to "pursue a voyage to the Southern Seas." Elizabeth actually placed one of her own armed vessels at his disposal; and encouraged in this, he commenced a career which the dispassionate reader must admit reflected dishonour and shame upon his patroness.

Having, with resources thus obtained, retired from the perilous expeditions on the high seas, Cumberland appeared in the smoother element of the Queen's Court. In the games of chivalry he bore off the prizes of courage and dexterity from the younger peers and courtiers; the fantastic band of knights-tilters boasted of him as one of their brightest ornaments; and Elizabeth condescended to "encourage his devotedness to her glory by an envied pledge of Royal favour." † As handsome Cumberland knelt before her Highness, she dropped her glove, perhaps not undesignedly; and, on his picking it up, she graciously desired him to keep

---

* Aikin's Court of Elizabeth, Vol. II.   † *Ibid*, Vol. II.

it. He caused the trophy to be encircled with diamonds, and ever after, at all tilts and tourneys bore it conspicuously placed in front of his high-crowned hat. He boasted frequently of the number of ladies who desired an alliance with him; yet many of the noted dames of the period rejected his addresses with scorn.

At the time of the Spanish Armada (1588) Lord Cumberland laid aside his knight-errantry for serious warfare. He joined the fleet appointed to hang upon the motions of the Spanish Armada, and harass it in its progress up the Channel; and on several occasions, especially in the last action, off Calais, he signalised himself by the most daring bravery. If, however, he had fallen into the hands of the Spaniards, no entreaty or remonstrance would have saved his life, for he had proved himself to be the most relentless pirate of the age—burning defenceless towns, and destroying all property, however valuable, when unable to carry it off. His ambition for glory as a combatant seems in him to have been subordinate to the love of gain and the desire for plunder, to which his profligate and extravagant habits had given the engrossing force of a passion.

Cumberland married the daughter of the Earl of Bedford, a lady described as of "strict propriety, benevolent and pious"—according to the morality of the times. As a husband, Cumberland proved unfaithful, and even cruel to his wife, who subsequently died in poverty.

Early in life Lord Cumberland sought an alliance with the beautiful daughter of Sir William Holles, of Haughton, in Nottinghamshire; but the good old knight indignantly refused consent to his daughter's marriage with a man whom he justly abhorred. For many years longer Elizabeth continued to shower favours upon this unworthy man.

I cannot pass over the name of HOLLES, which was so long associated with memories of all the better traits of the English character in high places. Sir William Holles was distinguished beyond any other Commoner, or perhaps any Peer in the realm, for boundless hospitality and the judicious mode in which he dispensed it. The ambassadors and other foreigners of distinction have been loud in praise of the generous table of the great Nottinghamshire knight. The historian of the family writes: "This most kind-hearted English gentleman began Christmas entertainments at Allhallowtide, and continued it until Candlemas. During this time any honest worthy man was permitted to stay three days, and enjoy prime 'belly cheer,' without being asked whence he came, or what he was like unto." The neighbouring squires, when pinched by debt, or having but small means, were sure of plenty of "belly cheer," and "good favour specially extended to them, because they were suffering from the frowns of the world." For each of the twelve days of Christmas Sir William Holles ordered a fat ox, two sheep, one hundred fowl, and a very large quantity of other provisions. The wines, spirits, ale and porter were also dispensed "with a hand that knew no stint," the maxim of the munificent host being that "good belly cheer deserved good drinking."

Sir William Holles never dined till some minutes *after* one of the clock—a late dinner hour in those times. Being asked by a guest why he preferred so late an hour, he replied that, "perhaps, for aught he knew, there might a friend come twenty miles to dine with him, and he would feel a double pleasure at meeting him at the dinner table, where all looked so merry and happy when the goblet went round."

The old English squires were admirable story-tellers, and

Sir William Holles stood in the front rank of that genial and amusing class.

At the coronation of Edward VI., Sir William Holles appeared with fifty followers, in blue coats and badges; the dress for "domestic attendants" of the House of Holles at that period. He never went to the sessions at Retford, though only four miles from his castle, without an escort of nearly forty men on horseback, accompanied by trumpeters. What was then very rare amongst the English nobles, or knights, he kept a respectable company of actors of his own, to perform plays and masques at festival times. The ancient May-day sports and ceremonies were also regularly carried out, as they might have been in the days of Henry III., who delighted in rustic amusements for the the people, and desired to add to their comforts.

This "grand old English knight" died at the age of ninety-two, in the year 1590. For more than a century and a half, the traditions of Nottinghamshire were full of interesting anecdotes of "Sir William, the squire of all squires, at hunting and jollification." The country folk raised their hats at the mention of his name.

I will place a few more particulars before the reader, of the descendants of Sir William Holles, on account of the strong light which they reflect on the manners and customs of the Elizabethan era.

The visitors at the castle, and its surroundings, were supplied with a variety of amusements. Sir William Holles also built a theatre, and kept a company of "merry men," who were supported at the castle, and liberally paid for their services. In summer those "funny folks" travelled through the country, and were well received by all conditions of people, who escorted them into town.

Sir William Holles was sincerely regretted by the lovers of field sports. In early life, Shakespeare, Ben Jonson, Spenser, and Raleigh were amongst the guests at Haughton; and the fame of the family hospitality was noted for several subsequent generations. In those times, all classes and parties were remarkable for hospitality. *Hospitality* is not, however, a virtue of party, creed, or country, but thorough good nature, and its history goes back to the most remote periods of the world.

Sir William Holles was succeeded in his estates and honours by his grandson, John Holles, who was one of the band of Gentlemen-pensioners to Queen Elizabeth. In the reign of James the First, Sir John Holles *purchased* from the Crown the title of Earl of Clare. A long and bitter feud existed between the Houses of Holles and Talbot of Shrewsbury. This ill-feeling had its origin in "a matrimonial disappointment." The first open rupture resulted in a duel between Orme, a gentleman attendant of Sir John Holles, and Mr. Pudsey, Master of the Horse to the Earl of Shrewsbury, in which the latter was mortally wounded. Shrewsbury prosecuted Orme, and sought to take away his life. In this effort he failed, as Sir John Holles conveyed his friend to Ireland, and subsequently obtained his pardon from Elizabeth. For his conduct in thus saving his friend, Holles was challenged by another county squire, Gervase Markham, "champion and gallant" to the Countess of Shrewsbury. Holles refused to fight on account of the demand of Markham that it should take place in a park belonging to his sworn enemy, the Earl of Shrewsbury, as he shrewdly suspected that treachery was meditated by the Talbots. Anxious to remove the aspersions cast upon his valour, Holles sought an encounter which might wear the appearance of an accident.

Soon after, having met Markham on the highway, they immediately dismounted, and "attacked each other with sharp swords." Markham fell, severely wounded; and the Earl of Shrewsbury lost no time in raising his tenantry and retainers to the number of two hundred men, in order to attack Holles and his followers, who quickly armed for the fray. On the other side, Lord Sheffield, the kinsman of Holles, appeared on the scene, accompanied by a considerable party of "madcaps," as duellists were styled by the Puritans of those times.

"I hear, good cousin," said Lord Sheffield, "that my Lord of Shrewsbury is prepared to trouble you; but take my word for it that before he or his tenants lay hands on you, it will cost them many a broken head, and many a sleepless night." Markham made a vow, "on bended knees, never to eat supper, or partake of the Sacrament of the Church of England, till he was revenged;" and it is added, "that he kept his vow for long years till the night of his death."*

It does not appear that Elizabeth or her Council took any steps to put down those deadly feuds amongst the jealous-minded nobles and squires, whose proceedings were described as emulating the barbarism of Sweden or Russia.

Gervase Markham, after a few years, "saw the error of his way," and, upon the advice of his old schoolmaster (Ascham), he studied literature, to the astonishment of the duellists and dicers with whom he had hitherto spent his time. He became the most voluminous miscellaneous writer of the age, writing on a vast variety of subjects, both in verse and prose; but his works on husbandry appear to have been the most useful, as

---

* Collins' Historical Collections; Tristram Hardy's Anecdotes of the Feuds of Old Families.

those on field sports were the most entertaining, to the English squires of that hilarious and reckless period.

Another of the family of Holles was destined to play a remarkable part under the Stuarts.

I conclude this volume with an anecdote of Queen Elizabeth which should have appeared in a preceding chapter. The Queen, seeing Sir Edward —— in her garden, one fine morning asked the knight in Italian, "What does a man think of when *he thinks of nothing?*" Sir Edward, who had not had the offer of some of the Queen's grants of land so soon as he had desired, paused a little, and then made answer: "Madam, he thinks of a *woman's promise.*" The Queen replied: "Well, Sir Edward, I must not confute *you*. Anger makes dull men witty, but, sometimes, it makes them *poor.*"

[The above anecdote has been recorded by Sir Nicholas Bacon, who was well acquainted with Queen Elizabeth.]

END OF THE THIRD VOLUME.

www.ingramcontent.com/pod-product-compliance
Lightning Source LLC
Chambersburg PA
CBHW020059020526
44112CB00032B/573